....

Economic Aspects of

ANTITRUST

Readings and Cases

....

HENRY ADLER EINHORN
U.S. Department of Commerce

WM. PAUL SMITH
Office of the Comptroller of the Currency

....

RANDOM HOUSE   New York

To Our Wives

Florence and Teresa

PREFACE

This book pleads no ideological cause. The authors seek neither the repeal of antitrust, as suggested by some, nor the critical beneficial prowess claimed by others. We do plead for the reexamination of antitrust laws, decisions, and consequences urged by many responsible commentators as indispensable to building a better society. This book is intended to assist in this examination process. The authors hope to achieve two objectives in this volume: (1) to introduce the student to antitrust, which has presented some of the more challenging aspects of Western sociojurisprudence, and (2) to focus on one of this subject's least mentioned features—the economic aspects of antitrust.

One of the basic attributes of antitrust jurisprudence is its dependence on adversary proceedings. As in all adversary litigation, defendant and prosecution plead the justice of their cause. Unfortunately, as in other adversary proceedings, truth lies somewhere in between—badly trampled. Our efforts are intended as first aid of sorts—the resuscitation of economic truth, the substitution of economic relevance for social fiction. To this end several of the principal antitrust issues are identified and treated separately. Our treatment of each issue generally is structured about a chronological presentation of the critical litigation of each issue. This legal chronology serves as the focus of a critical analysis of the economic issues inherent in each of five principal antitrust issues:

Monopoly
Oligopoly
Merger
Tying contracts
Exclusive dealing contracts

The social and legal importance of these issues are variable, changing as society changes. This volume is concerned with (1) the economic aspects of these specific issues and (2) the significance of economics in the continuing evolution of antitrust law.

Our approach assumes that antitrust is a reaction to particular economic conditions and situations. The noncompetitive attributes of these considerations frequently stimulate several forms of reaction—including antitrust laws. The concept of antitrust is, prima facie, appealing to many: if a member or portion of society does not conform to the standards of society, then some corrective policing action is necessary. In the economic realm competition is the accepted standard; if competition is not provided by those involved, then society must take corrective action—ergo, antitrust. Granted that this simplistic statement covers many sins, it does, however, indicate that antitrust is a society's answer to economic problems. This alone is neither right nor wrong, good nor bad. However, these value judgments can be applied to the enforcement of the antitrust policy statements.

If this enforcement is based on economic principles or reasoning designed to counter deviations and to restore competitive conditions and performance, then the enforcement can be labeled good. But, if the enforcement fails to provide these changes, some negative values seem to be in order.

Of course, to the extent that some noneconomic values are to be secured from antitrust enforcement, the promotion of these values should be considered in evaluating the antitrust enforcement. The authors do not argue whether these noneconomic, or social, values do or do not deserve a role in antitrust proceedings. We do, however, strongly suggest that they seldom are explicitly identified as such and that frequently economic concepts, arguments, and terminology are loosely applied to provide rationalization for noneconomic motivation. This practice amounts to little more than sophisticated hypocrisy. This book is intended as a step toward the more vigorous analytical treatment of the economic aspects of antitrust. If these are properly understood, the social values and goals can then be more clearly identified and obtained.

But, before starting this task, one pleasure awaits. The authors are indebted to Professors Donald Dewey and Harold F. Williamson, Sr. for their encouragement and sage counsel, to our students for their skepticism and trying questions, to Mrs. Gloria H. Brown and Mrs. Heather Seres for their translation of our illegible handscript into comprehensible typescript, and to our parents and lovers for their faith.

Insofar as our comments are controversial or injudicious and thus may have some merit, we insist that the credit is ours and not to be imputed to the federal agencies—the Department of Commerce, the Board of Governors of the Federal Reserve System, and the Office of the Comptroller of the Currency—with which we have been associated over the past four years.

CONTENTS

Economic Aspects
of Antitrust

1 INTRODUCTION

Since the Tower of Babel the success of joint ventures has depended on the effectiveness of communication between the parties. This is no less true in antitrust. Antitrust actions typically involve the evaluation of economic activity in a court of law. Even when an economist does not participate in the legal proceedings, the antitrust suit can be traced to its philosophical economic roots. Consequently, the implementation of an antitrust program, whatever its objectives, requires a common basis of intellectual—or at least conversational—exchange between the economic and the legal professions. To a large extent this common basis of understanding rests heavily on a common language or vocabulary.

The economist's terms "competition" and "monopoly" represent a useful point of departure for many examinations of antitrust and monopoly issues. In these lie the concept of a competitive system, with all of its alleged advantages, and the inferred restrictiveness and retrogression of monopoly that underlies the supposed efficacy of antitrust activity in the Western world. To economic theorists, the terms "competition" and "monopoly" have traditionally signified the ideal-type formulations of perfect competition or, conversely, perfect monopoly. Competition has been pictured in terms of many sellers with the absence of market power, the determination of prices through the operation of impersonal market processes, and the allocation of resources in such a manner that each factor of production, or resource, would receive only its "fair" return—the value of its contribution to total output. On the other hand, monopoly has been considered in terms of a single seller whose market power enables him to set a price that maximizes his profits, which often are thought to exceed any "normal" or "fair" return.

These concepts of competition and of monopoly were ideal characterizations, with no pretension of portraying real world situations. The dynamic possibilities of neoclassical economic theory were never as rigorously defined as were the static market models. Consequently, the 1930s witnessed numerous attempts to understand or portray models of less than perfect monopoly and less than perfect competition. Most notable were the theories of monopolistic and imperfect competition and of oligopoly that were proposed during this period. For the most part they were the product of efforts to build more meaningful theories or models of market processes. Their genesis, therefore, was a dissatisfaction, at least among economists, with the prevalent views of market processes rather than part of a direct concern with policy (of which antitrust activity was, and still is, only one facet) toward market processes per se.

One notable development of the late 1930s—J. M. Clark's idea of workable competition—was addressed to the problems of public policy toward market processes.[1] Clark argued that the absence of several elements of perfect competition was not fatal to a market condition that provided the basic competitive attributes; Clark termed this condition workable competition. A considerable degree of controversy arose from Clark's suggestions. In retrospect, the intervening years have witnessed a refined discernment of actual market conditions. Nonetheless, Clark's suggested formulation of workable competition comprises one aspect of the antitrust background, and it is these conceptual, or terminology, problems that are featured in the following material, excerpts from the 1955 *Report of the Attorney General's Committee to Study the Antitrust Laws*.[2] Many observers had hoped that the committee's report would provide a comprehensive statement guiding the development of antitrust laws and the government-business relationship. Regrettably, to many, the report merely described the evolution and

[1] J. M. Clark, "Toward a Concept of Workable Competition," *American Economic Review*, XXX (June 1940), 241–256.

[2] *Report of the Attorney General's Committee to Study the Antitrust Laws* (Washington, D.C., 1955).

status of antitrust law. For historical purposes, there are few sources of comparable value. However, despite a number of general observations it provided (along with comments from some individual committee members), the opportunity for a major bold policy analysis and statement was, on the whole, passed up.

The report's section on economic indexes of monopoly and competition is particularly relevant here. The interplay of economic analysis with relevant factual situations and the several antitrust statutes will be a major concern throughout this volume; the underlying factors are examined in the material immediately following.

....

Economic Definitions of "Monopoly," "Competition," and "Workable Competition"

....

I. GENERIC CONCEPTS OF COMPETITION AND MONOPOLY

The essence of full monopoly power resides in being the sole source of a product, so that the buyer must meet the seller's terms or go without. The essence of competition is to free the buyer from this power by access to alternative sources of the product. The same considerations apply where the problem is a buyer's monopoly.[1] The basic economic aspect of monopoly is the seller's power over the terms on which he trades. All the factors and ele-

---

[1] In this discussion, unless otherwise indicated, what is said of competition among sellers would apply equally where the restraints on competition exist or develop among buyers, and the pressure of these restraints is felt by sellers.

ments which constitute this idea are summed up by the convenient short-hand reference to monopoly power as power over price or power to exclude competitors. Monopoly power in this sense implies the monopoly seller's relative freedom from pressure to reduce costs, to develop new products, or otherwise to innovate, and to diffuse the benefits among customers.[2] The existence of monopoly power, lodged in private hands which are free to pursue their own advantage, is generally condemned by economists, aside from the question whether such power is used "reasonably" or "progressively." It is an unsafe power to lodge in private hands, making the monopolist a judge in his own case.

The idea of competition itself, as distinguished from the many variant technical concepts of competition, is not so easy to define. The literature of economics uses a good many concepts of "competition" for various purposes: perfect and imperfect competition, pure competition, monopolistic and workable competition, duopoly, oligopoly, and several others. Competition itself, as a generic concept embracing all its subdivisions, implies two ideas, which have a large common area but are not coextensive.

In the first sense, the word competition denotes only the presence of more than one seller in a market, and identifies a condition of rivalry among them—the self-interested and independent rivalry of two or more private competitors. But there is a second generic sense in which the word and the idea of competition are used, both in law and economics, and especially in the law. In this definition, "competition" is contrasted with "monopoly" with respect to the degree of market power possessed by a seller, or a group of sellers acting in concert. This second meaning of competition can be summed up as identifying a market condition in which the rivalry of sellers, of itself, prevents the existence of the discretionary market power of monopoly over price and output. Whether conditions in a given market are of the kind which tends typically to produce "competitive" or "monopolistic" market results in this latter sense depends in varying degrees upon the structure of that market, upon the way in which it conditions and influences the

[2] This does not imply that the presence of monopoly power in the economic sense constitutes "monopolization" under Section 2 of the Sherman Act.

decisions of businessmen as to price and output, upon the character of market incentives for innovation and cost reduction, and upon actual market behavior. To answer this central question, more evidence is needed than the simple fact that the market contains two or more sellers or buyers. One must consider the number and relative size of buyers and sellers, conditions affecting the entry of new firms and the growth of existing firms, relations among rivals in the process of making market decisions, as well as other market factors.)

These generic concepts of "competition" and "monopoly" are used in economics and the law in closely similar ways. Both in economics and in law, these are not concepts of all or none, as are the limiting cases of pure theory. . . . In utilizing economic concepts of "competition" and "monopoly" in the analysis of legal problems therefore, the task is twofold: (1) To isolate and define the economic concepts relevant in helping to answer questions posed by the law, and, to the degree to which they may be useful, to adapt them to the different standards established by different statutes, on the one hand; and (2) on the other, to examine the legal standards themselves in the light of economic knowledge in order to evaluate their appropriateness.

In seeking to clarify economic concepts which may be of use to the law in the analysis of market forces, a central preliminary task is to define the circumstances under which competition theoretically becomes "effective" from the economic point of view, in preventing a concern or a group of concerns acting in concert from having "effective" monopoly power. For this purpose, the issues center on "effective" or "workable" competition or its absence.

2. "WORKABLE" OR "EFFECTIVE" COMPETITION

The concept of "workable" or "effective" competition can perhaps best be described as the economists' attempt to identify the conditions which could provide appropriate leads for policy in assuring society the substance of the advantages which competition should provide. It is a kind of economist's "Rule of Reason"—

not, of course, to be confused with the legal rule of reason, but analogous to it in the sense that it is also an acknowledgment of the inevitability of the exercise of human judgment and discretion in classifying different forms of economic behavior.

The basic characteristic of effective competition in the economic sense is that no one seller, and no group of sellers acting in concert, has the power to choose its level of profits by giving less and charging more. . . . To bring this result about, it is necessary that rivals be free in fact to compete by lower prices and better service or products and selling activities, if they can achieve low enough costs to enable them to do so; and that no seller have power to limit this freedom of his rivals, and thus escape the pressures and penalties which effective competition imposes.

The market pressures which effective competition imposes upon each seller derive from the self-interested rivalry of his competitors. The essential character of this rivalry is to promote the competitor's economic interest by offering buyers inducements attractive enough to cause them to deal with him, in free bargaining, and in the face of inducements offered by his rivals.[3] . . .

Competitive rivalry in a given business situation may or may not be capable of developing enough force to deny any one seller or group of sellers acting in concert effective power to control the price they will charge, and other conditions of sale. Whether this condition is achieved normally depends on the character of the market. Active competition, for example, may involve initial moves by one competitor, the responses of the buyers, and the further responses of rival sellers. . . . The character of these responses may be affected not only by the aggressiveness and business policies of the rival sellers and buyers, but by their number, relative size and the nature of their expectations.

The market pressures of effective competition can be, and should properly be, quite severe. The firm rendering service inferior to that of its rivals would be seriously handicapped; and a firm maintain-

---

[3] The wording is intentionally chosen to avoid stating or implying that the customers *prefer* to deal with him, or that he offers or tries to offer *superior* inducements, such as *lower* prices. The definition should not be read to imply that A is not competing with B unless he invariably offers a lower price than B's. But he must be free to do so.

ing superiority over its rivals has a prospect of increasing its volume of trade progressively at their expense so long as it can maintain this superiority. . . .

a. Definition of "The Market"

In evaluating the market forces which together would characterize effective competition, the rivalry of close substitutes which may, for other purposes, be classified as belonging in other industries has, in varying degree, the same kind of effect as that of competing producers of the same or differentiated products or services classified within the same industry. . . .

For purposes of economic analysis, the "market" is the sphere of competitive rivalry within which the crucial transfer of buyers' patronage from one supplier of goods or services to another can take place freely. The boundaries of an "industry" or "market" will often be uncertain and controversial, and a definition appropriate in one case may be inappropriate in another. For our purposes, a market is an economic relationship among sellers and buyers, whose boundaries are not necessarily defined by geographical area alone, nor by conventional product classifications. To ascertain whether a firm or group of firms acting in concert has monopoly power, "the market" should include all firms whose production has so immediate and substantial an effect on the prices and production of the firms in question that the actions of the one group cannot be explained without direct and constant reference to the other. One should include in a market all firms whose products are in fact good and directly available substitutes for one another in sales to some significant group of buyers, and exclude all others. Where the products of different industries compete directly as alternatives for the same use, the market for that class of products should include the rival goods supplied by different industries. One should combine into one market two or more products (or two or more areas) if an appreciable fall in the price of one product (or in one area) will promptly lead to a relatively large diversion of purchasers from the other product (or area). The appropriate market area may be international, national, regional or local.

b. Tests of Performance

The economists' distinction between "effective monopoly" and "effective competition" does not turn on whether the industry in question is progressively managed or technologically advanced, nor on its policies with regard to wages, profits or high- or low-price programs. Effective competition is not a matter of the motives or policies of businessmen. The ultimate question in distinguishing "effective monopoly" from "effective competition" is whether the pressures of the market situation are such as tend of themselves to bring about the main beneficial effects which constitute the economic reasons why we try to maintain competition in our economy.

The process of adjusting the employment of resources to the pressures and demands of a workably competitive market is one of the chief means through which the diffusion of the benefits of competition takes place. In the long run, effective competition, implying the expansion (or contraction or withdrawal) of existing firms, or the entry of new ones, would reduce (or raise) the profit for a representative firm with respect to any particular product or service towards the point where bringing forth the supply earns no more than could be earned in alternative employments of the capital, labor, and management involved. The long-run tendency of effective competition to equalize the attractiveness of investment throughout the economy operates as among industries, as among the firms in any given industry, and within the business firm itself, which is guided by the relative profitability of the various products which it makes or can make. . . .

The impact of effective competition on profits throughout the economy, and thus on the flow of capital to alternative uses, is one of its most important functions. However, it is altogether normal in a competitive economy that a given industry or group of firms in an industry, each acting independently, can earn extremely high (or low) profits at any given time, and over considerable periods of time. For such profits are the signals through which a market economy attracts capital and other resources to more productive uses, and drives them out of less productive uses.

For these reasons reduction of costs and moderation of profits, like other tests of "progressive" performance in industry, do not prove the existence, nor their absence the lack, of effective competition. The rate of technical progress, and the level of profit in a firm or an industry, can reflect many forces other than the presence or absence of effective competition. In some cases, in conjunction with other more material facts, they may be considered to furnish collateral or corroborative evidence of the nature and significance of competitive forces in the industry.

. . . Our public policy, however, is founded on the economically sound assumption that competition will on the average result in much more progressiveness and efficiency than monopoly.

c. Summary of Factors Bearing on Identification of Workable Competition

What aspects of the market situation are significant in determining whether or not it is effectively competitive from the economic point of view? The short-hand legal definition of monopoly— "power * * * to raise prices or to exclude competition when it desired to do so" [4]—focuses directly on the ultimate economic elements of the problem. The economic definition of workable competition concentrates on the effective limits it sets on the power of a seller, or group of sellers acting in concert, over their price. That power cannot normally be retained for long without natural or imposed limitations on the opportunity for entry or growth of rivals. Restriction on the entry of rival firms is an integral part of the economic as it is of the legal definition of monopoly power, for competitive results are often less likely in a market where entry is not reasonably free. The factors listed below are considered some of the more important in summing up the economic aspects of workable competition. . . .

(1) A Number of Effective Competitive Sellers: The Issue of Relative Size.

The number and relative strength of firms necessary to effective competition cannot be compressed into a formula. The answer to the question depends also on other factors, including those hereafter discussed, so that a given number of firms might be

---

[4] *American Tobacco Co.* v. *United States,* 328 U.S. 781, 811 (1946).

compatible with effective competition in one industry and not in another. Size in the abstract is meaningless. Whatever significance it has exists only in relation to a particular market. Absolute size, as measured by number of employees, or dollars of assets, or similar formulae, has no significance in determining the presence or absence of workable competition. The interrelation and relative importance in different situations of the various factors bearing on the presence or absence of effective competition have not yet been fully isolated and measured by economics. However, where firms are few in number, special study would usually be needed to determine whether an industry were workably competitive.

Effective competition may be affected not only by the total number of sellers; their relative size and strength must also be considered. This does not mean that close equality of size among the various firms is essential for workable competition to exist, but only that the rivalry should not depend entirely upon sellers who are so weak or inefficient as to exist by sufferance. For such firms are not independent, and are not properly counted among the number of effectively competitive sellers. And as the number of independent sellers reaches unity, the market obviously reaches monopoly. The presence in any market of a unit much stronger than the others is a factor to be closely examined for its bearing on the workably competitive character of that market, and on the issue of whether any firm in fact exists only by sufferance, but by itself is not indicative of the absence of workable competition.

(2) Opportunity for Entry.   From the economic point of view, relative freedom of opportunity for entry of new rivals is a fundamental requisite for effective competition in the long run. Without this condition, it is idle to expect competition. The entry and withdrawal of firms, whether new firms or existing firms from other market areas, or other industries, or other stages of production and marketing, is the basic mechanism of the market for achieving its economic results. The cost of entry into the competitive area should not be impracticably high. This does not imply an absolute criterion for ease of entry in terms of a given number of dollars. Nor does it deny recognition to the fact that as a practical matter, the size of minimum adequate investment capital and other factors may make the entry of new firms into even a competitive industry a relatively slow or hazardous process. But it does mean that under prevailing conditions as to the availability of capital, an attempt by existing firms to raise prices considerably above the competitive norm would make it profitable and practicable for new firms or existing borderline firms to invade the field. In economic terms, this means that conditions of cost for a new firm should not be excessively higher, at least after a reasonable period of initial development, than conditions of cost for an existing member of the industry. . . .

Reasonable opportunity of outsiders with requisite skill to enter the market may appear dispensable, for if there are a sufficient number of competitors, and they compete vigorously, what purpose would be served by additional numbers? But if energetic and imaginative rivals cannot enter, the boldest and most rewarding innovations may be excluded.

(3) Independence of Rivals. A primary condition of workable competition in an economic sense is that there be genuine independence on the part of the business units in an industry, so that each firm pursues its own individual advantage. In industries with numerous sellers, concerted action is difficult to achieve without relatively visible machinery of cooperation. Where there are only a limited number of sellers, however, concerted action can be subtle and informal, and sometimes difficult to detect. In all industries, it is normal for sellers to try to take the reactions of rivals into account in determining their own competitive policies; where there are few sellers it may be easier to forecast such reactions. This may or may not impair competition, depending on whether or not the initiator of a competitive move can expect to retain an improved market position after his rivals have responded. Fewness of sellers does not necessarily lead to mutual interdependence of policies, but it may do so.

(4) Predatory Preclusive Practices. There should be no predatory preclusive tactics, such that their natural effect would be to enable the user to eliminate rivals without regard to their efficiency, or at least to place them under serious handicaps irrelevant to their efficiency. It should be noted as a practical matter that predatory competition in this sense can usually only be waged where a considerable degree of market power already exists, or where an attempt is being made to use a long purse in order to destroy or coerce rivals. Such conduct is regarded therefore as symptomatic either of monopoly or the intent to monopolize, or both, although it may not be necessary for those possessing market power in high degree to use such methods in order to gain or to keep monopolistic advantages from their position. Conversely, the accusation of "predatory" or "cutthroat" practices often turns out on examination not to stem from the abuse of significant degrees of market power, but from the uncomfortably active pressures of competition itself. . . . These facts bear not on the justification for predatory conduct—there is none—but on the issue of whether such conduct exists.

(5) *Rate of Growth of the Industry or Market.* The speed with which an industry is growing is not a direct economic indicator of the state of competition within it. An industry may be actually in decline and yet be actively competitive. . . . Rate of growth, however, is often important in determining the significance to be attached to other factors, and particularly to numbers and reasonable opportunity for entry.

The rate of growth or expansion of a market can, for example, strongly color the significance to competition of the number and relative size of the firms, and alter the effectiveness of barriers to entry. The expected rate of growth of the industry affects the attitudes and expectations of firms in the industry, the attractiveness of the industry to outside firms, and the possibility of maintaining positions of market power without severe restrictions on entry. . . .

(6) *Character of Market Incentives to Competitive Moves.* Competition may be effective or ineffective, depending upon how the market is organized and behaves, and according to what incentives there are for independent competitive actions: the hope of gain for the individual seller, and the risk of loss. The strength of these incentives may depend on factors which are in themselves neutral and become important only as they influence incentives. The intervals between a competitive move and the expected response, for example, are not themselves indicia of effective competition or its absence. But they come under study in seeking to determine whether incentives are relatively strong or weak.

In general, and outside of such specialized markets as organized exchanges and others of similar character, effective competition may hinge on the condition that the initiator of a competitive action can expect a gain in volume of business at least for a time. . . . The incentive to innovation, to price changes, or to other directly competitive moves is an interval during which an innovator may reasonably expect to have an advantage because his moves cannot be met and neutralized promptly enough by his rivals.

While information or continued price rigidities may be some indication of the existence or absence of incentives to competitive moves, such information cannot of itself be determined from an economic standpoint of either effective monopoly or effective competition. Monopolies may change prices in their own interests, and competitive industries may have periods of stable demand and supply conditions. Price changes, or the absence thereof, must therefore be considered in their market settings in order to evaluate their significance.

(7) Product Differentiation and Product Homogeneity. The definition of the word "market," and that of workable competition itself, both turn on the actual and direct competition a seller confronts from the closely related products of others. An important factor in determining the boundaries of the market is the knowledge of buyers as to the alternatives open to them. If other conditions are equal, it would seem for this reason to follow that the more homogeneous the product of rival sellers, the more easily buyers could switch from the output of one competitor to that of others; and therefore the wider the market and the greater the degree of competition in it.

The effect of product differentiation depends on the market setting in which it is placed. Extreme product differentiation, by tending to insulate the demand for one product against that for rival products, may allow real positions of monopoly to develop.

Relatively mild differentiation of products within a market otherwise effectively competitive, however, may be a factor favorable to the intensiveness of competition, including price competition and competition in quality. . . .

(8) *Meeting or Matching the Prices of Rivals.* The above analysis of the varying effects which product homogeneity and differentiation may have on competition in the economic sense in different market settings has a bearing also on the question of meeting or matching the prices of competitors. It is of the essence of effective competition that competitors should try to meet, or offer an equivalent for, any superior inducement which one of them offers. Meeting a rival's inducements is the means whereby competition diffuses the gains of productive efficiency. To forbid a seller to meet his rival's price would involve a *reductio ad absurdum,* so long as the market structure itself is untouched. . . .

However, effective competition also involves freedom to undercut rivals' prices. Thus an inflexible requirement that any existing price may be met, but not undercut, would mean that when demand falls off, or when there is a reduction in cost, the decline in price which would follow under effective competition might be aborted, because it would be to no one's interest to make the first move, since it would be matched forthwith. In many such situations, it would be to everyone's interest not to cut prices.

. . . But a rigid uniformity over periods of changing supply and demand, or a persistent failure by firms to increase or decrease prices when their independent self-interest would seem to dictate such a move, is not usually compatible with workable competition. This is a problem altogether distinct and apart from the legal question of whether a complex and rigid system of price-setting and price changing can only be explained by an agreement or conspiracy. The legal problem transcends although it includes the economic. But any rule, public or private, which forbade the meeting of prices, or one which forbade the undercutting of prices, would be a rule against workable competition.

A climate more stimulating to effective competition might be introduced into such a market in several possible ways, including: new entry, if large profits were being made; price discrimination;

variations in the product or in the other terms of the bargain; a change in the structure of the market, by an increase in the number of sellers; or utilization of other competitive devices such as product, service and customer relations improvement and more effective selling. This should not be interpreted as a general recommendation of a policy of discrimination, but is meant merely to point out some of the available alternatives in situations of this kind. Perhaps something could be accomplished by not preventing —and certainly by forbidding private groups the power to prevent —reasonable variety and variability in pricing practices.

(9) Excess Capacity. "Excess capacity" is a term difficult to define satisfactorily, and even more difficult to identify. The term is commonly used to describe capacity unused during a general depression, as well as "excesses" of capacity which may be generated by investment booms in competitive industries. Both these senses should be distinguished from the excess of capacity confronted by a declining industry. In a period of generally good business, for a growing or stable business, the existence of unused capacity, which could be utilized at or near prevailing costs, may help to demonstrate the presence of either effective monopoly or effective competition in connection with other facts. If the companies in an industry tend generally to pursue policies of making more money by charging high prices and restricting production, the industry may have chronic excess capacity as a result. The practice of a company purchasing and dismantling unused capacity in this sense— that is, capacity which could be utilized at normal costs—has always and rightly been considered strong evidence of attempt to monopolize. On the other hand, a moderate and varying amount of excess capacity naturally tends to develop from time to time as a result of expansion or in response to the rise and fall of demand in a competitive industry, or incident to competitive efforts of producers to increase their share of the market. And its presence is favorable to the effectiveness of competition, if other criteria of competition are present. It permits producers to handle added business at no great increase in unit cost of production, or even at a decrease in average unit costs, depending upon cost conditions at the time. And, as business approaches conditions in which efficient capacity is fully utilized at high profit, a failure on the part of the industry to expand in response to high levels of demand and profit might suggest the possibility of some restrictive arrangement to prevent the normal response of a competitive market.

(10) *Price Discrimination.* Some types of price discrimination may stimulate effective competition; others may be evidence of effective monopoly, in the economic sense. Before proceeding to examine the differences among the various types of price discrimination, a word of preliminary warning is in order.

Price discrimination as seen by an economist not only is not necessarily the same as "price discrimination" in the sense followed or applied in decisions under the Robinson-Patman Act, but it may be entirely antithetical. Furthermore, even when a price structure happens to be discriminatory in both senses, this may be evidence of either effectively monopolistic or effectively competitive forces, depending on its setting. Finally, even when price discrimination in an economic sense (whether or not in the sense proscribed under the Robinson-Patman Act) is evidence of departures from conditions of effective competition, it does not necessarily result in or denote violation of law.

Price discrimination, in the economic sense, occurs whenever and to the extent that there are price differences for the same product or service sold by a single seller, and not accounted for by cost differences or by changes in the level of demand; or when two or more buyers of the same goods and services are charged the same price despite differences in the cost of serving them. In order to know when there is or is not price discrimination, in the economic sense, between two or more buyers, it is necessary to know not only the price but also the total costs applicable to each class of transaction under comparison.

From the economic point of view, no particular definition of "price" is required; "price" is simply what the buyer has paid the seller as consideration for the goods and related services he has sought and purchased; nor is any close definition of the "goods" or "products" required except that there be some substantial elements of comparability. "Cost," for analysis of situations contemplated in this section of our Report, means average cost. . . .

And such cost differences as are relevant are those consistently characteristic of the categories of business being compared, not transitory or incidental differences. The actual lower costs of serving one or more buyers can arise from a great variety of circumstances. The product sold to some buyers may be physically somewhat different, in lacking certain appliances or finishing touches or quality. There may be differences in the services which go along with the goods to form the complete package for which consideration is given—such services as delivery, packaging, storage, credit extension, risk of default, handling, clerical attention, sales force attention, and many others. . . . These are all matters of factual detail.

Because many costs, particularly distribution costs, involve large elements of overhead, it may be difficult or impossible to estimate cost differentials with great precision. This is not to say, however, that the task should not be done, nor that cost differentials should be deemed not to exist, in the absence of precise estimates.

Price discrimination, in the economic sense, may be practiced by a monopolist or by a group of sellers acting in concert, because they wish to build up or protect the position of certain customers, and weaken that of others. But price discrimination may serve to promote competition, and it may be relevant evidence that competition exists and is effective. . . .

It is equally clear that in some cases differences in price not related to difference in cost may promote competition. Thus price discrimination may serve to disrupt or preclude any collusive or otherwise interdependent pricing. The very success of a concerted effort by a group of firms to raise prices above the competitive level by restricting output to less than the competitive level would make it attractive for some or all of the firms to offer better terms to some buyers. . . .

As has been pointed out several times in the preceding analysis, price discrimination may be the force which can increase the number of effective sellers in a market, or disrupt an otherwise effective system of monopoly pricing. Thus price discrimination is a fact of significance, to be considered in relation to other facts, in determining whether a market is workably competitive.

3. "WORKABLE" COMPETITION CONTRASTED WITH PURE OR PERFECT COMPETITION

"Workable" or "effective" competition supplies no formula which can substitute for judgment. It suggests leads to data of significance, and a means of organizing the data bearing on the question whether a given market of itself is sufficiently competitive in its structure and behavior to be classified as workably competitive. And it provides some bench-marks or criteria, representing somewhat different points of vantage, for the process of making that judgment.

The criteria it offers are not, of course, the criteria of pure or perfect competition. It may be useful at this point to clarify the role of these concepts in economics, and to distinguish them from the concepts used here.

The concepts of pure and perfect competition are tools of theoretical analysis. They are not intended to and do not constitute a description of reality. As a theoretical model, these ideas give economists means for rigorously exploring the interrelationships of certain specified market forces. And, as previously stated, they define rigidly the theoretical conditions necessary to a form of long-run equilibrium in which prices would equal costs, including the minimum economically necessary supply price of capital. Historically, the concept of perfect competition developed first as a series of conclusions about the cost-price relationships which competitive market pressures tend to produce; and later, as the cost-price results theoretically attributed to competition were more exactly defined, they assumed the character of limits, and economics produced a far more precise formulation of the conditions theoretically necessary to those results. These conditions are: (1) that the products of all the rival sellers in the market are precise substitutes for each other, and that all buyers and sellers have perfect knowledge of the market and complete indifference as to their customers or sources of supply; (2) that the number of sellers is so large that no one seller produces more than a negligible share of market supply; (3) that new firms can enter the industry with the same costs as existing firms; and (4) that all buyers and sellers in the market have mobility. To state these conditions is to make manifest their hypothetical character as tools of analysis, not descriptions of reality. As theoretical models, these concepts have facilitated analysis, and the study of real situations, by directing attention to key forces which lead actual markets to deviate in their results from those that it is believed would emerge under perfectly competitive conditions.

The concepts of pure and perfect competition have also clarified and helped to make more precise certain selected results centering on cost-price equilibrium which economists have long concluded should flow from competition. They have, however, neglected the requirements of competitive innovation in processes and products. They thus served to define, in theoretical terms, optimum conditions in the utilization of resources and the distribution of income, although in facilitating the study of optimal cost-price relations, and the relations between productivity and rewards, they may have, as stated, led some economists to neglect market forces inducing innovation in products and processes. It should be emphasized that pure and perfect competition are wholly theoretical standards, in that they are not intended *as such* to be guides to public policy. Nor should the courts be expected to be able to utilize pure and perfect competition concepts in adjudging any given market situation. They seek to define cost-price relations under conditions of equilibrium toward which certain markets tend to move, although in fact markets can never be expected to reach equilibrium. When taken out of context, the very precision of the theoretical standards of pure and perfect competition can be misleading. Nonetheless, these concepts, used in connection with the study of other factors outside their terms, have helped to orient economists' studies of actual situations, and have contributed, along with other influences, to the elaboration of the theory of workable competition, as an instrument for the direct study of market conditions.

Workable competition differs from pure and perfect competition in several ways. In the first place, the two theories have different purposes. The theory of pure and perfect competition is an instrument of theoretical analysis; the theory of workable competition seeks to provide a method for making necessarily less exact but more practical realistic judgments of actual market situations. Secondly, to the extent that the two theories are concerned with the same broad elements—the definition of the product and market, the number and relative size of sellers, and conditions of entry—the concept of workable competition posits a lesser degree of "perfection." Thus perfect competition would require an extremely large number of sellers. Criteria of workable competition, as is explained above, could be satisfied by a lesser number of sellers, some of whom may well produce significant fractions of total supply, provided they really compete and do not foreclose entry of new competitors, except by reason of their superiority. Pure and perfect competition would require that all sellers produce goods which were identical and that no buyers have preferences among sellers. The concept of workable competition is consistent with considerable product differentiation and recognizes the existence of buyer preference among sellers. As to entry, too, perfect competition contemplates complete freedom of entry by new firms, whereas workable competition is compatible with practical barriers to entry, such as considerable capital and even advertising requirements, and a period of higher costs while production is organized and management trained and shaken down. Thirdly, apart from these factors in market analysis which the two theories share, workable competition goes beyond the theory of perfect competition in certain respects. While the theory of perfect competition examines certain implications of the sellers' quest for profit under a limited set of assumptions, the literature of workable competition seeks to identify those aspects of competition which provide market incentives for innovation, including quality innovation as well as cost reduction, and taking directly into account other elements of the market situation which change through time. It is of importance, therefore, in using economic analysis of problems of market organization and behavior for antitrust purposes, that in each case the premises of analysis be made clear, and that economic theories not be applied beyond the limits of their own propositional base. Thus it does not follow that such technical economic terms as "elements of monopoly" or "market imperfections," which imply merely the absence of some of the conditions of pure or perfect competition, are for that reason monopoly situations in the antitrust sense, or even that they lessen the effectiveness of competition.

A few members stress that the "doctrine" of workable competition is only a rough and ready judgment by some economists, each for himself, that a particular industry is performing reasonably well—presumably relative to alternative industrial arrangements which are practically attainable. There are no objective criteria of workable competition, and such criteria as are proffered are at best intuitively reasonable modifications of the rigorous and abstract criteria of perfect competition.

Comparison of Legal and Economic Concepts of Competition and Monopoly

It seems clear that although there are some similarities between the legal concept of monopoly and competition and the economic concept of effective monopoly and effective competition, there are striking and substantial dissimilarities as well. Chief common ground is found in those instances where the law requires the examination of market situations both of structure and behavior and the marshaling and analysis of evidence relevant thereto, such as the problems of monopoly, substantial lessening of competition, or with regard to judgment as to the economic effect of practices classed as unreasonable *per se*.

One source of difference is the tendency of economists to examine the results to be expected from given conditions, which conditions may or may not be traceable to any one's actions; while the law deals with activities, or practices or courses of action which may be either directly harmful to competition or may be considered to bring about conditions viewed as probably having tendencies harmful to competition. Other differences arise from the particular language of statutes, and from the fact that, especially in the administration of a criminal statute, the law must give weight to concepts of intent and purposefulness of action, some of which have no counterpart in general economic analysis. Thus it is natural that economic theory has given little attention to the distinction between monopoly and monopolization, which has preoccupied the law under Section 2 of the Sherman Act. Again, the law cannot, save in the most obvious cases, assume that actual behavior in the market-place will in fact correspond to the pattern of competitive behavior that would theoretically be expected in a market of a given structure. The economic analysis of market theory, while it suggests important leads to relevant evidence, does not and cannot relieve the law of the necessity for searching out the evidence as to the kind of competitive behavior that actually occurs in a given instance. The law can learn from generalized studies of normal behavior, but it must always be guided by the established facts in the particular case at issue. The antitrust laws establish criminal guilt or civil responsibility; here as in all other phases of the law, legal responsibility is individual.

One of the interests of economics as a study is to reach conclusions about the respective social performance of different industries, and to draw conclusions as to whether a given market, whether competitive or monopolistic, is doing its social job well or not. The antitrust laws, however, are concerned with undue restraints of competition, with monopolization or attempts to monopolize, and with certain practices deemed especially injurious to competition.

Such conduct cannot be excused by proof it represents "progressive" managerial policy or, if defendant is a monopoly, it has been a good one, has performed acceptable social service, or even benefited the consuming public. Neither the Sherman Act nor economists generally discriminate between "good" or "bad" monopolization or undue restraints of trade; and likewise with violations of the Clayton Act. Though the "progressiveness" of business performance may sometimes be helpful in demonstrating the presence or absence of monopoly or undue restraint, its antitrust relevance has no bearing beyond these issues. However, whether conduct represents "progressive" or "unprogressive" managerial policy, performs an acceptable social service or benefits the consuming public may sometimes be helpful in demonstrating the presence or absence of monopolization or undue restraint of or injury to competition and can offer useful guideposts to antitrust officials in the selection of cases and to courts in the formulation of effective decrees. On the other hand, economic study of the social performance of business can make significant contributions to the antitrust laws in helping to clarify and to improve the theory on the basis of which antitrust statutes are drawn and assisting in long run improvements of this statutory system.

PART I *Monopoly*

2 MONOPOLY:

The Earliest Years of Antitrust

Monopoly, like sin, means all things to all people. However, we are not concerned with all people and their views but rather with economists, lawyers, and judges. Although antitrust proceedings and professional discussions often involve a confrontation of economists and lawyers and their views, their meanings of monopoly continue to diverge and, on occasion, the courts have accepted the definitions of neither. This divergence, as we shall see, has declined substantially during the past two decades. We must, nevertheless, devote some attention to terminology and the development of monopoly statutes and their interpretation.

Economists generally define monopoly in terms of the ability of an individual firm or a group to influence a product's price through output decisions. In the most obvious case monopoly power over price stems from the production and sale of a unique product by a single producer. The production of a unique product without good or close substitutes by a single producer, however, is seldom observed in our economy. Generically, the term "monopoly" has been applied to many situations in which a number of producers of identical or closely substitutable goods behave in a manner or enjoy power comparable to that expected of a classical monopolist. These powers include some control over the product's price and the terms of sale, discretions not found under the traditional expectations of a competitive system. The difficulties of determining what constitutes a close substitute are real indeed and increasingly important in antitrust cases. In many of the cases presented below, determination of close substitutes and thus the boundaries of the affected product market was a major factor in the court's consideration.

The discretion of monopolistic firms over product prices—that is, their ability to raise prices without an inordinate loss of sales— is critical to these firms' product output and resource employment decisions. Economists are concerned with the influence of monopoly and, alternatively, competition upon the allocation of resources: the employment of land, labor, capital, and various natural resources in the production of different commodities. The most frequently adopted norm or ideal for resource allocation is that resulting from the operation of a competitive industry. Structurally, a competitive industry is composed of a sufficient number of firms so that none can have appreciable discretion over price. While it is a moot point as to how many firms would suffice, economists are in general agreement about the implications of this competitive industry structure. Each individual firm would accept market prices as datum; its additional revenues from additional sales (marginal revenue) would be equal to, or not appreciably different from, market prices. Thus, as a profit maximizer, an individual firm would actively seek additional sales as long as its extra costs of production (marginal costs) do not exceed the market price. But firms with monopolistic power find that the price for both marginal and intramarginal units "turns against them" as sales expand; as profit maximizers, monopolists therefore restrict output to a level below a competitive level that equates marginal costs with price.

There has been a wide gulf between this analytical concern of economics with monopoly as a distortion of the competitive allocation of resources and the legal concern with monopoly. An examination of antitrust statutes and cases would reveal a primary concern with monopoly as a restriction on the rights of others. There is relatively little consideration of the allocative effects of particular alleged monopoly practices. Too often, the emphasis on the forms of behavior obscures consideration or even recognition of the effects of a particular act. Ideally, a joining of economic and legal analysis would involve a sharpening and application of the economist's analytical tools. These refinements would include better identification of market control and also the provision of tests to better determine the effects of various forms of behavior; that is, how, in the increasingly complex industrial relationships, do competitive versus noncompetitive results of a particular act balance out in determining the overall social desirability of that act?

However, the traditional forms of monopoly and competition are seemingly declining. Since our society is increasingly typified by industries whose structures are either oligopolistic or monopolistically competitive, the reconciliation of economic theory and legal restraints has become an even more difficult task. The following material highlights the evolution of American antimonopoly statutes by briefly outlining the development of common law principles and their effect on court and legislative law in the United States. The Sherman Act of 1890 is then examined briefly to indicate the conditions surrounding its passage and early effect as well as its philosophic approach. We then turn to a consideration of particular aspects of the act and its subsequent interpretation through the recent period; this examination is concerned primarily with economic aspects of the monopoly question.

A somewhat uncertain view exists as to the common law attitude on monopoly issues. This uncertainty reflects the paucity of surviving court records as well as the rather different economic issues and environment of earlier England.[1] Initially, monopoly referred to royal grants that provided exclusive rights to a receiver, but the term was later applied to similar dispensation received from Parliament. Both the control of price and quality of an item and the control of the work rights of others for their self-support were attributes of these early monopolies; however, the former two factors apparently were not necessary to establish a violation of common law on monopoly. Although the early records indicate that engrossing and forestalling were considered illegal, the issues, motivation, and penalties differ from their modern counterparts. The courts did not honor contracts in which a party promised not to follow a particular trade as, ostensibly, society would be deprived of their services. These contracts might have precluded a person from supporting himself, with the ensuing result that society would

[1] See Donald Dewey, *Monopoly in Law and Economics* (Chicago: Rand McNally, 1959).

have to provide for his maintenance through public institutions. This legal view was relaxed in later years, but only when it was recognized that such contractual forebearance was necessary to preserve the value of goods sold and the forebearance was limited.

Another legal ingredient in the monopoly doctrine evolution was the idea of conspiracy, which, like many other legal issues, had a rather sketchy and contradictory history. The concepts of conspiracy and monopoly were combined in the eighteenth century when they were applied primarily to labor rather than to manufacturers or other employers. Moreover, this conspiracy-to-monopolize concept affected only agreements limiting competition between two or more parties; the individual monopolists were not affected. As with contracts not to follow a particular trade, the courts' motivation seemed to be the prohibition of any act that might increase the public's welfare responsibility due to the foreclosure of opportunities for citizens to support themselves or secure food.

These issues are rather different from those of the modern industrial society, and in the adaptation process, courts often faced apparently contradictory common law precedents. Recent research in this area indicates that there was no settled precedent on conspiracy in restraint of trade or monopoly common law. The reasonableness of restraints as a permitting factor seemed limited to the contractual rights and property interests of the contracting parties rather than to any public interest. Considerations of public interest were restricted to instances of an individual's loss of support rather than to market control. Thus, the tendency of domestic courts to view contracts in restraint of trade as evidence of monopoly power required a modification of traditional law.

In the United States, as in England during the 1800s, the increasing number of monopoly suits and their growing complexity forced state courts to consider the circumstances of individual suits and to judge the legality of matters on this basis. This generated the "rule of reason" monopoly tradition in domestic courts. The use of "reasonableness" as a standard and the evolution of monopoly law were solely state court phenomena, thus providing no uniform decisions. Among the decisions assuming particular significance in later years, actions for damages due to contracts limiting trade were successful only when the defendant's actions were considered "criminal." The reasonableness principle, thus applied, permitted the courts to preserve the traditional law of contracts under drastically changed economic and social conditions by reconciling contractual rights with acts or effects of acts that were somehow contrary to the public interest.

The increasing industrialization, corporate organization, and consequent shifts in market power after the Civil War led to resentment and protests by several groups in society. Small businessmen, farmers, and workers felt an increasing disadvantage to the new large corporations. This discontent found its political expression in the 1880s and, as with much sustained political agitation, was vent at the state and federal levels. Much of this agitation was directed against the general social order although, eventually, specific targets were defined. These targets ranged from the legislative corruption associated with the railroad expansion, to the periodic business depressions, to the large consolidation movement that frequently involved fraud and misrepresentation as well as market domination by giant firms. The farm states generally, through granger acts, directed their attention to railroads; agitation culminated in the federal Interstate Commerce Act of 1887, but even this was of limited effect until some time after 1900.

State antimonopoly laws antedated federal laws in the United States, but their scope varied widely and they provided rather inadequate regulation. The more important desire to attract and retain industry was one cause of lax enforcement. Also, in the new economic society of industrialized America, comparatively few companies and markets fell within a single state's boundaries. The state laws, first passed in 1889, were a more local and immediate response to the same conditions that led to passage of the Sherman Act of 1890. The Sherman Act's key provisions are found in Sections 1 and 2, which were directed toward actual monopoly and conspiracies or agreements designed to secure monopoly power:

SECTION 1. Every contract, combination in the form of trust or otherwise, or conspiracy, in restraint of trade or commerce among the several States, or with foreign nations, is hereby declared to be illegal.

SECTION 2. Every person who shall monopolize, or attempt to monopolize, or combine or conspire with any other person or persons, to monopolize any part of the trade or commerce among the

several States, or with foreign nations, shall be deemed guilty of a
misdemeanor . . .

The Sherman Act departed from traditional antimonopoly law and,
in retrospect, treated monopoly more as a social than an economic
phenomenon. Although there is no clear statement of congressional
intent, the antitrust laws seemed to include few new ideas. According to Professor Donald Dewey, the debate on this bill revealed
how little the legislators knew of the common law on monopoly.[2]
However, the law's passage indicated an implicit realization that
traditional safeguards to competition were no longer sufficient and
that a new approach and action were necessary. The resulting
vagueness and uncertainty of scope of the act and standards clouded
its administration over the following years.

In the 1895 E. C. Knight [3] case, the first Sherman Act case reviewed by the Supreme Court, manufacturing was adjudged distinct
from commerce and thus not subject to the Sherman Act provisions.
However, the Court managed to ignore this ruling in subsequent
decisions, most of which involved railroads and unions rather than
manufacturing, which was presumably the original target of the
Sherman Act. Rate agreements were declared illegal in 1897 and
1898, while collusive bidding was held illegal in 1899. In its second and third antitrust rulings, the Trans-Missouri Freight Association[4] case of 1897 and the Joint Traffic Association[5] case of
1898, the Court held that railroads could not jointly determine the
freight rates to be charged to their customers. In the former, Justice
Peckham's majority decision held that contracts in restraint of trade
were illegal despite their possible reasonableness under common
law; repeatedly the courts ruled that joint price determination would
not be excused by a desire to avoid ruinous price warfare. In 1899
the Addyston Pipe & Steel Company[6] decision of Judge Taft held
that reasonableness was a common law excuse only under ancillary

[2] *Ibid.,* Chap. XI, especially pp. 143–144.

[3] United States v. E. C. Knight Company, 156 U.S. 1 (1895).

[4] United States v. Trans-Missouri Freight Association, 166 U.S. 290
(1897).

[5] United States v. Joint Traffic Association, 171 U.S. 505 (1898).

[6] Addyston Pipe & Steel Company v. United States, 175 U.S. 211 (1899).

effects and that such was the limit of any reasonableness doctrine under the Sherman Act; however, he held that an agreement to share markets and collude on price bids was not considered as ancillary under common law. The fifth Supreme Court case, in 1904, was the Northern Securities Company[7] decision permitting the federal government to dissolve combinations that were created or legally supported by a state charter if these combinations were in restraint of trade. This ruling permitted subsequent decisions involving holding companies, consolidations, and trade association activity.

However, the 1890–1910 period was characterized chiefly as an exploratory period in which the applicability and meaning of the Sherman Act were broadly outlined. In retrospect, the general philosophy was not determined until the Standard Oil[8] decision of 1911, which is described in the following chapter.

[7] Northern Securities Company v. United States, 193 U.S. 197 (1904).

[8] United States v. Standard Oil Co. of New Jersey, 221 U.S. 1 (1911).

3 STANDARD OIL:

Antitrust Reasonableness

The Standard Oil complex was one of the most important industrial enterprises formed during the nineteenth century; and the Court decision that led to the dissolution of this empire also was a most important antitrust decision.[1] In the 1911 Standard Oil decision Justice White enunciated the "rule of reason" that was to last until midcentury. Of more relevance here, however, was the Court's consideration of particular business practices and economic data, which, in light of recent examination, have become even more controversial.

The government alleged a conspiracy to restrain trade in petroleum or "crude oil," refined oil, and petroleum products during three periods 1870–1882, 1882–1899, and 1899 through the date of the suit. The 1870–1882 period was one in which the alleged conspiracy involved the Standard Oil Company of Ohio, which, with the individual defendants, founders of that company, purchased interests or entered into agreement with individuals in businesses concerned with the purchase, shipping, refining, and selling of petroleum and petroleum products. These purchases and agreements were undertaken allegedly to fix prices and control transport, restrain trade, and secure a monopoly in these areas. The Court described the problems involved in the latter two periods as follows:

Reiterating in substance the averments that both the Standard Oil Trust from 1882 to 1899 and the Standard Oil Company of New

[1] United States v. Standard Oil Co. of New Jersey, 221 U.S. 1 (1911).

Jersey since 1899 had monopolized and restrained interstate commerce in petroleum and its products, the bill at great length additionally set forth various means by which during the second and third periods, in addition to the effect occasioned by the combination of alleged previously independent concerns, the monopoly and restraint complained of were continued. Without attempting to follow the elaborate averments of these subjects spread over fifty-seven pages of the printed record, it suffices to say that such averments may properly be grouped under the following heads: Rebates, preferences and other discriminatory practices in favor of the combination by railroad companies; restraint and monopolization by control of pipe lines, and unfair practices against competing pipe lines; contracts with competitors in restraint of trade; unfair methods of competition, such as local price cutting at the points where necessary to suppress competition; espionage of the business of competitors, the operation of bogus independent companies, and payment of rebates on oil, with the like intent; the division of the United States into districts and the limiting of operations of the various subsidiary corporations as to such districts so that competition in the sale of petroleum products between such corporations had been entirely eliminated and destroyed; and finally reference was made to what was alleged to be the "enormous and unreasonable profits" earned by the Standard Oil Trust and the Standard Oil Company as a result of the alleged monopoly; which presumably was averred as a means of reflexly inferring the scope and power acquired by the alleged combination.[2]

Standard was alleged to have dominated the buying of crude oil, used its control of crude oil transportation in a manner that discriminated against its smaller competitors, and engaged in a wide variety of urban market practices including local discriminatory price cutting, bribery and threats, and questionable and secret rebates.

Some of these allegations indicate concern with economically meaningful conditions, but most of the charges seem to be taken up with "evil-men-and-good-friends" subject matter. The former include factors that involve some power or control over the structure or practices of an industry, including price control, product

2 *Ibid.,* 42–43.

quality and quantity, and conditions of entry and exit. However, the latter are repugnant and are condemned because they deviate from implicitly accepted social standards. These include acts by which, in the view of society, businessmen injure their fellowman solely for the sake of profit: that is, bogus patent suits, rebates, patent pools, food adulteration, and so on.

In the Standard Oil case only the alleged selective price cutting would appear to be an economic evil as such; other allegations would seemingly be violations of a criminal or tort nature or of society's mores. For example, the use of bogus companies to cut prices in some areas in order to deceive competitors and the public would not violate any economic requirement of competition or a legal prohibition. Bogus companies seem to have been condemned solely because their use did not seem quite "fair." Bribing of other companies' employees undoubtedly violated pre-existing law, and thus the application of antitrust laws and the dissolution of a business enterprise were not necessary to remedy conduct of this nature. The alleged unfairness of refusing to ship competitors' products over the Standard pipelines seemed to violate no existing statute since pipelines were not considered common carriers during most of the period. The use of rebates was allegedly an unfair method of competition, but this was an accepted business practice of the period. Standard, however, was possibly more effective in adapting this practice to domestic business. One important deviation was Standard's receipt of rebates for goods shipped by its competitors over the same lines in competition with Standard, but this practice alone would not normally support a full-scale attack upon a corporation and the "offense," if that term may be used, would probably come under the traditional common law or more specialized statutory prohibitions.

In a sense the extra rebates constitute an economic problem when viewed as a variety of price discrimination, with major consequent effects on resource allocation and consumption. Depending on the supply-and-demand functions in a particular market, the granting of favored discriminatory rates for one component resource of a final good can lead to lower prices and in turn greater consumption of that final good than might exist without such discriminatory treatment. Thus, marginal cost pricing by the railroads would have provided for lower prices and an increase in Standard's sales-production. Conceivably, with a more efficient use of fixed production facilities, this could have led to still lower average costs, and in turn lower prices and higher sales would follow (depending, of course, on demand elasticities). Under the hypothetical market the latter price reduction would not have been possible without the original rate discrimination. Unfortunately, such an analysis of the pricing policies and production costs was not attempted by the Court; instead, these rebates were considered solely in terms of "unfair competition" and of monopoly power as indicated by favored treatment.

Of all the allegations, the one of most economic substance was Standard's use of predatory price cutting as a device to secure complete market control. In such cases a company operating in two or more separate markets with varying competitive economic conditions may lower its prices in the competitive market in order to inflict sustained losses on the other (competitive) producers and thereby drive them from that market. Although the price-cutting firm will also be operating at a loss (assuming equal plant efficiency for all producers), its losses will be subsidized by its monopolistic profits in other markets. Moreover, when the other firms have been driven out of the originally competitive market, prices can then be raised to monopolistic levels. These tactics seem rather efficient on paper, and an examination of prices indicated that Standard in fact charged different prices in different markets. The final Supreme Court decision cited this factor, which has been a central issue in subsequent considerations of the case.

One notices that the Court's opinion is divided into four primary sections, a pattern that is followed in many of the following opinions. The first section is concerned with the statement of the Sherman Act and its meaning as reflected both by common law and by the congressional debates on the 1890 bill. The second issue receiving the Court's attention was the applicability of the statute to the alleged acts. At this stage the Court lays down its "rule of reason," which is designed to identify those conditions and behavior that are within the Sherman Act's jurisdiction. The decision that only unreasonable acts are prohibited marks a distinct break with prior decisions and served to guide future decisions for over forty years. The Court then turns to a determination of the facts of the case and the subsequent application of the statute. The importance of the Court's inferences is particularly evident here, especially as they follow the company's growth through a variety of legal structures. Last is a consideration of remedies, which, in this instance, were the general acceptance of those provided by the lower court. Of interest in this case was a partially dissenting opinion by Justice Harlan who, although concurring in the verdict, felt constrained to oppose the "rule of reason" concept, one of the landmark aspects of this decision.

···

STANDARD OIL COMPANY
OF NEW JERSEY
v.
UNITED STATES
221 U.S.1 (1911)

Mr. Chief Justice White delivered the opinion of the court:

The Standard Oil Company of New Jersey and thirty-three other corporations, John D. Rockefeller, William Rockefeller, and five other individual defendants, prosecute this appeal to reverse a decree of the court below. Such decree was entered upon a bill filed by the United States under . . . the anti-trust act, and had for its object the enforcement of the provisions of that act. . . .

    . . . The bill was divided into thirty numbered sections, and sought relief upon the theory that the various defendants were engaged in conspiring "to restrain the trade and commerce in petroleum, commonly called 'crude oil,' in refined oil, and in the other products of petroleum, among the several states and territories of the United States and the District of Columbia and with foreign nations, and to monopolize the said commerce." The conspiracy was alleged to have been formed in or about the year

1870 by three of the individual defendants, *viz.:* John D. Rockefeller, William Rockefeller, and Henry M. Flagler. The detailed
averments concerning the alleged conspiracy were arranged with
reference to three periods, the first from 1870 to 1882, the second
from 1882 to 1899, and the third from 1899 to the time of the
filing of the bill.

Indeed, so conclusive, it is urged, is the proof on these subjects,
that it is asserted that the existence of the principal corporate defendant,—the Standard Oil Company of New Jersey,—with the
vast accumulation of property which it owns or controls, because
of its infinite potency for harm and the dangerous example which
its continued existence affords, is an open and enduring menace
to all freedom of trade, and is a byword and reproach to modern
economic methods. On the other hand, in a powerful analysis of
the facts, it is insisted that they demonstrate that the origin and
development of the vast business which the defendants control was
but the result of lawful competitive methods, guided by economic
genius of the highest order, sustained by courage, by a keen in-
sight into commercial situations, resulting in the acquisition of
great wealth, but at the same time serving to stimulate and increase
production, to widely extend the distribution of the products of
petroleum at a cost largely below that which would have otherwise
prevailed, thus proving to be at one and the same time a benefac-
tion to the general public as well as of enormous advantage to
individuals. . . .

First. The text of the act and its meaning.

The debates show that doubt as to whether there was a common law of the United States which governed the subject in the
absence of legislation was among the influences leading to the
passage of the act. They conclusively show, however, that the main
cause which led to the legislation was the thought that it was required by the economic condition of the times; that is, the vast
accumulation of wealth in the hands of corporations and individuals, the enormous development of corporate organization, the
facility for combination which such organizations afforded, the
fact that the facility was being used, and that combinations known

as trusts were being multiplied, and the widespread impression that their power had been and would be exerted to oppress individuals and injure the public generally. . . .

In view of the common law and the law in this country as to restraint of trade, which we have reviewed, and the illuminating effect which that history must have under the rule to which we have referred, we think it results:

a. That the context manifests that the statute was drawn in the light of the existing practical conception of the law of restraint of trade, because it groups as within that class, not only contracts which were in restraint of trade in the subjective sense, but all contracts or acts which theoretically were attempts to monopolize, yet which in practice had come to be considered as in restraint of trade in a broad sense.

b. That in view of the many new forms of contracts and combinations which were being evolved from existing economic conditions, it was deemed essential by an all-embracing enumeration to make sure that no form of contract or combination by which an undue restraint of interstate or foreign commerce was brought about could save such restraint from condemnation. The statute under this view evidenced the intent not to restrain the right to make and enforce contracts, whether resulting from combinations or otherwise, which did not unduly restrain interstate or foreign commerce, but to protect that commerce from being restrained by methods, whether old or new, which would constitute an interference,—that is, an undue restraint.

c. And as the contracts or acts embraced in the provision were not expressly defined, since the enumeration addressed itself simply to classes of acts, those classes being broad enough to embrace every conceivable contract or combination which could be made concerning trade or commerce or the subjects of such commerce, and thus caused any act done by any of the enumerated methods anywhere in the whole field of human activity to be illegal if in restraint of trade, it inevitably follows that the provision necessarily called for the exercise of judgment which required that some standard should be resorted to for the purpose of determining whether the prohibition contained in the statute had or had not in any given case been violated. Thus not specifying, but indubitably contemplating and requiring a standard, it follows that it was intended that the standard of reason which had been applied at the common law and in this country in dealing with subjects of the character embraced by the statute was intended to be the measure used for the purpose of determining whether, in a given case, a particular act had or had not brought about the wrong against which the statute provided.

And a consideration of the text of the 2d section serves to establish that it was intended to supplement the 1st, and to make sure that by no possible guise could the public policy embodied in the 1st section be frustrated or evaded. . . .

Second. The contentions of the parties as to the meaning of the statute, and the decisions of this court relied upon concerning those contentions. rule of reason

In substance, the propositions urged by the government are reducible to this: That the language of the statute embraces every contract, combination, etc., in restraint of trade, and hence its text leaves no room for the exercise of judgment, but simply imposes the plain duty of applying its prohibitions to every case within its literal language. The error involved lies in assuming the matter to be decided. This is true, because, as the acts which may come under the classes stated in the 1st section and the restraint of trade to which that section applies are not specifically enumerated or defined, it is obvious that judgment must in every case be called into play in order to determine whether a particular act is embraced within the statutory classes, and whether, if the act is within such classes, its nature or effect causes it to be a restraint of trade within the intendment of the act. To hold to the contrary would require the conclusion either that every contract, act, or combination of any kind or nature, whether it operated a restraint on trade or not, was within the statute. . . .

We come, then, to the third proposition requiring consideration, *viz.:*

Third. The facts and the application of the statute to them.

Beyond dispute the proofs establish substantially as alleged in the bill the following facts:

1. The creation of the Standard Oil Company of Ohio.

2. The organization of the Standard Oil Trust of 1882, and also a previous one of 1879, not referred to in the bill, and the proceedings in the supreme court of Ohio, culminating in a decree based upon the finding that the company was unlawfully a party to that trust; the transfer by the trustees of stocks in certain of the companies; the contempt proceedings; and, finally, the increase of the capital of the Standard Oil Company of New Jersey and the acquisition by that company of the shares of the stock of the other corporations in exchange for its certificates.

The vast amount of property and the possibilities of far-reaching control which resulted from the facts last stated are shown by the statement which we have previously annexed concerning the parties to the trust agreement of 1882, and the corporations whose stock was held by the trustees under the trust, and which came therefore to be held by the New Jersey corporation. But these statements do not with accuracy convey an appreciation of the situation as it existed at the time of the entry of the decree below, since, during the more than ten years which elapsed between the acquiring by the New Jersey corporation of the stock and other property which was formerly held by the trustees under the trust agreement, the situation, of course, had somewhat changed,—a change which, when analyzed in the light of the proof, we think establishes that the result of enlarging the capital stock of the New Jersey company and giving it the vast power to which we have referred produced its normal consequence; that is, it gave to the corporation, despite enormous dividends and despite the dropping out of certain corporations enumerated in the decree of the court below, an enlarged and more perfect sway and control over the trade and commerce in petroleum and its products. The ultimate situation referred to will be made manifest by an examination of §§ 2 and 4 of the decree below, which are excerpted in the margin.

Giving to the facts just stated the weight which it was deemed they were entitled to, in the light afforded by the proof of other cognate facts and circumstances, the court below held that the acts and dealings established by the proof operated to destroy the "potentiality of competition" which otherwise would have existed to such an extent as to cause the transfers of stock which were made to the New Jersey corporation and the control which resulted over the many and various subsidiary corporations to be a combination or conspiracy in restraint of trade, in violation of the 1st section of the act, but also to be an attempt to monopolize and monopolization bringing about a perennial violation of the 2d section.

We see no cause to doubt the correctness of these conclusions, considering the subject from every aspect; that is, both in view of the facts established by the record and the necessary operation and effect of the law as we have construed it upon the inferences deducible from the facts, for the following reasons:

a. Because the unification of power and control over petroleum and its products which was the inevitable result of the combining in the New Jersey corporation by the increase of its stock and the transfer to it of the stocks of so many other corporations, aggregating so vast a capital, gives rise, in and of itself, in the absence of countervailing circumstances, to say the least, to the prima facie presumption of intent and purpose to maintain the dominancy over the oil industry, not as a result of normal methods of industrial development, but by new means of combination which were resorted to in order that greater power might be added than would otherwise have arisen had normal methods been followed, the whole with the purpose of excluding others from the trade, and thus centralizing in the combination a perpetual control of the movements of petroleum and its products in the channels of interstate commerce.

b. Because the prima facie presumption of intent to restrain trade, to monopolize and to bring about monopolization, resulting from the act of expanding the stock of the New Jersey corporation and vesting it with such vast control of the oil industry, is made conclusive by considering (1) the conduct of the persons or corporations who were mainly instrumental in bringing about the extension of power in the New Jersey corporation before the consummation of that result and prior to the formation of the trust agreements of 1879 and 1882; (2) by considering the proof as to what was done under those agreements and the acts which immediately preceded the vesting of power in the New Jersey corporation, as well as by weighing the modes in which the power vested in that corporation has been exerted and the results which have arisen from it.

Recurring to the acts done by the individuals or corporations who were mainly instrumental in bringing about the expansion of the New Jersey corporation during the period prior to the formation of the trust agreements of 1879 and 1882, including those agreements, not for the purpose of weighing the substantial merit of the numerous charges of wrongdoing made during such period, but solely as an aid for discovering intent and purpose, we think no disinterested mind can survey the period in question without being irresistibly driven to the conclusion that the very genius for commercial development and organization which it would seem was manifested from the beginning soon begot an intent and purpose to exclude others which was frequently manifested by acts and dealings wholly inconsistent with the theory that they were made with the single conception of advancing the development of business power by usual methods, but which, on the contrary, necessarily involved the intent to drive others from the field and to exclude them from their right to trade, and thus accomplish the mastery which was the end in view. And, considering the period from the date of the trust agreements of 1879 and 1882, up to the time of the expansion of the New Jersey corporation, the gradual extension of the power over the commerce in oil which ensued, the decision of the supreme court of Ohio, the tardiness or reluctance in conforming to the commands of that decision, the methods first adopted and that which finally culminated in the plan of the New Jersey corporation, all additionally serve to make manifest the continued existence of the intent which we have previously indicated, and which, among other things, impelled the expansion of the New Jersey corporation. The exercise of the power which resulted from that organization fortifies the foregoing conclusions, since the development which came, the acquisition here and there which ensued of every efficient means by which competition could have been asserted, the slow but resistless methods which followed by which means of transportation were absorbed and brought under control, the system of marketing which was adopted by which the country was divided into districts and the trade in each district in oil was turned over to a designated corporation within the combination, and all others were excluded, all lead the mind up to a conviction of a purpose and intent which we think is so certain as practically to cause the subject not to be within the domain of reasonable contention.

The inference that no attempt to monopolize could have been intended, and that no monopolization resulted from the acts complained of, since it is established that a very small percentage of the crude oil produced was controlled by the combination, is unwarranted. As substantial power over the crude product was the inevitable result of the absolute control which existed over the refined product, the monopolization of the one carried with it the power to control the other; and if the inferences which this situation suggests were developed, which we deem it unnecessary to do, they might well serve to add additional cogency to the presumption of intent to monopolize which we have found arises from the unquestioned proof on other subjects.

We are thus brought to the last subject which we are called upon to consider, *viz.:*

Fourth. The remedy to be administered.

In applying remedies for this purpose, however, the fact must not be overlooked that injury to the public by the prevention of an undue restraint on, or the monopolization of, trade or commerce, is the foundation upon which the prohibitions of the statute rest, and moreover that one of the fundamental purposes of the statute is to protect, not to destroy, rights of property.

Let us, then, as a means of accurately determining what relief we are to afford, first come to consider what relief was afforded by the court below, in order to fix how far it is necessary to take or add to that relief, to the end that the prohibitions of the statute may have complete and operative force.

Our conclusion is that the decree below was right and should be affirmed, except as to the minor matters concerning which we have indicated the decree should be modified. Our order will therefore be one of affirmance, with directions, however, to modify the decree in accordance with this opinion. The court below to retain jurisdiction to the extent necessary to compel compliance in every respect with its decree.

And it is so ordered.

Mr. Justice Harlan, concurring in part and dissenting in part:

A sense of duty constrains me to express the objections which I have to certain declarations in the opinion just delivered on behalf of the court.

I concur in holding that the Standard Oil Company of New Jersey and its subsidiary companies constitute a combination in restraint of interstate commerce, and that they have attempted to monopolize and have monopolized parts of such commerce,— all in violation of what is known as the anti-trust act of 1890. 26 Stat. at L. 209, chap. 647, U.S. Comp. Stat. 1901, p. 3200. The evidence in this case overwhelmingly sustained that view and led the circuit court, by its final decree, to order the dissolution of the New Jersey corporation and the discontinuance of the illegal combination between that corporation and its subsidiary companies.

In my judgment, the decree should have been affirmed without qualification. But the court, while affirming the decree, directs some modifications in respect of what it characterizes as "minor matters." It is to be apprehended that those modifications may prove to be mischievous . . .

. . . When counsel in the present case insisted upon a reversal of the former rulings of this court, and asked such an interpretation of the anti-trust act, as would allow reasonable restraints of interstate commerce, this court, in deference to establish practice, should, I submit, have said to them: "That question, according to our practice, is not open for further discussion here. This court long ago deliberately held (1) that the act, interpreting its words in their ordinary acceptation, prohibits all restraints of interstate commerce by combinations in whatever form, and whether reasonable or unreasonable; (2) the question relates to matters of public policy in reference to commerce among the states and with foreign nations, and Congress alone can deal with the subject; (3) this court would encroach upon the authority of Congress if, under the guise of construction, it should assume to determine a matter of public policy; (4) the parties must go to Congress and obtain an amendment of the anti-trust act if they think this court was wrong in its former decisions; and (5) this court cannot and will not *judicially legislate,* since its function is to declare the law, while it belongs to the legislative department to make the law." Such a course, I am sure, would not have offended the "rule of reason."

But my brethren, in their wisdom, have deemed it best to pursue a different course. They have now said to those who condemn our former decisions and who object to all legislative prohibitions of contracts, combinations, and trusts in restraint of interstate commerce, "You may *now restrain* such commerce, provided you are reasonable about it; only take care that the restraint is not undue." The disposition of the case under consideration, according to the views of the defendants, will, it is claimed, quiet and give rest to "the business of the country." On the contrary, I have a strong conviction that it will throw the business of the country into confusion and invite widely-extended and harassing litigation, the injurious effects of which will be felt for many years to come. When Congress prohibited *every* contract, combination, or monopoly, in restraint of commerce, it prescribed a simple, definite rule that all could understand, and which could be easily applied by everyone wishing to obey the law, and not to conduct their business in violation of law. But now, it is to be feared, we are to have, in cases without number, the constantly recurring inquiry—difficult to solve by proof—whether the particular contract, combination, or trust involved in each case is or is not an "unreasonable" or "undue" restraint of trade. Congress, in effect, said that there should be *no* restraint of trade, *in any form,* and this court solemnly adjudged many years ago that Congress meant what it thus said in clear and explicit words, and that it *could not* add to the words of the act. But those who condemn the action of Congress are now, in effect, informed that the courts will allow such restraint of interstate commerce as are shown not to be unreasonable or undue.

I do not stop to discuss the merits of the policy embodied in the anti-trust act of 1890; for, as has been often adjudged, the

courts, under our constitutional system, have no rightful concern
with the wisdom or policy of legislation enacted by that branch of
the government which alone can make laws.

For the reasons stated, while concurring in the general affirmance
of the decree of the Circuit Court, I dissent from that part of the
judgment of this court which directs the modification of the
decree of the Circuit Court, as well as from those parts of the
opinion which, in effect, assert authority in this court to insert
words in the anti-trust act which Congress did not put there, and
which, being inserted, Congress is made to declare, as part of the
public policy of the country, what it has not chosen to declare.

....

[Initially, the interpretations of law together with the statement and
the appraisal of facts given in the Standard Oil decision were largely
accepted at face value. The Court's "rule of reason," as we shall
see, proved inadequate for prosecution where size and economic
power were sometimes overwhelming but where conduct was not
blatantly predatory in nature. However, the Court's economic analysis of the facts in the Standard Oil case—especially concerning
Standard's supposed predatory price cutting—continued to be accepted even after the Court's interpretations of law were discarded.

The following analysis by Professor John S. McGee challenges
this traditional view of Standard's conduct and raises considerable
doubt as to the benefits of predatory price cutting to Standard. In
the excerpt given here, McGee argues that predatory price cutting
was not likely to be used by the pre-1911 Standard Oil enterprise
as a means of securing monopoly power. Only the first two parts of
McGee's article are presented here: the introductory statement concerning the predatory price cutting and Standard Oil, and McGee's
hypothesis concerning these issues. In a rather lengthy third section
Professor McGee described the results of his reexamination of the
voluminous Standard Oil trial record; these findings supported the
conclusions derived in the article's second section.]

....

Predatory Price Cutting:
the Standard Oil (N.J.) case
John S. McGee

....

> *He [Rockefeller] applied underselling for destroying his rivals' markets with the same deliberation and persistency that characterized all his efforts, and in the long run he always won.*—IDA TARBELL.

I. INTRODUCTION

The purpose of this paper is to determine whether the pre-dissolution Standard Oil Company actually used predatory price cutting to achieve or maintain its monopoly. This issue is of much more than antiquarian or theoretic interest. Settling it is of direct importance to present anti-trust policy. At the very least, finding the facts should aid in defining certain hazy notions that now figure in discussions of monopoly and its control.

The *Standard Oil* case of 1911[1] is a landmark in the development of anti-trust law. But it is more than a famous law case: it created a legend. The firm whose history it relates became the archetype of predatory monopoly.

It is sometimes said that *Standard Oil* was influential because it revealed deadly and reprehensible techniques by which Monopoly on a heroic scale could be achieved and, probably more important, perpetuated. Historians tell us that the facts revealed in *Standard Oil* were in good part responsible for the emphasis that the anti-

Abridged from John S. McGee, "Predatory Price Cutting: The Standard Oil (N.J.) Case," *The Journal of Law and Economics*, I (October 1958); 137–143.

[1] Standard Oil Co. of New Jersey v. United States, 221 U.S. 1 (1911).

trust laws came to place upon unfair and monopolizing business practices.

Perhaps the most famous of all of the monopolizing techniques that Standard is supposed to have used is local price cutting. Given the bad repute in which monopoly has long been officially held in this country, and the prominence of predatory pricing in *Standard Oil,* it is not surprising that the practice received special attention in the law. Monopoly was not new in 1911, but a predatory giant may have seemed novel. The vision of a giant firm that used a brutally scientific, and completely effective, technique for acquiring and maintaining monopoly must have aroused uncommon concern. Standard was invincible. Anything economists could say about the transience of monopoly must have seemed hopelessly unrealistic in view of the vigor and success with which Standard was said to have prevented entry.

In any case, by 1914, in the Clayton Act, predatory price discrimination was included among a select group of business practices the character or effect of which called for explicit statutory prohibition. The Robinson-Patman amendment of 1936 lengthened the list, but certainly did not weaken the hostility toward local price cutting. Indeed, its legislative history and subsequent interpretation reveal a continuing dread of the device.

Predatory discrimination thus occupies a special and almost unquestioned place in law and economics. This has led to a certain amount of difficulty, especially in connection with the Robinson-Patman Act. Some critics claim that this statute unnecessarily restricts rivalry, thereby softening competition. Yet even the critics apparently fear that if we permit the helpful kind of discrimination we will encourage the lethal kind. Most are obliged to rely on the tenuous standard of intent to distinguish one kind from the other.

This fearful ambivalence, in which the spectre of *Standard Oil* figures prominently, may be responsible for the continuing, and somewhat fruitless, arguments about the proper role of a "good faith" defense under Section 2(B) of the Robinson-Patman Act. It may also account for the popular view that disciplinary price cutting makes cartelization easier and its benefits more lasting. It surely has influenced thinking about small firms that face large rivals.

For these reasons, a re-examination of *Standard Oil* may be worthwhile.

II. PREDATORY PRICE CUTTING: SOME HYPOTHESES

According to most accounts, the Standard Oil Co. of New Jersey established an oil refining monopoly in the United States, in large part through the systematic use of predatory price discrimination. Standard struck down its competitors, in one market at a time, until it enjoyed a monopoly position everywhere. Similarly, it preserved its monopoly by cutting prices selectively wherever competitors dared enter. Price discrimination, so the story goes, was both the technique by which it obtained its dominance and the device with which it maintained it.

The main trouble with this "history" is that it is logically deficient, and I can find little or no evidence to support it.[2]

A brief examination of the logic of predatory price discrimination is helpful in interpreting the facts. In the beginning, oil refining in the United States apparently was competitive. Necessary capital was relatively slight, because of the modest quality demands imposed by consumer preferences and the primitive technological character of the refining process itself. The number of refiners was evidently large, since the Standard interests bought out more than a hundred of them. Standard Oil was not born with monopoly power: as late as 1870 it had only 10 per cent of the refining business.

The usual argument that local price cutting is a monopolizing technique *begins* by assuming that the predator has important mo-

[2] I am profoundly indebted to Aaron Director, of the University of Chicago Law School, who in 1953 suggested that this study be undertaken. Professor Director, without investigating the facts, developed a logical framework by which he predicted that Standard Oil had not gotten or maintained its monopoly position by using predatory price cutting. In truth, he predicted, on purely logical grounds, that they never systematically used the technique at all. I was astounded by these hypotheses, and doubtful of their validity, but was also impressed by the logic which produced them. As a consequence, I resolved to investigate the matter, admittedly against my better judgment; for, like everyone else, I knew full well what Standard had really done.

nopoly power, which is his "war chest" for supporting the unprofitable raids and forays. Evidently the technique could not be
used until the Standard interests achieved the necessary monopoly
power. Similarly, advantages from monopsonistic bargaining[3]
would not be available until the buyer attained considerable
stature.

A simpler technique did exist, and Standard used it. Unless
there are legal restraints, anyone can monopolize an industry
through mergers and acquisitions, paying for the acquisitions by
permitting participation of the former owners in the expected monopoly gains. Since profits are thus expanded, all of the participants can be better off even after paying an innovator's share to
the enterpriser who got the idea in the first place.

Under either competition or monopoly, the value of a firm is
the present worth of its future income stream. Competitive firms
can be purchased for competitive asset values or, at worst, for only
a little more. Even in the case of important recalcitrants, anything
up to the present value of the future monopoly profits from the
property will be a worthwhile exchange to the buyer, and a bounti-
ful windfall to the seller.

It is conceivable that Standard did not merge to the full size it
wanted, but did achieve whatever size was necessary to use predatory techniques to grow the rest of the way. How would it go about
using them? Assume that Standard had an absolute monopoly in
some important markets, and was earning substantial profits there.
Assume that in another market there are several competitors, all
of whom Standard wants to get out of the way. Standard cuts
the price below cost. Everyone suffers losses. Standard would, of
course, suffer losses even though it has other profitable markets:
it could have been earning at least competitive returns and is not.
The war could go on until average variable costs are not covered
and are not expected to be covered; and the competitors drop out.
In the meanwhile, the predator would have been pouring money
in to crush them. If, instead of fighting, the would-be monopolist
bought out his competitors directly, he could afford to pay them

---

[3] Example: railroad rebates. Although this subject lies outside the present
inquiry, I am convinced that the significance of railroad rebates has also
been misunderstood.

up to the discounted value of the expected monopoly profits to be gotten as a result of their extinction. Anything above the competitive value of their firms should be enough to buy them. In the purchase case, monopoly profits could begin at once; in the predatory case, large losses would first have to be incurred. Losses would have to be set off against the prospective monopoly profits, discounted appropriately. Even supposing that the competitors would not sell for competitive value, it is difficult to see why the predator would be unwilling to take the amount that he would otherwise spend in price wars and pay it as a bonus.

Since the revenues to be gotten during the predatory price war will always be less than those that could be gotten immediately through purchase, and will not be higher after the war is concluded, present worth will be higher in the purchase case. For a predatory campaign to make sense the direct costs of the price war must be less than for purchase. It is necessary to determine whether that is possible.

Assume that the monopolizer's costs are equal to those of his competitors. The market has enough independent sellers to be competitive. Otherwise the problem of monopolizing it ceases to concern us. This implies that the monopolist does not now sell enough in the market to control it. If he seeks to depress the price below the competitive level he must be prepared to sell increasing quantities, since the mechanism of forcing a lower price compels him to lure customers away from his rivals, making them meet his price or go without customers. To lure customers away from somebody, he must be prepared to serve them himself. The monopolizer thus finds himself in the position of selling more—and therefore losing more—than his competitors. Standard's market share was often 75 per cent or more. In the 75 per cent case the monopolizer would sell three times as much as all competitors taken together, and, on the assumption of equal unit costs, would lose roughly three times as much as all of them taken together.[4]

Losses incurred in this way are losses judged even by the standard of competitive returns. Since the alternative of outright pur-

---

[4] Any assumption that the monopolizer's size gives him sufficient cost advantage rapidly takes us away from a predatory price cutting example and into the realm of so-called natural monopolies.

chase of rivals would have produced immediate monopoly returns, the loss in view of the alternatives can be very great indeed.[5] Furthermore, at some stage of the game the competitors may simply shut down operations temporarily, letting the monopolist take all the business (and all the losses), then simply resume operations when he raises prices again. At prices above average variable costs, but below total unit costs, the "war" might go on for years.

Purchase has an additional marked advantage over the predatory technique. It is rare for an industrial plant to wear out all at once. If price does not cover average variable costs, the operation is suspended. This will often leave the plant wholly intact. In the longer run, it may simply be the failure of some key unit, the replacement of which is uneconomic at the present price level, that precipitates shut-down. In either case, physical capacity remains, and will be brought back into play by some opportunist once the monopolizer raises prices to enjoy the fruits of the battle he has spent so much in winning.

All in all, then, purchase would not be more expensive than war without quarter, and should be both cheaper and more permanent. It may at first be thought that predatory pricing more than makes up for its expense by depressing the purchase price of the properties to be absorbed. In effect, this requires that large losses reduce asset values less than smaller losses. This is not at all likely. Furthermore, assuming that the properties in question are economic,[6] it is unlikely that their long-run market value will be much reduced by an artificially low price that clearly will not be permanent. The owners can shut down temporarily, allowing the monopolist to carry all of the very unprofitable business, or simply wait for him to see the error of his ways and purchase. Even if there is widespread bankruptcy, wise men will see the value to the monopolist of bringing the facilities under his control, and find it profitable to purchase them at some price below what the monopolist can be expected to pay if he must. Since the monopolist is presumably

[5] It must not be supposed that, just because he enjoys profits elsewhere, anyone will be so stupid as to assume that it is costless to use them for anything but the best alternatives.

[6] If they are not, they need not concern us, since their extinction might be expected or welcomed under competition.

interested in profits, and has a notion of the effect of discount factors upon future income, he cannot afford to wait forever. Properties that a would-be monopolist needs to control can be an attractive investment.

Predation would thus be profitable only when the process produces purchase prices that are so far below competitive asset figures that they more than offset the large losses necessary to produce them. One empirical test, for those who suspect the logic, would be to examine prices paid for properties in cases where predatory pricing is alleged to have been practiced.

Some of the most strategic factors to be monopolized may be the skilled managerial and technical personnel of competitors. Reproducing them can be a much more formidable and longer job than the construction of physical facilities. But short of murder, the cost of which can also be expected to be high if undertaken in any quantity, the only feasible way of preventing their embarrassing and costly reappearance is to hire, retire, or share with them. None of these things can be accomplished well or permanently if these people are too much badgered in the process.[7]

There are two other crucial issues that must be examined, the first dealing with the extent to which monopolization is profitable; the second, with the necessary conditions for its success. Monopolization as such will be carried only so far as is necessary to maximize profits, since it inevitably involves certain expenses of planning, purchase, and rationalization. In the case of a vertically integrated industry the would-be monopolist will choose to monopolize the level that will produce the largest net profit. This requires choosing that one which is both cheapest to control and over which control is likely to endure. If a monopoly can be achieved at the refining level, for example, there is little sense trying to achieve one at the crude oil producing level, or marketing.

---

[7] "[A]s Mr. Rockefeller and Mr. Archbold testified, most of the concerns which were brought together continued to be operated and managed by the former owners." Brief for the U.S., Vol. 1, at 19.

Further, "There are only a few cases in which the Standard interests, during this period [1872–80], acquired stock in concerns without taking the former owners in as stockholders of the Standard, or bringing them into the combination by leaving them a minority interest in the original concern." Id., at 32.

Standard Oil of New Jersey achieved a refinery monopoly; anything more would have been redundant.[8]

This should not be taken to mean that the monopolist will not care what happens to the other levels; for he has every interest in seeing to it that the other levels are not monopolized by someone else. In marketing, for example, he would prefer that the product be distributed as cheaply as possible, since he can then extract full monopoly revenues from the level in his control. This point is important in interpreting the facts of the *Standard Oil* case.

Obstacles to entry are necessary conditions for success. Entry is the nemesis of monopoly. It is foolish to monopolize an area or market into which entry is quick and easy. Moreover, monopolization that produces a firm of greater than optimum size is in for trouble if entry can occur even over a longer period. In general, monopolization will not pay if there is no special qualification for entry, or no relatively long gestation period for the facilities that must be committed for successful entry.

Finally, it is necessary to examine certain data that are often taken to be symptomatic of predatory price cutting, when in fact they may be nothing of the sort. Assume that a monopolist sells in two markets, separated effectively by transport costs or other impediments to free interchange, and that he has a complete monopoly in both. Elasticity of demand is assumed to be the same in both markets, and monopoly prices are identical. Assume that, for some unknown reason, entry occurs in one market but not in the other. Supplies are increased in the first and price falls; price in the second remains unchanged. There are now two different prices in the two markets, reflecting the existence of alternative supplies in the first. The theory of the dominant firm, maximizing by taking into account the outputs of his lesser rivals at various prices, appears to fit the case. An objective fact-finder discovers that the monopolist is discriminating in price between the two

---

[8] This abstracts from any cost reductions that integration may make possible. These have nothing to do with the problem at hand.

See Bork, Vertical Integration and the Sherman Act, 22 U. of Chi. L. Rev. 157 (1954). Standard began producing crude oil in 1889, and by 1898 produced 33 per cent of the total. By 1906, its share declined to 11.11 per cent. Transcript of Record Vol., 19, at 626 (Def. Exh. 266).

markets. A bad theorist then concludes that he is preying on some-body. In truth, the principle established is only that greater sup-plies bring lower prices.

Compare this example with another. Assume that we have two separate markets, and that each is in short-run competitive equi-librium with firms earning super-normal returns. Assume that, for some reasons, entry takes place in one market but not in the other. Supply increases and price falls in one but not in the other. From this evidence of price changes in both the monopoly and compe-tition examples, the inference is simply that greater supplies lower prices. We should not infer fom the price data that either case has anything to do with predatory price cutting.

To sum up: (1) Predatory price cutting does not explain how a seller acquires the monopoly power that he must have before he could practice it. (2) Whereas it is *conceivable* that someone might embark on a predatory program, I cannot see that it would pay him to do so, since outright purchase is both cheaper and more reliable. (3) Because monopolization by any technique al-ways involves some expense, a firm *qua* monopolizer will carry it to the one securest level in an integrated industry, not to all. (4) Actual variations in prices among markets may be accounted for in terms of variations in demand elasticities, but do not imply or establish that anybody is preying on anybody else.

4 MONOPOLY:

From Common Law to Economics

McGee's analysis now appears compelling to a great many economists, and to some his conclusions are "beyond question." But his study is a recent one, which clearly could not have affected the course of early monopoly prosecution. As noted earlier, after the Standard Oil case the most general view of monopoly was in terms of patterns of predatory behavior—such as the so-called predatory price cutting. This behavior was presumably followed with an intent to restrain the degree of competition among established firms, to forestall the emergence of new competitors and new competition, and to drive out competitors. It is not inconceivable that if McGee's article had appeared four and a half decades earlier, it would have successfully challenged the analysis adopted in the Standard Oil case.

To be sure, the rejection of the Court's analysis in the Standard Oil case is not tantamount to a rejection of either the Court's conclusion or the remedies in the case. After all, in many areas of the country and in a number of important product lines, Standard was a dominant firm that possessed great power to affect prices, output, and the allocation of resources within this sector generally.

The adherence to the predatory-behavior view of monopoly, however, proved to be the Achilles' heel of early twentieth-century antitrust prosecution. In the minds of many students of antitrust activity, both in law and in economics, the 1920 United States

Steel[1] decision most dramatically reveals the inadequacies of the "rule of reason."

In the United States Steel case the Court again adopted and applied the "rule of reason," with the views of monopoly in terms of predatory behavior embedded in that rule. U.S. Steel was organized in 1901 through the combination of several large steel companies, themselves the result of earlier consolidations. At the time of its formation, U.S. Steel was popularly known as "the World's greatest corporation" (that is, the *largest*). U.S. Steel was then preeminent among domestic steel producers, but while it expanded greatly during the next decade, its market share in several important product lines declined considerably. The District Court's review of the period from 1901 to 1911, when the suit was initiated, clearly revealed how the growth of smaller producers had outstripped that of U.S. Steel in several basic product lines.

. . . in 1911 the finished rolled product—which excludes pig iron, steel castings, and ingots—of the United States . . . was 19,000,000 tons. Of this tonnage the competitors of the Steel Corporation produced 54 per cent., or 10,300,000 tons, while the Steel Corporation made 8,700,000 tons; but not only did its competitors produce in 1911 the major part of the country's finished rolled product, . . . but judging from the past, the present proportionate lead of the competitors bids fair to increase. In 1901 . . . the total finished roll product . . . was substantially divided between 49.9 per cent. made by its competitors, and 50.1 per cent. by the Steel Corporation. While both together have since increased the nation's product from 13,000,000 to 19,000,000 tons, yet of this 6,000,000 increase its competitors produced 3,400,000 tons to the Steel Company's 2,600,000 tons.

Taking steel ingots, another basic supply on which great numbers of finishing industries are ultimately dependent, we find . . . that while in 1901, of the 13,000,000 tons of the total American ingot production, the competitors of the Steel Company only made 4,500,000 tons, as against the Steel Company's 8,500,000, yet by 1911 . . . the competitors had increased their production by 6,500,000 tons, while the Steel Company had only increased 4,500,

[1] United States v. United States Steel Corporation, 251 U.S. 417 (1920).

000. In other words, while the Steel Company produced in 1901, 66 per cent. of the country's ingot production, it was producing but 54 per cent. in 1911.[2]

In other product lines, however, U.S. Steel's share of domestic output increased during the period. Nevertheless, in a number of these instances, the evidence indicated that U.S. Steel's domestic *sales* relative to other American producers had fallen. This result reflected the Steel Corporation's dramatic success in the export markets. Thus, with respect to these product lines, the District Court also concluded that the market positions of the independent steel producers had improved during the 1901–1911 period.

Most economists would maintain, however, that the market position held by U.S. Steel in 1911 remained sufficient to give the company appreciable control, or at least influence, of a monopolistic nature—over the prices, output, and general resource allocation in this sector of the economy. The Supreme Court was wedded to a construction of the law that relied on incidents of behavior rather than patterns of results.

> The corporation is undoubtedly of impressive size, and it takes an effort of resolution not to be affected by it or to exaggerate its influence. But we must adhere to the law, and the law does not make mere size an offense or the existence of unexerted power an offense. It . . . requires overt acts, and trusts to its prohibition of them and its power to repress or punish them. It does not compel competition, nor require all that is possible.[3]

In turning to "overt acts" for evidence of possible unlawful monopoly, the Supreme Court was again utilizing the interpretation of the Sherman Act that had been applied in the earlier Standard Oil case. But, unlike Standard Oil, to quote a summary of the District Court opinion with which the Supreme Court concurred, U.S. Steel

---

[2] United States v. United States Steel Corporation, 223 Fed. Rep. 55 (1915), 65.

[3] *Op. cit.,* 451.

. . . did not at any time abuse the power or ascendancy it possessed. It resorted to none of the brutalities or tyrannies that the cases illustrate of other combinations. It did not secure freight rebates; it did not increase its profits by reducing the wages of its employees,—whatever it did was not at the expense of labor; it did not increase its profits by lowering the quality of its products, nor create an artificial scarcity of them; it did not oppress or coerce its competitors,—its competition, though vigorous, was fair; it did not undersell its competitors in some localities by reducing its prices there below those maintained elsewhere, or require its customers to enter into contracts limiting their purchases or restricting them in resale prices; it did not obtain customers by secret rebates or departures from its published prices; there was no evidence that it attempted to crush its competitors or drive them out of the market, nor did it take customers from its competitors by unfair means, and in its competition it seemed to make no difference between large and small competitors.[4]

In short, the Steel Corporation was one of the "good guys" that colluded with rather than crushed rivals. Rather than engage in predatory behavior, U.S. Steel "combined its power with that of its competitors. It did not have power in and of itself [to fix and maintain prices], and the control it exerted was only in and by association with its competitors." The point that the ability of U.S. Steel to induce and maintain price increases, which in turn led to restricted output, was a reflection of monopoly power was lost to the Court. From the Court's viewpoint, "the government's contention that the acceptance of the corporation's [higher] prices is the submission of impotence to irresistible power is, in view of the testimony of the competitors, untenable." Today the Court's logic seems quaint and naïve; one would hardly expect rivals to view higher prices in the same fashion that drowning men view more

---

[4] *Ibid.*, 440–441. There were two opinions by the District Court in the United States Steel case. Both came to the conclusion that U.S. Steel did not possess an unlawful monopoly, but on the basis of rather different logic. Briefly, two of the District Court judges contended that the corporation was organized in an effort to realize economies of operation rather than to obtain a monopoly position, while two judges contended that the intent was to gain a monopoly position. But all agreed that U.S. Steel had not had, by itself, an unlawful monopoly.

water. Thus, in relying on predatory conduct as the exercise of monopoly power, the Court failed to perceive that higher prices might also reflect monopoly power.

The Court's indulgence of the "good trust" in the United States Steel case was extended in the 1927 International Harvester case.

It does not appear that . . . the International Company has used its capital and resources,—which, although much larger than those of any single competitor, are but little larger than the aggregate capital and resources of all its competitors, and are in large part employed in its foreign trade,—its subsidiary companies, or incidental advantages, for the purpose or with effect of restraining and suppressing the interstate trade in harvesting machinery; that it has at any time reduced the prices of harvesting machines below cost, for the purpose of driving out its competitors; or that it has at any time controlled and dominated the trade in harvesting machinery by the regulation of prices. . . . It has not . . . attempted to dominate or in fact controlled or dominated the harvesting machinery industry by the compulsory regulation of prices. The most that can be said as to this, is that many of its competitors have been accustomed, independently and as a matter of business expediency, to follow approximately the prices at which it has sold its harvesting machines; but one of its competitors has habitually sold its machines at somewhat higher prices. The law, however, does not make the mere size of a corporation, however impressive, or the existence of unexerted power on its part, an offense, when unaccompanied by unlawful conduct in the exercise of its power. *United States* v. *United States Steel Corp.,* 251 U.S. 417 . . . And the fact that competitors may see proper, in the exercise of their own judgment, to follow the prices of another manufacturer, does not establish any suppression of competition or show any sinister domination.[5]

With the 1927 International Harvester decision embellishing the position taken in the United States Steel, the possibility of a vigorous antitrust policy was relegated to limbo. Its resurrection in part awaited the development of a new interpretation of the Sherman

[5] United States v. International Harvester Company, 274 U.S. 693 (1927), 707–709.

Act. This new view of the law, one that has a firm basis in economic analysis, was not forthcoming until the Alcoa decision almost two decades later.

THE ALUMINUM CASE AND THE NEW ANTITRUST POLICY

During the 1930s and the early 1940s, enforcement of the antitrust statutes was often secondary to other social and economic policies. Both the severity of the Depression and the urgency of the World War II efforts led to the primacy of other conflicting policies. During this period, therefore, the objectives of antitrust policy were not motivated by a single overriding goal. Moreover, there was considerable variation in the particular forms of the legislation regulating business and in the enforcement of these laws. During its early years the Roosevelt administration encouraged cooperation between businesses under the aegis of the National Recovery Administration's codes of industry practice.[6] This extensive effort at industry rationalization in order to encourage business recovery was essentially antithetical to a vigorous antitrust policy. For example, the NRA codes often limited the permissible dimensions of rivalry among the industry members by setting minimum prices, common lists of extras, and so on. After only a few years of operation, the Supreme Court declared this legislation unconstitutional. However, shortly afterward, the exigencies of World War II required materials on such vast scales that only big-business enterprises could provide the required military production. As a result, enforcement of the antitrust statutes in large part was held in abeyance until the termination of the war.

The immediate postwar period, however, brought further developments in some of the few cases that were initiated during the earlier period as well as an end to the prevailing gentleman's agreement toward nonenforcement of the antitrust laws. The most im-

---

[6] An excellent and most thorough review of the varied policies toward competition, and mitigation of it, is contained in Ellis W. Hawley's recent study, *The New Deal and the Problem of Monopoly: A Study in Economic Ambivalence* (Princeton: Princeton University Press, 1966).

portant decision of the immediate postwar period was in the Aluminum Company of America[7] case, which was initially filed by the Government in 1937. This 1945 decision seemingly marked new directions in the legal or judicial interpretation of the antitrust statutes and narrowed the gap between the judicial and the economic views of monopoly.

The Alcoa case largely turned on the critical definition of the line of commerce and the market involved in the alleged monopolization. Thus the issues were those that an economist would consider in determining the existence of monopoly. In contrast, in the earlier Sherman Act cases the courts had relied on evidence as to behavior designed to exclude competitors. Furthermore, and more important for its legal precedent, the opinion held that size or condition of monopolization would, by itself, indicate the necessary intent to monopolize since "no monopolist monopolizes unconscious of what he is doing."

These issues, and the logic of the Court's treatment of them, emerge clearly from Judge Learned Hand's opinion, of which excerpts follow. Afterward we will turn to an economist's analysis of, and suggested alternatives to, the eventual remedies in this case. But first, it would be well to consider the Court's major findings.

In determining that Alcoa possessed an unlawful monopoly in virgin aluminum ingot, the Court eschewed many of the previously utilized judicial indexes of monopoly. Much of Judge Hand's opinion in the case turned on the definitions of products and markets. It is most interesting to follow the logic of the product-market delineation in the case. The most crucial issues concerned whether the relevant ingot market should include the virgin ingot used internally by Alcoa for its production of other products and whether secondary aluminum ingot also should be included. In the minds of most economists, Judge Hand properly included Alcoa's entire production of virgin ingot, whether sold as ingot or further processed by Alcoa. Economists would be less approving of his arguments in support of limiting the market definition to virgin aluminum ingot. Judge Hand thereby disregarded secondary

[7] United States v. Aluminum Company of America *et al.*, 148 F. 2d 416 (1945).

ingot, which was freely interchangeable with the virgin ingot for a great many, if not all, purposes. The importance of the product-market definition in this case is partly reflected by the Court's frequently quoted statement that over 90 percent of the market "is enough to constitute a monopoly; it is doubtful whether sixty or sixty-four percent would be enough; and certainly thirty-three percent is not."

After settling the issues of product definitions and permissible market positions, the court turned to the more traditional indexes of monopoly. It argued that a showing of monopoly and not of its abuse was required to indicate a Sherman Act violation; and Judge Hand stated that this could be inferred, under some conditions, by size. Thus the District Court ruled that Alcoa's profits were not monopolistic, but Judge Hand held that "it is no excuse for 'monopolizing' a market that the monopoly has not been used to extract from the consumer more than a 'fair' profit." The Court, therefore, enunciated a view that monopoly itself was bad, not simply as it ended or precluded competition. In other words, Congress "did not condone 'good trusts' and condemn 'bad' ones; it forbad all." In its defense Alcoa argued that its monopoly position had been thrust upon it and was not the result of attempts to monopolize. Alcoa's anticipation of increased demand and the expansion of its facilities in advance of such developments were viewed as an indication of monopolistic intent by the Court rather than as proof of successful competitive behavior. Of first importance was the Courts' ruling that the "power and intent" requirement of the Sherman Act's Section 2 was met by monopoly size alone: " 'Alcoa' meant to keep, and did keep, that complete and exclusive hold upon the ingot market with which it started. That was to 'monopolize' that market, however innocently it otherwise proceeded." [8]

---

[8] In addition the court ruled on charges that Alcoa also engaged in unlawful practices designed "to suppress competitors." These allegations covered the securing of bauxite and water-power sites, suppression of efforts to compete with Alcoa in ingot and fabricated products, and dominating the aluminum markets. The appellate court's opinion held that the government failed to prove these allegations, but the court did say that, in the issue of an alleged price squeeze between aluminum ingot and sheet, the facts warranted different interpretation by the trial judge. The court also

talk about remedy

....

UNITED STATES
v.
ALUMINUM CO. OF AMERICA et al.
148 F. 2d 416 (1945)

Before L. Hand, Swan, and Augustus N. Hand, Circuit Judges:

L. Hand, Circuit Judge.

This appeal comes to us by virtue of a certificate of the Supreme Court, under the amendment of 1944 to § 29 of 15 U.S.C.A. The action was brought under § 4 of that title, praying the district court to adjudge that the defendant, Aluminum Company of America, was monopolizing interstate and foreign commerce, particularly in the manufacture and sale of "virgin" aluminum ingot, and that it be dissolved; and further to adjudge that that company and the defendant, Aluminum Limited, had entered into a conspiracy in restraint of such commerce. . . . We may divide these, as the district judge did, into four classes: Aluminum Company of America, with its whòlly owned subsidiaries, directors, officers and shareholders. (For convenience we shall speak of these defendants collectively as "Alcoa," that being the name by which the company has become almost universally known.) Next, Aluminum Limited, with its directors, officers, and shareholders. (For the same reason we shall speak of this group as "Limited.") Third: the defendant, Aluminum Manufactures, Inc., which may be treated as a subsidiary of "Alcoa." Fourth: the defendant, Aluminum Goods Manufacturing Company, which is independent of "Alcoa," as will appear. The action came to trial on June 1, 1938, and proceeded without much interruption until August 14, 1940, when the case

---

directed its attention to the relationships between Alcoa and Aluminum, Ltd., holding that, despite common ownership, the two were separate and independent companies following Alcoa's divestiture of Aluminum, Ltd., as a subsidiary. However, the court held that Aluminum had entered into cartel agreements that violated domestic antitrust laws by affecting domestic imports.

was closed after more than 40,000 pages of testimony had been taken. The judge . . . entered final judgment dismissing the complaint on July 23rd, of 1940. . . . Although the plaintiff challenged nearly all of the 407 findings of fact, with negligible exceptions these challenges were directed, not to misstatements of the evidence, but to the judge's inferences—alleged to be "clearly erroneous." For convenience we have divided our discussion into four parts: ①️ whether "Alcoa" monopolized the market in "virgin" aluminum ingot; ② whether "Alcoa" was guilty of various unlawful practices, ancillary to the establishment of its monopoly; ③ whether "Limited" and "Alcoa" were in an unlawful conspiracy; and whether, if not, "Limited" was guilty of a conspiracy with foreign producers; ④ what remedies are appropriate in the case of each defendant who may be found to have violated the Act.

"ALCOA'S" MONOPOLY OF "VIRGIN" INGOT

"Alcoa" is a corporation, organized under the laws of Pennsylvania on September 18, 1888; its original name, "Pittsburgh Reduction Company," was changed to its present one on January 1, 1907. It has always been engaged in the production and sale of "ingot" aluminum, and since 1895 also in the fabrication of the metal into many finished and semi-finished articles. It has proliferated into a great number of subsidiaries, created at various times between the years 1900 and 1929, as the business expanded. . . .

. . . The most important question in the case is whether the monopoly in "Alcoa's" production of "virgin" ingot, secured by the two patents until 1909, and in part perpetuated between 1909 and 1912 by the unlawful practices, forbidden by the decree of 1912, continued for the ensuing twenty-eight years; and whether, if it did, it was unlawful under § 2 of the Sherman Act . . . It is undisputed that throughout this period "Alcoa" continued to be the single producer of "virgin" ingot in the United States; and the plaintiff argues that this without more was enough to make it an unlawful monopoly. It also takes an alternative position: that in any event during this period "Alcoa" consistently pursued unlawful exclusionary practices, which made its dominant position certainly unlawful, even though it would not have been, had it been retained only by "natural growth." Finally, it asserts that many of these practices were of themselves unlawful, as contracts in restraint of trade under § 1 of the Act . . . "Alcoa's" position is that the fact that it alone continued to make "virgin" ingot in this country did not, and does not, give it a monopoly of the market; that it was always subject to the competition of imported "virgin" ingot, and of what is called "secondary" ingot; and that even if it had not been, its monopoly would not have been retained by unlawful means, but would have been the result of a growth which the Act does not forbid, even when it results in a monopoly. We shall first consider the amount and character of this competition; next, how far it established a monopoly; and finally, if it did, whether that monopoly was unlawful under § 2 of the Act.

From 1902 onward until 1928 "Alcoa" was making ingot in Canada through a wholly owned subsidiary; so much of this as it imported into the United States it is proper to include with what it produced here. In the year 1912 the sum of these two items represented nearly ninety-one per cent of the total amount of "virgin" ingot available for sale in this country. This percentage varied year by year up to and including 1938: in 1913 it was about seventy-two per cent; in 1921 about sixty-eight per cent; in 1922 about seventy-two; with these exceptions it was always over eighty per cent of the total and for the last five years 1934–1938 inclusive it averaged over ninety per cent. The effect of such a proportion of the production upon the market we reserve for the time being, for it will be necessary first to consider the nature and uses of "secondary" ingot, the name by which the industry knows ingot made from aluminum scrap. This is of two sorts, though for our purposes it is not important to distinguish between them. . . . In spite of this, as in the case of clippings and trimmings, the industry will ordinarily not accept ingot so salvaged upon the same terms as "virgin." There are some seventeen companies which scavenge scrap of all sorts, clean it, remelt it, test it for its composition, make it into ingots and sell it regularly to the trade. . . .

There are various ways of computing "Alcoa's" control of the aluminum market—as distinct from its production—depending upon what one regards as competing in that market. The judge figured its share—during the years 1929–1938, inclusive—as only about thirty-three per cent; to do so he included "secondary," and excluded that part of "Alcoa's" own production which it fabricated and did not therefore sell as ingots. If, on the other hand, "Alcoa's" total production, fabricated and sold, be included, and balanced against the sum of imported "virgin" and "secondary," its share of the market was in the neighborhood of sixty-four per cent for that period. The percentage we have already mentioned—over ninety—results only if we both include all "Alcoa's" production and exclude "secondary." That percentage is enough to constitute a monopoly; it is doubtful whether sixty or sixty-four per cent would be enough; and certainly thirty-three per cent is not. Hence it is necessary to settle what he shall treat as competing in the ingot market. That part of its production which "Alcoa" itself fabricates, does not of course ever reach the market as ingot; and we recognize that it is only when a restriction of production either inevitably affects prices, or is intended to do so, that it violates § 1 of the Act. . . . However, even though we were to assume that a monopoly is unlawful under § 2 only in case it controls prices, the ingot fabricated by "Alcoa," necessarily had a direct effect upon the ingot market. All ingot—with trifling exceptions—is used to fabricate intermediate, or end, products; and therefore all intermediate, or end, products which "Alcoa" fabricates and sells, pro tanto reduce the demand for ingot itself. . . . We cannot therefore agree that the computation of the percentage of "Alcoa's" control over the ingot market should not include the whole of its ingot production.

As to "secondary," as we have said, for certain purposes the industry will not accept it at all; but for those for which it will, the difference in price is ordinarily not very great; the judge found that it was between one and two cents a pound, hardly enough margin on which to base a monopoly. Indeed, there are times when all differential disappears, and "secondary" will actually sell at a higher price: i.e., when there is a supply available which contains just the alloy that a fabricator needs for the article which he proposes to make. Taking the industry as a whole, we can say nothing more definite than that, although "secondary" does not compete at all in some uses (whether because of "sales resistance" only, or because of actual metallurgical inferiority), for most purposes it competes upon a substantial equality with "virgin." On these facts the judge found that "every pound of secondary or scrap aluminum which is sold in commerce displaces a pound of virgin aluminum which otherwise would, or might have been, sold." We agree: so far as "secondary" supplies the demand of such fabricators as will accept it, it increases the amount of "virgin" which must seek sale elsewhere; and it therefore results that the supply of that part of the demand which will accept only "virgin" becomes greater in proportion as "secondary" drives away "virgin" from the demand which will accept "secondary." (This is indeed the same argument which we used a moment ago to include in the supply that part of "virgin" which "Alcoa" fabricates; it is not apparent to us why the judge did not think it applicable to that item as well.) . . .

In the case of a monopoly of any commodity which does not disappear in use and which can be salvaged, the supply seeking sale at any moment will be made up of two components: (1) the part which the putative monopolist can immediately produce and sell; and (2) the part which has been, or can be, reclaimed out of what he has produced and sold in the past. By hypothesis he presently controls the first of these components; the second he has controlled in the past, although he no longer does. . . . The competition of "secondary" must therefore be disregarded, as soon as we consider the position of "Alcoa" over a period of years; it was as much within "Alcoa's" control as was the production of the "virgin" from which it had been derived. . . .

We conclude therefore that "Alcoa's" control over the ingot market must be reckoned at over ninety per cent; that being the proportion which its production bears to imported "virgin" ingot. If the fraction which it did not supply were the produce of domestic manufacture there could be no doubt that this percentage gave it a monopoly—lawful or unlawful, as the case might be. The producer of so large a proportion of the supply has complete control within certain limits. It is true that, if by raising the price he reduces the amount which can be marketed—as always, or almost always, happens—he may invite the expansion of the small producers who will

90%

try to fill the place left open; nevertheless, not only is there an inevitable lag in this, but the large producer is in a strong position to check such competition; and, indeed, if he has retained his old plant and personnel, he can inevitably do so. There are indeed limits to his power; substitutes are available for almost all commodities, and to raise the price enough is to evoke them.

The case at bar is however different, because, for aught that appears there may well have been a practically unlimited supply of imports as the price of ingot rose. . . . Thus there is a distinction between domestic and foreign competition: the first is limited in quantity, and can increase only by an increase in plant and personnel; the second is of producers who, we must assume, produce much more than they import, and whom a rise in price will presumably induce immediately to divert to the American market what they have been selling elsewhere. It is entirely consistent with the evidence that it was the threat of greater foreign imports which kept "Alcoa's" prices where they were, and prevented it from exploiting its advantage as sole domestic producer; indeed, it is hard to resist the conclusion that potential imports did put a "ceiling" upon those prices. Nevertheless, within the limits afforded by the tariff and the cost of transportation, "Alcoa" was free to raise its prices as it chose, since it was free from domestic competition, save as it drew other metals into the market as substitutes. Was this a monopoly within the meaning of § 2? The judge found that, over the whole half century of its existence, "Alcoa's" profits upon capital invested, after payment of income taxes, had been only about ten per cent, and, although the plaintiff puts this figure a little higher, the difference is negligible. The plaintiff does indeed challenge the propriety of computing profits upon a capital base which included past earnings that have been allowed to remain in the business; but as to that it is plainly wrong. . . . "Alcoa's" earnings belonged to its shareholders, they were free to withdraw them and spend them, or to leave them in the business. If they chose to leave them, it was no different from contributing new capital out of their pockets. This assumed, it would be hard to say that "Alcoa" had made exorbitant profits on ingot, if it is proper to allocate the profit upon the whole business proportionately among all its products—ingots, and fabrications from ingot. A profit of ten per cent in such an industry, dependent, in part at any rate, upon continued tariff protection, and subject to the vicissitudes of new demands, to the obsolescence of plant and process—which can never be accurately gauged in advance—to the chance that substitutes may at any moment be discovered which will reduce the demand, and to the other hazards which attend all industry; a profit of ten per cent, so conditioned, could hardly be considered extortionate.

There are however, two answers to any such excuse; and the first is that the profit on ingot was not necessarily the same as the profit of the business as a whole, and that we have no means of allocating its proper share to ingot. It is true that the mill cost appears; but obviously it would be unfair to "Alcoa" to take, as the measure of its profit on ingot, the difference between selling price and mill cost; and yet we have nothing else. It may be retorted that it was for the plaintiff to prove what was the profit upon ingot in accordance with the general burden of proof. We think not. Having proved that "Alcoa" had a monopoly of the domestic ingot market, the plaintiff had gone far enough; if it was an excuse, that "Alcoa" had not abused its power, it lay upon "Alcoa" to prove that it had not. But the whole issue is irrelevant anyway, for it is no excuse for "monopolizing" a market that the monopoly has not been used to extract from the consumer more than a "fair" profit. The Act has wider purposes. Indeed, even though we disregarded all but economic considerations, it would by no means follow that such concentration of producing power is to be desired, when it has not been used extortionately. Many people believe that possession of unchallenged economic power deadens initiative, discourages thrift and depresses energy; that immunity from competition is a narcotic, and rivalry is a stimulant, to industrial progress; that the spur of constant stress is necessary to counteract an inevitable disposition to let well enough alone. . . . True, it might have been thought adequate to condemn only those monopolies which could not show that they had exercised the highest possible ingenuity, had adopted every possible economy, had anticipated every conceivable improvement, stimulated every possible demand. No doubt, that would be one way of dealing with the matter, although it would imply constant scrutiny and constant supervision, such as courts are unable to provide. Be that as it may, that was not the way that Congress chose; it did not condone "good trusts" and condemn "bad" ones; it forbad all. Moreover, in so doing it was not necessarily actuated by economic motives alone. It is possible, because of its indirect social or moral effect, to prefer a system of small producers, each dependent for his success upon his own skill and character, to one in which the great mass of those engaged must accept the direction of a few. These considerations, which we have suggested only as possible purposes of the Act, we think the decisions prove to have been in fact its purposes.

But we are not left to deductive reasoning. Although in many settings it may be proper to weigh the extent and effect of restrictions in a contract against its industrial or commercial advantages, this is never to be done when the contract is made with intent to set up a monopoly. . . . Perhaps, it has been idle to labor the point at length; there can be no doubt that the vice of restrictive contracts and of monopoly is really one, it is the denial to commerce of the supposed protection of competition. To repeat, if the earlier stages are proscribed, when they are parts of a plan, the mere projecting of which condemns them unconditionally, the realization of the plan itself must also be proscribed.

We have been speaking only of the economic reasons which forbid monopoly; but, as we have already implied, there are others, based upon the belief that great industrial consolidations are inherently undesirable, regardless of their economic results. . . . Throughout the history of these statutes it has been constantly assumed that one of their purposes was to perpetuate and preserve, for its own sake and in spite of possible cost, an organization of industry in small units which can effectively compete with each other. We hold that "Alcoa's" monopoly of ingot was of the kind covered by § 2.

It does not follow because "Alcoa" had such a monopoly, that it "monopolized" the ingot market: it may not have achieved monopoly; monopoly may have been thrust upon it. If it had been a combination of existing smelters which united the whole industry and controlled the production of all aluminum ingot, it would certainly have "monopolized" the market. In several decisions the Supreme Court has decreed the dissolution of such combinations, although they had engaged in no unlawful trade practices. . . . We may start therefore with the premise that to have combined ninety per cent of the producers of ingot would have been to "monopolize" the ingot market; and, so far as concerns the public interest, it can make no difference whether an existing competition is put an end to, or whether prospective competition is prevented. . . . Persons may unwittingly find themselves in possession of a monopoly, automatically so to say: that is, without having intended either to put an end to existing competition, or to prevent competition from arising when none had existed; they may become monopolists by force of accident. Since the Act makes "monopolizing" a crime, as well as a civil wrong, it would be not only unfair, but presumably contrary to the intent of Congress, to include such instances. A market may, for example, be so limited that it is impossible to produce at all and meet the cost of production except by a plant large enough to supply the whole demand. Or there may be changes in taste or in cost which drive out all but one purveyor. A single producer may be the survivor out of a group of active competitors, merely by virtue of his superior skill, foresight and industry. In such cases a strong argument can be made that, although, the result may expose the public to the evils of monopoly, the Act does not mean to condemn the resultant of those very forces which it is its prime object to foster: finis opus coronat. The successful competitor, having been urged to compete, must not be turned upon when he wins. The most extreme expression of this view is in United States v. United States Steel Corporation. . . . But, whatever authority it does have was modified by the gloss of Cardozo, J., in United States v. Swift & Co., . . . when he said, "Mere size * * * is not an offense against the Sherman Act unless magnified to the point at which it amounts to a monopoly * * * but size carries with it an opportunity for abuse that is not to be ignored when the opportunity is proved to have been utilized in the past." "Alcoa's" size was "magnified" to make it a "monopoly"; indeed, it has never been anything else; and its size, not only offered it an "opportunity for abuse," but it "utilized" its size for "abuse," as can easily be shown.

It would completely misconstrue "Alcoa's" position in 1940 to hold that it was the passive beneficiary of a monopoly, following upon an involuntary elimination of competitors by automatically operative economic forces. . . . This increase and this continued and undisturbed control did not fall undesigned into "Alcoa's" lap; obviously it could not have done so. It could only have resulted, as it did result, from a persistent determination to maintain the control, with which it found itself vested in 1912. There were at least one or two abortive attempts to enter the industry, but "Alcoa" effectively anticipated and forestalled all competition, and succeeded in holding the field alone. True, it stimulated demand and opened new uses for the metal, but not without making sure that it could supply what it had evoked. There is no dispute as to this; "Alcoa" avows it as evidence of the skill, energy and initiative with which it has always conducted its business; as a reason why, having won its way by fair means, it should be commended, and not dismembered. We need charge it with no moral derelictions after 1912; we may assume that all it claims for itself is true. The only question is whether it falls within the exception established in favor of those who do not seek, but cannot avoid, the control of a market. It seems to us that that question scarcely survives its statement. It was not inevitable that it should always anticipate increases in the demand for ingot and be prepared to supply them. Nothing compelled it to keep doubling and redoubling its capacity before others entered the field. It insists that it never excluded competitors; but we can think of no more effective exclusion than progressively to embrace each new opportunity as it opened, and to face every newcomer with new capacity already geared into a great organization, having the advantage of experience, trade connections and the elite of personnel. Only in case we interpret "exclusion" as limited to manoeuvres not honestly industrial, but actuated solely by a desire to prevent competition, can such a course, indefatigably pursued, be deemed not "exclusionary." So to limit it would in our judgment emasculate the Act; would permit just such consolidations as it was designed to prevent.

We disregard any question of "intent." Relatively early in the history of the Act—1905—Holmes, J., in Swift & Co. v. United States, supra, . . . explained this aspect of the Act in a passage often quoted. Although the primary evil was monopoly, the Act also covered preliminary steps, which, if continued, would lead to it. These may do no harm of themselves; but, if they are initial moves in a plan or scheme which, carried out, will result in monopoly, they are dangerous and the law will nip them in the bud. For this reason conduct falling short of monopoly, is not illegal unless it is part of a plan to monopolize, or to gain such other control of a market as is equally forbidden. To make it so, the plaintiff must prove what in the criminal law is known as a "specific intent"; an intent which goes beyond the mere intent to do the act. By far the greatest part of the fabulous record piled up in the case at bar, was concerned with proving such an intent. . . . In order to fall within § 2, the monopolist must have both the power to monopolize, and the intent to monopolize. To read the passage as demanding any "specific," intent, makes nonsense of it, for no monopolist monopolizes unconscious of what he is doing. So here, "Alcoa" meant to keep, and did keep, that complete and exclusive hold upon the ingot market with which it started. That was to "monopolize" that market, however innocently it otherwise proceeded. So far as the judgment held that it was not within § 2, it must be reversed.

"ALCOA'S" UNLAWFUL PRACTICES

As we have said, the plaintiff also sought to convict "Alcoa" of practices in which it engaged, not because they were necessary to the development of its business, but only in order to suppress competitors. Since we are holding that "Alcoa" "monopolized" the ingot market in 1940, regardless of such practices, these issues might be moot, if it inevitably followed from our holding that "Alcoa" must be dissolved. It could be argued that the new companies which would then emerge, should not be charged in retrospect with their predecessor's illegal conduct; but should be entitled to start without the handicap of injunctions, based upon its past. Possibly that would be true, except that conditions have so changed since the case was closed, that, as will appear, it by no means follows, because "Alcoa" had a monopoly in 1940, that it will have one when final judgment is entered after the war. That judgment may leave it intact as a competing unit among other competing units, and the plaintiff might argue, and undoubtedly will, that, if it was in the past guilty of practices, aimed at "monopolizing" the ingot market, it would be proper and necessary to enjoin their resumption, even though it no longer will have a monopoly. For this reason it appears to us that the issues are not altogether moot. In spite of the prolixity of the evidence, the challenged practices can be divided into three classes: (a) the "preemption" of bauxite deposits and water power; (b) the suppression of several efforts by competitors to invade either the ingot market, or some of the markets for fabricated goods; (c) the "domination" of the markets for such goods, and particularly of the markets for "sheet" and "cable."

[The opinion here included a rather lengthy discussion of these issues; the Court held that the government failed to provide its allegations in these matters. The opinion did say that, in the issue of a possible price squeeze between ingot and sheet, the facts presented warranted different treatment by the trial judge. However, because these matters were peripheral issues, they are not described at greater length in these excerpts.]

"LIMITED"

"Limited" was incorporated in Canada on May 13, 1928, to take over those properties of "Alcoa" which were outside the United States. Only two were excepted: a Dutch company which owned bauxite deposits in Dutch Guiana; and a Canadian power transmission company, which supplied "Alcoa's" Massena plant. . . . In exchange for all the properties conveyed, "Limited" issued all its common shares to "Alcoa's" common shareholders in the proportion of one for every three; and it thus resulted that the beneficial ownership remained what it had been, except for the interest of "Alcoa's" preferred shareholders, who were apparently considered amply protected by the properties in the United States. . . .

The companies had a number of transactions with each other, upon which the plaintiff relies to prove that they did not deal at arms length, but that "Limited" was organized only as a creature of "Alcoa." . . .

There was also some evidence that "Alcoa" took part in the formation of the "Alliance," a foreign "cartel" which we shall describe later. . . .

The Davises in answer to all this evidence swore that "Limited" had been organized for three reasons, quite different from controlling prices in the United States. First, there was at that time a growing nationalism in the British Empire—where "Alcoa" sold most of its foreign aluminum—which manifested itself in the slogan: "Buy British," and which would be better satisfied, if the properties were owned by a Canadian corporation, even though its shareholders were American. Next, "Alcoa" had neglected its foreign properties—relatively—and they would better prosper under a management, singly devoted to them. Finally, the time was coming when Arthur V. Davis wished to take a less active part in affairs; and there would be embarrassment in choosing between Hunt and Edward K. Davis, as his successor. . . .

Upon the whole evidence the judge found that by 1935 "Limited" had become altogether free from any connection with "Alcoa," and that "Alcoa" had had no part in forming the "Alliance," or in any effort at any time to limit imports, to fix their price, or to intervene in price fixing "cartels" in Europe—except the early ones. In short, he again felt persuaded by the testimony against any inferences to be drawn from the conceded facts, and from the declarations put in the mouths of the Davises. . . . It was not unreasonable to believe that Arthur V. Davis and the Mellons, seeing that some kind of "cartel" might be an inescapable incident to continuing business abroad, wished in 1931 to keep "Alcoa" as far removed from it as possible.

Even so, the question remains whether "Alcoa" should be charged with the "Alliance" because a majority of its shareholders were also a majority of "Limited's" shareholders; or whether that would be true, even though there were a group, common to both, less than a majority, but large enough for practical purposes to control each. . . . Except when there was evidence that those in nominal control of one of the two corporations, exercised no independent decision, but followed the directions of the other, they were treated as juridically separate. Indeed, were it not so, a minority of shareholders would always be compelled to see to it that a majority—perhaps even a controlling fraction—of the shares did not pass to a confederated group who had a similar control over another corporation. For these reasons we conclude that "Alcoa" was not a party to the "Alliance," and did not join in any violation of § 1 of the Act, so far as concerned foreign commerce.

Whether "Limited" itself violated that section depends upon the character of the "Alliance." . . .

The agreement of 1936 abandoned the system of unconditional quotas, and substituted a system of royalties. Each shareholder was to have a fixed quota for every share it held, but as its production exceeded the sum of its quotas, it was to pay a royalty, graduated progressively in proportion to the excess; and these royalties the "Alliance" divided among the shareholders in proportion to their shares. . . .

Did either the agreement of 1931 or that of 1936 violate § 1 of the Act? The answer does not depend upon whether we shall recognize as a source of liability a liability imposed by another state. On the contrary we are concerned only with whether Congress chose to attach liability to the conduct outside the United States of persons not in allegiance to it. . . .

Both agreements would clearly have been unlawful, had they been made within the United States; and it follows from what we have just said that both were unlawful, though made abroad, if they were intended to affect imports and did affect them. . . .

The judge also found that the 1936 agreement did not "materially affect the * * * foreign trade or commerce of the United States"; apparently because the imported ingot was greater in 1936 and 1937 than in earlier years. We cannot accept this finding, based as it was upon the fact that, in 1936, 1937 and the first quarter of 1938, the gross imports of ingot increased. . . .

. . . It will be remembered that, when the defendants in that case protested that the prosecution had not proved that the "distress" gasoline had affected prices, the court answered that that was not necessary, because an agreement to withdraw any substantial part of the supply from a market would, if carried out, have some effect upon prices, and was as unlawful as an agreement expressly to fix prices. The underlying doctrine was that all factors which contribute to determine prices, must be kept free to operate unhampered by agreements. For these reasons we think that the agreement of 1936 violated § 1 of the Act.

THE REMEDIES

Nearly five years have passed since the evidence was closed; during that time the aluminum industry, like most other industries, has been revolutionized by the nation's effort's in a great crisis. That alone would make it impossible to dispose of the action upon the basis of the record as we have it; and so both sides agree; both appeal to us to take "judicial notice" of what has taken place meanwhile, though they differ as to what should be the result. The plaintiff wishes us to enter a judgment that "Alcoa" shall be dissolved, and that we shall direct it presently to submit a plan, whose execution, however, is to be deferred until after the war. It also asks a termination of all shareholding in common between "Alcoa" and "Limited"; and that injunctions shall go against any resumption of the putative unlawful practices. On the other hand, "Alcoa" argues that, when we look at the changes that have taken place— particularly the enormous capacity of plaintiff's aluminum plants —it appears that, even though we should conclude that it had "monopolized" the ingot industry up to 1941, the plaintiff now has in its hands the means to prevent any possible "monopolization" of the industry after the war, which it may use as it wills; and that the occasion has therefore passed forever which might call for, or justify, a dissolution: the litigation has become moot. "Limited" on its part argues that, so far as concerns the "Alliance" —the only practice which we are holding unlawful—the war has killed it forever; and, more particularly, that the decision in United States v. Hamburg-Amerikanische Packet-Fahrt, 239 U.S. 466, 36 S.Ct. 212, 60 L.Ed. 387, is on all fours. We do not agree with either side; but, before giving our reasons, we must determine for what purposes we may look outside the record.

After doing so, it is impossible to say what will be "Alcoa's" position in the industry after the war. The plaintiff has leased to it all its new plants and the leases do not expire until 1947 and 1948, though they may be surrendered earlier. No one can now forecast in the remotest way what will be the form of the industry after the plaintiff has disposed of these plants, upon their surrender. It may be able to transfer all of them to persons who can effectively compete with "Alcoa"; it may be able to transfer some; conceivably, it may be unable to dispose of any. The measure of its success will be at least one condition upon the propriety of dissolution, and upon the form which it should take, if there is to be any. It is as idle for the plaintiff to assume that dissolution will be proper, as it is for "Alcoa" to assume that it will not be; and it would be particularly fatuous to prepare a plan now, even if we could be sure that eventually some form of dissolution will be proper. Dissolution is not a penalty but a remedy; if the industry will not need it for its protection, it will be a disservice to break up an aggregation which has for so long demonstrated its efficiency. The need for such a remedy will be for the district court in the first instance, and there is a peculiar propriety in our saying nothing to control its decision, because the appeal from any judgment which it may enter, will perhaps be justiciable only by the Supreme Court, if there are then six justices qualified to sit.

But there is another, and even more persuasive, reason why we should not now adjudge a dissolution of any kind. The Surplus Property Act of 1944 provides the method by which the plaintiff's "surplus" properties shall be disposed of: "aluminum plants and facilities" among the rest, § 19(a) (1). The "Surplus Property Board," § 5(a), is to "designate one or more Government agencies to act as disposal agencies," § 10(a), and they are to "have responsibility and authority for the disposition of such property and for the care and handling of such property, pending its disposition," § 11(d), subject to the Board's regulations. These "agencies" may dispose of the properties "by sale, exchange, lease, or transfer, for cash, credit, or other property, with or without warranty, and upon such other terms and conditions, as the agency deems proper" § 15(a). The following, among other "objectives," are to "regulate the orderly disposal of surplus property": "(b) to give maximum aid in the reestablishment of a peacetime economy of free independent private enterprise"; "(d) to discourage monopolistic practices and to strengthen and preserve the competitive position of small business concerns in an economy of free enterprise"; "(p) to foster the development of new independent enterprise"; "(r) to dispose of surplus property as promptly as feasible without fostering monopoly or restraint of trade * * *." So far as consistent "with the usual and customary commercial practice" preference is to be given to smaller purchasers, § 18(b); to whom, when proper, money may be lent § 18(f). Finally, no "disposal agency" shall even "begin negotiations" to sell a plant which has cost over a million dollars without advising the Attorney General of "the probable terms or conditions" of the sale; and he in turn must tell the "agency" whether "the proposed disposition will violate the antitrust laws." The act must not be read to "impair, amend, or modify" those laws, or to "prevent their application" to purchasers of surplus property. In view of these declarations of the purpose of Congress, the "agency" which the Board "designates" to dispose of the plaintiff's "aluminum plants and facilities" may well believe that it cannot do so without some plan or design for the industry as a whole, some comprehensive model which shall, so far as practicable, re-establish "free independent private enterprise," "discourage" monopoly, "strengthen" small competitors, "foster" independents and not foster "monopoly or restraint of trade." If it should find this method desirable, it would have to learn what purchasers were in the market, how strong they were, what units they could finance and operate, and in what position they would be to compete. In such a model or design the "agency" would have to assign a place to "Alcoa," and that place no one of course can now anticipate. Conceivably "Alcoa" might be left as it was; perhaps it might have to be dissolved; if dissolved, the dissolution would depend upon how the other plants were distributed. If the "agency" should find it wise to proceed in this way, it may succeed in inducing "Alcoa" to accept the place assigned to it, particularly if the plan has not been prepared ex parte. If it does not succeed, then, but then only, will it be appropriate for the district court to act. We do not of course mean that in deciding whether to dissolve "Alcoa," or how to do it, that court must be governed by any plan which the "agency" may have devised, if it does devise one. But, plan or no plan, it must wait until it learns what the "agency" has in fact done. Moreover, if the "agency" does form a plan, it will have been an attempt to realize the same "objectives" for which the court itself must strive; and the court may well feel that it should accord to the "agency's" plan that presumptive validity which courts are properly coming more and more to recognize in the decisions of specialized tribunals. Nothing which we now say ought in any measure to limit the discretion of the "agency" to proceed in this way. Therefore we shall merely reverse the judgment, so far as it held that "Alcoa" was not "monopolizing" the ingot market, and remand the case to the district court.

....

[The court, in reversing judgment and remanding the case "for further proceedings not inconsistent with the foregoing," also refused to order shareholders of both Alcoa and Aluminum, Ltd. to divest themselves of one of these issues. The court also directed the District Court to form an injunction to preclude Alcoa from renewing an alleged earlier "price squeeze" between ingot and sheet. This was described as a precautionary insurance even though Alcoa claimed it had been discontinued for twelve years and could not be renewed since the sheet producers were given access to ingot at competitive prices. The court also enjoined Aluminum from entering into any further international cartel agreements covering United States imports.

The following material is the major portion of John V. Krutilla's examination of the aluminum industry and the disposal program suggested for surplus government aluminum plants. Krutilla's consideration of economic conditions in this industry leads to a suggestion of an alternative remedy for this industry. The omitted portions of the article contain a very brief summary of Alcoa's history, case comments, and Krutilla's comments.]

....

Aluminum—a Dilemma For Antitrust Aims?

John V. Krutilla

....

I. INTRODUCTION

The problem for Government policy in antitrust prosecution has often been posed as a dilemma involving a choice between two desirable objectives. Allocation of resources in the interest of efficiency requires an effective degree of price competition which is dependent on the existence of many sellers, no one of which can exercise a perceptible influence on market price. Yet modern industrial nations contain within their economic fabric activities which can be performed most efficiently by enterprise of great size. Since markets for industries characterized by increasing returns to scale are often insufficient to sustain a large number of Gargantuan firms, elements of monopoly emerge within these areas. Government policy, therefore, becomes impaled on the horns of a dilemma, i.e., whether to preserve efficiency within a firm at the expense of a socially more efficient allocation of resources, or to sacrifice efficiency in individual cases in the interest of competition. But must economists concede the necessity for this choice?

This paper explores the question mainly as it relates to the aluminum industry. It is appropriate to suggest, however, that the problem analyzed is not restricted to the aluminum industry. The conclusions of this paper, therefore, have implications also for other industries in which parallels with the aluminum case exist.

Abridged from John V. Krutilla, "Aluminum—A Dilemma for Antitrust Aims?" *Southern Economic Journal,* XXII (October 1955), 164–175.

II. BACKGROUND OF THE PROBLEM

Three stages are required in the production of aluminum: (1) the chemical refining of ore (alumina) from bauxite, (2) electrolytic reduction of alumina to metallic aluminum, and (3) the fabrication of aluminum into industrial shapes and forms and into end items for ultimate consumption. Given the present organization of the industry, three factors are of primary importance in the production of aluminum: (1) sources of aluminum bearing ore, (2) a commercially feasible process for extracting alumina, and (3) large blocks of inexpensive electrical energy.

III. IMPLICATIONS OF DISPOSAL PROGRAMS FOR FUTURE COMPETITION

The manifold expansion of aluminum capacity during World War II was accomplished principally by the Government's construction program. This program left the Government in possession of 52 per cent of the alumina capacity, 58 per cent of the reduction capacity, and 40 per cent of the sheet, plate, and strip fabricating capacity. Directed to sell these facilities so as to foster competition, and confronted with an existing firm of enormous size and degree of integration, the Government employed these facilities to create competitors of equivalent size and integration.

Underlying the rationale of this program was the assumption that competition could not develop in the industry unless alumina were available to new firms independently of Alcoa. This assumption led to the belief that only integrated firms could compete, and a policy was therefore adopted which led to the creation of large completely integrated competitors. This decision seriously limited the number of new entrants since only two alumina plants were available for disposal. Kaiser obtained alumina capacity of approximately 700,000 tons per year, vastly exceeding the requirements of its 130,000 ton reduction capacity. Reynolds likewise, although already an integrated producer, obtained a set of completely integrated operations with alumina capacity far exceeding its requirements.[1]

It is doubtful if those expecting a competitive industry to emerge as result of the Government's disposal program took comfort in the creation of one additional producer. Certainly from the standpoint of alternatives which could have been considered, the results achieved were less than gratifying. Existence of but three producers in the field provides an excellent environment in which the Chamberlinian situation of a "recognized mutual dependence" is realized, and although the producers may act as independent entities, the results remain the same as though restrictive agreements were adhered to by them.[2]

It was not realistic to assume that the new market structure created by the Government's disposal program would have promoted anything approaching competitive behavior on the part of the Big Three.[3] Moreover, a limitation on entrance of new firms resulted from the Government's policy of creating huge integrated operations. Except in time of war, or preparation for war, the normal growth in demand for aluminum is gradual and can be met easily by the addition of new potlines to existing reduction capacity—provided excess alumina capacity exists.[4] This contrasts with the difficulty of entering the market with a completely integrated operation of economical scale. Thus the opportunity for the

[1] Reynolds obtained the 750,000 ton per year Hurricane Creek, Arkansas, alumina plant; the Jones Mills, Arkansas, and Troutdale, Oregon, reduction mills (145,000–150,000 tons annual capacity); and the McCook, Illinois, rolling mill (144,000 tons per year capacity).

[2] Edward H. Chamberlin, *The Theory of Monopolistic Competition,* Sixth Edition (Cambridge, 1948), pp. 46–51.

[3] For an interesting account of the failure of the Government's plan for competition, see the testimony of Arnold Troy in *Study of Monopoly Power,* Hearings before the Subcommittee on Study of Monopoly Power, of the Committee of the Judiciary, House of Representatives, 82nd Congress, 1st session, Serial No. 1, Part 1, Aluminum, pp. 314–352.

[4] For example, additions of a seventh and eighth potline to Kaiser's Spokane reduction mill was achieved at a nominal investment by use of equipment from dismantled uneconomic wartime built Government reduction mills. In Alcoa's case, an expansion of a relatively small amount was accomplished by the substitution of the larger Point Comfort, Texas, plant for the small obsolete Niagara Falls plant.

Big Three to expand by relatively small increments as postwar demand increased made it virtually impossible for new firms to enter the industry. For the latter, no opportunity existed in the absence of a sharply increased demand sufficient to accommodate expansion by established producers as well as the entire output of new, completely integrated operations of economical scale.

A second impediment to competition was the artificial reduction in fixed costs for the Big Three resulting from their purchase of Government facilities. Possessing facilities of yet undetermined peacetime value, and faced with a competitor of Alcoa's magnitude, the Government made the plants available ultimately at a figure approximately 37 per cent of original cost. Kaiser, for example, obtained ore refining, reduction, and fabricating facilities for $36 million—or roughly only 20 per cent of current replacement cost.[5]

By contrast, during 1951 through 1953 the Government sought to encourage new producers to enter the aluminum field by granting comparatively limited inducements. Accelerated amortization and markets guaranteed for a five-year period were provided. The guaranteed market, however, afforded a price equivalent to the average of the prices established by the Big Three.[6] Under such conditions the Big Three alone were in a favorable position to participate in the program by virtue of (1) their practice of administered pricing, coupled with, (2) their artificially low cost at existing facilities, and (3) their comparative ease in obtaining financing. Having a substantial block of low-cost capacity, established producers were able to obtain low interest money for expansion and to take full advantage of accelerated amortization on new facilities while maintaining stable prices on virgin aluminum. Prospective new producers, however, discovered accelerated amortization and guaranteed markets to be of dubious value because of (1) inflated original costs, (2) inadequate collateral to provide low-cost financing for a large integrated operation,[7] and

---

[5] Equity 85–73 Defendant's Exhibit No. 158, p. 24498, In the Case of United States v. Aluminum Company of America, et al. District Court of the United States, Southern District, New York.

[6] *Study of Monopoly Power*, Part 1, Aluminum, pp. 600–1.

[7] For these operators, Government guaranteed loans increased money

(3) the administered prices on pig and ingot. Testimony presented by one such prospect suggests that the stipulated stockpile price would have provided a return of some $40 per ton *less* than estimated production costs.[8] As a result, the Big Three have obtained the preponderant share of the defense certified new capacity. Jointly Alcoa, Reynolds, and Kaiser obtained over 800,000 tons of the total 875,000 tons certified by DPA under the first two rounds of expansion. Anaconda Copper Mining Company obtained the remaining 8 per cent, representing the sole new entrant under the expansion program. A third round, authorizing 214,000 tons allocated to Harvey Machine Company, Olin Industries, and the Wheland Company, has recently been canceled after these firms encountered financing difficulties, the same problem that attended Harvey's and Apex Smelting Company's attempts to enter the first round of expansion more than three years earlier. Under the circumstances the recent Government attempt to promote competition in the industry promises little more success than was achieved by its disposal program.

A legitimate concern for the need to preserve economies of scale doubtless influenced both the action of the Court and the Surplus Property Board in their stewardship of the public trust. It is appropriate to suggest, however, that neither adequately perceived the nature of these economies—in particular, the stage in the process where the economies appear. Failing to recognize that scale economies occurred almost exclusively in the initial production stage, i.e., in the refining of alumina, the Government did not perceive the opportunity provided for positive antitrust policy. It thereby eliminated a set of possibilities for creating an industry of many firms without destructive consequences for productive efficiency.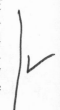

---

costs to 5 per cent per annum in contrast to the 3 to 3½ per cent interest loans available to established producers.

[8] *Study of Monopoly Power,* Part 1, Aluminum, p. 596.

IV. VARIATION IN SCALE ECONOMIES
AMONG PRODUCTION STAGES

Typical of many chemical processes, the extraction of alumina is attended by substantial economies of scale.[9] But huge reduction and fabricating facilities are required (from the standpoint of efficiency within an integrated firm) only to enable a scale of total operations which will realize economies of scale at the alumina stage. If there were a competitive market in alumina from which small independent firms could obtain refined ore in small quantities at costs equivalent to those obtained by any operator irrespective of size, there would be little justification for the massive superstructure of related facilities integrated through successive stages.

At the fabricating stage, the variety of end products required to serve the ultimate market permits economical operation of rolling mills over a wide range of capacities. Aluminum Products of La Grange, Illinois, for example, operates rolling facilities of only 2,000 tons annual capacity, while Alcoa's largest rolling mill (located in Tennessee) has an annual rated capacity of 300,000 tons. Within this range exists an opportunity for a variety of different sized rolling mills depending on the ultimate product markets to be served. Similar conclusions apply to other fabricating operations such as extruding, forging, casting, etc. The existence of some 17,000 independent aluminum fabricators utilizing largely secondary metal attests to the feasibility of small-scale full- and semi-fabrication.[10]

There is general agreement that economies of scale are of negligible importance in the reduction stage as well, where the refined ore is reduced to metallic form.[11] Aluminum is reduced in a series of identical electrolytic cells of quite limited size. For all practical purposes, these correspond to the economic case of perfect divisibility. In practice, a small number of joint facilities are required which provide a limited opportunity for economizing investment

[9] Engle, Gregory and Mossé, *Aluminum, An Industrial Marketing Appraisal* (Chicago, 1945), pp. 219–222.

[10] *Study of Monopoly Power,* Part 1, Aluminum, pp. 315, 326.

[11] Donald H. Wallace, *Market Control in the Aluminum Industry,* pp. 190–1. Also, Engle, et al., *op. cit.,* p. 221.

with increasing scale; yet even these facilities represent but a minor part of total investment. Total capital outlays, hence, tend to rise almost proportionally with capacity.[12]

At the ore refining stage, however, economies of scale are substantial. According to a study made by Engle, Gregory, and Mossé, the difference in the cost of production between a 100,000 and a 500,000 ton per year alumina plant amounted to approximately 20 per cent at early 1940 price levels.[13] An additional difference, not observed by the authors, ordinarily appears in raw material handling costs. Where the size of a plant will not justify investment in bulk unloading facilities, discharging bauxite from ore carriers will approximate a dollar to a dollar and a half more per ton if gondolas must be relied on. This represents an additional $4 to $6 difference in the final cost per ton of aluminum.[14]

Further evidence regarding scale economies is indirectly suggested in the engineering studies undertaken at the request of the Surplus Property Board preparatory to its disposal of Government facilities. The Dorr Company, which conducted a study of the Baton Rouge alumina plant, estimated the cost of producing

[12] Cecil H. Chilton, "Sixth Tenth Factor Applies to Complete Plant Costs," *Chemical Engineering,* Vol. 57, No. 4 (April 1950) pp. 112–114. The rule that "costs at a second [plant] X times the first may be obtained by multiplying the known cost by $X^{0.6}$" is developed from data on a variety of chemical process industries. For aluminum reduction, however, doubling the size of a given plant requires approximately a 90 per cent increase in capital outlays (p. 112).

[13] Engle, et al., *op. cit.,* pp. 219–223.

[14] Professor Wallace in his monumental work (*op. cit.,* p. 193 N 193 and 194) suggests that after an alumina plant "has become large enough to utilize fully the best size and type of boilers, kilns and pumping system, further enlargements result only in duplication . . . enlargement beyond a scale designed for an output of 50 tons of alumina a day (15,000–18,000 tons per year) brings no savings in cost of capital equipment per unit of output, and offers very little opportunity for economizing labor." Professor Wallace came to these conclusions on the basis of information obtained from *Aluminum Industry* (published 1930), a description of the Salindres plant in *Engineering* CVI (August 1918), a personal visit to a plant and an authoritative opinion.

Judging from the experience in the domestic aluminum industry in recent years (1940–present) where newly built plants have exceeded 400,000 tons annual capacity and from recently published works by consulting engineers (Aries and Newton, *Chemical Engineering Cost Estimation,* New York, 1951, pp. 62–63, and Chilton, *op. cit.*) additional economies of scale appear to be realized far beyond the level estimated by Wallace.

alumina at three alternative levels, 300, 500, and 1000 tons per day.[15] Although this is not the same as estimating costs for separate facilities specifically designed to operate at these levels, the estimated charges on plant and equipment excluded all facilities not required at the lower production levels.[16] Fifteen of twenty-three items of cost revealed differentials among the three operating levels. Average unit cost for the 500 and 300 tons per day production level were, respectively, 14 and 27 per cent above unit cost for the 1000 ton per day operating level.[17] Again these estimates make no allowances for differential unloading charges between large plants using bulk unloading facilities, and small ones for which such facilities would not be justified or at least substantially underutilized.

The evidence available does not permit determining the precise level at which scale economies are fully realized in the production of alumina. It does establish, however, that a substantially smaller number of alumina plants than aluminum reduction mills are required to serve a given market economically. Accordingly, it appears that the "Dilemma of Antitrust Aims" in the aluminum field could be resolved if a large number of competing nonintegrated aluminum producers could draw on a smaller number of competing large-scale alumina plants for their ore requirements. The question then becomes: What arrangements could be conceived whereby efficiently scaled alumina plants could produce refined ore for sale in a competitive market to a larger number of independent reduction mills, thereby preserving efficiency in production and realizing the benefits of competition?

V. ALTERNATIVE POLICY FOR COMPETITION IN THE ALUMINUM INDUSTRY

What alternatives might the Government have adopted to encourage growth of an efficient competitive aluminum industry?

[15] *Baton Rouge Alumina Plant*. E. O. 1432, Report of the Dorr Company to the Surplus Property Board, unpublished Government document.

[16] *Ibid.*, pp. 62–66.

[17] *Ibid.*, p .69.

Considering that the Government petition for relief in its antitrust suit was developed along with its disposal program, a horizontal rather than a vertical divestiture would have seemed more appropriate.[18] Had the Government pressed for divestiture along these lines, concurrently offering assistance in organizing a competitive market in alumina through its disposal program, a much more convincing rationale for divestiture would have existed for the Court to consider.[19] Four separate alumina plants would have been available initially, with sufficient capacity to supply the eleven existing economic reduction mills, and ten to twenty additional small smelters.

At the reduction stage sixteen plants were in existence following the war. Alcoa owned five with an annual economic capacity of approximately 332,750 tons.[20] Reynolds owned two small plants with a combined annual economic capacity of approximately 80,000 tons.[21] The remaining four economic mills representing 272,000 tons[22] were available to establish four additional independent operators, while the 368,000 tons of new Government-built capacity, which was uneconomically located in high cost power areas, was available for dismantling and relocation to more economic sources of power. This could have provided the basis for assistance to

[18] The term "vertical divestiture" is used in this context to correspond to Judge Knox's use of the term. That is, severance of Alcoa vertically to produce two vertically integrated firms. Horizontal divestiture will be used here to mean the separation of the ore refining facilities from the reduction and further stages of production.

[19] The economic feasibility of the Justice Department's actual proposal was subject to considerable question. One of the two integrated firms to be created from the facilities owned by Alcoa would have received the obsolete and high cost East St. Louis plant at which variable costs alone exceeded by approximately 35 per cent total costs at more recently built plants. It is certainly open to legitimate skepticism whether a weakened Alcoa, or the second firm to have been created from the remnants of Alcoa's facilities, would have had the vitality to reorganize the disparate parts into an efficient system.

[20] 91 Federal Supplement No. 3, pp. 365–6. Economic capacity as derived by Judge Knox represented that portion of total rated capacity for which there existed an economic supply of power.

[21] *Ibid.*, p. 367.

[22] See "Aluminum Plants and Facilities," *Report of the Surplus Property Board to the Congress,* September 21, 1945, Appendix 15c, pp. 116–118.

additional new firms. Conceivably a dozen new firms could have been induced to enter the field, given the facilities with which the Government had to work and provided a competitive supply of alumina were available. Could such a competitive supply have been established?

The practical task for professional economists was to propose some scheme for successful organization of a dependable competitive supply of alumina. The scheme should have been conceived to serve both the ends of efficiency and competition. Two such schemes are advanced below. It is not suggested that these exhaust the possibilities. They are presented primarily to outline an approach to the antitrust problem and to stimulate further discussion.[23]

Government Operation of Alumina Plants. In order to separate ore refining from successive stages, a public corporation could have been established and authorized to produce alumina for sale on a competitive basis to any aluminum producer. Such a corporation would have been able to meet the pooled requirements of the industry from the operation of the two wartime built Government alumina plants. This would have enabled a relatively large number of small metal producers to obtain alumina from a dependable source in small quantities at costs competitive with Alcoa's. This plan could have been implemented without any disruption of Alcoa's operation, and yet removed one of the important economic barriers to growth of competition.

However, unless the reduction capacity brought into operation through the disposal program would have equaled the total Government capacity (economic and otherwise) a significant amount of excess alumina capacity would have existed initially both within the Government's, as well as Alcoa's, block of capacity. A pooling of production facilities at the ore refining stage, accomplished

---

[23] A general scheme requiring considerable modification for application to specific industries has been advanced by Alfred Oxenfeldt, "Monopoly Dissolution: A Proposal Outlined," *American Economic Review,* June 1946, pp. 384–391. A plan involving some features in common with Oxenfeldt's was advanced by an independent fabricator at the Celler Committee Hearings (*Study of Monopoly Power,* Aluminum, p. 352). Both plans have merit but also contain a number of shortcomings which the proposals outlined below avoid.

through divestiture of Alcoa's alumina plants, represented an alternative with the public corporation achieving a monopoly in the production and marketing of alumina.

The plan to permit a Government monopoly in the refining stage could have led to efficient utilization of capacity under ideal management. It may be objected, however, that there would have been no "economic" incentive to achieve lowest costs within plants and further might have been quite disruptive of productive efficiency during the plan's implementation. But of equivalent importance is the prevalent political objection to any extension of governmental operations into fields which private enterprise can manage. In view of the critical significance of aluminum in our economy, particularly for defense purposes, and the legitimate concern over the monopolistic character of the industry, a justification for governmental intervention might have been made, provided no alternative existed. It appears, however, an alternative scheme could have been advanced.

Multiple Producer Cooperatives in Alumina. As an alternative to a Government monopoly in alumina production and marketing, or a public corporation established to provide an alternative source from which non-integrated producers could buy independently of Alcoa, a special adaptation of the cooperative arrangement could have been considered. Admittedly, the plan would have lacked the simplicity and would have been more difficult to implement than either the actual disposal program or a governmental operation. But the results obtained would have approached more closely the objectives of governmental antitrust and disposal program policies, with a minimum of governmental intervention. Essential features of such a proposal would have been:

1. Separation of ore refining from higher stages
2. Organization of producer cooperatives at the ore refining stage each consisting of one alumina plant (with a possible exception) and several reduction operator-owners
3. Government retention of all shares representing excess capacity for sale at request of any future new producer
4. Distribution of shares in cooperative among members commensurate with each member's requirements

5. Restriction of shares to only one alumina cooperative for each member
6. Provision of only one vote for each member irrespective of number of shares held
7. Value of shares to reflect capitalized prospective earnings of each plant
8. Adoption of a uniform system of accounts open to inspection
9. Sharing of profits by members in proportion to shares held
10. No restriction on members with respect to alumina cooperative from which ore is purchased
11. Restriction of purchases to spot transactions, with identical prices f.o.b. refining plant, to all purchasers
12. Qualification of new producers for purchase of alumina to consist of prior purchase of shares in a cooperative commensurate with producer's ore requirements

Minimum Disturbance to Existing Operations. Divestiture of Alcoa's ore refining facilities along with retention by the Government of its wartime built alumina plants would have provided for the separation of stages and provided the facilities about which producer cooperatives could have been organized. In the interest of maintaining uninterrupted levels of production, one producer cooperative could have been established consisting of Alcoa and three to five additional small producers,[24] based on the refining capacity previously held by Alcoa.[25] Two additional cooperatives could have

[24] To have been created from the Government's surplus reduction capacity and Government-held shares in excess refining capacity.

[25] This capacity was represented by the 600,000 (plus) tons annual capacity of the Mobile, Alabama, and roughly 400,000 tons annual capacity of the East St. Louis plants. A cooperative involving the two formerly owned Alcoa alumina plants might have represented the only exception to the rule that one cooperative would be organized about each refining plant.

Alternatively, a plan could have been developed around a single large alumina producer cooperative involving all of the ore refining plants, with the provision that members share in the profits in relation to purchases. The latter stipulation would promote sales competition, conceivably, but the scheme would not incorporate sufficient incentives to strive for intra-plant economies, and also would represent an invitation to restrict output to affect prices at the final stage.

been formed using the Government's Hurricane Creek and Baton Rouge refining facilities in a manner to achieve a relatively equal distribution of reduction operators between them.[26]

Ease of Entry. With the Government holding shares representing excess capacity in alumina and required to make these available on request of any prospective producer, any small firm could have obtained alumina for a small reduction operation as economically from the market as it could have through integrating on a grand scale. This would have enabled a number of relatively small concerns to enter the field with $5–$12 million in lieu of the $150–$225 million required for an economically scaled set of completely integrated facilities. Small firms manifesting interest in the recent expansion program[27] thus could have competed in a meaningful way for the three-quarters of a million tons of certified capacity which went by default to the Big Three during the recent Government expansion program.

Incentives to Compete. On the reduction level, the larger number of reduction operators would have been a long stride toward sufficient numbers to provide unqualified competition. At the alu-

[26] The provision that value of shares in cooperatives reflect capitalized prospective earnings of individual plants would have led to indifference on the part of reduction mill operators as regards the cooperative to which they would be assigned. This would have permitted freedom in the organization of cooperative memberships.

Theoretically, since transportation costs could not be incorporated easily into the determination of individual plant's going concern value for individual reduction operators, reluctance on the part of some reduction operators might have developed regarding assignment to a particular cooperative. Practically speaking, however, this was not likely to have happened. Refining facilities were clustered either at the source of domestic bauxite or on the Gulf Coast ports of entry for imported bauxite. Reduction mills, on the other hand, were clustered in areas where electrical energy was available at low rates. The difference in freight rates on alumina from alternative refining plants to any particular reduction mill would have been negligible (because of the negotiated nature of freight rates governing alumina movements) or could have been equalized by negotiations with carriers where differences appeared probable. Cf. Ex Parte 175a and 175b; T.C. 1-A, B, and C; C.F.A., 218-N; and N.O.F.T.B. 3-B.

[27] Apex Smelting Company, Eastern Metal Products Company, Independent Aluminum Company, National Aluminum, Spartan Aircraft, Harvey Machine Company, Olin Industries and The Wheland Company.

mina stage, Government ownership of shares in each of the three cooperatives (to the extent of initial excess capacity) would have been an effective barrier, originally, to collusion among members of separate cooperatives. However, governmental participation in the ownership would not have been necessary to preclude collusion as other provisions would have promoted self policing.

The provision that no aluminum producer could have held shares in more than one cooperative would have erected an obstacle to restrictive agreements (governing both refining and reduction) through contacts established at the refining stage. With this obstacle to collusion among producers of different cooperatives no incentive would remain for restrictive agreements among members within any cooperative. Competition among aluminum producers of different sets would result in losses to participants of "within set" agreements. And a precaution against any one producer's dominating the policy of his cooperative would have been provided by the limitation on voting to a single vote irrespective of number of shares held.[28]

Incentives to Efficiency.   With excess capacity initially in refining and marked differences in cost among plants[29] efficient resource allocation demanded that only the plants with the lower variable costs be operated. Furthermore, since variable costs at these plants were higher for low levels of operation than at levels nearer those for which the plants were designed,[30] operation of all plants at a fraction of capacity actually resulted in avoidable excess costs.[31]

Competition among reduction operators would have ensured that no alumina plant would have remained in operation so long as its

[28] Since Alcoa would have provided the bulk of financial resources for the cooperative of which it would have been a member, but would have been entitled to no greater voice in management than any of the remaining three to five cooperating members, consideration might have been given to providing Alcoa with an option. It could have been authorized to elect dissolution into as many independent firms as it possessed reduction mills. If the stockholders elected to do so, presumably it would be in their interest, and certainly in the interest of a competitive industry.

[29] "Alumina Plants and Facilities," *op. cit.,* Appendix 15b, 112–115; also 91 Federal Supplement No. 3, p. 368.

[30] Dorr Company Report to the Surplus Property Board, *op. cit.,* p. 69.

[31] See notes 33 and 34 following.

average variable cost exceeded the market price.[32] Idling of the extra-marginal plant, therefore, would have reallocated the market requirement among the remaining low variable cost plants. This would have led to greater economy at those plants as production volume expanded to points lower along the declining portion of the average cost curve at plants left in operation.[33] Moreover, competition from reduction operators of different cooperatives would exert pressure on the managements of alumina plants to achieve maximum intraplant economies.[34]

This plan would overcome the objectionable economic features of the Government-operated alumina plants since economic incentives would exist both for purchases from the most economical

[32] The larger number of independent reduction operators along with other features of the proposal (3, 5, 8 and 10–12) would have provided the environment for competition on the reduction level. If this would have been achieved, managers of intra-marginal alumina plants would have been faced with a horizontal demand curve and would have operated at capacity or where marginal costs equaled price. The marginal plant, providing the incremental supply, would have been faced with a sloping demand curve and on it would have devolved the task of appraising the market for alumina and adjusting quantity in accordance with its appraisal of market demand. For this cooperative, the intersection of marginal cost and marginal revenue would have dictated the quality to be produced and, indirectly, the offer price. The marginal firm, however, would have had the role of only qualified price leadership for, whenever the price determined by the intersection of marginal cost and revenue at the marginal plant exceeded the average variable cost at the extra-marginal plant, the marginal cooperative would face a restraint on its ability to control the incremental supply.

[33] Since 1) delivered cost of alumina to Alcoa's reduction mills was less than production costs (even omitting capital charges) alone at its East St. Louis plant, and 2) the Government's alumina plants together with Alcoa's Mobile plant represented between 1.9 and 2.1 million tons of alumina capacity, whereas the total ore requirements of all economic reduction mills was in the neighborhood of only 1.4 million tons annually, the East St. Louis plant would have been the extra-marginal plant. Records indicate that the Hurricane Creek and Mobile plants would have been the lowest variable cost plants whereas the Baton Rouge plant would have been marginal.

[34] Profits from the operation of alumina cooperatives would have been shared by reduction operators in proportion to shares held. Being in competition with reduction operators with shares in other cooperatives, members of each cooperative would have incentive to reduce costs at their own cooperative.

source irrespective of ownership, and for insistence that management of cooperatives achieve maximum operating efficiency within
individual alumina plants. Furthermore, ownership and control of
refining facilities by the ultimate users of alumina would have ensured that the major economies available through vertical integration
would be preserved.[35] This plan also is more consistent with the
prevalent feeling that private arrangements should be sought to
achieve socially desirable ends in preference to the extension of
Government participation in the economic sphere.

Equalization of Initial Advantage.   The value of shares in
alumina cooperatives could have been adjusted to provide for capi-
talizing anticipated earnings; otherwise variation in costs among
plants would have operated to the disadvantage of those reduction
operators assigned to the higher cost alumina plants. After operating experience regarding production costs had been obtained,
renegotiation of the initial terms at which shares were made available could have been considered because of the difficulties inherent
in estimating earnings in advance of operation. In this manner,
otherwise unjustified economic rents could have been applied to
recovering the Government's investment in the facilities it had provided. This would have provided relatively equal opportunity for
all new producers, and made it a matter of indifference (economically) to aluminum producers as regards which alumina
cooperatives they would join.[36]

[35] Cf. Wallace, *op. cit.,* pp. 182 and 188.
[36] For more extended discussion of this point see note 26 above.

5 THE CELLOPHANE CASE:

How Do You Wrap Up a Market?

The previous cases, taken in order, indicate the evolution of (domestic) antitrust (law pertaining to) prosecution in monopoly situations. The extension of these principles to oligopolistic situations and the development of the treatment of other antitrust situations will be considered in later chapters. The material immediately following, however, indicates the importance of carefully marshaling and presenting economic evidence in an antitrust suit. This material pertains to the Government's suit against E. I. du Pont de Nemours & Company for alleged monopolization of the cellophane market. It has been suggested that the government's failure to marshal an economic description of the relevant product market was in large part responsible for the subsequent decision. The following material is an analysis of the issues as presented by two distinguished economists. The report is introduced at length, as it effectively presents the economic material involved in this particular monopoly topic: line of commerce, market area, intent, and so on.

In the du Pont (Cellophane)[1] case the question of monopoly centered about the product line's definition: whether the product was cellophane or flexible wrapping papers. The lower court found that flexible wrapping papers was the relevant line of commerce,

---

[1] United States v. du Pont and Co., 351 U.S. 377 (1956).

that du Pont's development of cellophane did not constitute an attempt to monopolize, and that du Pont's cellophane production did not amount to a monopoly output. In considering the relevant product line, the Supreme Court held that fungibility was not required in order to group several items into a single product line; additionally, it stated that production of almost 75 percent of one among several alternative differentiated products did not constitute monopoly where that particular product totaled less than 20 percent of the entire class of goods. The Supreme Court relied on the reasonable interchangeability of goods in use as its primary factor in determining the relevant line of commerce. It specifically held that price differentials between cellophane and other flexible packaging materials did not preclude this competitiveness. It attributed the large profits in cellophane to the very large growth in demand, as marketing and other technology changed, rather than to any monopolistic position of du Pont. The lower court had ruled that a high cross-elasticity of demand existed between cellophane and other flexible packaging materials, and the Supreme Court sustained this finding. The overlapping use of competitive flexible packaging materials in such markets as candy and meats was cited as reflective of competition by the several packaging materials to meet packaging needs. The trial court had found that du Pont could not exclude competitors from the manufacture of cellophane and that no evidence showed du Pont received any higher rate of return than other manufacturers of flexible packaging materials. The following excerpts from the Supreme Court's opinion provide a background for the sharply critical analysis by Stocking and Mueller that follows the opinion.

••

UNITED STATES
v.
DU PONT & CO.
351 U.S. 377 (1956)

If cellophane is the "market" that du Pont is found to dominate, it may be assumed it does have monopoly power over that "market." Monopoly power is the power to control prices or exclude competition. It seems apparent that du Pont's power to set the price of cellophane has been limited only by the competition afforded by other flexible packaging materials. Moreover, it may be practically impossible for anyone to commence manufacturing cellophane without full access to du Pont's technique. However, du Pont has no power to prevent competition from other wrapping materials. The trial court consequently had to determine whether competition from the other wrappings prevented du Pont from possessing monopoly power in violation of § 2. Price and competition are so intimately entwined that any discussion of theory must treat them as one. It is inconceivable that price could be controlled without power over competition or vice versa. This approach to the determination of monopoly power is strengthened by this Court's conclusion in prior cases that, when an alleged monopolist has power over price and competition, an intention to monopolize in a proper case may be assumed.

Determination of the competitive market for commodities depends on how different from one another are the offered commodities in character or use, how far buyers will go to substitute one commodity for another. . . .

But where there are market alternatives that buyers may readily use for their purposes, illegal monopoly does not exist merely because the product said to be monopolized differs from others. If it were not so, only physically identical products would be a part of the market. To accept the Government's argument, we would

have to conclude that the manufacturers of plain as well as moistureproof cellophane were monopolists, and so with films such as
Pliofilm, foil, glassine, polyethylene, and Saran, for each of these
wrapping materials is distinguishable. These were all exhibits in
the case. New wrappings appear, generally similar to cellophane:
is each a monopoly? What is called for is an appraisal of the
"cross-elasticity" of demand in the trade. . . . The varying circumstances of each case determine the result. In considering what
is the relevant market for determining the control of price and
competition, no more definite rule can be declared than that commodities reasonably interchangeable by consumers for the same
purposes make up that "part of the trade or commerce," monopolization of which may be illegal. As respects flexible packaging materials, the market geographically is nationwide.

But, despite cellophane's advantages, it has to meet competition
from other materials in every one of its uses. . . .

An element for consideration as to cross-elasticity of demand
between products is the responsiveness of the sales of one product
to price changes of the other. If a slight decrease in the price of
cellophane causes a considerable number of customers of other
flexible wrappings to switch to cellophane, it would be an indication that a high cross-elasticity of demand exists between them;
that the products compete in the same market. The court below
held that the "[g]reat sensitivity of customers in the flexible packaging markets to price or quality changes" prevented du Pont from
possessing monopoly control over price. . . .

We conclude that cellophane's interchangeability with the other
materials mentioned suffices to make it a part of this flexible packaging material market.

The "market" which one must study to determine when a producer has monopoly power will vary with the part of commerce
under consideration. The tests are constant. That market is composed of products that have reasonable interchangeability for the
purposes for which they are produced—price, use and qualities
considered. While the application of the tests remains uncertain,

it seems to us that du Pont should not be found to monopolize cellophane when that product has the competition and interchangeability with other wrappings that this record shows.

•••

[The Stocking and Mueller article is concerned first with the selection of those factors identifying monopoly and with an examination of cellophane's development. This is followed by a consideration of possible market models and an examination of du Pont's behavior and performance to determine which market model best corresponds to the facts of this case. Thus, the authors attempt to evaluate the evidence with an intent to determine whether, despite du Pont's contentions, cellophane was produced and sold under monopolistic conditions. To this end an examination of the markets for cellophane was required, and this included the views of du Pont, its customers, and potential producers of cellophane. In turn, these views reflect an interpretation of physical characteristics, prices, and packaging needs. Profits are also considered, not only as an indicator of monopoly return, but in relation to price changes in order to determine whether the price changes are consistent with any of the economic models considered. The authors suggest that if cellophane's higher prices reflected higher costs, then "monopolistic" cellophane profits would disappear if cellophane did, in fact, compete with other flexible packaging materials. However, if the price differentials reflected only the higher quality of cellophane, then the existence of a monopoly position would permit the continuance of unusually high profits. Although one may differ with some of the judgments involved, the study is a model for economic analysis of monopolistic issues.]

....

The Cellophane Case
and the New Competition

George W. Stocking and
Willard F. Mueller

....

On December 13, 1947 the Department of Justice instituted civil proceedings against E. I. du Pont de Nemours & Company, charging du Pont with having monopolized, attempted to monopolize, and conspired to monopolize the manufacture and sale of cellophane and cellulose caps and bands in the United States in violation of section 2 of the Sherman Act. Almost precisely six years later Paul Leahy, Chief Judge of the United States District Court for the District of Delaware, rendered a decision in the matter.[1] He pointed out that the charge against du Pont of having monopolized cellophane involved two questions: "1. does du Pont possess monopoly powers; and 2., if so has it achieved such powers by 'monopolizing' within the meaning of the Act and under *United States* v. *Aluminum Company of America* [?]" He concluded that "unless the first is decided against defendant, the second is not reached." Judge Leahy did not need to reach the second question for he found the defendant not guilty. In doing so he concluded

Abridged from George W. Stocking and William F. Mueller, "The Cellophane Case and the New Competition," *The American Economic Review,* XLV, No. 1 (March 1955), 29–63.

[1] *United States* v. *E. I. du Pont de Nemours & Co.,* 118 F. Supp. 41 (D. Del. 1953). This study is based largely on the testimony and exhibits in this case, but it does not consider cellulose caps and bands. Du Pont discontinued making caps before the government filed its complaint, and the district court, as with cellophane, found no monopolizing of bands. [The Supreme Court affirmed the District Court decision on review. 351 U.S. 377 (1956).] References to the government's exhibits will be designated as GX, to the defendant's exhibits as DX, and to the transcript of testimony as T.

that "[f]acts, in large part uncontested, demonstrate du Pont cellophane is sold under such intense competitive conditions acquisition of market control or monopoly power is a practical impossibility." In reaching this conclusion Judge Leahy reviewed at length evidence introduced by the defendant to show that du Pont behaved like a competitor, not like a monopolist. The court found that du Pont conducted research to improve manufacturing efficiency, to reduce cost of production, and to improve the quality and develop new types of cellophane. It promoted the development and use of packaging machinery that could handle both cellophane and other flexible wrapping materials. In doing so it not only helped to increase cellophane sales but stimulated improvement in rival flexible wrapping materials. It supplied customers with technical services to help them solve problems created by the use of cellophane. It developed over fifty types of cellophane tailored to meet the special wrapping needs of particular products. It studied the buying habits of the public. It conducted market studies to determine the effect on sales of packaging a product in cellophane. It promoted sales by educating potential cellophane users to the sales appeal of a transparent wrapping material. It reduced prices to get into new and broader markets. The court found that in response to price and quality changes buyers at times shifted from cellophane to competing products and back again. The court concluded that "[t]he record reflects not the dead hand of monopoly but rapidly declining prices, expanding production, intense competition stimulated by creative research, the development of new products and uses and other benefits of a free economy."

Detecting monopoly is simpler than measuring it. While economists recognize that few if any industrial markets are free entirely from the influence of monopoly, by studying the structure and behavior of markets they can generally isolate characteristics which taken together will permit them to classify markets as effectively competitive or noncompetitive. In trying to classify du Pont's market for cellophane, we shall rely primarily on three criteria: (1) What role has business strategy played in du Pont's production and sales policies? (2) Is cellophane sufficiently differentiated from rival products to have a distinct market, or is its market that of all flexible wrapping materials? (3) Do the trend and level of its earnings reflect monopoly power or competition? [2]

I. BUSINESS STRATEGY AS EVIDENCE OF MONOPOLY

Economists have said a good deal about the role which strategy plays among oligopolists jockeying for market position. They have said less about the significance of business strategy as a basis for classifying an industry as monopolistic or workably competitive. We believe it is an important criterion. Purely competitive markets do not generally confront buyers and sellers in the business world. Frequently sellers are few, products are differentiated, knowledge is imperfect, obstacles to the movement of factors exist. Business firms from time to time make deliberate adjustments in both their price and production policies; they resort to strategy to improve their lot. Strategy may be directed to other than price and production policies. Business executives are constantly alert for any business advantage that will make their market position more secure or isolate them from the impact of competitive forces. They seek control of the sources of the best raw materials and the richest natural resources. They try to improve their products and processes

[2] Clair Wilcox uses the following criteria in classifying markets in his TNEC study, *Competition and Monopoly in American Industry* (1940): (1) the number of producers and the extent of industrial concentration, (2) uniformity of price quotation, (3) degree of price flexibility, (4) volume of production and extent of utilization of capacity, (5) rate of profit, and (6) rate of business mortality. Alone no one of these is a satisfactory index, and together they may be misleading unless perchance there is a consistency among the several indexes. We place considerable emphasis on two factors not included in Wilcox's list, business strategy and product differentiation, and we consider only incidentally if at all most of the factors on which Wilcox relied. Applying Wilcox's criteria to our conception of the cellophane market, we find that producers are few, concentration is high, profits are high, turnover of producing units is low, business mortality is low. These criteria suggest monopoly power. On the other hand, cellophane prices have been flexible and surplus capacity has been negligible. These characteristics suggest competition. Whether or not the factors we have chosen are adequate to answer the question we have raised we leave to the reader.

or to discover and develop new and better ones. They try to protect their accumulated know-how as business secrets or, where they can, to obtain patents that legalize monopoly.

Economists recognize these practices as manifestations of business rivalry, as aspects of the sort of competition that characterizes modern industrial markets. Business rivalry is itself a symptom of the absence of pure competition. Farmers who, lacking government aid, sell in competitive markets do not regard each other as business rivals but as neighbors. But even when businessmen forego active price competition, they generally do not abandon all rivalry. Correctly, economists have concluded that this rivalry may protect the public interest. It leads to technological innovation and to economic progress. Although economists recognize that business strategy may lead to monopoly, some economists believe that in a dynamic capitalistic society monopoly is inevitably short-lived. It is continually being undermined by the rivalry of other firms. The better product, the better process of today gives way to the better product, the better process of tomorrow. Only the imperfections and mortality of monopoly make it tolerable. Businessmen striving for monopoly promote the public welfare by failing to achieve their goal. Where they achieve it, either by independent business strategy or by collusive action, the public interest may not be served.

Du Pont became acquainted with cellophane through its production of artificial silk. In 1920 it had entered into a contract with the Comptoir des Textiles Artificiels, a French corporation, which through its affiliates was then an important manufacturer of rayon in France, Switzerland, Belgium, and Italy, for the joint operation of an American rayon company using the viscose process. . . . Aware of the affinity of rayon and cellophane processes and impressed by the prospects of large cellophane sales in the American market, du Pont in 1923 signed an option contract with Arena Trading Corporation, a Delaware corporation which was acting for itself and its associates, including La Cellophane, Société Anonyme, the Comptoir's affiliate which made cellophane. Under the option Arena provided du Pont with all relevant economic and technical information to enable it to decide within four months whether it wished to make and sell cellophane in North and Central America through a corporation jointly owned by it and La Cellophane. . . .

On June 9, 1923 du Pont entered into an organizational agreement providing for the transfer to the new company, Du Pont Cellophane Company, Inc., of "an unqualified, unrestricted and exclusive right to use all and every process now owned" by Arena "or which may hereafter be acquired by it . . . in connection with the manufacture of cellophane."

Du Pont the Sole Domestic Producer

Du Pont became the sole domestic producer of cellophane and thereby a monopolist in its sale. The Department of Justice contended that it was an unlawful monopolist from the outset, but the district court decided otherwise. Whether lawful or not, du Pont was a monopolist in producing cellophane, and it anticipated and in fact earned monopoly profits from the outset.

This is a characteristic of any successful innovation. . . . But . . . we must distinguish between justifiable monopoly revenue— returns to the innovator—and what Knight calls monopoly gains. Monopoly gains according to Knight are monopoly revenues that are "too large or last too long." What is too long or too large Knight does not say, but he clearly implies that the procedure by which they are made large and perpetuated may convert justifiable monopoly revenue into socially unjustifiable monopoly gains.

Having achieved at the outset a monopoly in producing and selling cellophane in the American market, du Pont took steps to protect its position.

One of its first strategic moves was to obtain an increase in the tariff. This became urgent in 1925, when Société Industrielle de la Cellulose (SIDAC) completed a cellophane plant in Belgium and began exporting cellophane to the American market at cut-rate prices. Du Pont first considered a patent infringement suit against Birn & Wachenheim, SIDAC's American distributors, but fearful that it would lose such a suit decided against it and in favor of a try for higher duties. . . .

Du Pont won the field so completely from imported cellophane that its cellophane sales for 1929 represented 91.6 per cent of the total business in the United States, whereas importers had had 21 per cent in 1927 and 24 per cent in 1928. The Tariff Act of 1930 fixed the duty on imported cellophane at 45 per cent ad valorem, and cellophane imports were never again significant. In no year between 1930 and 1947 did they amount to 1 per cent of cellophane consumption in the United States.

Division of World Markets

La Cellophane's plan to develop the American market through a single company jointly owned by it and a domestic firm was not unique. Before transferring to Du Pont Cellophane Company, Inc., its rights to the American market, La Cellophane had made a similar agreement with Kalle & Company (hereinafter Kalle) covering the German market. Ultimately Kalle obtained exclusive rights to La Cellophane's process and patents for the manufacture and sale of cellophane in Germany, Austria, Hungary, Czechoslovakia, Yugoslavia, Poland, Russia, Romania, China, Denmark, Sweden, Norway, and Finland.

Although La Cellophane had agreed to furnish du Pont with such technological information and patent rights as it might later acquire from its other licensees, du Pont sought to fortify its market position through a direct agreement with Kalle. On May 7, 1929 both parties agreed to exchange free of charge except for patent fees all patent rights and technical data covering cellophane that they then had or might later get. . . . Du Pont assigned its moistureproof patent rights in the countries in Kalle's territory to Kalle or gave it implied licenses under which Kalle took out patents in its own name.

Five years later du Pont entered a technical exchange and license agreement with British Cellophane Limited (hereinafter BCL), a La Cellophane licensee, which specifically delineated the territories within which each party would operate. . . .

Meanwhile all the world's leading cellophane producers except du Pont had tried to establish an international cartel to assign territories and fix quotas among themselves. . . . Nevertheless the [cartel] agreement recognized the North American market as belonging to du Pont and Sylvania. . . .

In 1934 du Pont relied on the 1930 cartel agreement in asserting its right to the West Indies as against BCL, to which La Cellophane had granted a license and with which du Pont was then negotiating its technical agreement. . . .

The cartel's course was not an easy one. World depression and the pressure of totalitarian governments for foreign exchange turned members' eyes toward South American markets, and even with agreements and quotas South American prices were unstable. Du Pont's sales there under its 1930 agreement with La Cellophane (discussed in the following subsection) were particularly disturbing to cartel members. On September 6, 1938 La Cellophane wrote du Pont that "it is apparently impossible to bring about a price accord for South America in our Convention." The second world war weakened still further agreements to divide markets. Du Pont's agreements with Kalle and BCL were to run twenty years, subject to renewal, but in 1940 du Pont disavowed all formal territorial limitations, not only with these companies but with Canadian Industries Limited and La Cellophane as well, "in the light of legal developments in this country."

SIDAC Competes with La Cellophane and with du Pont

Although La Cellophane had promised du Pont a monopoly in making and selling cellophane in the United States, it could not fulfill the promise. As du Pont feared, neither its patents nor its know-how was sufficient to protect it from competition. In 1925 two former employees of La Cellophane, using La Cellophane's trade secrets, helped establish SIDAC, which began to sell in the rich American market. It made its first sales through Birn & Wachenheim, who had handled La Cellophane's business in the United States before the organization of Du Pont Cellophane. In 1929 SIDAC established an American subsidiary, the Sylvania Industrial Corporation of America, and quit exporting cellophane to the United States. By this time it had subsidiaries in England and Italy and competed in La Cellophane's export markets. La Cellophane sued SIDAC for patent infringement and in settlement accepted a stock interest in SIDAC; thus indirectly it became through Sylvania du Pont's competitor in the American market, in violation of its 1923 agreements with du Pont.

Negotiations over this matter were prolonged. Du Pont conceived its problem to be how to "accept reparations and at the same time protect its future position without contravening American statutes." In lieu of reparations La Cellophane lifted the 1923 restriction limiting du Pont to the North and Central American markets. La Cellophane granted it equal rights with itself in Japan and South America. La Cellophane also agreed to keep technical information, patents, and other data which it received from du Pont from going directly or indirectly to SIDAC or Sylvania.

Du Pont Seeks Patent Protection

When du Pont obtained its option to participate jointly with La Cellophane in developing the American market, it had not investigated the validity of La Cellophane's patent claims. The terms of the option had been "predicated on the practical absence of serious competition on the part of other manufacturers either in this country or other countries." Shortly after its organization Du Pont Cellophane launched a research program designed to strengthen its market position by improving cellophane. One of its chief defects was its permeability to moisture. Du Pont promptly attacked this problem and by 1927 had developed a moisture-proofing process and had applied for patents. Its basic patent covering moistureproof cellophane, . . . was a product patent broad in scope and extensive in claims.[3] J. E. Hatt, general manager of

[3] A problem arising during the second world war when the government needed more moistureproof laminated products than du Pont could supply directly, reflects the breadth of the patent claims. Hines of du Pont posed the problem in this way: "What is the best procedure to give the Government these laminated products necessary to win the war and, having decided on that, what can be done to preserve du Pont's position in a postwar economy?" Recognizing that the government's interest might best be served by allowing converters to make them, du Pont feared that the converters might "at the end of the war, be possessed of a great deal of information with respect to the preparation of moistureproofing compositions and the technique of moistureproofing film with them and would be disposed to continue in such a business on a peace-time basis to the detriment of the

Du Pont Cellophane's cellophane department, [in 1930] described patent applications that du Pont had filed and quoted patent counsel's opinion that they promised "important and substantial additional protection." Between 1930 and 1934 Du Pont Cellophane authorized a research project further to bolster its patent position. . . .

These steps proved adequate to forestall other domestic competition[4] and to bring Sylvania Industrial Corporation to terms when it invaded the American market.

Sylvania Reaches Accord with du Pont

Sylvania completed its Virginia plant for making cellophane in 1930. Apparently its early experimental research to develop a moistureproof cellophane rested, as did du Pont's, on the use of a nitrocellulose base to which gum, wax, and plasticizer were added. When du Pont's Charch and Prindle patent covering moistureproof cellophane was issued, du Pont advised Sylvania informally of its claims and Sylvania after considering them "felt obliged to discard the work they had done up to that time, and approach the subject from a new angle." Their new angle substituted a vinyl resin base for the nitrocellulose base. Du Pont, regarding this as an infringement, advised Dr. Wallach, Sylvania's president, that "we would be obliged to enforce our patent" and eventually filed an infringement suit against Sylvania. In the anti-

---

Company's interests." Memorandum dated January 26, 1942 from du Pont's patent service to du Pont's cellophane research section, GX 2497, pp. 3255–57.

[4] Du Pont's strong patent position may not have been wholly responsible for the reluctance of other domestic companies to produce cellophane. Apparently Union Carbide & Carbon Corporation in the 1930's considered entering the cellophane field. It purchased rights to a process for making a transparent wrapping material similar to cellophane. Lammot du Pont in a letter of December 2, 1931 to L. A. Yerkes, president of Du Pont Cellophane, stated that in the course of an hour's conversation on this topic with Messrs. Jesse Ricks and Barret of Union Carbide & Carbon "[t]hey assured me repeatedly they did not wish to rush into anything, most of all a competitive situation with du Pont. Their whole tone was most agreeable. . . . In the course of the conversation, various efforts at co-operation between Carbide and du Pont were referred to, and in every case assurances of their desire to work together, given." GX 4381, p. 4300.

trust proceedings against du Pont the government contended that the "entire infringement suit was nothing more than a harassing action designed to coerce Sylvania into entering a highly restrictive agreement." The district court in finding for du Pont rejected this contention. Since the court has spoken, we do not express judgment on this issue. But we wish to review briefly evidence that throws some light on du Pont's strategy.

The record indicates that (1) du Pont in negotiating for reparations following SIDAC's entry into the American market considered and rejected a proposal that it grant Sylvania a license which would restrict its output; (2) after warning Sylvania that it would defend its patents and learning that Sylvania challenged their validity, du Pont postponed action while entrenching its patent position; (3) although professing confidence in its ability to establish its patents' validity, du Pont offered to settle the issue by granting a license limiting Sylvania's production of moistureproof cellophane to 10 per cent of the companies' combined output; (4) on Sylvania's rejecting this offer du Pont formally notified Sylvania that it was infringing du Pont's moistureproofing patents and asked that it cease; (5) upon its refusal to desist du Pont formally inaugurated infringement proceedings; and (6) before the proceedings were carried to completion du Pont and Sylvania settled the suit by a patent exchange and licensing agreement.

Both parties no doubt thought that they stood to gain by a settlement. If Sylvania lost the suit, it would be forced to stop producing moistureproof cellophane or to produce it on such terms as du Pont might offer. If it won, anyone with adequate resources could produce cellophane, and selling cellophane would become a competitive enterprise. . . . With neither side ready to test the validity of du Pont's patents, the parties compromised. The compromise constituted no threat to du Pont's dominant market position.

Until June, 1951 du Pont and Sylvania were the only producers of cellophane in the American market. Between 1933 and 1945 (when they contracted for smaller royalties and abandoned penalties for exceeding their quotas), with Sylvania's output geared to du Pont's, du Pont could determine how much cellophane should come on the market. Actually the penalty provision of the agreement never operated and its deletion from the 1945 agreement produced no marked effect on Sylvania's production. The court found that "[i]ts policies as to expansion in no way changed following the termination of the 1933 agreement in 1945." Although their shares varied from time to time, du Pont supplied about 76 per cent and Sylvania 24 per cent of the market from 1933 to 1950. But gearing Sylvania's production to du Pont's must have lessened Sylvania's incentive to independent, vigorous rivalry, price or non-price, and the record indicates that until January 1, 1947 Sylvania's quoted prices were generally identical with du Pont's.

Conclusion

Du Pont's moves and countermoves to protect its domestic market were the strategy of a producer operating in a monopolistic, not a competitive, market. Its agreements with foreign producers to license patents and exchange technical data, its domestic patent program, its effort to get higher tariffs, its restrictive market agreement with Sylvania, all reflect du Pont's effort to preserve what it apparently regarded as a monopoly market, That du Pont and Sylvania (whose production was geared to du Pont's and whose quoted prices were generally identical with du Pont's) together monopolized the market for cellophane seems scarcely debatable. That du Pont acted as though in its monopoly of cellophane it had a valuable property right which it sought to exploit is equally clear. But was du Pont mistaken? Were available substitutes so similar that du Pont's monopoly of cellophane was in reality a mirage or a phantasy? Is there in fact no distinct market for cellophane, but only a larger market for flexible wrapping materials with producers so numerous that none can make monopoly profits? Let us turn to that question.

II. CELLOPHANE—A DIFFERENTIATED PRODUCT?

For several years du Pont was the sole domestic producer of cellophane and for a quarter of a century Sylvania and du Pont were the only producers. But buyers of flexible wrapping material need not rely solely on these two suppliers. Several hundred rivals produced flexible wrapping materials, in many uses substitutes for cellophane. May not these have converted a monopolistic market into one of workable competition? Let us examine briefly the relevant theory and then the facts.

Price Theory and Product Differentiation

Although others have made important contributions to an understanding of the significance of interproduct competition, Chamberlin, the pioneer, offers a good starting point for this discussion. Chamberlin has recognized that "[a]s long as the substitutes are to any degree imperfect, he [the seller] still has a monopoly of his own product and control over its price within the limits imposed upon any monopolist—those of the demand." [5] But Chamberlin also recognized that rival products, where entry is free and differentiation not marked, could eliminate excess profits even in the "monopolized" field. Expressing his findings diagrammatically, he concluded that the sloping demand curve facing the producer of a differentiated product may become tangent to the cost curve somewhere above lowest average cost. Chamberlin regarded this as a "sort of ideal" solution. As he put it, "With fewer establishments, larger scales of production, and lower prices it would always be true that buyers would be willing to pay more than it would cost to give them a greater diversity of product; and conversely, with more producers and smaller scales of production, the higher prices they would pay would be more than such gains were worth." [6]

Chamberlin's conclusion that the entry of producers of substitute products will eliminate monopoly profits is based upon two im-

[5] E. H. Chamberlin, *The Theory of Monopolistic Competition* (5th ed., Cambridge, Mass., 1947), p. 67.

[6] *Ibid.*, p. 94. This assumes, of course, that buyers know what they get and get what they want in buying a differentiated product. This is a dubious assumption. Years ago a well-known pharmaceutical company by its advertising endeavored to create a widespread fear of halitosis. "Not even your best friends will tell you." Having created a fear of halitosis, it provided a product to dissipate it, thereby rendering the buyer a service for which he was willing to pay.

portant assumptions: (1) his uniformity assumption—"both demand and cost curves for all the 'products' are uniform throughout the group";[7] and (2) his symmetry assumption—"any adjustment of price or of 'product' by a single producer spreads its influence over so many of his competitors that the impact felt by any one is negligible and does not lead him to any readjustment of his own situation."

If cost and demand curves are not uniform, or if the "group" of firms producing the substitute products is sufficiently small to introduce the oligopoly problem, we may expect a divergence from the above solution. As for the uniformity assumption, Chamberlin says: "[I]n so far as substitutes of such a degree of effectiveness may not be produced, the conclusions are different—demand curves will lie to the right of the point of tangency with cost curves, and profits will be correspondingly higher. This is the explanation of *all* monopoly profits, of whatever sort." [8] Thus, unless effective substitutes exist, Chamberlin argues that monopoly profits may be "scattered throughout the group." [9] If Chamberlin's symmetry assump-

[7] *Ibid.,* p. 82. To simplify his exposition Chamberlin first assumes uniformity in cost and demand curves. Later he abandons this assumption in the interest of reality. In abandoning it he reaches the conclusion indicated in the text: where sufficiently effective substitutes are not offered in the market, monopoly profits result.

[8] *Ibid.,* p. 111. Emphasis in original. This statement of the problem seems to make it similar to if not identical with the conventional, neoclassical conception of monopoly. Richard T. Ely for example pointed out: "The use of substitutes is consistent with monopoly, and we nearly always have them. For almost anything we can think of, there is some sort of a substitute more or less perfect, and the use of substitutes furnishes one of the limits to the power of the monopolist. In the consideration of monopoly we have to ask, what are the substitutes, and how effective are they?" *Monopolies and Trusts* (New York, 1912), pp. 35–36.

[9] Chamberlin, *op. cit.,* p. 113. By the "group" Chamberlin apparently means firms making products which although differentiated are designed for the same use, e.g., toothpaste manufacturers. In his "Monopolistic Competition Revisited," *Economica,* Nov., 1951, N.S. XVIII, 352, 353, he abandons the group concept, arguing that "competition is always a matter of substitutes, and . . . substitutes are always a matter of degree." In abandoning the group concept, he does not abandon the conclusion that where substitutes are similar enough and entry is free, monopoly profits will disappear and the demand curve will be tangent to the cost curve at some point above minimum cost. But he also recognizes that the "isolated" monopolist, in spite of close substitutes, may find the demand for his own product strong enough to yield him "profits in excess of the minimum."

tion is not fulfilled, an oligopoly solution may be expected.[10] In either case monopoly profits result.

In applying Chamberlin's theory to the flexible packaging materials market and to cellophane's position in it, the empirical issue revolves about (1) the degree of effectiveness of substitutes and (2) the number of rival firms. If substitutes are not effective enough to eliminate monopoly profits, it is not necessary to consider the oligopoly problem.

Clark's analysis leads to similar conclusions, viz., that competition among substitutes may eliminate monopoly profits; but Clark goes further than Chamberlin in finding these results salutary. According to Clark the high cross elasticity of demand tends to flatten the monopolist's demand curve. Moreover, the monopolist's fear of potential competition may lead him to behave as though potential competition had become a reality. These two restraining forces, rival substitute products and potential competition, may yield cost-price relationships similar to those of pure competition. They may make imperfect competition workable.

An increasing number of economists have come to believe this. Robertson develops the idea somewhat further. In reviewing the significance of interproduct and interindustry competition he concludes that we really need not worry about monopoly for "there is probably not much of it." There is not much of it because the "old-fashioned apparatus of competition works in new ways to save us."

Moreover, this new apparatus of competition once more makes relevant a theory of competition based on large numbers.

> To assess the competitive situation of a firm we must still resort to counting numbers. We cannot do away with the group, for the group exists in the real world. Yet counting only those firms which are within the "industry" tells us very little. We must do our counting by taking categories of uses for the output of an industry, considering what products of other industries directly compete within these categories.

Since a monopolist's product may serve in a great variety of uses, a monopolist may find it "profitable to forego monopoly control

[10] *Monopolistic Competition,* p. 102.

in one use in order to push the commodity into many uses." Thus monopoly serves the public by serving itself and in doing so loses its power over the market.

What Robertson has discovered for the economists, businessmen had already professed. David Lilienthal, writing about the "new competition," said:

> I am not saying that active competition between the producers of the same product is of no present consequence. It certainly is. My point is that under present-day conditions it is often the least significant form. The competition between alternative materials, or ways of satisfying human needs and desires, has become a new dimension of competition.

It was on such principles that Judge Leahy relied in reaching his conclusions in the Cellophane case.

This calls for a more careful consideration of the uniqueness of cellophane, of du Pont's pricing policies in selling it, and of the rate of earnings realized in doing so. If cellophane is sufficiently differentiated from other flexible wrapping materials, its demand curve may "lie to the right of the point of tangency with its cost curve" and its producer may receive monopoly profits in making and selling it. If cellophane is a less highly differentiated product within Chamberlin's conception of the term and if entry to the manufacture of rival wrapping materials is not blocked, the maker of cellophane will be faced by a sloping demand curve; but the curve will be tangent to the cost curve at some point above lowest average cost, and the seller will not make a monopoly profit. If the differentiation is so slight and potential competition so imminent as to bring it within Clark's concept of the term, the seller's long-run demand curve will be close to the horizontal (his control over price will be slight) and prices will be close to lowest average cost. If the cellophane market conforms to Robertson's model, cellophane's differentiation will be too slight to count, monopoly profit will not exist, and its price will be competitive. To which of these models does the market for cellophane conform?

The Market for Cellophane

As a first step in answering this question we will examine briefly the flexible packaging materials market. The district court in determining whether du Pont monopolized the market for cellophane concluded that "the relevant market for determining the extent of du Pont's market control is the market for flexible packaging materials." In this broad market the court found several hundred firms selling a variety of differentiated products for an even wider variety of uses. They sold either directly to packagers or to converters who prepared packaging materials for special uses. The court found that in 1949 du Pont cellophane accounted for only 17.9 per cent of the total square yardage of domestic output and imports of flexible packaging materials. (Apparently this did not include kraft paper.) Such a small percentage scarcely demonstrates that du Pont had monopolized the *flexible packaging materials* market. Nor had it. But in passing judgment on the validity of the court's view that there is a single market for flexible packaging materials it may be helpful to classify the major contemporary materials according to their special qualities and major uses.

Cellophane is a thin, transparent, nonfibrous film of regenerated cellulose. It comes in two major types: plain and moistureproof. Moistureproof cellophane far outsells plain. In 1950 plain cellophane sales totalled $12,005,737; moistureproof cellophane sales, $116,660,209. Because moistureproof cellophane sales are over nine times those of plain, our analysis will give primary consideration to moistureproof. Moistureproof cellophane is highly transparent, tears readily but has high bursting strength, is highly impervious to moisture and gases, and is resistant to grease and oils. Heat sealable, printable, and adapted to use on wrapping machines, it makes an excellent packaging material for both display and protection of commodities.

Other flexible wrapping materials fall into four major categories: (1) opaque nonmoistureproof wrapping *paper* designed primarily for convenience and protection in handling packages; (2) moistureproof *films* of varying degrees of transparency designed primarily either to protect, or to display and protect, the products they encompass; (3) nonmoistureproof transparent *films* designed primarily to display and to some extent protect, but which obviously do a poor protecting job where exclusion or retention of moisture is important; and (4) moistureproof *materials* other than films of varying degrees of transparency (foils and paper products) designed to protect and display.

Kraft paper is the leading opaque nonmoistureproof wrapping paper. For general wrapping it has no equal. It is cheap, strong, and pliable and gives adequate protection. On a tonnage basis it easily tops all other packaging materials in total sales. But it is neither designed for nor adapted to the special uses for which cellophane was created and, as one market expert has put it, "in the true sense" does not compete with cellophane. More accurately, we think, cellophane does not compete with it. On a cost basis it cannot compete. At less than one cent per thousand square inches, kraft paper sells for less than cellophane's manufacturing cost.

The leading moistureproof *films* which might compete with cellophane include polyethylene, Saran, and Pliofilm. Relatively these are newcomers in the packaging field. In some qualities they match or even excel cellophane. But we have it on the authority of du Pont market analysts that these films have offered little or no competition to cellophane in its major markets. . . .

About these several films du Pont in its 1948 market analysis concluded:

> The principal markets for non-viscose films have been competitive with Cellophane only to a very minor degree up to this time. Some are used very little or not at all in the packaging field—others are employed principally for specialty uses where Cellophane is not well adapted—none have been successfully introduced into any of Cellophane's main markets due to their inherent shortcomings.[11]

On the superiority of cellophane as compared with other films for most of cellophane's uses, the experts apparently agreed. Olin Industries, Inc., later to become the third domestic cellophane producer, after investigation reported: "According to du Pont,

[11] DX 595, p. 1147.

Cellophane is considered the only all purpose film, and any product to be *truly competitive* with Cellophane must have the following attributes: (1) low cost, (2) transparency, (3) operate with a high efficiency on mechanical equipment, (4) print well both as to speed and appearance." [12] Olin concluded:

> There are no films currently marketed which are potentially competitive to any substantial degree in Cellophane's major markets when measured by the above attributes necessary for wide usage. Other transparent films will find their place for those low volume uses which can absorb the additional cost of the film and which necessitate certain physical properties not possessed by Cellophane. [13]

Consumer decisions confirmed the judgment of the experts. In 1949 converters used roughly fourteen times as much cellophane as all other packaging films. [14]

Apparently cellophane has no effective rival in another segment of the flexible packaging material market, the outer wrapping of packaged cigarettes. Clear as plate glass, flexible, easily ripped open, moistureproof, it displays and protects with such perfection that except when they can't get it cigarette makers use no other overwrap. [15] The court recognized this, noting however that makers of Pliofilm, glassine, and aluminum foil keep trying to break into this market. They have not succeeded.

The court to the contrary notwithstanding, the market in which cellophane meets the "competition" of other wrappers is narrower than the market for all flexible packaging materials. Cellophane dominates the market for cigarette overwraps, it does not compete with kraft paper for general wrapping, and in its more specialized markets the nonviscose films do not compete with cellophane except in fringe uses.

[12] Report on "the evidence in support of entry by Olin Industries into the Cellophane business, based on the purchase of patent license and 'know-how' from du Pont," December 15, 1948, GX 566, p. 7575.

[13] *Loc. cit.*

[14] DX 985. This is a market analysis prepared for du Pont by Robert Heller & Associates.

[15] A shortage of cellophane in the mid-forties forced some cigarette makers to use other materials. Brown and Williamson Tobacco Company once experimented with selling Kools and Raleigh cigarettes in a one-piece foil package. 118 F. Supp. at 108.

Food Packaging

In 1949, 80 per cent of du Pont's cellophane sales were for packaging food products; here cellophane encounters its most vigorous rivalry, "competing" with vegetable parchment, grease-proof paper, glassine, wax paper, and aluminum foil. Each of these wrapping materials is a differentiated bundle of qualities, competing in a wide variety of uses. Users attach a different importance to the several qualities. Many value transparency highly, a quality in which cellophane is outstanding. Some, however, regard transparency as a disadvantage. All are likely to rate moisture protection as important, but wax paper, aluminum foil, and some types of glassine are about as good as cellophane in this. Food packagers in selecting wrapping material no doubt consider carefully the unique combination of qualities represented by each of these materials. They resell the product they wrap and they are cost-conscious. Presumably they try to select the material that, quality considered, will give the greatest value. In determining values they must consider consumer response to the several materials. In any event, some buyers of packaging materials changed from one kind to another in trying to get their money's worth. Some candy makers and some bread makers, for example, operating on narrow margins, in the mid-thirties switched from cellophane to a less costly wrapper when their other production costs mounted. The court concluded from the evidence that "shifts of business between du Pont cellophane and other flexible packaging materials have been frequent, continuing and contested." In no one of the more important uses for packaging foods did cellophane in 1949 supply as much as 50 per cent of the total quantity (in square inches) of wrapping materials used (see Table). Only in the packaging of fresh produce did cellophane sales top the list. Its percentage of total sales varied from 6.8 per cent for packaging bakery products to 47.2 per cent for fresh produce. Like du Pont's percentage of total sales of all flexible wrapping materials, these specific figures scarcely demonstrate that du Pont has monopolized the sale of flexible packaging material to food packagers.

Such facts apparently led the court to conclude that du Pont, although selling about 76 per cent of the cellophane and together

Comparison by Percentages of Total Quantity of Selected
Flexible Packaging Materials, Classified by End Uses

Type of Material	Bakery Products	Candy	Snacks	Meat and Poultry	Crackers and Biscuits	Fresh Produce	Frozen Food Excluding Dairy Products
Cellophane	6.8	24.4	31.9	34.9	26.6	47.2	33.6
Foil	.2	32.5	.8	.1	.2	.1	.7
Glassine	4.4	21.4	62.8	2.7	10.0	.1	2.1
Papers	88.6	21.6	4.4	57.5	63.2	45.6	60.3
Films	.0	.1	.1	4.8	.0	7.0	3.3
Total	100.0	100.0	100.0	100.0	100.0	100.0	100.0

NOTE: Based on 1949 sales (in millions of square inches) of nineteen major converters "representing a substantial segment" of the converting industry, *United States* v. *E. I. du Pont de Nemours & Company,* 118 F. Supp. 41, 113 (D. Del. 1953). G. W. Bricker of Robert Heller and Associates, management consultants employed by du Pont, testified that the above data covered two-thirds of du Pont's and Sylvania's cellophane. T. 4474.

with Sylvania—whose production was geared to du Pont's—selling all of it, had not monopolized the market for *all* flexible wrapping materials. No one is likely to quarrel with this finding. But in an economic sense a firm may have a monopoly of a differentiated product, that is, it may behave like a monopolist and enjoy the fruits of monopoly in selling it, even though it meets the rivalry of substitutes. That is the economic issue here. Is cellophane so highly differentiated that du Pont in selling it can follow an independent pricing policy, that is, is the cross elasticity of demand for cellophane so low that du Pont, while pricing it independently, can enjoy a monopoly profit in its sale? Let us examine this issue.

When du Pont first marketed cellophane, it apparently thought cellophane had unique qualities and it adopted a strategy designed to prevent competition from any other producer, in short, to protect its monopoly.[16] It also priced cellophane from the outset to

[16] If cellophane had encountered the effective competition of rival wrapping materials, du Pont would have had nothing to gain by impeding entry. That is to say, if cellophane were merely one of many substitutable products among which effective competition prevails, the price of each would be driven down to a competitive (cost-remunerative) level and it should be

yield monopoly revenue. Its long-run aim in selling cellophane was apparently that of any monopolist, viz., to maximize revenues. But the maximization of revenues over time even by a monopolist may call for a farsighted and vigorous policy in exploiting a product. Monopolists, although they can restrict output and charge relatively high prices, may not find it profitable to do so. Du Pont argued and the court concluded that the test of monopoly is the power to exclude competition and the power to raise prices. A more logical test is the power to exclude competition and the power to *control* prices. That a monopolist may find it profitable to lower prices, increase sales, and reduce costs, even though the public benefits, does not necessarily mean, as Robertson suggests, that he has relinquished monopoly power. To use monopoly power rationally is not to forego it.

President Yerkes of the Du Pont Cellophane Company, Inc., concluded as early as 1924 that to maximize earnings du Pont should reduce cellophane prices. . . .

Walter S. Carpenter, Jr., chairman of du Pont's board of directors, expressed a similar idea when he testified in the Cellophane case . . .

The Yerkes-Carpenter philosophy apparently prevailed. The price of cellophane, which averaged $2.508 a pound in 1924, was reduced in every year until 1936, when it averaged 41.3 cents a pound. With minor interruptions the decline continued until cellophane sold for an average price of 38 cents a pound in 1940. Inflation accompanying the Second World War reversed the trend. With few exceptions cellophane prices moved upward until 1950, when they averaged 49 cents a pound. But despite the reductions moistureproof cellophane (300 MST-51, the principal type) sold at from two to seven times the price of 25# bleached glassine and from two to four and a half times the price of 30# waxed paper, its most important rivals.

Du Pont's Independent Pricing Policy

On its face du Pont's pricing policy was consistent with that of a monopolist. Other evidence supports this conclusion. Had cello-

---

a matter of indifference to du Pont whether this results from rival products or from new producers of cellophane.

cellophane operating investment. In 1934 it earned $6,000,000 and in 1940, $12,000,000. Although its annual rate of earnings before taxes declined somewhat from a high of 62.4 per cent in 1928, in only two years between 1923 and 1950 inclusive did the rate fall below 20 per cent.

Du Pont's cellophane pricing policy is consistent with the economists' assumption that a rational monopolist aims to maximize profits. This did not always call for a price reduction. In 1947 du Pont earned only 19.1 per cent before taxes and only 11.2 per cent after taxes on its cellophane investment—the postwar low. Raising the average price of cellophane from 41.9 cents a pound in 1947 to 46 cents a pound in 1948 paid off. By May, 1948 du Pont's operative earnings had increased to 31 per cent. At that time its division manager announced that "if operative earnings of 31 per cent is [*sic*] considered inadequate, then an upward revision in prices will be necessary to improve the return." He suggested a schedule of prices which would increase operative earnings to about 40 per cent. This was not put into effect until August, 1948. Operative earnings for 1948 averaged only 27.2 per cent; but by 1949 they had increased to 35.2 per cent and by 1950 to 45.3 per cent. Operative earnings after taxes yielded 20 per cent on du Pont's investment in 1950.

Du Pont's pricing policy in the postwar inflation is also consistent with the theory of monopolistic behavior, but the record indicates that profit maximization was not the sole factor affecting price decisions. The division manager in suggesting price increases called attention to other relevant factors:

---

expenditures conducted within and for the particular division. Du Pont calculates its rate of operating earnings on the basis of its working and fixed investment allocated to its cellophane operations.

Net cellophane earnings are calculated by allowing for federal income taxes, capital stock tax, franchise, state income, and foreign taxes, "B" bonus, and fundamental research by the chemicals department. Federal income and other taxes constituted the great bulk of these deductions: 90 per cent as early as 1935 (GX 490, p. 6506) and during the Second World War practically all, when the company was paying large excess profits taxes. Consequently, cellophane operating earnings may be thought of as primarily representing earnings on total cellophane investment before taxes, and cellophane net earnings as earnings after taxes.

2. What effect, if any, will a price increase have on our case when it is heard before the Federal Judge? I have not covered this with our Legal Department but in view of the position they took last July and August prior to the October increase, I am inclined to think they should be brought in for a discussion on this matter.

3. The du Pont Company may get some undesirable publicity from the press. A price increase on Cellophane could be looked upon as added fuel to the present recent spurt in the inflationary spiral and add to the present pressure for an increase in wages. This question is currently a live one at several of our Cellophane plants. Probably it would be in order to discuss this with Mr. Brayman.

After considering these questions du Pont executives decided on the price increase.

Cellophane's earnings record offers persuasive if not convincing evidence that du Pont has had monopoly power in selling cellophane. A comparison of du Pont's earnings from cellophane with its earnings from rayon lends force to this conclusion.[18] Despite the dissimilarity of the end products, several factors justify the comparison. Cellophane and rayon stem from the same basic raw materials. Both are radical innovations. Both were initially manufactured under noncompetitive conditions and both enjoyed substantial tariff protection. The same business management produced both products. The French Comptoir shared in the management of both Du Pont Cellophane and Du Pont Rayon until 1929. Yerkes, president of Du Pont Cellophane, was also president of Du Pont Rayon. Presumably du Pont in controlling business policy for both companies was actuated by similar business motives. Both products have had several reasonably close substitutes. The production and consumption of both increased phenomenally. Cellophane and rayon have been similarly characterized by rapidly developing technology, rapid reduction in costs, and rapid decline in prices. The chief difference in the manufacture and sale of the

[18] Data are not available to compare du Pont's earnings from cellophane with the earnings of producers of other wrapping materials. These are without exception diversified firms producing a variety of products. However, the record discloses that in every year from 1935 through 1942 du Pont failed to cover costs in selling cellulose acetate film, which it sold in competition with two other concerns (GX 490 through GX 497).

two products significant to the course of profits apparently lies in the structure of the rayon and cellophane industries. Although rayon manufacture began in this country as a monopoly, rival firms came into the industry promptly. American Viscose Corporation began as the sole domestic producer of rayon shortly before the First World War and du Pont followed in 1920. By 1930 these concerns had eighteen rivals. As late as 1949 fifteen firms occupied the field. Although the four largest firms in recent years have usually accounted for about 70 per cent of the total output and although most of the firms have generally followed a price leader, Markham from his painstaking and exhaustive study concludes that freedom of entry and the pressure of substitute products have made the rayon industry workably or effectively competitive. The course of both du Pont's and the industry's rate of earnings support this conclusion. Federal Trade Commission data reveal that in 1920, when du Pont first produced rayon, American Viscose Corporation, until then the country's sole producer, realized 64.2 per cent on its investment. Although du Pont showed a loss in 1921, its rate of earnings rose to 38.9 per cent by 1923. Thereafter its rate of earnings and those of the industry declined until by 1929 they had fallen to 19.0 and 18.1 per cent, respectively. When six more firms entered the industry in 1930, average industry earnings fell to 5.0 per cent and du Pont suffered a loss of 0.9 per cent. During the following eight years du Pont averaged only 7.5 per cent on its rayon investment, and the industry as a whole put in a similar performance.

In striking contrast, du Pont with only a single rival in producing cellophane (and that rival's output closely geared to du Pont's) earned less than 20 per cent on its cellophane investment in only one depression year. From the beginning of the depression in 1929 through the succeeding recovery and the 1938 recession du Pont averaged 29.6 per cent before taxes on its cellophane investment. On its rayon investment it averaged only 6.3 per cent.

IV. CONCLUSIONS

Apparently the cellophane market does not conform to the Chamberlinian model in which substitutes are so close that no producer may long enjoy monopoly returns—a "sort of ideal" equilibrium adjustment with the demand curve tangent to the cost curve at some point above lowest average cost. It does not conform to Clark's model of workable competition wherein rival products and potential competition reduce the slope of the demand curve, or to Robertson's model wherein substitutes are so close as to result in a competitive price. Rather, cellophane is so differentiated from other flexible wrapping materials that its cross elasticity of demand gives du Pont significant and continuing monopoly power.

Du Pont has used its power with foresight and wisdom. It has apparently recognized that it could increase its earnings by decreasing its costs and prices, by educating its potential customers to the benefits of wrapping their products in cellophane, by improving machinery for packaging, by helping converters and packagers solve their technical problems. It has built a better mousetrap and taught people how to use it.

But du Pont has not surrendered its monopoly power. Its strategy, cellophane's distinctive qualities, and the course of its prices and earnings indicate this. Du Pont's strategy was designed to protect a monopoly in the sale of a product it regarded as unique, and its pricing policies reflected the judgment of its executives on how best to maximize earnings. We think its earnings illustrate Knight's distinction between justifiable profits to the innovator and unjustifiable monopoly gains. They have been "too large" and have lasted "too long."

PART II *Oligopoly*

6 OLIGOPOLY AND THE AMERICAN TOBACCO CASE

Monopoly was once commonly visualized in terms of a single dominant firm, especially one using allegedly predatory practices to vanquish its rivals. But few firms now utilize these more blatant predatory practices. Also, sizeable competitors have emerged in most modern industries to compete with, and survive along side of, the industry's most prominent member. The growth of an industrial structure that is often largely oligopolistic has raised important questions concerning the continuing relevance of the Sherman Act. The decline of predatory practices further undermines a possibly once valid view of "monopoly," a point that emerges from the 1920 U.S. Steel decision and the later decisions based on the same logic.

Our sense of fair play and our compassion for striving entrepreneurs may now be less strained; however, the emergence of gentlemanly conduct and of friendly "competitors" has not necessarily corrected the economic misallocations of resources arising from the same underlying monopoly situations. A wide and meaningful enforcement of the Sherman Act therefore necessitated a break with the logic of the earlier cases. As indicated earlier, the Alcoa decision represented a major advance toward relying on evidence of market position instead of predatory behavior in dominant firm situations. Nevertheless, the Alcoa case was only one

brought before WWII 1937

decision by a particular court, albeit a court with final appellate
standing. Realistically, then, the Alcoa case scarcely signaled a
full-blown acceptance of an economic view of monopoly, even in
a single-seller situation. In this situation, monopoly is still monopoly, be it ever so genteel. Moreover, acceptance by the courts of
the economic analysis of the Alcoa case still left many conceptual
hurdles (both in law and in economics) to the application of the
Sherman Act to modern oligopolistic industry situations.

By contrast to the pre-World War II aluminum industry, the
industry involved in the 1946 American Tobacco[1] case was an
oligopoly with no clearly dominant firm and in which there was
little evidence of either open collusion or predatory conduct as
such. Like the Alcoa case, this suit was also initiated during a
brief period of aggressive antitrust activity shortly before World
War II. The American Tobacco case was the first attempt to apply
the Sherman Act to precisely those oligopolistic situations that are
seemingly so common, but which were largely immune to prosecution under the "rule of reason."

According to modern oligopoly theory, the structures of such
oligopolistic industries—few sellers and a high degree of concentration—tend to lead to parallel action on the part of the member
firms. This parallel action stems from the vulnerability of individual
firms to the actions of others—especially, price changes—and, in
turn, the threat of retaliation. Members of such oligopolistic industries, therefore, often pursue policies designed to mitigate, if not
eliminate, price competition. As an end result, firms in such industries are often led to collude, either tacitly or overtly, on prices
and other possible dimensions of rivalry. Such collusion has taken
many forms, ranging from overly zealous trade-association activities, market-sharing agreements, and more extensive cartel agreements to gentlemen's agreements, the mere recognition of communities of interest, and following a recognized price leader—no doubt
the most common procedure utilized in cases of tacit collusion. Irrespective of the form, such collusion has as natural goals to avoid
breaks in the industry's price structure or to otherwise preserve and
enhance firm, and industry, profits.

---

[1] American Tobacco Company v. United States 328 U.S. 781 (1946).

settled after war 1946

The end result of the parallel action stemming from implicitly agreed-upon communities of interest and from explicit agreements is largely the same: increased prices, restricted output, possibly a limited variety of services, and so forth. Nevertheless, explicit agreements were vulnerable to attack under the Sherman Act as a "conspiracy in restraint of trade" or to "monopolize," but, as the U.S. Steel decision might suggest, parallel action in the absence of overt collusion was largely free from antitrust prosecution.

This situation was broached in the American Tobacco case. In deciding this case the Supreme Court ruled that a conspiracy to monopolize could be inferred from a pattern of action or behavior over time and that a formal agreement to a conspiracy was unnecessary. That is, a common purpose or a "meeting of the minds" could be inferred from the parties' conduct. Thus the case seemingly held important implications for the future of those industries in which price leadership is a characteristic feature.

In this case the American Tobacco Company, Liggett and Meyers Tobacco Company, R. J. Reynolds Tobacco Company, and some officials and a subsidiary were charged with a number of violations of Sections 1 and 2 of the Sherman Act, generally covering the period 1937 through 1939. But evidence on earlier years also was introduced to indicate the patterns of behavior during the relevant years. The key issues related to the dominance and control over leaf tobacco purchases and the sale of the finished product, cigarettes. The evidence indicated that Reynolds had previously been an active competitor of the other two firms, but that, upon its growth, Reynolds had ceased its independent competitive policies.

The Court examined the size and behavorial patterns of the cigarette manufacturers to determine whether the three largest companies dominated the industry. Each of these companies was over twice the size of others in the industry. The Court felt that, other considerations aside, large-scale firms could most easily dominate the industry. It especially emphasized the very large size of the net annual returns and advertising expenditures of these firms; the latter in particular was cited as a barrier to entry into the industry. The trial jury had also found that the defendants had conspired to control prices and other aspects of the leaf tobacco market as well as the sale and distribution of cigarettes. In addition to these

barrier to entry

findings and that of conspiring to monopolize these markets, the court found that the defendants had the power and the intent to exclude competition from the industry. This decision of the trial jury was based on the cigarette companies' parallel behavior patterns rather than on specific contracts or oral agreements between the defendants. The prevalence and persistence of this behavior presumably provided a substantial barrier to the entry of potential competitors. On review, the Supreme Court held that it was not unreasonable for the lower court to conclude that the three defendants (which produced over two-thirds of all cigarettes, over 80 percent of comparable cigarettes, and faced competition from very small companies only) conspired in restraint of trade and to monopolize the industry.

The following excerpts from the Supreme Court's opinion indicate its reasoning concerning four charges of monopoly and conspiracy. These excerpts are followed by an article by William H. Nicholls that analyzes the implications of the Court's arguments, specifically whether oligopolistic situations constitute monopoly simply by having market power (with intent inferred from concerted action) and whether parallel action constitutes evidence of conspiracy.

Nicholls then considers the possible economic significance of such a precedent, pointing out the difficulties of proper remedies. It should be mentioned that, in retrospect, the Court did not intend to rule against monopolies per se, but to indicate that structural plus behavorial conditions in a given industry context might provide the conditions under which the intent could be inferred. Also, the Court did not indicate the conspiracy to monopolize could be indicated solely by parallel price action; rather, inferred conspiracy had to involve behavior of greater import than pricing.

●●

AMERICAN TOBACCO COMPANY
v.
UNITED STATES
328 U.S. 781 (1946)

Mr. Justice Burton delivered the opinion of the Court.

The petitioners are The American Tobacco Company, Liggett & Myers Tobacco Company, R. J. Reynolds Tobacco Company, American Suppliers, Inc., a subsidiary of American, and certain officials of the respective companies who were convicted by a jury, in the District Court of the United States for the Eastern District of Kentucky, of violating §§ 1 and 2 of the Sherman Anti-Trust Act, pursuant to an information filed July 24, 1940, and modified October 31, 1940.

Each petitioner was convicted on four counts: (1) conspiracy in restraint of trade, (2) monopolization, (3) attempt to monopolize, and (4) conspiracy to monopolize. Each count related to interstate and foreign trade and commerce in tobacco. . . .

. . . It long has been settled, however, that a "conspiracy to commit a crime is a different offense from the crime that is the object of the conspiracy.". . .

Although there is no issue of fact or question as to the sufficiency of the evidence to be discussed here, nevertheless, it is necessary to summarize the principal facts of that conspiracy to monopolize certain trade, which was charged in the fourth count. These facts demonstrate also the vigor and nature of the intent of the petitioners to exclude competitors in order to maintain that monopoly if need or occasion should offer itself to attempt such an exclusion. To support the verdicts it was not necessary to show power and intent to exclude *all* competitors, or to show a conspiracy to exclude *all* competitors. The requirement stated to the jury and contained in the statute was only that the offenders shall "monopolize any part of the trade or commerce among the several States, or with foreign nations." This particular conspiracy may well have derived special vitality, in the eyes of the jury, from the fact that its existence was established, not through the presentation of a formal written agreement, but through the evidence of widespread and effective conduct on the part of petitioners in relation to their existing or potential competitors.

. . . The fact, however, that the purchases of leaf tobacco and the sales of so many products of the tobacco industry have remained largely within the same general group of business organizations for over a generation, inevitably has contributed to the ease with which control over competition within the industry and the mobilization of power to resist new competition can be exercised. A friendly relationship within such a long established industry is, in itself, not only natural but commendable and beneficial, as long as it does not breed illegal activities. Such a community of interest in any industry, however, provides a natural foundation for working policies and understandings favorable to the insiders and unfavorable to outsiders. The verdicts indicate that practices of an informal and flexible nature were adopted and that the results were so uniformly beneficial to the petitioners in protecting their common interests as against those of competitors that, entirely from circumstantial evidence, the jury found that a combination or conspiracy existed among the petitioners from 1937 to 1940, with power and intent to exclude competitors to such a substantial extent as to violate the Sherman Act as interpreted by the trial court. [The court here included two tables and the court's interpretation to show the dominance of the "Big Three" in cigarette production from 1931 through 1939.]

With this background of a substantial monopoly, amounting to over two-thirds of the entire domestic field of cigarettes, and to over 80% of the field of comparable cigarettes, and with the opposition confined to several small competitors, the jury could have found from the actual operation of the petitioners that there existed a combination or conspiracy among them not only in restraint of trade, but to monopolize a part of the tobacco industry. The trial court described this combination or conspiracy as an "essential element" and "indispensable ingredient" of the offenses charged. It is therefore only in conjunction with such a combination or conspiracy that these cases will constitute a precedent. The conspiracy so established by the verdicts under the second count appears to have been one to fix and control prices and other material conditions relating to the purchase of raw material in the form of leaf tobacco for use in the manufacture of cigarettes. It also appears to have been one to fix and control prices and other material conditions relating to the distribution and sale of the product of such tobacco in the form of cigarettes. The jury found a conspiracy to monopolize to a substantial degree the leaf market and the cigarette market. The jury's verdicts also found a power and intent on the part of the petitioners to exclude competition to a substantial extent in the tobacco industry.

. . . A correct interpretation of the statute and of the authorities makes it the crime of monopolizing, under § 2 of the Sherman Act, for parties, as in these cases, to combine or conspire to acquire or maintain the power to exclude competitors from any part of the trade or commerce among the several states or with foreign nations, provided they also have such a power that they are able, as a group, to exclude actual or potential competition from the field and provided that they have the intent and purpose to exercise that power.

It is not the form of the combination or the particular means used but the result to be achieved that the statute condemns. It is not of importance whether the means used to accomplish the unlawful objective are in themselves lawful or unlawful. Acts done to give effect to the conspiracy may be in themselves wholly innocent acts. Yet, if they are part of the sum of the acts which are relied upon to effectuate the conspiracy which the statute forbids, they come within its prohibition. No formal agreement is necessary to constitute an unlawful conspiracy. Often crimes are a matter of inference deduced from the acts of the person accused and done in pursuance of a criminal purpose. Where the conspiracy is proved, as here, from the evidence of the action taken in concert by the parties to it, it is all the more convincing proof of an intent to exercise the power of exclusion acquired through that conspiracy. The essential combination or conspiracy in violation of the Sherman Act may be found in a course of dealings or other circumstances as well as in an exchange of words. . . . Where the circumstances are such as to warrant a jury in finding that the conspirators had a unity of purpose or a common design and understanding, or a meeting of minds in an unlawful arrangement, the conclusion that a conspiracy is established is justified. Neither proof of exertion of the power to exclude nor proof of actual exclusion of existing or potential competitors is essential to sustain a charge of monopolization under the Sherman Act.

The precise question before us has not been decided previously by this Court. However, on March 12, 1945, two weeks before the grant of the writs of certiorari in the present cases, a decision rendered in a suit in equity brought under §§ 1 and 2 of the Sherman Anti-Trust Act against the Aluminum Company of America closely approached the issue we have here. That case was decided by the Circuit Court of Appeals for the Second Circuit under unique circumstances which add to its weight as a precedent. United States v. Aluminum Co. of America, 148 F 2d 416. That court sat in that case under a new statute authorizing it to render a decision "in lieu of a decision by the Supreme Court" and providing that such decision "shall be final and there shall be no review of such decision by appeal or certiorari or otherwise."

We find the following statements from the opinion of the court in that case to be especially appropriate here and we welcome this opportunity to endorse them:

"Many people believe that possession of unchallenged economic power deadens initiative, discourages thrift and depresses energy; that immunity from competition is a narcotic, and rivalry is a stimulant, to industrial progress; that the spur of constant stress is necessary to counteract an inevitable disposition to let well enough alone. . . . These considerations, which we have suggested only as possible purposes of the Act, we think the decisions prove to have been in fact its purposes.

"Starting, however, with the authoritative premise that all contracts fixing prices are unconditionally prohibited, the only possible difference between them and a monopoly is that while a monopoly necessarily involves an equal, or even greater, power to fix prices, its mere existence might be thought not to constitute an exercise of that power. That distinction is nevertheless purely formal; it would be valid only so long as the monopoly remained wholly inert; it would disappear as soon as the monopoly began to operate; for, when it did—that is, as soon as it began to sell at all—it must sell at some price and the only price at which it could sell is a price which it itself fixed. Thereafter the power and its exercise must need coalesce. Indeed it would be absurd to condemn such contracts unconditionally, and not to extend the condemnation to monopolies; for the contracts are only steps toward that entire control which monopoly confers: they are really partial monopolies.

"It does not follow because 'Alcoa' had such a monopoly, that it 'monopolized' the ingot market: it may not have achieved monopoly; monopoly may have been thrust upon it. If it had been a combination of existing smelters which united the whole industry and controlled the production of all aluminum ingot, it would certainly have 'monopolized' the market. In several decisions the Supreme Court has decreed the dissolution of such combinations, although they had engaged in no unlawful trade practices. . . . We may start therefore with the premise that to have combined ninety per cent of the producers of ingot would have been to 'monopolize' the ingot market; and, so far as concerns the public interest, it can make no difference whether an existing competition is put an end to, or whether prospective competition is prevented. The Clayton Act itself speaks in that alternative: 'to injure, destroy, or prevent competition.'

"It insists that it never excluded competitors; but we can think of no more effective exclusion than progressively to embrace each new opportunity as it opened, and to face every newcomer with new capacity already geared into a great organization, having the advantage of experience, trade connections and the elite of personnel. Only in case we interpret 'exclusion' as limited to manoeuvres not honestly industrial, but actuated solely by a desire to prevent competition, can such a course, indefatigably pursued, be deemed not 'exclusionary.' So to limit it would in our judgment emasculate the Act; would permit just such consolidations as it was designed to prevent.

"In order to fall within § 2, the monopolist must have both the power to monopolize, and the intent to monopolize. To read the passage as demanding any 'specific' intent, makes nonsense of it, for no monopolist monopolizes unconscious of what he is doing."

In the present cases, the petitioners have been found to have conspired to establish a monopoly and also to have the power and intent to establish and maintain the monopoly. To hold that they do not come within the prohibition of the Sherman Act would destroy the force of that Act. Accordingly, the instructions of the trial court under § 2 of the Act are approved and the judgment of the Circuit Court of Appeals is affirmed.

. . . . .

The Tobacco Case of 1946
William H. Nicholls

. . . . .

THE SIGNIFICANCE OF THE TOBACCO DECISIONS

It is the task of the law of monopoly to distinguish between business practices which are in the public interest and those which are not. In carrying out this difficult problem of evaluation, the courts have had to devise and apply tests capable of differentiating between approved and disapproved practices. As elsewhere in the law, the law of monopoly has reflected the perennial conflict between certainty and change. Two tests of monopoly have become

Abridged from William H. Nicholls, "The Tobacco Case of 1946," *The American Economic Review*, XXXIX, No. 3, Proceedings (May 1949), 284–296.

traditional: (1) On the question of conspiracy, does the evidence show that competitors actually agreed? (2) On the question of monopolization, was there overt predatory action to exclude competition? These two tests had the advantages of certainty—they could be applied with sufficient consistency to assure equality of treatment before the law; and they were sufficiently concrete to indicate the practices which must be avoided to escape condemnation under the law. Unfortunately, however, these tests have become increasingly inadequate as the structure and practices of American industry have taken new and more subtle forms. Thus, the need for change—for adapting the law to a new industrial environment—has become more and more apparent.

In the *Tobacco* case,[1] at the neccessary cost of new uncertainties, the courts finally met this need for change in two ways. First, the Court of Appeals brought wholly tacit, nonaggressive oligopoly fully within the reach of the conspiracy provisions of the Sherman Act. Prior law already had made clear that—in the absence of "formal agreement"—an unlawful conspiracy can be inferred from "concert of action," "unity of purpose," or "a common design." Furthermore, in the *Tobacco* case, there was plentiful and undisputed evidence that the three defendant dominant firms had behaved identically with regard to prices, terms of sale, and general business practices. Nevertheless, the case was probably unique in that there was not a whit of evidence that a common plan had even been contemplated or proposed. The government's evidence was admittedly *wholly* circumstantial. The fact of identity of behavior was offered as the basis for inferring both the existence and the elements of the alleged common plan and the defendants' knowledge of that plan. Each was alleged to have acted similarly with the knowledge that the others would so act, to their mutual self-interest. Thus, the *Tobacco* case brought the basic assumption of modern oligopoly theory squarely before the courts. In finding in the facts a reasonable basis for the jury's inference of unlawful conspiracy, the Court of Appeals accepted the practical implications of that assumption; namely, that a few dominant firms will, perhaps

---

[1] *American Tobacco Co., et al.,* v. *U.S.,* 147 F. 2d 93 (1944); 328 U.S. 781 (1946).

independently and purely as a matter of self-interest, evolve non-aggressive patterns of behavior. Thus, attention was shifted from form to probable results. Upon final appeal, the Supreme Court refused to review this part of the lower court's findings.

Second, in the *Tobacco* case, the existence of power to exclude competition, not the abuse of that power, became the new test of illegal monopolization. Thus, the recent *Aluminum* doctrine[2] was approved and was extended to conspiratorial oligopoly. Accepting without review the judgments below that a conspiracy had been established, the Supreme Court held that neither the exertion of power to exclude nor the actual exclusion of competitors is necessary to the crime of monopolization. Existence of the power and intent to exclude will suffice. Since the Court was willing to infer intent from the concerted action of the conspirators, the power to exclude—as shown by degree of market control of the combination —was made the crucial issue. Thus, attention was shifted from monopolization as an *action* to monopoly as a *condition*. The Supreme Court explicitly limited the precedential significance of this decision to cases in which conspiracy is an essential ingredient. Nevertheless, so broad was the lower court's application of the law of conspiracy to the facts that, if it were generally followed, the behavior of few oligopolies could probably escape condemnation as "conspiratorial."

It should be obvious that the *Tobacco* decisions of 1946 must be given a prominent place in the historical development of the case law of the antitrust acts. And, if my interpretation of their legal implications is correct, the *Tobacco* decisions have gone far to close the wide gap between the legal and economic concepts of monopoly, which became so apparent to economists during the thirties.[3] In accepting detailed similarity of behavior among a few dominant firms as a reasonable basis for inferring illegal conspiracy, the courts have finally brought the law of conspiracy into harmony with the economics of oligopoly. Furthermore, the legal and economic concepts of monopoly (including conspiratorial group monopoly)

[2] *U.S.* v. *Aluminum Co.,* 148 F. 2d. 416 (1945), the Circuit Court serving as the final court of appeal.

[3] Cf. E. S. Mason, "Monopoly in Law and Economics," *Yale Law Journal,* Vol. 47 (1937–38), pp. 34–49.

have been brought closer together. Thus, Rostow is correct in finding, on the basis of the *Aluminum* and *Tobacco* cases, that "market control is now a far more important theme in Sherman Act cases than handicaps on an individual's power to do business. The old preoccupation of judges with evidence of business tactics they regarded as ruthless, predatory and immoral has all but disappeared. . . . We are close to the point of regarding as illegal the kind of economic power which the economist regards as monopolistic." [4] That the *Aluminum* and *Tobacco* decisions have revitalized the Sherman Act, especially Section 2, seems beyond serious doubt. Furthermore, economists can rejoice that the precepts of modern economic analysis have so quickly found their way into the case law of monopoly.

Unlike lawyers of the Antitrust Division, however, economists cannot be satisfied simply by the scoreboard of cases won by the government. Although some important legal "twilight zones" remain, the widespread application of the new tests of monopoly to oligopolistic industries should lead to a high proportion of government victories from now on. It is clear, however, that without remedial action, these legal victories will be of relatively little economic or social consequences. And, if remedial action is taken, it is by no means certain that the economic consequences will always be in the public interest.

THE PROSPECTS OF GOVERNMENT "VICTORY"

With regard to the *Tobacco* decision, counsel for Reynolds Tobacco Company argued that:

> . . . the significance of these convictions extends far beyond the immediate consequences to petitioners and the tobacco industry. . . . For, *if these convictions be lawful, the pattern of prosecution is applicable—with the result of almost certain and repeated convic-*

[4] Eugene V. Rostow, "The New Sherman Act: A Positive Instrument of Progress," *University of Chicago Law Review,* Vol. 14 (1946–47), pp. 574–75 *et seq.* For a more cautious appraisal of these two cases, cf. Edward H. Levi, "The Antitrust Laws and Monopoly," *ibid.,* pp. 172–81.

> *tion—to every other executive and corporation in a mass production industry* . . . in which, as a matter of common knowledge, economic forces have produced identities or close similarities in manufacturing, packaging, pricing, advertising, marketing and even raw material acquisition.

The present writer is willing to accept this appraisal as being at least within the realm of possibility. Given the widespread pattern of domination-by-a-few in modern American industry, counsel for Liggett and Myers was also probably correct in arguing that "the common practices of the tobacco industry are in many instances usual features of business life today, and in all instances practices which businessmen guided by . . . self-interest, acting reasonably and in the absence of agreement, might adopt." In view of this fact, the conviction of the major tobacco companies suggests at least a presumption in favor of the view that the Antitrust Division's ability to find and prosecute monopolies successfully is now largely limited only by the extent of its own resources in bringing cases to trial.

Nevertheless, we must recognize that at least two important questions are as yet unanswered. First, what types of similarity of behavior among oligopolistic competitors will the courts hold to be insufficient to sustain an inference of illegal conspiracy? In the *Tobacco* case, the circumstantial evidence supporting such an inference was very strong—considerably stronger than the evidence which could be marshaled against many other oligopolistic industries. However, the extent to which the courts are willing to go in finding illegal conspiracy among oligopolists will depend at least as much upon their judgment and preconceptions as upon the facts of any specific case before them. The conspiracy doctrine of the *Tobacco* case certainly permits them to go about as far as they like in this direction. Second, what is the legal status of a single dominant firm of intermediate size (say, controlling 50–65 per cent of an industry), such as was involved in the *Steel* and *Harvester* cases? Until the courts explicitly apply recent doctrine to a situation of this sort, the law will continue to treat loose "conspiracies" more severely than (within certain limits) such a single dominant firm with an equal or greater degree of market control.

Despite these remaining "twilight zones," the conclusion is apparent: in antitrust action against oligopolistic industries, the prospects of government victory are now relatively bright.

"VICTORY" WITHOUT REMEDIAL ACTION

It is the writer's belief that, in the *Tobacco* case, the courts reached a conclusion which—in the main—economic analysis would support. Nevertheless, the fact remains that the court in effect condemned the natural, normal, and intelligent consequences of an oligopolistic market structure. The difficult question of appropriate remedial action was therefore placed in bold relief. As a criminal prosecution, the *Tobacco* case provided no remedial action. Thus far, therefore, the government's victory has been (apart from a quarter-million dollars of fines) almost an empty one.

Given the present structure of the industry, until now left untouched by the government, the writer must admit a feeling of some sympathy for the arguments of counsel for the tobacco companies. Thus, counsel claimed that, even if guilty, they were "entirely without guide as to how they may lawfully avoid the creation of evidence of future Sherman Act violations against themselves, unless they cease business altogether." For example, must Reynolds refrain from "percentage buying" of leaf? And if it does, and its competitors do likewise, "will it or they not then be accused of manipulating prices, allocating tobaccos, and discriminating against growers through intermittent buying . . . ?" Or "must Reynolds desist from charging for its product the price charged for a competitive product, and must Reynolds, by prosecution or otherwise, attempt to prevent a competitor from selling at Reynolds' price?" Or again:

> What are the specific policies and practices we must abandon, modify, or adopt in order to conduct our business according to law? . . . Presumably, the appellants were convicted of agreement, not of the particular operations alleged to constitute agreement. Yet, on the Government's theory, continuation by more than one of the appellants of the operations alleged is evidence of a further Sherman Act agreement. . . . If this is so, how is Liggett & Myers to carry on? Must it start all over again with new manage-

ment, with a new system? Is everything the appellants do illegal, or evidence of illegality, if done by more than one of them?

Since neither the prosecution nor the courts provided an answer, the major tobacco companies have themselves done so; namely, to follow essentially the same cigarette price policies since the trial that they followed before. The evidence upon which the *Tobacco* decision was based extended only through July, 1940. . . .

[At this point Professor Nicholls discussed the prices charged by the cigarette companies and the factors bearing on these prices from July 1940 through 1948.]

. . . Insofar as price differences among the standard brands do now exist, it is obvious that they are of no practical importance, being too small to be reflected in different retail prices. Furthermore, there have been no changes in the customary discounts to wholesalers. Hence, even though very minor price differences may have resulted from the *Tobacco* decision, they are significant only as a means of attempting to avoid the absolute price identity there condemned. In fact, with the minor exceptions noted, the list prices, terms of trade, and timing of price changes are probably more nearly identical today—if one considers all of the standard brands—than prior to 1940.

This limited evidence supports the view that, if there was illegal conspiracy before 1940, there is still illegal conspiracy today. Furthermore, if the economic power of the three major companies combined constituted illegal monopolization before 1940, it does so *a fortiori* at the present time. Between 1939 and 1947, during which domestic cigarette sales nearly doubled, the three defendant companies expanded their share of the domestic cigarette market from 68 to more than 85 per cent. Thus, they appear to be fast approaching their position of 1931, when they sold 91 per cent of the nation's cigarettes. Meanwhile, the economy brands' share of the domestic market has dropped from 14 to about 1 per cent in the face of high consumer incomes, high manufacturing costs, and a narrowing price differential below the standard brands. As a consequence, the smaller companies which grew rapidly on economy brands during the thirties have lost much ground since 1939, their standard brands (if any) failing to share sufficiently in the shift to a higher-priced product to compensate for their declining low-priced market. Apart from Philip Morris (which has not quite held its own despite its purchase of Axton-Fisher in 1944), all companies other than the Big Three have suffered moderate to severe losses of market position since 1939. Within the Big Three, Liggett and Myers' share dropped slightly while American's jumped from 22.7 to 36.1 per cent, and Reynolds' from 23.7 to 28.8 per cent. Not since 1931 have one or two companies been so dominant. The two recent price changes suggest that American—now that it has again clearly established itself as the nation's largest cigarette manufacturer—has displaced Reynolds as the recognized price leader of the industry. It is even possible that Reynolds has voluntarily abdicated its traditional position as price leader in order that it can be certain to avoid the absolute price identity so recently condemned.

Despite the absence of any fundamental changes in their historical pattern of similar price behavior and despite their recrudescent degree of market control, the three convicted tobacco companies nevertheless appear to have followed a more moderate price policy since 1946 than that of earlier years. Net prices to the major manufacturers are now only about 33 per cent above 1939 and the Big Three's rates of profits are currently running at about 13–16 per cent (1948) as compared with 14–18 per cent in 1939 and 17–22 per cent in 1931. (Meanwhile, Lorillard's rate of profits has increased slightly to 10 per cent [1948] and Philip Morris' has fallen from 25.2 per cent in 1939 to 8.6 per cent in 1947.) This more moderate price policy is probably in part due to the Big Three's desire to fend off the existing and potential competition which they found so unexpecedly strong in the thirties. Apparently such price policies—in conjunction with the continued powerful differential advantage of their highly advertised brands—promise to maintain or increase the Big Three's market control where the more grasping price policies of the past failed to do so. Undoubtedly, present cigarette prices also still reflect to some extent the long period of controlled prices. Finally, because of the legal doubts which it cast upon the whole fabric of traditional cigarette price policies, recent antitrust action should probably receive part of the credit for these more moderate prices. If so, however, until effective remedial action is taken, the Antitrust Division's victory at best may have brought somewhat lower cigarette prices (at least in the short run) at the cost of that increasing concentration of economic power which it so much abhors. With this possible exception, the current history of the tobacco industry suggests that the widespread conviction of oligopolistic industries, though now legally possible, will produce only relatively unimportant economic consequences unless accompanied by measures to change the underlying industrial structure which makes the condemned behavior almost inevitable. Thus the difficult problem of evaluation and prescription in the public interest still remains.

consent decree

THE PROBLEM OF REMEDIAL ACTION *dissolution*

The Antitrust Division has certainly not been unaware of the need for remedial action in the tobacco industry. In response to warnings from the Department of Justice following the 1946 decision, the convicted companies claim to have made changes in their policies which eliminate the possibility of further violations of the antitrust laws. That the Antitrust Division has not yet been convinced is indicated by the fact that, during the last year, it has held several conferences with the three companies to consider the terms of a proposed consent decree.[5] I am extremely skeptical, however, about the efficacy of any consent decree which falls short of dissolution. And even with the bargaining strength which its recent successful criminal action gives the Division, we can hardly expect the companies to agree to dissolution in such an out-of-court settlement. Yet in the civil suit recently instituted against the four major meat packers, the Division reveals that it considers dissolution the appropriate remedy for oligopoly. In this suit, patterned in detail after the *Tobacco* decision, the Division seeks dissolution of the four principal firms into fourteen companies.[6] Why, then, has

[5] R. J. Reynolds Tobacco Co., Prospectus on an Issue of Debentures, September 29, 1948, pp. 27–28.

[6] In the Dist. Ct. of the U.S., Northern Dist. of Ill., Eastern Division, *U.S.* v. *Armour, Swift, Cudahy, and Wilson,* Civil Action No. 48C 1351, September 15, 1948. The complaint alleges that, as a continuing offense since 1893, the four defendants have (1) refrained from competition among

barriers to dissolution

not the Antitrust Division brought a civil suit seeking dissolution of the major tobacco companies?

I suspect that the principal reason, apart from the need for economizing resources, is that the Division recognizes the difficulties involved in formulating a dissolution plan for the tobacco industry. Each of the three companies has three to four cigarette manufacturing plants which could be made into separate firms. Furthermore, it is almost certain that the principal economies of scale, beyond those of the individual plant, are those of advertising and market control; hence are private rather than social. Nevertheless, there are at least two important barriers to dissolution. First, each of the three firms has concentrated wholly (Reynolds) or largely (85 per cent or more) upon a single brand of cigarettes. Since a single brand of cigarettes could hardly be divided among several successor companies, the present major brands would probably have to be abolished. The original Tobacco Trust, having a multiplicity of brands, did not present this difficulty to those responsible for developing the details of its dissolution. Second, the paramount importance of advertising and sales effort in the industry cannot be overlooked. As Jones once pointed out, the dissolution of the Tobacco Trust "led to a duplication of selling organization and an increased overhead expense; and the result was a general *increase* in selling costs." Between 1910 and 1913, the selling costs of the successor cigarette companies increased by 85 per cent, and the advertising expenditures more than doubled, in comparison with those of the Trust.[7] True, the dissolution ushered in a decade of innovation and price competition which was strongly in the public interest. Thereafter, however, the industry settled down into a pattern of non-price competition which it is doubtful that even a

---

themselves by market sharing (constant percentages) in the purchase of livestock and the sale of meats, and by identical cost-figuring, prices, and terms of trade for both livestock and meats; (2) restrained competition by independents through the formulation of policies which the latter were urged to follow; and (3) excluded competitors by purchase or by resisting expansion of independents. As relief, the government asks (1) that each defendant be enjoined from following each of the practices complained of and (2) that Swift and Armour each be dissolved into five companies, and Cudahy and Wilson be dissolved into two companies.

[7] Eliot Jones, *The Trust Problem in the United States* (1922), pp. 40–44.

second dissolution could fully avoid. In other words, the cigarette industry is of such a nature that competition, at best, must continue to have important imperfections. Nonetheless, despite such difficult problems as these, a workable plan of dissolution could probably be devised upon the basis of a careful study of the structure of the tobacco industry.

other

Whether or not dissolution is resorted to, however, supplementary techniques should not be ignored. Although lying outside of the limits of antitrust action, two other measures deserve consideration as means of encouraging competition in the tobacco industry. First, a sharply progressive tax might be imposed upon the individual firm's total expenditures for advertising. Ideally, the tax should apply only to advertising expenditures greater than those already being made by firms of intermediate size, thereby permitting small firms to expand their advertising outlays somewhat but forcing the largest firms to curtail theirs considerably. Such a tax should go far toward eliminating the overwhelming advantages which large-scale advertising gives to giant firms, both in holding their market position against existing small firms and in limiting the entry of new firms. If clear limits were established on the extent of advertising, resort to price competition should also be encouraged. The great practical obstacles to this proposal are obvious. First, since such a tax might have to apply to all industries nondiscriminately, it would be difficult to make due legislative allowances for important differences between industries in the absolute and relative levels of advertising costs. Second, insofar as large firms lost business as a result of the lower advertising expenditures caused by the tax, a question of constitutionality under the "due process" clause might be invoked. Third, one could hardly expect the press and radio to support such a tax with enthusiasm or complete objectivity. Nevertheless, this proposal does center attention upon one of the key problems involved in introducing a modicum of competition into industries—such as tobacco, liquor, drugs, cosmetics, etc.—which rely heavily upon advertising.

A second measure for encouraging competition in the tobacco industry would be the sharp reduction or elimination of the federal and state cigarette taxes. These taxes have now reached so high a proportion of the final retail price as to make price competition among cigarette manufacturers almost prohibitive. Thus, at the present time, in a state levying a three-cent-per-package cigarette tax in addition to the federal tax of seven cents, a manufacturer would have to cut his final net price by about 15 per cent to lower the retail price by 5–6 per cent (or one cent a package). Since distributing margins are very small, the elimination of the cigarette tax would bring these two percentages very close together and make price competition among manufacturers much more attractive. Valuable though cigarette (and liquor) taxes may be as a lucrative source of governmental revenues, that they strongly foster monopolistic price policies has been almost wholly overlooked. . . . The present flat tax per thousand cigarettes is inexcusably burdensome upon the economy brands, which are the only real element of price competition in the industry. While a graduated tax, based upon two or more price classes, has been frequently proposed, it has never met with Congressional favor.[8] Far better than such a graduated tax would be a straight ad valorem tax which would encourage a full continuum of possible prices, thereby helping to undermine the present pattern of virtual price identity for both standard brands and economy brands.

In spite of its apparent reticence to dissolve the major cigarette companies, the Antitrust Division may be expected to use dissolution proceedings much more frequently in the future than it has previously done. Unfortunately, drastic though it may be, dissolution appears to be the only really effective remedy for oligopoly which lies within the limits of antitrust action per se. If the current suit against the meat packers is indicative, the Division may even be launching an unprecedented drive toward atomization of American industry. The economic consequences of such remedial action, if generally executed, would certainly be far reaching. Whether they would always be in the public interest as well is less easy to foresee. The danger is that the well-known antibigness bias of the Antitrust

[8] See, for example, Senate Committee on Finance (73d Cong., 2d sess.), *Hearing on Reduction of Tax on Cigarettes,* 1934. In December, 1948, the House Select Committee on Small Business recommended to Congress "a graduated ad valorem rate of tax" on cigarettes. *Report of House Select Committee on Small Business, Problems of Small Business Resulting from Monopolistic and Unfair Trade Practices* (80th Cong., 2d sess.), pp. 10–11 and 26.

Division will lead to an overzealous disregard for economies of scale and other basic economic realities in at least some of its dissolution proposals.

CONCLUSION

The *Tobacco* case is clearly a legal milestone in the social control of oligopoly. By permitting the inference of illegal conspiracy from detailed similarity of behavior and by shifting attention from the abuse of power to its mere existence (as indicated by degree of market control), the courts have at last brought oligopolistic industries within reach of successful prosecution under the antitrust laws. This is all to the good. The economic consequences will depend, however, upon whether government victories are accompanied by appropriate remedial action. If they are not, such victories will be nearly futile. On the other hand, if remedial action is taken, the Antitrust Division must assume a new and heavy responsibility to restrain the narrowly punitive spirit to which its antibigness bias so easily leads; and to prescribe remedies solely with a view to their contribution to the public interest, broadly conceived and based upon thoroughgoing economic analysis. Although the courts now may have largely abandoned the "rule of reason," the Antitrust Division—in deciding what industries to prosecute and in preparing appropriate corrective measures—must develop a "standard of reasonableness" of its own if the public interest is to be properly served. Finally, it must be recognized that other legislative reforms —though lying outside the bounds of antitrust action—can do much to supplement or complement the antitrust laws in attaining the goal of a more competitive economy.

The *Tobacco* case is indeed a legal milestone. Whether it will be an economic milestone—or millstone—will depend upon the judiciousness with which its doctrines are applied. Certainly, the law and economics alike should combine their best efforts in meeting the new challenge which the *Tobacco* decision has so forcefully laid down.

7 THE OLIGOPOLISTIC CONUNDRUM

As Nicholls indicated, the Tobacco decision presented very pregnant possibilities of antitrust prosecution. In retrospect these possibilities never materialized, largely because the two "dubious assumptions" specified by Nicholls were not realized: (1) The courts did not say what Nicholls believed they said: they did not infer illegal conspiracy from highly similar conduct; that is, the abuse of power was not inferred from its existence. (2) The legal implications that Nicholls read into the decision were not carried to their logical conclusion; that is, the courts have not been willing to provide the appropriate remedial action required for any economically meaningful relief. Subsequent interpretation of the Tobacco decision restricted its effect, and there was no resultant realignment of the domestic industrial structure.

In the following article, written somewhat later than the Nicholls' one, Jesse W. Markham considers the meaning of the Tobacco decision, specifically in regard to instances of parallel price behavior. Markham examines three particular price-leadership models in an attempt to identify those factors that might be affected by the decision. His views as to the likely effects of the case conclude the article. Some aspects of oligopoly theory and of business behavior have been suggested by previous material but are highlighted in Markham's article. One aspect is the profusion of considerations that enters into oligopoly analysis. The great number of considerations and our inability to identify them clearly in any given instance serve to weaken the usefulness of oligopoly theory to problems of market control. In addition, the importance of nonprice behavioristic considerations in the business decision-making process further weakens the argument for applying rigid oligopoly-model conclusions to antitrust issues. In an important sense Markham's analysis questions the usefulness or relevance of contemporary analysis to antitrust problems. Does the neoclassical statement of the 1930s offer the most fruitful basis for an analysis of antitrust issues in the real world of law and economics?

· ·

The Nature and Significance of Price Leadership

Jesse W. Markham

· ·

That the Supreme Court's decision in the *Tobacco* case of 1946 attaches a new significance to price leadership in oligopolistic markets seems beyond reasonable doubt. The *Tobacco* decision constitutes a reversal of the stand taken by the Court in the *U.S. Steel* and *International Harvester* cases, where the Court ruled that the acceptance of a price leader by the rest of the industry did not constitute a violation of the Sherman Act by the price leader. If we accept the full meaning of what the Court has really said, that parallel pricing, whether implemented by an agreement or not, is now illegal, pricing policies prevailing in markets where sellers are few will henceforth be subjected to a much closer examination than they have been in the past.

If the legal implications of the *Tobacco* decision as interpreted by Professors Rostow, Nicholls and others be accepted, the eco-

Abridged from Jesse W. Markham, "The Nature and Significance of Price Leadership," *The American Economic Review*, XLI (1951), 891–905.

nomic consequences of price leadership and the specific conditions
likely to render it an effective weapon against price competition in
oligopolistic markets need to be re-examined. Because the courts
have not yet faced up to the problem of providing appropriate
remedies, the question of wherein lies the most fruitful remedial
action should at least be raised. It is primarily to this task that this
article is addressed. Since, however, there is always the danger of
assigning unwarranted homogeneity to such an economic phenomenon, its significance will be appraised on the basis of (1) the particular types of price leadership which prevail in industrial markets and
(2) the extent to which each type might conceivably circumvent
forces of competition.

Professor Stigler has distinguished between two kinds of price
leadership: (1) that associated with a dominant firm and (2) that
of the barometric type.[1] Since, however, one of the market conditions that the barometric firm's price is supposed to reflect is both
secret and open price cutting,[2] it is not always possible to determine
whether the barometric firm should be viewed as the "price leader"
or as one of the first "price followers." Hence, for purposes of this
discussion, the above otherwise satisfactory dichotomy will be aug-
mented by a third type of price leadership which may be viewed
either as an extreme form of the barometric type or simply as price
leadership in lieu of overt collusion.

"MODELS" OF PRICE LEADERSHIP

Although most of the vast volume of economic literature on price
practices and policies conveys the impression that price leadership
is a logical and effective means for eliminating price competition
among rival sellers, theoretical treatment of the topic has been cast
in rather simple static terms and limited to three special cases.[3]

[1] George J. Stigler, "The Kinky Oligopoly Demand Curve and Rigid
Prices," *Journal of Political Economy,* Vol. LV (October, 1947), pp. 444–45.

[2] See Professor Stigler's illustrative case, *ibid.,* p. 445.

[3] The number of institutional and other conditions under which the prices
set by one firm in an industry might be used by all others is probably very
large, but only three sets of conditions seem to make price leadership of
some sort inevitable and at the same time identify the price leader.

Perhaps the most familiar theoretical model of price leadership is centered upon the dominant firm or partial monopolist. Starting from the assumption that an industry comprises one large producer and a number of smaller ones, no one of which produces a high enough percentage of total output to influence the price, it logically follows that the role of price making falls to the dominant firm. This is true because each small firm regards its own demand schedule as perfectly elastic at the price set by the dominant firm and thus behaves as though it operates under conditions of perfect competition. The dominant firm might set any price it chooses, but presumably would set one which maximizes its profits by equating its own marginal cost with its marginal revenue as derived from the market demand schedule and the summation of the individual marginal cost curves of the independent small producers.

Professor Boulding[4] has presented two other theoretical models of price leadership. One relates to an industry comprising one low-cost high-capacity firm and one or more high-cost low-capacity firms, the other to an industry comprising at least two firms having identical cost curves but different shares in the market. In the former case, because no price can equate marginal cost with marginal revenue for both (or all) firms, a conflict in price policy inevitably arises. However, since the price preferred by the low-cost high-capacity firm is lower than the price preferred by the high-cost low-capacity firm (or firms), the low-cost firm can impose its price policy on the industry. In the other case, under assumptions described by Professor Boulding as "rather peculiar," that marginal cost curves for all firms are identical and that each firm's relative share in the market is different from that of all other firms and remains unchanged over the entire range of possible prices, marginal cost and marginal revenue are equated at a lower price for the firm having the smallest share in the market than for any other firm. Hence, the firm having the smallest share in the market at all possible prices can impose the price most acceptable to it on the rest of the industry. Professor Boulding makes no claim that the latter model is built upon sufficiently realistic assumptions to throw much

[4] Kenneth E. Boulding, *Economic Analysis* (rev. ed.; New York, 1948). For a diagrammatical presentation of the two models, see pp. 582, 586.

light upon price policies generally but suggests that it might explain price behavior in the retail gasoline industry.

It is worthwhile to point out that in none of the above three models is price leadership a result of collusion; in fact, in each of the models price leadership is an inevitable consequence of a particular cost or demand phenomenon which precludes price collusion among sellers as a possible solution. Moreover, in none of the three models is the absence of competition attributable to the presence of a price leader. In each of the three cases, conditions in either the factor or product market are already assumed to be inconsistent with the assumptions associated with highly competitive industries. Since the empirical evidence presented in a later section also suggests that effective price leadership, for the most part, is a result of monopoly rather than a cause of it, it is important that these two observations be borne in mind when it comes to prescribing appropriate remedies for industries having price leaders.

DOMINANT FIRM PRICE LEADERSHIP

Contrary to the general belief that price leadership, because it eliminates the kink in the oligopoly demand curve, makes for a higher degree of price flexibility, Professor Stigler has presented evidence to show that "except for the number of price changes of two-firm industries . . . , the prices of industries with price leaders are less flexible than those of industries without price leaders." [5] Significant though this discovery may be as evidence of the nonexistence of kinked oligopoly demand curves, it should be pointed out that the basic conclusion reached by Professor Stigler applies to a particular type of oligopolistic market and, hence, is not conclusive evidence that price leadership, regardless of types, leads to less flexible prices. For example, Professor Stigler limits the industries characterized by price leadership to those in which a dominant firm (one that produces a minimum of 40 per cent of the total output of an industry and more if the second largest firm is large) is present. Hence, industries char-

[5] Stigler, *op. cit.,* p. 446.

acterized by other types of price leadership were included among those having no price leader. Moreover, the average number of firms in industries classified as having a price leader was slightly less than one-half of the average number of firms in industries not so classified. It is not surprising, therefore, that the former group shows a higher degree of price inflexibility than the latter for two reasons.

First, the rationale of price making by the dominant firm or partial monopolist differs but little from that employed by the pure monopolist. They both, presumably, have complete control over prices, but the partial monopolist, unlike the pure monopolist, must take account of the quantity that the competitive sector of the industry will offer at any price he may set. However inadequate classical theory might be in explaining the rigidity of monopoly prices, given the empirical evidence that monopoly prices are relatively inflexible, it probably follows that prices controlled by partial monopolists assume similar rigidities.

Secondly, the greatest number of firms in any industry classified among those having a price leader was four; the average number of firms in such industries was three. On the other hand, one industry not classified among those having a price leader contained as many as twelve firms and another contained eleven; the average number of firms in industries classified as having no price leader was over six. However, since many of the excluded industries such as the rayon, newsprint, copper, gasoline, plate glass, window glass and plow industries possess barometric price leaders and a larger number of firms than those having a partial monopolist, Professor Stigler's findings could also be interpreted as evidence that (1) prices are more flexible under barometric than dominant firm price leadership and (2) price flexibility increases as the number of firms is increased. Professor Stigler isolated and very adequately treated the latter relationship himself; the former will be discussed more fully below.

In the light of the formal theoretical construction employed to explain the rationale of dominant firm price leadership, a fairly strong argument can be made against even including markets where prices are set by a dominant firm among those containing a "price leader." Formal solutions which yield an equilibrium price in such markets preclude all possibilities of the failure of small firms to follow the dominant firms' price change, and, hence, from the viewpoint of the dominant firm, increase the probability of their following to absolute certainty. That is to say, whether the dominant firm attempts to maximize profits in the short run by equating its own marginal cost and derived marginal revenue schedules or pursues some other price policy, so long as it produces at a rate of output which clears the market at its own price, the remaining firms in the industry have no choice but to equate their marginal costs with the price it sets. Essentially, therefore, the pure dominant firm market presents a problem of monopoly price control rather than one of price leadership.

For purposes of public policy, to draw such a distinction between monopoly pricing and price leadership involves more than a mere question of definition. Price "leadership" in a dominant firm market is not simply a *modus operandi* designed to circumvent price competition among rival sellers but is instead an inevitable consequence of the industry's structure. Hence, the only obviously effective remedy for such monopoly pricing is to destroy the monopoly power from which it springs, *i.e.,* dissolve, if economically and politically feasible, the dominant firm. Public policy should hardly be directed toward this end, however, before the foundations of the dominant firm's existence have been thoroughly examined. Nearly every major industry in the American economy has, in its initial stages of development, been dominated by a single firm—the Slater Mill in cotton textiles, the Firestone Company in rubber tires, Birdseye in frozen foods, the American Viscose Corporation in rayon yarn, etc., to mention only a few. The monopoly power of the initial dominant firm in most industries, however, was gradually reduced by industrial growth and the entrance of new firms. It is not at all certain that public policy measures could have either hastened or improved upon the process. Where forces of competition do not eliminate such power, however (Professor Stigler has suggested the aluminum and Scotch tape industries to me as possible examples), it is highly improbable that a mere declaration of the illegality of price leadership by the courts offers itself as a sufficient or even a possible remedial measure. The dominant firm would simply be confronted with the dilemma of ① changing prices frequently and reminding the public with each price change that it sets the price for the industry or ② simply varying its output and risk the attendant onus of price fixing. Hence, should all dominant firms accept the implications of the recent *Tobacco* decision at their face value, there would be no reason to conclude *a priori* whether prices in markets dominated by a particular firm would henceforth be more or less flexible, or would more closely approximate prices which one would expect under more competitive conditions.

BAROMETRIC FIRM PRICE LEADERSHIP

Unlike price leadership of the dominant firm type, there is no explanatory hypothesis which identifies the barometric price leader. In contrast to the dominant firm, the barometric firm "commands adherence of rivals to his price only because, and to the extent that, his price reflects market conditions with tolerable promptness." [6] Hence, the reasons why a particular firm is the barometric firm must be found in the historical background of an industry and the institutional and other features which have shaped its development.

Patently, it is not possible in every case to judge when barometric price leadership is monopolistic and when it is competitive in character without making a thorough investigation, but there are certain visible market features associated with competitive price leadership. For example, unless a particular firm has demonstrated unusual adeptness at adjusting prices to market forces, in the absence of conspiracy one would certainly expect occasional changes in the identity of the price leader. Moreover, unless the lines of price communication are extremely efficient, prices are not likely to be uniform among sellers in a specific market area for a short period immediately following the date the price leader announces a new price. A "wait and see" policy on the part of several sellers not only gives rise to occasional price differentials, but also suggests the absence of even tacit collusion. Furthermore, if new

[6] *Ibid.*, p. 446.

prices are communicated among buyers more rapidly than among sellers, there would be frequent changes in the ratios of sales (and, depending upon inventory policies, of production) of particular firms to the total volume of sales (or production) for the industry as a whole. In the rayon and textile industries, where each large fabricator buys yarn and cloth from several sellers simultaneously, this is usually the case. Buyers iron out price differentials among sellers by refusing to buy at old prices if the price leader has announced a price reduction and buy heavily at old prices if the price leader has announced a price increase.

Barometric price leadership which follows the above lines probably does not greatly circumvent the public interest nor is it likely that the *Tobacco* decision has brought this type of price leadership within the reach of the antitrust laws. The barometric firm possesses no power to coerce the rest of the industry into accepting its price and, in most such industries, it simply passes along information to the "Big Three" or the "Big Four" on what the rest of the industry is doing in a declining market, and proceeds with initiating price increases in a market revival only so rapidly as supply and demand conditions dictate.

For purposes of prescribing appropriate remedial action it is important also to differentiate between actual collusive price leadership and "apparent" collusive price leadership which stems more from overt selling arrangements than from simply following price changes announced by a rival firm. In the steel, cement, glass container, and fertilizer industries, what has appeared at times to be barometric price leadership was in fact a natural consequence of basing point and zone pricing systems. Under a single basing point system, if recognized and adhered to by all producers, giving the appearance of following a price leader is inevitable since the pricing policies of all sellers are unalterably geared to the base mill. The same is true of a multiple basing point system if all base mills are owned by a single seller. Identical prices among producers in an industry operating under a multiple basing point system where the base mills are owned by different producers is not clearly a necessary consequence of the basing point system, but one should, on economic grounds, expect all prices at least to move in the same direction. A decrease in the base price in one area allows all producers abiding by this base price to further invade adjacent areas until mills in adjacent areas meet the price reduction; an increase in the base price in one area increases the demand for the commodity from mills in adjacent areas, thereby encouraging corresponding price increases. Hence, a sufficient explanation for similar price movements among producers abiding by a basing point system is the presence of the basing point system itself. The best evidence that this is so is the undisciplined pricing which occurs when the basing point system temporarily breaks down.[7]

For the most part, therefore, the barometric price leader, as defined by Professor Stigler and as visualized for purposes of this paper, appears to do little more than set prices that would eventually be set by forces of competition. In such industries as the copper and rayon industries, *i.e.,* oligopolies within monopolistically competitive markets, these prices are largely dependent upon the prices of closely competing products. In more clearly delineated oligopolistic industries, particularly where the number of firms is fairly large, price leadership of the barometric type has seldom if ever been a sufficiently strong instrument alone to insure price discipline among rivals. Price leadership in the steel and fertilizer industries has been a subordinate feature of a basing point system. The glass container industry implemented price leadership by inaugurating a zone pricing and market sharing system. In spite of this, many firms were not faithful price followers.[8] . . .

From the standpoint of public policy the real problem in such markets as those discussed above, therefore, centers upon economic forces which support price leadership rather than upon price leadership *per se*. In industries dominated by a strong partial monopolist, parallel pricing among firms stems from the monopoly power possessed by the partial monopolist and not from the tacit adoption of a price leader to circumvent price competition. The competitive sector of the industry often has no choice but to accept

[7] *Cf*. Temporary National Economic Committee, Monograph No. 42, p. 3.

[8] *Cf*. Robert L. Bishop, "The Glass Container Industry," in *The Structure of American Industry,* edited by Walter Adams (New York, 1950), pp. 407–8.

the partial monopolist's price. In oligopolies which form segments of larger monopolistically competitive industries, such as those which conform to the pattern of the rayon and copper industries, the barometric firm "leads" price changes only in the limited sense that its price movements are presumed by its rivals to have resulted from a synthesis of all the available market information. Price decreases initiated by firms selling closely competing products and by smaller firms within its own segment of the industry usually prompt downward list-price revisions by the barometric firm. List-price increases occur only after the market forces have been reversed. In most markets of an intermediate character the evidence indicates that price leadership has been decidedly a subordinate feature of a pricing policy built upon the much stronger foundations of trade association activity, zone pricing, basing point agreements, etc.[9]

A comprehensive study embracing the tacit and overt pricing arrangements among sellers in a wide variety of industries more or less oligopolistic in character would undoubtedly point up to more meaningful conclusions than those suggested by the above evidence. Nevertheless, there is some basis for believing that the mere adoption of a price leader is not nearly such an effective means for eliminating price competition among the few as many economists are prone to believe. Except for the type of price leadership discussed below, the evidence suggests that the power of the price leader to preserve price discipline derives less from his ostensible status as the barometric firm than from the more overt arrangements which support it. Where such supporting arrangements are not found, the barometric firm seems to do little more than respond to forces of competition. If this is so, the *Tobacco* decision may have far less importance than has been attributed to it, but at the same time the search for remedial action in similar future cases may not be nearly so fruitless as is generally believed.

---

[9] An examination of recent industry studies [including those reproduced in part in *The Structure of American Industry, op. cit.,* and in Walter Adams and Leland E. Traywick, *Readings in Economics* (New York, 1948)] reveals little evidence that price leadership, when not buttressed by stronger means of preserving price discipline, prevented price competition among oligopolists in times of market crisis.

The elimination of supports to effective price leadership, most of which are not particularly elusive targets, might very well eliminate the effectiveness of price leadership itself.

PRICE LEADERSHIP IN LIEU OF AN OVERT AGREEMENT

In industries which possess certain specific features, however, one would expect *a priori* a type of price leadership of a much different nature and considerably more inimical to the public interest than that of the barometric type discussed above. In such industries price leadership may conceivably be so effective as to serve all the ends of a strong trade association or of a closely knit domestic cartel and, hence, in a political environment where overt collusion is illegal, may be the only feasible means of assuring parallel action among sellers. In view of the foregoing discussion, the most important market features prerequisite to effective price leadership of this type would seem to be as follows:

1. Firms must be few in number and each firm must be sufficiently large to be compelled to reckon with the indirect as well as the direct effects of its own price policy. If there are several very small firms in the industry but no dominant firm, they, through ignoring their indirect influence on price, are likely to engage in promiscuous price cutting whenever market crises occur and, hence, at least for downward price adjustments, usurp the role of price leader. Moreover, such firms are not likely to follow the lead in upward price revisions unless they are completely satisfied with their expected volume of sales at the new price.

2. Entry to the industry must be severely restricted if the price set by the price leader is to remain close to a rationalized oligopolistic price for any significant length of time. If the long-run cost curve for the new entrant is substantially the same as those which confront entrenched firms, price rationalization can be only temporary since the rationalized price will attract new entrants which, in turn, will bid the price down.[10] If, however, the time lag

---

[10] For an imperfect example, see discussion of cigarette industry, *infra*.

between investment decisions and actual investment in the industry is significant, price rationalization for the duration of the lag may suggest itself as a profitable possibility.

3. The "commodity" produced by the several firms need not be perfectly homogeneous but each producer must view the output of all other firms as extremely close substitutes for his own. If this condition is not fulfilled, each producer is likely to view his product as distinctive in character and the "market" will not be characterized by a single price policy but by several. Examples of such individual pricing policies may be found in the automobile and brand-name men's clothing markets. Where the output of each firm is differentiated to the extent that it is only a moderately good substitute for the output of other firms, price leadership, of course, is meaningless.

4. The elasticity of the market demand schedule for the output of the industry as described in (3) above must not greatly exceed unity. If demand for the output of the industry is elastic because the oligopoly is only a segment of a larger monopolistically competitive market, the prices of closely competing products severely limit or possibly even eliminate the gains to be derived from adopting a price leader. Moreover, if demand for the output of the oligopoly is highly elastic, firms are not likely to adhere to the price leader's price if to do so would result in substantially less than capacity operations, since each firm could still stimulate its own sales considerably by lowering its price, even though all other firms met the new price. The price history of the domestic rayon industry and the postwar price history of the copper industry furnish particularly good evidence of the validity of this point. Whenever declining silk and cotton prices have commenced to reduce the volume of rayon sales at existing list prices, rayon producers, if the price leader has not already reduced his price, have sold at less than list price in order to move accumulating inventories and to maintain operations at near-capacity output. Similarly, copper producers appear to follow the price leader only if they believe his new price is in line with prevailing scrap, aluminum, and tin prices.

5. Individual-firm cost curves must be sufficiently similar so that some particular price allows all firms to operate at a satisfactory rate of output. If, for example, the industry is composed

of several high-cost low-capacity firms and several low-cost high-capacity firms, the resulting conflict in price and output policies cannot be resolved by adopting a price leader so long as all firms remain in the industry.[11] Low-cost firms will not accept the price leadership of high-cost firms since there is a better option in the form of a lower price and a higher rate of output open to them. They can therefore force the high-cost sector of the industry to adopt the lower price but, if the differences in costs between high-cost and low-cost firms are significant, high-cost firms will not recover full costs and will gradually be eliminated from the industry. Hence, the conflict will have been resolved and the condition that all producers be confronted with reasonably similar cost curves will then be fulfilled.

It might be argued that the foregoing conditions are fully as necessary for any form of effective parallel action, such as price maintenance agreements, strong trade associations, or even unimplemented oligopolistic rationalization, as they are for effective price leadership. Such an argument, of course, would be entirely valid for, it will be recalled, the type of price leadership being examined is but one of a number of possible forms of conscious parallelism, all of which presumably stem from a common source, namely, the identity between the long-run interests of each individual firm and those of the industry as a whole.

Moreover, conditions other than those discussed above bear significantly upon the likelihood of effective price leadership ever arising and maintaining price discipline in an industry. Among those that first come to mind are the extent of tariff protection, the rate of technological change, the stability of demand, and the aggressiveness of management. An examination of the available price histories of industries in which the number of sellers is not large indicates, however, that price leadership is most likely to serve the ends of a collusive agreement when the above five conditions are fulfilled. Or, stated another way, effective price discipline seems to have been rarely achieved by the tacit means of price

---

[11] For the theoretical analysis relevant to an industry containing several firms but only one low-cost high-capacity firm, see Boulding, *supra,* fn. 4.

leadership alone when one or several of these conditions did not exist.

THE TOBACCO DECISION REAPPRAISED

Had the Department of Justice diligently searched the American economy for an industry which most nearly contained all the conditions prerequisite to effective price leadership, it could hardly have found a better example than the cigarette industry. The entrenched position of the "Big Three brand-names had made entry to the cigarette industry exceedingly difficult. Moreover, parallel action in the leaf tobacco market had insured fairly comparable if not equal cost conditions among the three large cigarette producers; and, although each of them viewed the output of the other two as such perfect substitutes for his own that none would risk a retail price differential, demand for their output collectively, at least in the short run, was inelastic. Furthermore, in 1929 the Big Three controlled over 90 per cent of the domestic cigarette market and, with Lorillard, they controlled 98 per cent. Hence, for all practical purposes, the number of cigarette producers was very small. Also, the large cigarette producers had had ample opportunity as well as compelling reasons for working out a *modus operandi* which would identify their individual interests with those of the Big Three collectively. In substance, counsel for Liggett and Myers probably described the attitude of all the large producers of cigarettes when he stated, ". . . in making price decisions the management of Liggett and Myers has acted in response to a long experience of non-identical prices as well as identical prices." [12]

In spite of such ideal conditions for securing parallel action by adopting a price leader, however, the Big Three soon discovered that even their market was subject to economic forces that put an upper limit on exploitation. The *long-run* demand for their collective output was elastic, hence complete exploitation of the ciga-

---

[12] *American Tobacco Company* v. *United States,* 147 F. 2d 93 (6th Cir., 1944), Liggett and Myers' Brief, p. 264; *ibid.,* Reynolds' Brief, p. 390; and American Tobacco's Brief, pp. 94–95.

rette market was limited to a short-time period. With low tobacco prices and high cigarette prices in the latter half of 1931 and 1932, competitive forces began to assert their influence. Whereas the 10-cent brands had been virtually unknown (accounting for only 1.5 per cent of all cigarettes sold) in the first half of 1931, output of small independents began to increase rapidly after the price increase led by Reynolds in June, 1931. By December, 1932, they accounted for 22 per cent of total cigarette sales. In the meantime, the sales of Reynolds, American, Liggett and Myers and Lorillard had been drastically reduced. By February, 1933, their vulnerability to competition had become sufficiently evident to the Big Three to induce reductions in popular brand cigarette prices to the lowest level since 1918. Hence, simple price leadership, even under such ideal conditions as those afforded by the cigarette industry, had failed to preserve the rationalized oligopoly (or monopoly) market solution.

In the light of their alleged strategy after 1933, perhaps no one was more aware than the Big Three themselves of the long-run ineffectiveness of price leadership when not implemented by other safeguards from competition. Although price leadership continued to play an important role in cigarette pricing, its effectiveness after 1933 was largely dependent upon the successful effort of the Big Three to manipulate the leaf tobacco market.

If unimplemented price leadership proved to be an exploitative weapon of limited effectiveness in the cigarette industry, and its usefulness confined to a time period scarcely exceeding several years, it is highly improbable that tacit parallel pricing in oligopolistic markets offers itself *per se* as either a fruitful or fertile field for antitrust investigation. Hence the *Tobacco* decision, particularly when viewed against a background in which appropriate remedial action is conspicuously absent, is not likely to have far-reaching consequences. The appropriate question before economists, the business community, and the courts alike, therefore, is not how far tacit parallel pricing in oligopolistic markets can proceed before it becomes illegal, but rather what implementing devices and market conditions make price leadership both possible and effective. In most oligopolistic industries where the record of pricing techniques is fairly complete, there are good reasons for suspecting that price leadership is essentially a shadow of more insidious pricing devices and trade restraints. When the devices which buttress price leadership have been destroyed, price leadership as an exploitative practice may well have been emasculated.

In view of the extraordinary conditions prerequisite to the more effective type of price leadership, it is not likely that the *Tobacco* decision, as a legal precedent, can or will measurably influence the behavior of prices in markets where sellers are few in numbers; nor will it greatly broaden the scope of the antitrust laws. Along these lines, the recent basing point and similar future decisions would appear to be a much more profitable line of approach to monopoly problems posed by industries comprising relatively few sellers.

8 OLIGOPOLY TREATMENT:

A Guide to the Perplexed

As is evident in the preceding selections, the legal treatment of oligopoly defies a simple statement. The legal emphasis in oligopolistic situations has vacillated between the structural and the behavioral issues. The Court's hesitancy in choosing and maintaining a position has been exceeded only by the failure of economists to identify unambiguously the attributes of oligopolistic markets. In law, as in economics, monopoly has been attacked in its single-seller form and also in those instances in which companies expressly agreed to act as one. Yet in industries composed of few firms that operated without explicit agreements, the courts faced an ambiguous situation with, conceptually, competition as the only alternative to monopoly. Consequently many mergers of large companies were condoned upon a showing that several large companies survived in the industry. Thus an anomolous situation developed whereby the antitrust laws may permit the development of oligopoly through "structural change—a unification of firms by merger or holding company control—where it would not tolerate restrictive agreements between the same firms, although the market control involved in the latter arrangement is far less comprehensive and enduring . . ." One perennial antitrust conundrum, therefore, is the extent to which antitrust traditions have encouraged the development of oligopoly by their ambivalent merger-collusion attitude.

Few economists seriously suggest exemption of oligopolies from antitrust coverage on grounds that unfettered oligopolistic situations are desired to realize the benefits of scale economies. Neither have jurists or legislators suggested a revision of the traditional monopoly or behavioral aspects of antitrust law in order to provide a firm and rational treatment of oligopoly. Conceptually it would be possible to treat oligopolistic situations through extensive government control of businesses or the regulation of their price-quantity decisions. Of course, this would extend the regulation that is now generally limited to the public utilities and transportation industries. However, such government control has traditionally been antithetical to the basic values held by our society. Generally, Americans have favored markets free of either government or private controls.

In the following selection Louis B. Schwartz, a professor of law, grapples with the need to develop a law for the treatment of oligopoly that can be clearly stated and equitably administered and that is consistent with legal traditions and economic analysis. Schwartz asserts that all too frequently oligopoly cases are decided on the basis of legal fictions designed to provide equitable rather than legal consistency. Following his examination of our legal experience with oligopolies, Schwartz offers specific proposals for a legislative supplement to the Sherman Act. These proposals represent criteria for a possible triggering of efforts to reorganize a firm; and, Schwartz argues, they have a foundation in economic analysis and offer a consistency with legal tradition. It is problematical whether these suggestions are more acceptable now than, for the sake of argument, they might have been or will be in 1890, 1911, 1927, 1945, or "1984."

....

New Approaches to the Control of Oligopoly

Louis B. Schwartz

....

Every undertaking to prohibit, regulate, or control monopoly and restraint of trade must approach the subject from two points of view: structure and practices. From the point of view of structure, legislation must seek to prevent concentration of private control of markets into too few hands—that is, to prevent mergers and other relatively rigid unifications of interest and management, and to break up existing excessive concentrations. From the point of view of practices, the aim must be to prevent certain types of concerted action by agreement or understanding among independent firms whose size alone presumably does not offend the rules as to industry structure.

It is remarkable that this two-level operation of the antitrust laws may permit a structural change—a unification of firms by merger or holding company control—where it would not tolerate restrictive agreements between the same firms, although the market control involved in the latter arrangement is far less comprehensive and enduring and presumably, therefore, less dangerous. The explanation for this paradox is said to be that unifications often have technological justifications, especially economies of scale, which we do not wish to limit by law. A startling consequence of this paradox of antitrust regulation is that the enactment of a law preventing temporary combinations is likely to lead to a wave of mergers and permanent consolidations to replace the newly forbidden restrictive agreements. The process of consolidation will go on to the limit of the law. Where this limit is high, as it has been

Abridged from Louis B. Schwartz, "New Approaches to the Control of Oligopoly," *The University of Pennsylvania Law Review,* 109 (November 1960), 31–53.

in the United States, major industries will typically come to be dominated by two, three, or four firms—that is, by an oligopoly. Economists tell us that oligopolies function like monopolies, or as if there were agreements among the leading firms even though no such agreements exist. Through price leadership, mutual deference, fear, or simple recognition of what is in their common interest, they will maintain prices above competitive levels, refuse to supply new distributors, and postpone introduction of new and cheaper techniques involving the rapid obsolescence of old investment.

Faced with this situation, a government having an antitrust policy must make up its mind whether: (1) to revise the structural part of its antitrust law so that it does not tolerate "oligopoly"; (2) to revise the practices part of its antitrust law so that coordinated action which would be illegal when done by agreement becomes illegal without proof of agreement; (3) to do nothing about the situation, on the theory that concentration to the level of oligopoly is necessary to achieve economies of scale and thus serves the public interest notwithstanding the impairment of competition; or (4) to establish public control of price and other economic decisions of "oligopolists" to prevent abuse of the monopolistic power which it is said they inherently possess.

When is an industry properly characterized as oligopolistic or dangerously oligopolistic? As might be expected, no firm and clear answer can be given. The variables in the economic formula are too numerous and each of the variables is difficult to measure. In the first place, there are the difficulties of defining an "industry" and securing the relevant statistics.[1] The more firms and products we lump together in a single industry, the smaller will seem the share of any one firm or group of firms. Are steel, aluminum, and

---

[1] As to the various bases on which concentration may be calculated, *compare* FTC, REPORT ON THE CONCENTRATION OF PRODUCTIVE FACILITIES (1947) (percentage of industry's net capital assets), *with* KAYSEN & TURNER, ANTITRUST POLICY: AN ECONOMIC AND LEGAL ANALYSIS (1959) (percentage of total market sales). . . . See also the three articles in NATIONAL BUREAU OF ECONOMIC RESEARCH, BUSINESS CONCENTRATION AND PRICE POLICY (1955): Miller, *Measures of Monopoly Power and Concentration: Their Economic Significance* at 119; Rosenbluth, *Measures of Concentration* at 57; and Scitovsky, *Economic Theory and the Measurement of Concentration* at 101.

copper separate industries? Or are they, because of a degree of interchangeability, to be considered a single field of "basic metals"? Or should we draw the industry boundaries with reference to particular forms of fabrication, so that we differentiate an iron industry from a steel industry, and treat "wire and cable" as one industry embracing products made of steel, aluminum, or copper? [2]

When we have determined what products and firms to consider as single industries, we must also calculate the geographic boundaries of their "markets," because firms making even identical products in different territories, isolated from each other, do not act as competitive checks upon each other. The important word here is *"isolated"*: market regions may be isolated or partially isolated by geographic remoteness entailing prohibitive freights, or by political barriers such as tariffs, quotas, or exchange controls. Markets may also be effectively segregated by private cartels or unspoken understandings under which potentially competitive international firms do not challenge each other's dominance in particular export markets. In some instances markets can be made to appear larger than their natural boundaries, as where trade association adherence to a system of basing point prices keeps delivered prices high enough to enable firms to do business in localities remote from their plants.[3] Such difficulties and uncertainties severely restrict the utility of "oligopoly" as a regulatory concept.[4]

The best effort to date to translate the nebulous concept of oligopoly into specific guides for administrative action is the 1959 book by Professors Kaysen and Turner, *Antitrust Policy: An Economic and Legal Analysis.* . . .

It should be emphasized that the <u>Kaysen-Turner criterion of undue concentration—that the eight largest sellers have more than</u>

[2] On the problems of industry and business classification, see Conklin & Goldstein, *Census Principles of Industry and Product Classification, Manufacturing Industries,* in NATIONAL BUREAU OF ECONOMIC RESEARCH, *op. cit. supra* note 1, at 15, and the comments which follow by Fabricant at 36, Kottke at 40, and Suits at 48.

[3] See FTC v. Cement Institute, 333 U.S. 683 (1948); FTC v. A. E. Staley Mfg. Co., 324 U.S. 746 (1945).

[4] *Cf.* NATIONAL BUREAU OF ECONOMIC RESEARCH, *op. cit., supra* note 1, at 57–140, where leading economists, especially Fellner at 113, Kaysen at 116–18, and Miller at 119, express pervasive skepticism regarding the significance of various indices of concentration.

one third of the business—rests upon their judgment that "in a majority of the markets with which we are familiar" the large sellers are "likely" to recognize the interaction of their own behavior "to a significant degree." Inasmuch as the empirical basis for this judgment is not set forth, its reliability even for the United States is subject to challenge. Obviously, the judgment does not have even prima facie validity in other countries where entirely different relationships between market structure and firm behavior might be observed. But the Kaysen-Turner criterion is put forward not to condemn all concentrations above this level, but merely to identify areas in the economy where official inquiry appears to be justified. For this limited purpose, tests which are easy to apply may be satisfactory, even though the determination of the critical point on the spectrum of concentration depends largely on the subjective reactions of experienced persons. An example of such a crude index may be found in the third table appended to this Article; the table is based on the Federal Trade Commission's 1947 report on the concentration of productive facilities.[5] The FTC considers as "extreme" concentration any situation in which the three largest companies control more than sixty per cent of the "net capital assets" in the industry.[6]

With this brief summary of the state of American economic thought on oligopoly, let us turn to a review of the law relating to oligopoly. It is notable, in the first place, that neither American nor typical European legislation speaks in terms of "oligopoly." This is entirely understandable in view of the lack of specific content which can be given to the term. Nor do American statutes use words like "concentration" or "dominant firm," such as are found in European law. One might even conclude from certain statements and decisions of our Supreme Court that there is a positive determination to refrain from giving legal effect to the state of concentration in an industry. "Mere size . . . is not an offense against the Sherman Act unless magnified to the point at which it amounts to a monopoly . . . ,"[7] declared Mr. Justice Cardozo in 1932. And earlier, the Supreme Court had declined to order dissolution

---

[5] FTC, *op. cit., supra* note 1, at 21.

[6] FTC, *op cit., supra* note 1, at 17.

[7] United States v. Swift & Co., 286 U.S. 106, 116 (1932).

of the United States Steel Corporation although the company was the result of an illegal consolidation of numerous, huge, fully integrated steel plants into a single organization with fifty per cent of the national steel capacity.[8] In *United States v. National Lead Co.,*[9] the Court rejected a dissolution proposal with the comment that there had been "no showing that four major competing units would be preferable to two. . . ."[10] And Judge Learned Hand's famous opinion in *United States v. Aluminum Co. of America*[11] declared that even one hundred per cent control would not necessarily violate the Sherman Act, if, for example, the defendant achieved this position without purposeful action designed to exclude others. Assuming such baneful purpose, it would still be necessary to find virtually complete and unified control of the relevant business in order to convict the defendant as a monopolist; ninety per cent of the market would be enough, but "it is doubtful whether sixty or sixty-four percent would be enough; and certainly thirty-three percent is not."[12] It would be difficult to imagine a greater contradiction than we find between this judicial declaration that the law permits one firm to control a third of the business in aluminum and the Kaysen-Turner hypothesis that a business is prima facie overconcentrated if eight firms together control a third of the business.

The divergence, however, is not as great as appears on its face. The doctrine that "size alone is not an offense" is a misleading statement of the actual position of American law, which, after all, does give significant effect to dominance and concentration. The original pronouncement of the innocence of large size was itself coupled with the qualification that "size carries with it an opportunity for abuse that is not to be ignored. . . ."[13] This opens the door to something like the Kaysen-Turner proposal that special scrutiny be given to situations involving large firms—that is, to industries evidencing an unusual degree of concentration. A strik-

---

[8] See United States v. United Steel Corp., 251 U.S. 417 (1920).

[9] 332 U.S. 319 (1947).

[10] *Id*. at 352.

[11] 148 F.2d 416 (2d Cir. 1945).

[12] *Id*. at 424.

[13] United States v. Swift & Co., 286 U.S. 106, 116 (1932); *cf*. United States v. Griffith, 334 U.S. 100, 107 n.10 (1948).

ing application of this principle is provided by the *Alcoa* case, where Judge Hand—having first performed some remarkable manipulations in market analysis to bring the company within range of his "monopoly" standard [14]—went on to scrutinize the company's behavior so rigorously as to make even its active, expansionist policy a dereliction.

A classic reason for opposing monopoly is that it tends to restrict supply, yet here, paradoxically, foresighted expansion of capacity is the element of behavior seized upon to put the company in violation of the law. Similarly, it is often said that the General Motors Corporation must "voluntarily" refrain from cutting prices lest it force some of its competitors out of business. Such propositions, so evidently at variance with the rationale of free competition, can be understood only as circumlocutions for an unspoken but nevertheless active concern about industry structure and concentration. We are formally committed to a law which forbids only monopolization or evil practices; and bound as we are by this formal commitment, a way—a fiction if necessary—must be found to attribute evil to giant organizations which manage to avoid our ordinary list of proscribed commercial restraints.

This attributive process may be seen operating in *United States v. E. I. du Pont de Nemours & Co.,*[15] where an alleged preemption by Du Pont of General Motors' purchases of automotive finishes and fabrics was made the basis for interdicting Du Pont stock control of General Motors. It is easy to criticize the market analysis expounded by Mr. Justice Brennan writing for the majority in that case. The dissenting Justices persuasively demonstrate that Du Pont did not actually exert control over GM purchases and that, in any event, the Clayton Act was not intended to apply retroactively to a purchase of stock twenty years before, when the transaction was lawful. But back of the majority view was the

---

[14] Although Alcoa had been the sole domestic producer of virgin aluminum, its sales of that product were in competition with "secondary" aluminum, *i.e.,* that recovered by the scrap industry. To arrive at a figure of 90% control for Alcoa, Judge Hand treated this secondary aluminum as a part of the supply controlled by the company, even though the company had sold the original material from five to twenty-five years earlier. See 148 F.2d at 422–25.

[15] 353 U.S. 586 (1957).

good

commonsense recognition that an antitrust law which cannot pre-vent integration of two such financial and industrial colossi as General Motors and Du Pont would be a farce with which no Con-gress ever intended to entertain the American people.

The doctrine of "internal conspiracy" must also be viewed as an indirect attack on the giant firm. Under this doctrine separately incorporated units of an enterprise which is economically and func-tionally a single firm may be guilty of an illegal "conspiracy" when they concert their price and other policies.[16] I have not seen this doctrine applied to any but very large organizations.

As might be expected, a legal policy against concentration which can be given effect only indirectly and through fictions is likely to operate erratically. In some sectors of American antitrust law the judges have evolved rules dealing more explicitly with dominance and oligopoly. Thus, in interpreting section 3 of the Clayton Act which forbids exclusive dealing arrangements "where the effect may be to substantially lessen competition," the defendant's lead-ing position in its market and the adherence of major competitors to parallel policies have become crucial factors. In *Standard Oil Co. v. United States*,[17] the defendant's exclusive dealing contracts were held illegal where it appeared that defendant was the largest seller in its region—controlling twenty-three per cent of the sales —and that all other "major suppliers" followed similar practices, thus "collectively, even though not collusively, preventing a late arrival from wresting away more than an insignificant portion of the market." [18]

---

[16] Kiefer-Stewart Co. v. Joseph E. Seagram & Sons, Inc., 340 U.S. 211 (1951); *cf.* Distillers Corp.-Seagrams, Ltd., 50 F.T.C. 738 (1954) (sub-sidiaries and parent ordered not to collaborate in pricing). *But cf.* United States v. Arkansas Fuel Oil Corp., TRADE REG. REP. (1960 Trade Cas.) ¶ 69619, at 76496 (D.C. Okla. 1960), where discussion of a price increase with an officer of one's parent corporation was held to be "mere approval by a parent corporation . . . [which] does not constitute a *per se* violation of the Sherman Act." See the discussion of this case in text . . . *infra.* See also Schwartz, *Relations with Affiliated Customers*, in N.Y. STATE BAR ASS'N SECTION ON ANTITRUST LAW, ANTITRUST LAW SYMPOSIUM 214 (1952); Note, *Intra-Enterprise Conspiracy under the Sherman Act*, 63 YALE L.J. 372 (1954).

[17] 337 U.S. 293 (1949).

[18] *Id.* at 309. See Dictograph Prods., Inc. v. FTC, 217 F.2d 821, 827 (2d

In recent years American merger law has given evidence of special sensitivity to the acquisition of lesser companies by leading firms, even when the resulting combinations do not approach the minimum level of concentration which Judge Hand deemed necessary to constitute a monopoly.[19] But, in contrast to the exclusive dealing cases, there seems to be no tendency to make market dominance or leadership a sufficient circumstance, standing alone, to establish a violation or prima facie violation of the merger provisions of section 7 of the Clayton Act.[20] The size of firms involved and the structure of the industry are merely circumstances to be considered with many others in determining whether the merger will probably impair competition "substantially."

Although oligopolistic structure appears to be significant in varying degrees with respect to exclusive dealing and mergers, it receives almost no recognition in our laws dealing with price discrimination—and this despite the fact that the relevant language

---

Cir. 1954), where it was said in interpretation of the *Standard Oil* case: "Where the alleged violator dominated or was a leader in the industry, proof of such fact was, at an early stage, determined to be sufficient predicate from which to conclude that the use of exclusive-dealing contracts was violative of Section 3 and other factors appear to have been largely ignored. . . . More recently, the Supreme Court extended the rule to business organizations enjoying a powerful, though clearly not dominant position. . . ." *Cf.* Schwartz, *Potential Impairment of Competition—The Impact of Standard Oil Co. of California v. United States on the Standard of Legality Under the Clayton Act*, 98 U. Pa. L. Rev. 10 (1949).

[19] See, *e.g.,* American Crystal Sugar Co. v. Cuban-American Sugar Co., 259 F.2d 524 (2d Cir. 1958) (combination would be fourth largest in country, supplying 13% of sugar in its region); United States v. Brown Shoe Co., 179 F. Supp. 721 (E.D. Mo. 1959), *prob. juris. noted*, 363 U.S. 825 (1960) (fourth largest shoe producer having 5% of total production combining with another firm having 0.5% of total production and 1.2% of total retail shoe sales, the latter attribute making it the largest family shoe chain retailer); United States v. Bethlehem Steel Corp., 168 F. Supp. 576 (S.D.N.Y. 1958) (combination of second and sixth largest steel firms); Hamilton Watch Co. v. Benrus Watch Co., 114 F. Supp. 307 (D. Conn.), *aff'd*, 206 F.2d 738 (2d Cir. 1953) (combination controlling 20% of nationally advertised jeweled watches).

[20] For a criticism of the FTC's failure—notwithstanding the parallel language of §§ 3 and 7—to conform merger law to exclusive dealing law in this respect, see STAFF OF SUBCOMM. NO. 5, HOUSE COMM. ON THE JUDICIARY, 84TH CONG., 1ST SESS., INTERIM REPORT ON CORPORATE AND BANK MERGERS 19–25 (Comm. Print 1955).

of section 2 of the Clayton Act, as amended by the Robinson-Patman Antidiscrimination Act, is parallel to that of sections 3 and 7. A dominant petroleum firm may justify discrimination among its customers on the ground that it is meeting a competitive offer.[21] . . .

Still another way in which American antitrust law has adapted itself to the phenomenon of oligopoly is by the doctrine of "conspiracy" based on "conscious parallel action." Firms which persistently follow parallel business policies will be treated as if they had agreed upon those policies, at least where there is some evidence that they consciously faced the policy issue as a common problem.[22] On the other hand, the inference of conspiracy from parallel action can be rebutted by showing that identical commercial conditions facing the separate firms compelled them to act identically.[23]

Closely related to the doctrine of conspiracy based on conscious parallel action is the proposal to make "price leadership" presumptive evidence of conspiracy between the price leader and his followers.[24] In *American Tobacco Co. v. United States,*[25] the three largest cigarette companies were convicted of jointly monopolizing

[21] Standard Oil Co. v. FTC, 340 U.S. 231 (1951). Perhaps the disapproval of "systematic" discrimination, allegedly to meet competition, operates with special force against oligopolies. See FTC v. Cement Institute, 333 U.S. 683 (1948); FTC v. A. E. Staley Mfg. Co., 324 U.S. 746 (1945); Moog Indus., Inc. v. FTC, 238 F.2d 43 (8th Cir. 1956), *aff'd per curiam,* 355 U.S. 411 (1958).

[22] Interstate Circuit, Inc. v. United States, 306 U.S. 208 (1939) (common terms of licensing second-run showings of films of dominant movie producers); Milgram v. Loew's, Inc., 192 F.2d 579 (3d Cir. 1951), *cert. denied,* 343 U.S. 206 (1952) (denying first-run showings to drive-in theaters). See Givens, *Parallel Business Conduct Under the Sherman Act,* 5 ANTITRUST BULL. 273 (1960); Note, *Conscious Parallelism—Fact or Fancy?,* 3 STAN. L. REV. 679 (1951).

[23] Pevely Dairy Co. v. United States, 178 F.2d 363 (8th Cir. 1949), *cert. denied,* 339 U.S. 942 (1950) (identical pricing by "competing" milk companies explicable by uniform federally regulated price paid to farmers for raw milk, uniform wages paid to workers represented by single union, standardized product, and production conditions regulated by health ordinances).

[24] HANDLER, A STUDY OF THE CONSTRUCTION AND ENFORCEMENT OF THE FEDERAL ANTITRUST LAWS 44 (TNEC Monograph No. 38, 1941).

[25] 328 U.S. 781 (1946).

the cigarette business by employing, in common, certain buying practices allegedly designed to prevent the manufacture of cheaper cigarettes and by slavishly imitating each other's price moves in the distribution of cigarettes. The companies' insistence that identity of price movement was compelled by competition rather than a manifestation of monopoly was rendered somewhat ridiculous when the president of the American Tobacco Company testified that not only was he compelled to reduce his price whenever his rivals announced a reduction, lest he lose sales, but also that he was compelled to increase prices when Reynolds raised theirs, since otherwise Reynolds' increased profits would enable them to spend more money on advertising and so again deprive him of sales.[26] Absurd as this seems, economists would probably support the proposition that oligopolists in this situation have no alternative but to arrive, with or without agreement, at a common price, and that it will be a high price in relation to cost. Indeed, a study of the sequel to the *Tobacco* case revealed that the companies followed essentially the same price policies after the case as they did before, and increased their combined share of the national market from sixty-eight per cent to seventy-six per cent.[27]

One trouble with inferring or presuming conspiracy from parallel action is that it seems to lead logically to remedial action directed against the presumed conspiracy. It assumes that if the parties are compelled to act "independently" they will behave differently. But we know that in a sufficiently concentrated oligopoly the distinction between independent and concerted action tends to evaporate.[28] The theoretical error in diagnosing the problem as one of conspiracy rather than of structure is accompanied by a practical problem of devising effective controls. One can hardly order the "leader" to stop setting and publicizing its own prices. It would be equally difficult and unfair to enjoin "followers" from charging as much as their big leader—and they obviously cannot charge more.

[26] *Id*. at 805.

[27] Nicholls, Price Policies in the Cigarette Industry 402 (1951).

[28] See Att'y Gen. Nat'l Comm. Antitrust Rep. 326 (1955): "When sellers are few, even in the absence of conspiracy, the market itself may not show many of the characteristics of effective competition, and in fact may not be effectively competitive in the economic sense."

A final illustration of the equivocal and ineffective response of American law to the problem of oligopoly and parallel pricing is provided by the so-called fair trade laws which authorize suppliers to set resale prices. These laws reinforce the tendency of concentrated industries to operate on the basis of parallel high pricing by the large firms. They do this by eliminating an important source of pressure for independent, competitive, downward price adjustments at the producer level—namely, pressure by retailers whose profit margin has been cut by the competition of other retailers. It has often been observed, for example, that gasoline "price wars" at the retail level precipitate competitive wholesale price reductions, which the supplier is compelled to make in order to enable his distributor to maintain his gallonage. "Fair trade" helps, therefore, to reduce the number of entrepreneurs whose decisions must be aligned in order to stabilize prices. In cigarettes, toothpaste, liquor, and consumer durables, the number of price makers is reduced by fair trade to fewer than a half-dozen giant producers. Inasmuch as these producers have already succeeded in partially insulating their products from competition with each other by heavy advertising expenditures designed to persuade the consumer that each trademark identifies a unique product, the insistence of the fair trade laws that products be in "free and open competition with products of the same general class" is rendered ineffective.[29]

In sum, the failure of American legislation to deal explicitly with the problem of oligopoly has not wholly prevented the judicial development of legal answers to oligopoly but has made that development inconsistent and unpredictable. Even legislation especially designed to slow up the process of economic concentration, like recent antimerger laws, has fallen short of its goal because of the failure of antitrust proponents to face up directly to the problem of oligopoly. These antimerger laws may actually aggravate the evils at which they were aimed, because only future mergers are affected. The great combines in steel, motors, and banking have their domi-

---

[29] *Cf.* Eastman Kodak Co. v. Home Util. Co., 138 F. Supp. 670, 677 (D. Md.), *aff'd in part, modified in part, remanded,* 234 F.2d 766 (4th Cir. 1956) (manufacturer's fair-traded product in free and open competition with others in its class despite substantially complete fair trade coverage of all similar products).

nance confirmed by antimerger acts which inhibit the amalgamation of smaller units but fail to provide for dissolution of the very amalgamations whose formation stimulated enactment of the laws. This has been the history of the Clayton Act and its amendments as well as of recent legislation[30] against holding company expansion in the fields of banking and savings and loan associations. Only in the field of public utility holding companies did the Roosevelt administration succeed in pushing through a divestiture program to confine each enterprise to "a single integrated public-utility system" or, with special approval, contiguous systems where the combined operation "is not so large . . . as to impair the advantages of localized management, efficient operation, or the effectiveness of regulation." [31]

Nothing could be further from American antitrust ideology than the idea of official intervention in pricing and other economic decisions of enterpreneurs where no malpractice or evil intent appears. Yet, just as we have arrived by indirection at a rough policy relating to oligopoly and parallel action (although our statutes do not speak in these terms), so we are beginning to impose upon powerful corporations affirmative obligations not unlike those expressly provided for in advanced European legislation. Thus, a giant integrated aluminum company may be required to maintain a margin between the price at which it sells sheet aluminum and the price at which it sells fabricated products sufficient to permit independent fabricators to survive.[32] The officials of a mammoth broadcasting network, which owns TV stations and at the same time provides network programs on a contract basis to hundreds of affiliated stations, have avowed that whenever the network proposes to buy an affiliated station it pays the first price asked by the

[30] Bank Holding Company Act, 70 Stat. 133 (1956), 12 U.S.C. §§ 1841–48 (1958), 26 U.S.C. §§ 1101–03 (1958); 73 Stat. 691 (1959), 12 U.S.C. § 1730 (a) (Supp. 1959) (saving and loan holding companies).

[31] Public Utility Holding Companies Act of 1935, § 11(b)(1), 49 Stat. 820, 15 U.S.C. § 79k (1958).

[32] United States v. Aluminum Co. of America, [148 F.2d 416, 447 (2d Cir., 1945)].

owner.[33] This appears to be a recognition that its economic position, based on the power to discontinue the vital affiliation, is so overwhelming that the network stands in jeopardy under the antitrust laws if it tries to bargain for a lower purchase price. The dominant position of the Eastman Kodak Company in production of color film led to an antitrust decree requiring it to desist from including a processing charge in the price of film so that film users would be free to patronize independent processors.[34] The right of large firms to select their customers—for example, to refrain from dealing with distributors who cut resale prices—has been under attack in Congress and has been whittled down in recent Supreme Court decisions.[35]

On the other hand, there are notable cases where American tribunals have failed to intervene effectively to control the exercise of oligopoly power. Thus, the General Electric Company was permitted to dictate the price at which retailers sold its electric lamps, as well as the price of electric lamps manufactured and sold by its giant competitor-licensee, Westinghouse,[36] although the Court might well have drawn a distinction between the right of small patentees to include price-fixing clauses in patent licenses and the right of industrial giants to dominate a market through contractual arrangements based on patents. The *General Electric* case has never been directly overruled, although its authority is much shaken by later decisions which do give effect to oligopoly considerations.[37]

[33] Brief for Appellants, pp. 23–24, Poller v. Columbia Broadcasting Sys., *appeal docketed,* No. 15379, D.C. Cir., Sept. 25, 1959 (quoting depositions). For an illustration of the allegedly coercive use of network broadcasting power, see United States v. Radio Corp. of America, 358 U.S. 334 (1959).

[34] United States v. Eastman Kodak Co., 1954 Trade Cas. ¶ 67920 (W.D.N.Y.).

[35] See United States v. Parke, Davis & Co., 362 U.S. 29 (1960); STAFF OF SENATE SELECT COMM. ON SMALL BUSINESS, 86TH CONG., 1ST SESS., THE RIGHT TO BUY (Comm. Print 1959). See also A. C. Becken Co. v. Gemex Corp., 272 F.2d 1 (7th Cir. 1959); United States v. United Shoe Mach. Corp., 110 F. Supp. 295 (D. Mass. 1953), *aff'd per curiam,* 347 U.S. 521 (1954).

[36] United States v. General Elec. Co., 272 U.S. 476 (1926); United States v. General Elec. Co., 82 F. Supp. 753, 817–27 (D.N.J. 1949).

[37] United States v. New Wrinkle, Inc., 342 U.S. 371 (1952); United States v. Line Material Co., 333 U.S. 287 (1948) (four Justices favored overruling

   The leading case of *Associated Press v. United States*[38] presented
in reality a problem in oligopoly control of national and international news, for such news was available from only three agencies of which AP was by far the most powerful. Yet, the matter
was disposed of on the narrow basis of a "conspiracy" among the
newspaper members of AP to "discriminate" against competitors
of existing members in passing on the competitors' applications to
join AP. Accordingly, although AP was convicted of violating the
Sherman Act, the Court's order went no further than to prohibit
the discrimination, leaving undisturbed AP's exclusive right to distribute news originating with its powerful membership and its exclusive arrangements with foreign news syndicates. It is not surprising that the number of American news syndicates was soon
reduced to two.[39]

   The uneasy and inadequate use of the antitrust laws to impose
affirmative controls on oligopoly has led to a variety of proposals
to change and supplement the law. Some seek to inaugurate a
program of deconcentration. Kaysen and Turner, for example, call
for a declaration that "an unreasonable degree of market power
as such [is] illegal." [40] They propose that, in passing upon the
legality of mergers, a twenty per cent share of a market be considered prima facie excessive concentration.[41] "Market power shall
be conclusively presumed where, for five years or more, one com-

---

General Electric); United States v. Masonite Corp., 316 U.S. 265 (1942);
Newburgh Moire Co. v. Superior Moire Co., 237 F.2d 283 (3d Cir. 1956)
(price alignment of three-fifths of industry invalidates licensing agreement).

   [38] 326 U.S. 1 (1945).

   [39] See 1958–1 TRADE REG. REP. ¶ 4207.105, reporting Department of
Justice approval of merger of United Press and International News Service,
the latter being in "failing circumstances." *Cf.* Times-Picayune Publishing
Co. v. United States, 345 U.S. 594 (1953), where it was held that a newspaper publisher with half the readership and 40% of the advertising in New
Orleans was not so "dominant" as to require it to desist from using the "unit
rule" in the sale of advertising. Under this rule an advertiser who wished
space in the publisher's morning paper had to buy space also in his afternoon paper. The competing afternoon paper soon expired. See *Death of the
Times-Star,* Time, Aug. 4, 1958, p. 47.

   [40] KAYSEN & TURNER, ANTITRUST POLICY: AN ECONOMIC AND LEGAL
ANALYSIS 111 (1959).

   [41] *Id.* at 99, 133; *cf.* Stigler, *Mergers and Preventive Antitrust Policy,* 104
U. PA. L. REV. 176, 182 (1955).

pany has accounted for 50 percent or more of annual sales in the market, or four or fewer companies have accounted for 80 percent of such sales." [42] Although endorsing divestiture and dissolution as remedies, they provide a number of defenses under which considerable concentration could be justified as reasonable—for example, where concentration is necessary to achieve economies of scale, or dissolution of a firm concentrated in a single plant is not physically practicable.

I have a mild preference for supplementing section 2 of the Sherman Act with a legislative program that differs somewhat from the Kaysen-Turner proposal. I would begin with a narrower class of enterprises. A firm would be subject to reorganization if: (1) it has assets in excess of one billion dollars; (2) it operates in a basic industry; and (3) it has twenty per cent of the national market or is one of the four leading firms which in the aggregate have fifty per cent of the market. The statute would specify the industries which the legislature deems basic—for instance, steel and automobiles.

There is nothing magical about the requirement of assets in excess of one billion dollars. I am less concerned with the precise figure than with indicating the principle of the legislation. The figure might be a half billion, either generally or in selected industries which Congress might designate on the basis of past antitrust experience. In determining a firm's assets, it would be necessary to have rules declaring what affiliations between separately incorporated firms should cause them to be treated as a single enterprise.

The firms thus singled out should be reorganized under a criterion stiffer than the Kaysen-Turner standard of "unreasonable market power." The test should be whether they are larger than can be justified by economies of scale in production and distribution, with the burden of proof placed on the firm; that is, if a firm falls within the standards I have formulated, it must prove that its size leads to lower costs of production or distribution, or it will be reorganized into smaller business units.

This proposal places no absolute limit on size of firm, but merely institutes inquiry where industrial giants operate in overly concen-

[42] KAYSEN & TURNER, *op. cit., supra* note 40, at 98.

trated basic industries. Firms of more than a billion dollars in assets would be left untouched if such size is shown to be economical. A superbillion firm, which is not dominant in a basic industry, is left free to expand in fields dominated by other giants, thus encouraging these powerful units to invade each other's markets.

The proposed billion-dollar figure is not an imputation of evil beginning at that level, but only a device to limit the initial administrative effort to a reasonable number of cases where economic power has most obviously gone very far. Experience with these firms should equip the regulatory agency to expand controls if that should prove desirable. Naming a figure like one billion dollars will also enable management and counsel to plan a firm's development with an eye to the law's requirements. Thus, as the critical size is approached, consideration may be given to voluntary divestiture of peripheral activities, by "spinning off" or other arrangements. Or expansion can be directed into areas where the firm will not be one of the dominant oligopolists.

The deconcentration program I envision would be carried out by an administrative agency, presumably the Federal Trade Commission, in civil proceedings. The criminal and treble-damage provisions of the Sherman and Clayton Acts are inappropriate to cases of this character involving no imputations of misbehavior or illicit monopolistic intent. Initially, at least, the program would be confined to the manufacturing and mining industries, in view of the special considerations applicable to regulated transportation businesses and public utilities. Insurance and banking, where some of the very largest firms are found,[43] present some unique problems as to both the efficacy of present regulation and the measurement of concentration, so that further inquiry may be needed before assigning responsibility for a deconcentration program in these fields.

To restrain the power of very large organizations that would remain in existence under any conceivable decentralization program, there is need for a statutory declaration that exclusive deal-

---

[43] *E.g.,* Metropolitan Life Ins. Co. (over $15 billion in assets); Bank of America (over $10 billion in assets).

ing, mergers, price discrimination, restrictive patent licensing, and other anticompetitive practices are illegal when engaged in by dominant or leading firms, although smaller firms might be able to justify the same practices as reasonable or involving only minimal effect on competition.[44]

Such proposals, however strongly they may be resisted in the United States, remain in the mainstream of antitrust tradition, strengthening the proscriptions against concentration of economic power and unfair practices. In quite a different tradition are pending proposals to subject price increases in major concentrated industries to a preaudit by an administrative agency or legislative committee.[45] Such a measure was suggested by Professor Galbraith in the course of Senator Kefauver's hearings on administered prices.[46] These hearings disclosed, for example, that the steel companies did not offer each other rivalry in pricing but, on the contrary, were able through the price leadership of the United States Steel Corporation to raise prices more quickly than costs increased, even in a declining market—a classic example of oligopolistic parallel pricing.

The pending price-notification bill [47] falls somewhere between the British Monopolies Commission postaudit of oligopoly pricing, which leads to "voluntary" price reductions, and the strong Dutch provisions for regulated pricing and production. I wish that I could be more hopeful that the bill would make an effective contribution to solution of the problem of parallel pricing by dominant firms. It seems more likely to set up a perpetual and inconclusive political

[44] See ATT'Y GEN. NAT'L COMM. ANTITRUST REP. 392 (1955) (dissent of L. B. Schwartz).

[45] See S. 1237, 86th Cong., 1st Sess. (1959), which would, if enacted, amend the Employment Act of 1946, 60 Stat. 23, 15 U.S.C. §§ 1021–24 (1958), to read in part: "It shall be the duty and function of the [Council of Economic Advisers] to hold public hearings concerning (a) price increases, proposed in industries where most of the output is produced by relatively few firms, which increases appear to threaten economic stability. . . ."

[46] See Subcomm. on Antitrust and Monopoly of the Senate Comm. on the Judiciary, *Report on Administered Prices in the Steel Industry,* S. REP. No. 1387, 85th Cong., 2d Sess. (1958); Schwartz, *Administered Prices, Oligopoly and the Sherman Act,* in 12 ABA ANTITRUST SECTION REP. 17 (1958).

[47] S. 1237, 86th Cong., 1st Sess. (1959).

debate. But if the government, having exhausted its best efforts to maintain workable competition, must inquire into pricing, it seems obvious that continuous administrative supervision is essential and that the mission of an agency charged with such supervision should be clearly and narrowly defined. It should be directed to concern itself primarily with large, basic, and highly concentrated industries, to report regularly to the legislature on such matters as costs, profits, and freedom of entry, and to make recommendations on reorganization, taxation (to recapture excess profits), tariff policy (to dilute the oligopoly by encouraging foreign competition), and procurement (so that government purchasing does not reinforce oligopoly). The very prospect of this kind of supervision and publicity would do much to induce moderation in the exercise of oligopoly power, while the information obtained would lay the basis for the continuous evolution of rational legal control of over-concentrated industries.

Although the price-notification bill has its difficulties and breaks with the antitrust tradition, it contains an idea that may be seminal for the future development of antitrust law. It suggests that the signal for governmental concern and the starting point of official inquiry should be how the prices of important products are actually behaving. If they are rigid, or move in disregard of costs, or are set at levels that discourage a desirable expansion of demand, may we not move from that observation directly to an appropriate official response without going through the intermediate steps of determining the "boundaries" of a "market," making the difficult measurement of "concentration" in the market, and adopting some controversial criterion of excessive concentration? [48] It will be recalled that Kaysen and Turner arrive at their criterion of dangerous degree of concentration by observing that most markets concentrated to that degree are "likely" to behave oligopolistically "to

[48] Compare the complete integration of "antitrust" regulation into a general regime of price regulation in Norway. The Norwegian authorities, looking primarily at price behavior rather than at structure, may even encourage consolidations, agreements to curtail price competition, or group boycotts of foreign firms, where they believe such action is beneficial to the public interest. See Eckhoff, *Norway,* in ANTITRUST LAWS—A COMPARATIVE SYMPOSIUM 281, 298–305 (Friedmann ed. 1956).

a significant degree." If economists can recognize oligopolistic, antisocial pricing, a law of the future may well provide that appropriate counter-measures be taken, including but not by any means limited to reorganizing the leading firms.

....

PART III *Mergers*

9 MERGERS

Our concern with mergers as an area of antitrust activity reflects the frequency of their consummation and their effects on competition. Scholars generally recognize three widespread domestic merger movements, although some question may exist as to whether these reflect actual increases in merger or merely better reporting of mergers by the business community.[1] The first of these periods, 1887–1904, coincides with the passage and formative years of the Sherman Act while the other two periods, 1919–1930 and 1940–1947, figure prominently in subsequent Clayton Act merger-law litigation.

The government's attempt to apply the Sherman Act to mergers failed to generate an effective merger policy. The Northern Securities case of 1904 was the most successful application of Sherman Act enforcement to mergers. The Court ruled that a holding company that controlled the stock of two competing railroads could be dissolved if that company was formed specifically to restrict competition between the previously independently operated companies.

Specific merger legislation in the United States dates from the original Clayton Act of 1914. This act was a response to the Standard Oil and Tobacco[2] cases of 1911 as well as to general public

---

[1] See Jesse W. Markham, "Survey of the Evidence and Findings on Mergers," *Business Concentration and Price Policy* (Princeton: Princeton University Press, 1955); and Ralph L. Nelson, *Merger Movements in American Industry, 1895–1956* (Princeton: Princeton University Press, 1959).

[2] United States v. American Tobacco Company, 221 U.S. 106 (1911).

sentiment that some activities of industrial firms should be specifically prohibited. The Clayton Act was intended to preclude the emergence of monopoly situations rather than withhold action until a full-blown monopoly situation developed.[3] Section 7 of the Clayton Act precluded the purchase of stock in other companies whenever trade might be restrained or monopoly created in any domestic market. The original Section 7 of the Clayton Act reads as follows:

> SECTION 7.   That no corporation engaged in commerce shall acquire, directly or indirectly, the whole or any part of the stock or other share capital of another corporation engaged also in commerce where the effect of such acquisition may be to substantially lessen competition between the corporation whose stock is so acquired and the corporation making the acquisition or to restrain such commerce in any section or community or tend to create a monopoly of any line of commerce.
>
> No corporation shall acquire, directly or indirectly, the whole or any part of the stock or other share capital of two or more corporations engaged in commerce where the effect of such acquisition or the use of such stock by the voting or granting of proxies or otherwise may be to substantially lessen competition between such corporations, or any of them, whose stock or other share capital is so acquired, or to restrain such commerce in any section or community or tend to create a monopoly of any line of commerce.

The applicability of Section 7 was severely limited by the Supreme Court's views that asset acquisitions would not fall under the Clayton Act provisions. This view of Section 7, which was developed in a series of decisions from 1923 through 1934, effectively permitted mergers without fear of prosecution simply by selling the assets of the company rather than the shares of ownership.[4] The legality of a merger thus had nothing to do with the economic effects—only with the legal path chosen.

[3] An excellent review of the considerations involved in the passage of the Clayton Act and in the enforcement of the act is found in David Dale Martin's book, *Mergers and the Clayton Act* (Berkeley and Los Angeles: University of California Press, 1959).

[4] Cf. Martin, *Mergers and the Clayton Act;* and Donald Dewey, *Monopoly in Law and Economics* (Chicago: Rand McNally, 1959).

Two additional factors also seemingly limited the prosecution of mergers under Section 7. One was the question as to congressional intent to lower the standards for merger violations of the antitrust law; this was compounded by the government's apparent selection of economically weak industries in which the suits were brought. Second, the extension of merger prosecution to the Federal Trade Commission apparently was a factor in the courts' rejections of these suits and judgments since the courts were being asked to define in addition a rival jurisdiction for these equity suits.

Briefly, the key decisions and their importance were as follows. First, the Supreme Court's 1923 decision in the FTC's action against the Aluminum Company of America upheld the commission's order requiring Alcoa's divestiture of the recently acquired stock interest in the Aluminum Rolling Mill Company.[5] However, the force of this action was nullified when Alcoa subsequently acquired and retained the rolling company's assets. In 1926 there was a temporary gain in the FTC's efforts to establish effective jurisdiction over merger cases and the acceptance of its power to force divestiture of the acquired companies. However, the year was dominated by a sharp FTC setback in the Thatcher Manufacturing Company[6] case. In this case the Court ruled that the commission could not require divestiture of either stock or assets whenever the assets had been merged into the acquiring corporation prior to the FTC's action; in such instances, the Court held, the government would have to seek its relief in the courts. In 1934 the Supreme Court acknowledged its rout of the FTC with the Arrow-Hart & Hegemann Electric Company[7] decision. In this case the Court ruled that the FTC was powerless when, after the FTC's complaint but before its hearing, the acquiring company integrated the acquired company's assets and dissolved the acquired company. Other instances could be cited of similar FTC rebuffs; the Justice Department filed very few merger suits during this period, but it did lose those few

[5] Federal Trade Commission v. Aluminum Company of America, 299 Fed. Rep. 361 (1924).

[6] Thatcher Manufacturing Co. v. Federal Trade Commission, 272 U.S. 554 (1926).

[7] Arrow-Hart & Hegemann Electric Company v. Federal Trade Commission, 291 U.S. 587 (1934).

filed. According to Dewey, only two industrial mergers seemed to have been stopped by the Clayton Act between 1914 and 1950.[8]

The apparently culminating blow to the usefulness (or effectiveness) of the antitrust laws concerning mergers and acquisitions came in 1948 with the Columbia Steel case.[9] This case, which Justice Douglas labeled "the most important antitrust case which has been before the Court in years," was filed under Sections 1 and 2 of the Sherman Act; since the matter was an asset acquisition, the Clayton Act did not apply. The suit was brought in an effort to prevent a United States Steel Corporation subsidiary, the Columbia Steel Corporation, from acquiring the assets of Consolidated Steel Corporation, the largest independent steel fabricator in the eleven-state West Coast market area. United States Steel was the country's largest producer of rolled steel products and also a fabricator of these into finished structural fabricated items, but it did not fabricate the rolled steel into finished plate fabricated items. All fabricated products are produced for specific purposes, but the "facilities required for structural fabrication are quite different from those required for plate fabrication." Columbia Steel was the largest West Coast producer of rolled steel; it also sold United States Steel's fabricated products, but no United States Steel subsidiary produced these items in Consolidated's eleven-state market. Prior to World War II rolled steel was sold on the West Coast at a price computed on the basis of Eastern cities basing points, thus putting independent West Coast fabricators at a relative disadvantage. However, the base for postwar price was Geneva, Utah, where United States Steel owned the largest war surplus rolled steel producing plant that the government had built in the West Coast area. This plant was sold to United States Steel after the Attorney General advised that its acquisition would not violate the antitrust laws even though it would increase United States Steel's share of the West Coast capacity to 39 percent from 17.3 percent (United States Steel estimated it would have 51 percent of the market's capacity after the acquisition; its share of the total United States capacity rose from 31.4 to 32.7 percent).

---

[8] Dewey, *op. cit.*, p. 221.

[9] United States v. Columbia Steel Co., 334 U.S. 446 (1948).

Testimony indicated that United States Steel wanted to assure itself a market for Geneva's plates and shapes. By contrast, Consolidated wanted to escape the cyclically oriented fabrication business "at a time when a favorable price could be realized," while much of the case turned on the government's charge that the merger would "lessen competition by excluding producers of rolled steel products other than United States Steel from supplying the requirements of Consolidated." Not surprisingly, the parties differed widely on the possible competitive effects of the merger. These differences largely stemmed from a "sharp dispute as to the size and nature of the market for rolled steel products with which Consolidated's consumption is to be compared." United States Steel contended that "rolled steel products are sold on a national scale, and that for the major producers the entire United States should be regarded as the market." However, the government argued "that the market must be more narrowly drawn, and that the relevant market to be considered is the eleven-state area in which Consolidated sells its products . . ." With the broader market definition, "Consolidated's requirements are an insignificant fraction of the total market, less than ½ of 1%" but if "all sales of rolled steel products in the Consolidated market are considered, Consolidated's purchases . . . represent a little more than 3% of the total . . ." However, if the market is "restricted to the consumption of plates and shapes in the Consolidated market, figures for 1937 indicate that Consolidated's consumption of plates and shapes was 13% of the total."

For the Court, the proper delineation of the product market was not easy. The problem was the same one that is met in many cases involving an economic analysis of an actual market situation:

> . . . the record furnishes little indication as to the propriety of considering plates and shapes as a market distinct from other rolled steel products. If rolled steel producers can make other products as easily as plates and shapes, then the effect of the removal of Consolidated's demand for plates and shapes must be measured not against the market for plates and shapes alone, but for all comparable rolled products. The record suggests, but does not conclusively indicate, that rolled steel producers can make other products interchangeably with shapes and plates, and that therefore we

should not measure the potential injury to competition by considering the total demand for shapes and plates alone, but rather
compare Consolidated's demand for rolled steel products with the
demand for all comparable rolled steel products in the Consolidated
marketing area.[10]

In this case the Supreme Court followed the findings of the
District Court in concluding that "rolled steel production and
consumption in the Consolidated marketing area is the competitive
area and the product for consideration." Thus the Supreme Court
ruled that the relevant market was that for rolled steel products
in the eleven-state area. Some horizontal integration was also
affected in fabricated structural products. But the Court found
that prewar competition in steel products had been national, since
half of the ten largest sellers "in the Consolidated market perform
their fabrication outside the area." The government argued that
the merger would eliminate any competition previously existing
between Consolidated and United States Steel, especially within
individual product lines. The opinion cited evidence on competition
in particular product lines that supported the trial court's findings
that "competition between the two companies in the manufacture
and sale of fabricated steel products was not substantial." The
trial court also held that the acquisition was completed for sound
business reasons and not with the intent to monopolize the
production and distribution of fabricated steel products.

The government alleged that the vertical integration aspects were
per se illegal, relying on an earlier Yellow Cab[11] decision. However, the Court held that the Yellow Cab case did not declare
vertical relationships illegal per se, but only where they unreasonably restricted the chances of competitors to sell their product.
After reviewing the economic evidence in the case, and previous
opinions dealing with antitrust considerations of vertical integration,
the Court concluded "that the so-called vertical integration resulting from the acquisition of Consolidated does not unreasonably
restrict the opportunities of the competitor producers of rolled
steel to market their product."

[10] *Ibid.*, 510–511.
[11] United States v. Yellow Cab Co., 332 U.S. 218 (1947).

Thus, in affirming the merger's validity, the Court based its decision on such factors as Consolidated's share of the Western states' rolled steel products market (and its consequent negligible vertical aspects), the rather negligible horizontal aspects of the acquisition, the growing future of the steel industry, and the industry's need for such large-sized companies. The Court further stated that size and a prior merger history were insufficient to prove intent to monopolize, especially in view of a declining share of total capacity.

In examining the allegation of an intent to "monopolize the production and sale of fabricated steel products in the Consolidated Market," the Court also considered the circumstances surrounding United States Steel's acquisition of the Geneva plant. Here the Court noted that the "bid of United States Steel for the Geneva plant emphasized the importance of erecting finishing facilities to assure a market for Geneva's production." The majority argued further that

> . . . it is doubtful whether objections could be raised if United States Steel proposed to build instead of buy from a competitor fabricating facilities similar to those possessed by Consolidated. The reasons given by Consolidated and United States Steel for the purchase and sale of assets here involved seem not to involve any action condemned by the Sherman Act. Granting that the sale will to some extent affect competition, the acquisition of a firm outlet to absorb a portion of Geneva's rolled steel production seems to reflect a normal business purpose rather than a scheme to circumvent the law.[12]

The Court thus seemed to say that this acquisition, in absence of proof of an intent to monopolize, was to be considered in the same light as *de novo* construction of a comparable plant.

To most economists, the Court's treatment of the construction of a plant as parallel to acquisition is difficult to understand if not totally incredulous. No doubt the Court was led astray on this point by its deference to "a normal business purpose" for the transaction. From the viewpoint of the expanding firm, the

---

[12] *Op. cit.*, 533–534.

business motivations and result are similar if not identical, irrespective of how the expansion is accomplished. In either case, United States Steel would have obtained fabrication facilities within the eleven-state area that would have served as a captive market for the Geneva plant's ingot production. From a social standpoint, however, the construction and the acquisition of facilities are not at all parallel in effect. Construction expands the productive capacity of the industry in general, as well as that of the individual firm. By contrast, acquisition merely involves a transfer of control from one enterprise to another without affecting the industry's overall capacity to produce. More important, acquisitions of this sort eliminate an established competitor, thereby affecting the nature and degree of competition within that market. Of course, this is likely to be of greatest importance where an independent competitor is eliminated through acquisition of the industry's dominant firm. In the minds of many economists along with the dissenting minority in this case, the Court's acceptance of the merger based on the argument that large size was a necessary characteristic of the industry is similar, and equally unfortunate.

The dissent by Justice Douglas (with three other justices concurring) provides a contrast and reflects some of the earlier Alcoa arguments and, in itself, highlights the problem of applying the Sherman Act to mergers. It mentions the gradual evolution of concentrated conditions due to mergers, each of which might be justified by "sound business reasons." But the minority argued that irrespective of how

. . . the acquisition may be rationalized, the effect is plain. It is a purchase for control, a purchase for control of a market for which United States Steel has in the past had to compete but which it no longer wants left to the uncertainties that competition in the West may engender. This in effect it concedes. It states that its purpose in acquiring Consolidated is to insure itself of a market for part of Geneva's production of rolled steel products when demand falls off.

But competition is never more irrevocably eliminated than by buying the customer for whose business the industry has been competing. The business of Consolidated amounts to around $22,000,000 annually. That the competitive purchases by Consolidated are over

$5,000,000 of commerce is immaterial. It plainly is not *de minimus.* . . . it can be said here, as it was in *International Salt Co.* v. *United States,* . . . that the volume of business restrained by this contract is not insignificant or insubstantial. United States Steel does not consider it insignificant, for the aim of this well-conceived project is to monopolize it. If it is not insubstantial as a market for United States Steel, it certainly is not from the point of view of the struggling western units of the steel industry.[13]

Justice Douglas then turned to the question of the relevant market for appraising the competitive impact of the merger. Somewhat pragmatically, he argued for a much more narrow market definition than the majority accepted. In particular, Justice Douglas argued that:

The largest market which must be taken for comparison is the market actually reached by the company which is being absorbed. In this case Consolidated's purchases of rolled steel products are a little over three per cent of that market. . . . Yet consideration of the case from that viewpoint puts the public interest phase of the acquisition in the least favorable light. A surer test of the impact of the acquisition on competition is to be determined not only by consideration of the actual markets reached by Consolidated but also by the actual purchases which it makes. Its purchases were predominantly of plates and shapes—76 per cent from 1937–1941. This was in 1937, 13 per cent of the total in the Consolidated market. That comparison is rejected by the Court or at least discounted on the theory that competitors presently selling to Consolidated can probably convert from plates and shapes to other forms of rolled steel products. But a surer test of the effect on competition is the actual business of which competitors will be deprived.[14]

The dissenting opinion thus clearly embodies a much more narrow product-market definition than that adopted by the majority. A number of contrasts are striking, but the most telling seemingly results from the weight given to possible flexibility of productive

---

[13] *Ibid.,* 537–538.
[14] *Ibid.,* 538–539.

<u>facilities.</u> As noted earlier, the majority's definition of the relevant product encompassed the rolled steel products sold in the eleven-state area. In large part this definition was based on the possibility that producers of shapes and plates such as those purchased by Consolidated would shift to the production of other rolled steel products. Justice Douglas, however, chose to restrict the markets considered not only to "the actual markets reached by Consolidated but also by the actual purchases which it makes," which were predominantly plates and shapes.

These diverging views on market delineation together with the concomitant conclusions pose an uncomfortable paradox for a great many economists. As a rule, economists would delineate the boundaries of a market on the basis of substitutability of products, both in production and in consumption. Thus economists at least would be sympathetic, and would probably subscribe, to the product definitions that the majority relied upon in this case. But, at the same time, economists most likely would join with Justice Douglas insofar as conclusions are concerned.

On the surface at least, this paradox is not easily resolved. Indeed, a compelling resolution of the paradox that is directly responsive to only these considerations may not be possible. However, this particular situation may be best visualized by casting it in a somewhat different light: Does not the acquisition of Consolidated also involve the elimination of United States Steel as a potential entrant (as a "buyer" of ingot and as a seller of fabricated products) into the area? Should we not also consider how the acquisition augments United States Steel actual and potential market position in the area and nationally? That is, the impact on competition of the elimination of a firm accounting for 3, or 13, percent of the market may depend more upon the attributes of the acquiring firm than upon the acquired firm itself. Justice Douglas, in the concluding paragraph of the dissent, broaches this point. After contending that the "monopoly of this substantial market for rolled steel products is in itself an unreasonable restraint of trade," Justice Douglas then argued:

> The result might well be different if Consolidated were merging with or being acquired by an independent west coast producer for the

purpose of developing an integrated operation. The purchase might then be part of an intensely practical plan to put together an independent western unit of the industry with sufficient resources and strength to compete with the giants of the industry. Approval of this acquisition works in precisely the opposite direction. It makes dim the prospects that the western steel industry will be free from control of the eastern giants. United States Steel, now that it owns the Geneva plant, has over 51 per cent of the rolled steel or ingot capacity of the Pacific Coast area. This acquisition gives it unquestioned domination there and protects it against growth of the independents in that developing region. That alone is sufficient to condemn to purchase. Its serious impact on competition and on the economy is emphasized when it is recalled that United States Steel has one-third of the rolled steel production of the entire country.[15] . . .

The essence of the dissent thus goes to the heart of the purposes of the Clayton Act: a plea to prevent the further decline of competition and the spread of monopoly. As a corollary, Justice Douglas argued that the showing of intent to monopolize is not required in a Sherman Act case if the monopoly or restraint follows directly and necessarily from the act. The dissent held this to be the case in the acquisition of Consolidated and that, moreover, it was not necessary to "hold that vertical integration is *per se* unlawful in order to strike down" the acquisition.

The Columbia Steel case emphasized the failure of either Sherman or Clayton Acts sections to cover the incipient stages of possible monopoly or noncompetitive conditions; consequently, it proved to be the final impetus required for congressional amendment of the Clayton Act's merger provisions. The amendment was passed in 1950 and is termed the Celler-Kefauver Bill. The revised Section 7 is presented below, with underlined sections representing those portions added to the original.

Celler-Kefauver Act, 1950
Amending Section 7 of the Clayton Act

SECTION 7. That no corporation engaged in commerce shall acquire, directly or indirectly, the whole or any part of the stock or

[15] *Ibid.*, 539–540.

other share capital *and no corporation subject to the jurisdiction of the Federal Trade Commission shall acquire the whole or any part of the assets* of another corporation engaged also in commerce, where in line of commerce in any section of the country, the effect of such acquisition may be substantially to lessen competition, or to tend to create a monopoly.

No corporation shall acquire, directly or indirectly, the whole or any part of the stock or other share capital and no corporation . . . shall acquire the whole or any part of the assets of one or more corporations engaged in commerce, where in any line of commerce in any section of the country, the effect of such acquisition, of such stocks or assets, or of the use of such stock by the voting or granting of proxies or otherwise, may be substantially to lessen competition, or to tend to create a monopoly.

Shortly after Section 7 was amended, the Court acted in the federal government's suit to require divestiture of E. I. du Pont de Nemours & Company's large holdings of GM stock. This suit was first filed under the Sherman and original Clayton Acts, and the decision raised speculation concerning new powers in the Clayton Act; this is discussed in the Harbeson article below. Divestiture was urged in order to halt the alleged monopolization of specific markets in which GM was the dominant purchaser, and du Pont supposedly had an unfair advantage through its stock-holding. Although technically this case revolved about monopolization and the case was argued primarily on the grounds of a Sherman Act violation, the decision was based on Section 7 of the original Clayton Act. Because the Clayton Act was included in the complaint almost as an afterthought and the government stressed the Sherman Act aspects of the case, the use of the Clayton Act as the basis of the Court's decision was rather surprising. It is possible that the Supreme Court stretched some points to find an antitrust violation by these two inordinately large companies.

10 THE DU PONT (GENERAL MOTORS) CASE:

More on Wrapping up a Market

In the development of the courts' delineation of markets and analysis of the areas of competition, two cases involving E. I. du Pont de Nemours & Company occupy a prominent place. The first, the du Pont (cellophane) case considered earlier, was brought under the Sherman Act. In the cellophane decision the relevant product was defined by the Court in terms of substitute or reasonably interchangeable goods that were available for the same general purpose.

The present case, *United States v. E. I. du Pont de Nemours & Company* et al.,[1] involved an alleged violation of the original Section 7 of the Clayton Act stemming from du Pont's acquisition of General Motors stock following World War I. The du Pont (GM) case also revolved about the definition of the market concerned, since "[d]etermination of the relevant market is a necessary predicate to a finding of a violation of the Clayton Act because the

---

[1] United States v. E. I. du Pont de Nemours & Company *et al.*, 353 U.S. 586 (1957).

threatened monopoly must be one which will substantially lessen competition 'within the area of effective competition.' " This case may thus be compared with the du Pont (cellophane) decision. In the du Pont (GM) case, the relevant product was defined by the Supreme Court as those goods designed for particular uses and thus had peculiar characteristics.

Specifically, the Court applied these standards to goods sold by du Pont to General Motors; it then concluded that automotive finishes and fabrics both represented distinct product lines and that the automotive market was the relevant market for application of Section 7 in this case. Extracts from the Court's findings of fact and its views are presented below, followed by an analysis of the case by Professor Robert W. Harbeson. The extracts from the opinion stress the Court's reasoning in this case, which was not convincing to Justices Burton and Frankfurter. As the excerpts from Justice Burton's opinion indicate, these two members of the Court contended that Section 7 was not applicable to vertical acquisitions.

••

UNITED STATES
v.
E. I. DU PONT
DE NEMOURS & COMPANY et al.
353 US 586 (1957)

Mr. Justice Brennan delivered the opinion of the Court.

This is a direct appeal . . . from a judgment of the District Court for the Northern District of Illinois, dismissing the Government's action brought in 1949 under § 15 of the Clayton Act. The complaint alleged a violation of § 7 of the Act resulting from the purchase by E. I. du Pont de Nemours and Company in 1917–1919 of a 23% stock interest in General Motors Corporation. This appeal is from the dismissal of the action as to du Pont, General Motors and the corporate holders of large amounts of du Pont stock, Christiana Securities Corporation and Delaware Realty & Investment Company.

The primary issue is whether du Pont's commanding position as General Motor's supplier of automotive finishes and fabrics was achieved on competitive merit alone, or because its acquisition of the General Motors' stock, and the consequent close intercompany relationship, led to the insulation of most of the General Motors' market from free competition, with the resultant likelihood, at the time of suit, of the creation of a monopoly of a line of commerce.

Section 7 is designed to arrest in its incipiency not only the substantial lessening of competition from the acquisition by one corporation of the whole or any part of the stock of a competing corporation, but also to arrest in their incipiency restraints or monopolies in a relevant market which, as a reasonable probability, appear at the time of suit likely to result from the acquisition by one corporation of all or any part of the stock of any other corporation. The section is violated whether or not actual restraints or monopolies, or the substantial lessening of competition, have occurred or are intended. Acquisitions solely for investment are excepted, but only if, and so long as, the stock is not used by voting or otherwise to bring about, or in attempting to bring about, the substantial lessening of competition.

We are met at the threshold with the argument that § 7 before its amendment in 1950, applied only to an acquisition of the stock of a competing corporation, and not to an acquisition by a supplier corporation of the stock of a customer corporation—in other words, that the statute applied only to horizontal and not to vertical acquisitions. This is the first case presenting the question in this Court. . . .

The first paragraph of § 7, written in the disjunctive, plainly is framed to reach not only the corporate acquisition of stock of a competing corporation, where the effect may be substantially to lessen competition between them, but also the corporate acquisition of stock of any corporation, competitor or not, where the effect may be either (1) to restrain commerce in any section or community, or (2) tend to create a monopoly of any line of commerce. The amended complaint does not allege that the effect of du Pont's acquisition may be to restrain commerce in any section or community but alleges that the effect was ". . . to tend to create a monopoly in particular lines of commerce. . . ."

We hold that any acquisition by one corporation of all or any part of the stock of another corporation, competitor or not, is within the reach of the section whenever the reasonable likelihood appears that the acquisition will result in a restraint of commerce or in the creation of a monopoly of any line of commerce. Thus, although du Pont and General Motors are not competitors, a violation of the section has occurred if, as a result of the acquisition, there was at the time of suit a reasonable likelihood of a monopoly of any line of commerce. . . .

Appellees argue that there exists no basis for a finding of a probable restraint or monopoly within the meaning of § 7 because the total General Motors market for finishes and fabrics constituted only a negligible percentage of the total market for these materials for all uses, including automotive uses. . . .

Determination of the relevant market is a necessary predicate to a finding of a violation of the Clayton Act because the threatened monopoly must be one which will substantially lessen competition "within the area of effective competition." Substantiality can be determined only in terms of the market affected. The record shows that automotive finishes and fabrics have sufficient peculiar characteristics and uses to constitute them products sufficiently distinct from all other finishes and fabrics to make them a "line of commerce" within the meaning of the Clayton Act. Thus, the bounds of the relevant market for the purposes of this case are not coextensive with the total market for finishes and fabrics, but are coextensive with the automobile industry, the relevant market for automotive finishes and fabrics.

The market affected must be substantial. . . . Moreover, in order to establish a violation of § 7 the Government must prove a likelihood that competition may be "foreclosed in a substantial share of . . . [that market]." Both requirements are satisfied in this case. The substantiality of a relevant market comprising the automobile industry is undisputed. The substantiality of General Motors' share of that market is fully established in the evidence.

. . . Because General Motors accounts for almost one-half of the automobile industry's annual sales, its requirements for automobile finishes and fabrics must represent approximately one-half of the relevant market for these materials. Because the record clearly shows that quantitatively and percentagewise du Pont supplies the largest part of General Motors' requirements, we must conclude that du Pont has a substantial share of the relevant market.

The appellees argue that the Government could not maintain this action in 1949 because § 7 is applicable only to the acquisition of stock and not to the holding or subsequent use of the stock. This argument misconceives the objective toward which § 7 is directed. . . .

. . . None of these cases holds, or even suggests, that the Government is foreclosed from bringing the action at any time when a threat of the prohibited effects is evident.

The du Pont Company's commanding position as a General Motors supplier was not achieved until shortly after its purchase of a sizable block of General Motors stock in 1917. . . .

At least 10 years before the stock acquisition, the du Pont Company, for over a century the manufacturer of military and commercial explosives, had decided to expand its business into other fields. . . .

We agree with the trial court that considerations of price, quality and service were not overlooked by either du Pont or General Motors. Pride in its products and its high financial stake in General Motors' success would naturally lead du Pont to try to supply the best. But the wisdom of this business judgment cannot obscure the fact, plainly revealed by the record, that du Pont purposely employed its stock to pry open the General Motors market to entrench itself as the primary supplier of General Motors' requirements for automotive finishes and fabrics.

Similarly, the fact that all concerned in high executive posts in both companies acted honorably and fairly, each in the honest conviction that his actions were in the best interests of his own company and without any design to overreach anyone, including du Pont's competitors, does not defeat the Government's right to relief. It is not requisite to the proof of a violation of § 7 to show that restraint or monopoly was intended.

The statutory policy of fostering free competition is obviously furthered when no supplier has an advantage over his competitors from an acquisition of his customer's stock likely to have the effects condemned by the statute. We repeat, that the test of a violation of § 7 is whether at the time of suit there is a reasonable probability that the acquisition is likely to result in the condemned restraints. The conclusion upon this record is inescapable that such likelihood was proved as to this acquisition. The fire that was kindled in 1917 continues to smolder. It burned briskly to forge the ties that bind the General Motors market to du Pont, and if it has quieted down, it remains hot, and, from past performance, is likely at any time to blaze and make the fusion complete.

The judgment must therefore be reversed and the cause remanded to the District Court for a determination, after further hearing, of the equitable relief necessary and appropriate in the public interest to eliminate the effects of the acquisition offensive to the statute. The District Courts, in the framing of equitable decrees, are clothed "with large discretion to model their judgments to fit the exigencies of the particular case." . . .

The motion of the appellees Christiana Securities Company and Delaware Realty and Investment Company for dismissal of the appeal as to them is denied. It seems appropriate that they be retained as parties pending determination by the District Court of the relief to be granted.

It is so ordered.

Mr. Justice Clark, Mr. Justice Harlan and Mr. Justice Whittaker took no part in the consideration or decision of this case.

Mr. Justice Burton, whom Mr. Justice Frankfurter joins, dissenting.

. . . On the basis of this evidence, the District Court found that the Government had failed to prove its case and, specifically, that (a) du Pont did not control General Motors, (b) there had been "no limitation or restraint upon General Motors' freedom to deal freely and fully with competitors of du Pont" or upon its "freedom . . . to deal with its chemical discoveries," and (c) after 30 years in which no such restraint had resulted, there was no "basis for a finding that there is or has been any reasonable probability of such a restraint within the meaning of the Clayton Act." . . .

The Court's decision is far reaching. Although § 7 of the Clayton Act was enacted in 1914—over 40 years ago—this is the first case in which the United States or the Federal Trade Commission has sought to apply it to a vertical integration. Likewise, this appears to be the first case in which it ever has been argued that § 7 is applicable to a stock acquisition which took place many years before. . . .

For the reasons given below, I believe that the Court had erred in (1) applying § 7 to a vertical acquisition; (2) holding that the time chosen by the Government in bringing the action is controlling rather than the time of the stock acquisition itself; and (3) concluding, in disregard of the findings of fact of the trial court, that the facts of this case fall within its theory of illegality.

I.

. . . This paragraph makes unlawful only those intercorporate stock acquisitions which may result in any of three effects: (1) substantially lessen competition between the acquiring and the acquired corporations; (2) restrain commerce in any section or community; or (3) tend to create a monopoly of any line of commerce. The Government concedes that General Motors and du Pont have never been in competition with each other. Since the substantially lessen competition clause applies only to acquisitions involving competing corporations (generally referred to as horizontal acquisitions), that clause concededly is not applicable to this case. . . .

Section 7 never has been authoritatively interpreted as prohibiting the acquisition of stock in a corporation that is not engaged in the same line of business as the acquiring corporation. Although the language of the Act is ambiguous, the relevant legislative history, administrative practice, and judicial interpretation support the conclusion that § 7 does not apply to vertical acquisitions.

A reading of the legislative history of the bill leaves the distinct impression that intercorporate relationships between buyers and sellers which resulted in noncompetitive preferences were intended to be dealt with exclusively by the provision forbidding interlocking directorates (§ 8 of the Clayton Act), if not covered by the specific prohibitions of certain price discriminations (§ 2), and of certain exclusive selling or leasing contracts (§ 3).

Assuming that the three unlawful effects mentioned in § 7 are not entirely synonymous with each other, such an assumption does not require the conclusion that § 7 was intended to apply to vertical acquisitions as well as to horizontal acquisitions. . . .

Finally, this Court has twice construed old § 7 as applying only to stock acquisitions involving competing corporations. . . .

The legislative history, administrative practice, and judicial interpretation of § 7 provide the perspective in which the Government's present assertion that § 7 applies to vertical acquisitions should be viewed. Seen as a whole, they offer convincing evidence that § 7, properly construed, has reference only to horizontal acquisitions. I would so hold. However, even if the opposite view be accepted, the foregoing views of the enforcing agencies and the courts are material to a proper consideration of the other issues which must then be reached.

II.

In this case the Government is challenging, in 1949, a stock acquisition that took place in 1917–1919. The Court, without advancing reasons to support its conclusion, holds that in determining the effect of the stock acquisition is such as to violate § 7, the time chosen by the Government in bringing its suit is controlling rather than the time of the acquisition of the stock. This seems to me to ignore the language and structure of § 7, the purpose of the Clayton Act, and all existing administrative and judicial precedents.

. . . The offense described by § 7 is the acquisition, not the holding or the use, of stock. When the acquisition has been made, the offense, if any, is complete. The statutory language is unequivocal. It makes the test the probable effect of the acquisition at the time of the actual acquisition, and not at some later date to be arbitrarily chosen by the Government in bringing suit.

The distinction carefully made in the several paragraphs of § 7 between an unlawful acquisition and an unlawful use of stock reinforces this conclusion. . . .

The Clayton Act was not intended to replace the Sherman Act in remedying actual restraints and monopolies. Its purpose was to supplement the Sherman Act by checking anticompetitive tendencies in their incipiency, before they reached the point at which the Sherman Act comes into play. . . .

III.

The remaining issues are factual: (1) whether the record establishes the existence of a reasonable probability that du Pont's competitors will be foreclosed from securing General Motors' trade, and (2) whether the record establishes that such foreclosure, if probable, involves a substantial share of the relevant market and significantly limits the competitive opportunities of others trading in that market. In discussing these factual issues, I meet the Court on its own ground, that is, I assume that the old § 7 applies to vertical acquisitions, and that the potential threat at the time of suit is controlling. Even on that basis the record does not support the Court's conclusion that § 7 was violated by this 1917–1919 stock acquisition.

A. Foreclosure of Competitors

. . . Du Pont is primarily a manufacturer of chemicals and chemical products. Thousands of its products could be used by General Motors in manufacturing automobiles, appliances and machinery. Despite du Pont's sales efforts over a period of 40 years, General Motors buys many of the commodities produced by du Pont from du Pont's competitors. The Court, ignoring the many products which General Motors declines to buy from du Pont or which it buys only in small quantities, concentrates on the few products which du Pont has sold in large volumes to General Motors for many years—paints and fabrics. Before examining the history of those large-volume purchases, it is essential to understand where and by whom purchasing decisions within General Motors have been made.

The record discloses that each division buys independently, that the pattern of buying varies greatly from one division to another, and that within each division purchases from du Pont have fluctuated greatly in response to price, quality, service and other competitive considerations. . . .

1. Paints. Du Pont, for many years, has had marked success in the manufacture and sale of paints, varnishes, lacquers and related products. . . . Although du Pont has been General Motors' principal supplier of paint for many years, General Motors continues to buy about 30% of its paint requirements from competitors of du Pont. Moreover, the sales of paint from du Pont to General Motors do not bulk large in the respective total sales and purchases of either company. In 1948, du Pont's finish sales to General Motors were only 3% of its total sales of all products; they were an infinitesimal percentage of General Motors' total purchases.

Two products account for a high proportion of these finish sales to General Motors: "Duco," a nitrocellulose lacquer invented and patented by du Pont, and "Dulux," a synthetic resin enamel developed by du Pont. However, Duco and Dulux did not come into commercial use until 1924 and 1931, respectively, and du Pont's position as a principal manufacturer of finishes was attained much earlier.

The invention and development of Duco in the early 1920's represented a significant technological advance. . . .

Finally, the success of Duco has never been confined to the General Motors' car divisions. . . .

As the District Court found, *"In view of all the evidence of record, the only reasonable conclusion is that du Pont has continued to sell Duco in substantial quantities to General Motors only because General Motors believes such purchases best fit its needs."* (Emphasis supplied.) . . .

The second largest item which General Motors buys from du Pont is Dulux, a synthetic enamel finish used on refrigerators and other appliances. . . . Since its development, Dulux has been used *exclusively* by all the major manufacturers of refrigerators and other appliances—General Electric, Westinghouse, Crosley, and many others—except Frigidaire, which continues to finish part of its refrigerators with porcelain. . . . Several representatives of competitive refrigerator manufacturers testified that they purchased 100% of their requirements from du Pont. *"There is no evidence that General Motors purchased from du Pont for any reason other than those that prompted its competitors to buy Dulux from du Pont—excellence of product, fair price and continuing quality of service."* (Emphasis supplied.) . . .

The Court fails to note that du Pont's efforts to sell paints other than Duco and Dulux to General Motors have met with considerably less success. . . .

The District Court did not err in concluding, on the basis of this evidence, that du Pont's success in selling General Motors a substantial portion of its paint requirements was due to the superior quality of Duco and Dulux and to du Pont's continuing research and outstanding service, and that *"du Pont's position was at all times a matter of sales effort and keeping General Motors satisfied. There is no evidence that General Motors or any Division of General Motors was ever prevented by du Pont from using a finish manufactured by one of du Pont's competitors; nor is there any evidence that General Motors has suffered competitively from its substantial use of Duco."* (Emphasis supplied.) . . .

2. Fabrics. The principal fabrics which du Pont has sold to General Motors are imitation leather (du Pont's "Fabrikoid" and "Fabrilite") and top material for open cars and convertibles (du Pont's "Pontop," "Everbright" and "Teal"). . . .

In addition to the mass of evidence supporting the District Court's finding that *"such purchases of fabrics as the General Motors divisions have made from du Pont from time to time were based upon each division's excercise of its business judgment and are not the result of du Pont domination"* (emphasis supplied), the record clearly indicates that du Pont's fabrics can and have made their way in the automotive industry on their merits. Prior to the early 1920's, du Pont was the principal supplier of coated fabrics to all three of the then major producers—Ford, Willys-Overland and General Motors. . . . Du Pont likewise has supplied, over the years, a considerable part of the coated and combined fabrics of most of the smaller automobile companies.

The District Court did not err in concluding that *"Du Pont, the record shows, has maintained its position as the principal fabric supplier to General Motors through its early leadership in the field and by concentrating upon satisfactorily meeting General Motors' changing requirements as to quality, service and delivery."* (Emphasis supplied.) . . .

3. Other Products. The Court concludes only that du Pont has been given an unlawful preference with respect to paints and fabrics. By limiting the issue to these products, it eliminates from deserved considerations those products which General Motors does not buy in large quantities or proportions from du Pont. Yet the logic of the Court's argument—that the stock relationship between du Pont and General Motors inevitably has or will result in a preference for du Pont products—requires consideration of the total commercial relations between the two companies. Du Pont "influence," if there were any, would be expected to apply to all products which du Pont makes and which General Motors buys.

The record supports the conclusion of the District Court:

"All of the evidence bearing upon du Pont's efforts to sell these various miscellaneous products to General Motors supports a finding that the latter bought or refused to buy solely in accordance with the dictates of its own purchasing judgment. There is no evidence that General Motors was constrained to favor, or buy, a product solely because it was offered by du Pont. On the other hand, the record discloses numerous instances in which General Motors rejected du Pont's products in favor of those of one of its competitors. *The variety of situations and circumstances in which such rejections occurred satisfies the Court that there was no limitation whatsoever upon General Motors' freedom to buy or to refuse to buy from du Pont as it pleased.*" (Emphasis supplied.) . . .

B. Relevant Market

Finally, even assuming the correctness of the Court's conclusion that du Pont's competitors have been or will be foreclosed from General Motors' paint and fabric trade, it is still necessary to resolve one more issue in favor of the Government in order to reverse the District Court. It is necessary to hold that the Government proved that this foreclosure involves a substantial share of the relevant market and that it significantly limits the competitive opportunities of others trading in that market.

The relevant market is the "area of effective competition" within which the defendants operate. . . . "[T]he problem of defining a market turns on discovering patterns of trade which are followed in practice." . . . "Determination of the competitive market for commodities depends on how different from one another are the offered commodities in character or use, how far buyers will go to substitute one commodity for another." . . . This determination is primarily one of fact.

The Court holds that the relevant market in this case is the automotive market for finishes and fabrics, and not the total industrial market for these products. The Court reaches that conclusion because in its view "automotive finishes and fabrics have sufficient peculiar characteristics and uses to constitute them products distinct from all other finishes and fabrics. . . ." . . . We are not told what these "peculiar characteristics" are. Nothing is said about finishes other than that Duco represented an important contribution to the process of manufacturing automobiles. Nothing is said about fabrics other than sales to the automobile industry are made by means of bids rather than fixed price schedules. Dulux is included in the "automobile" market even though it is used on refrigerators and other appliances, but not on automobiles. So are other finishes and fabrics used on diesel locomotives, engines, parts, appliances and other products which General Motors manufactures. Arbitrary conclusions are not an adequate substitute for analysis of the pertinent facts contained in the record.

The record does not show that the fabrics and finishes used in the manufacture of automobiles have peculiar characteristics differentiating them from the finishes and fabrics used in other industries. What evidence there is in the record affirmatively indicates the contrary. The sales of the four products principally involved in this case—Duco, Dulux, imitation leather, and coated fabrics—support this conclusion.

The Court might be justified in holding that products sold to the automotive industry constitute the relevant market in the case of products such as carburetors or tires which are sold primarily to automobile manufacturers. But the sale of Duco, Dulux, imitation leather, and coated fabrics is not so limited.

The burden was on the Government to prove that a substantial share of the relevant market would, in all probability, be affected by du Pont's 23% stock interest in General Motors. The Government proved only that du Pont's sales of finishes and fabrics to General Motors were large in volume, and that General Motors was the leading manufacturer of automobiles during the later years covered by the record. The Government did not show that the identical products were not used on a large scale for many other purposes in many other industries. Nor did the Government show that the automobile industry in general, or General Motors in particular, comprised a large or substantial share of the total market. What evidence there is in the record affirmatively indicates that the products involved do have wide use in many industries, and that an insubstantial portion of this total market would be affected even if an unlawful preference existed or were probable.

For the reasons stated, I conclude that § 7 of the Clayton Act, prior to its amendment in 1950, did not apply to vertical acquisitions; that the Government failed to prove that there was a reasonable probability at the time of the stock acquisition (1917–1919) of a restraint of commerce or a tendency toward monopoly; and that, in any event, the District Court was not clearly in error in concluding that the Government failed to prove that du Pont's competitors have been or may be foreclosed from a substantial share of the relevant market. Accordingly, I would affirm the judgment of the District Court.

The Clayton Act:
sleeping giant of antitrust?

Robert W. Harbeson

Thus, over 40 years after the enactment of the Clayton Act, it now becomes apparent for the first time that Section 7 has been a sleeping giant all along. Every corporation which has acquired a stock interest in another corporation after the enactment of the Clayton Act in 1914, and which has had business dealings with that corporation is exposed, retroactively, to the bite of the newly discovered teeth of Section 7.[1]

The foregoing passage from the minority opinion of the United States Supreme Court in *United States v. E. I. du Pont de Nemours*

Abridged from Robert W. Harbeson, "The Clayton Act: Sleeping Giant of Antitrust?" *The American Economic Review,* XLVIII, No. 1 (March 1958), 92–104.

[1] *U. S. v. E. I. du Pont de Nemours and Co. et al.,* 353 U.S. 586 (1957), at p. 611; hereafter cited as *U.S. v. du Pont.*

and Company et al., handed down June 3, 1957, suggests the great legal and economic significance which at least some members of the Court attach to this decision. A similar view has been widely echoed in the business and financial press. For example, *Fortune* comments editorially that the decision is "potentially the most important antitrust development since Justice Edward Douglass White enunciated the 'rule of reason' in the Standard Oil Case in 1911." [2] The important word in this statement is "potentially"; without minimizing the importance of the increased scope which this decision gives to the antitrust laws it seems likely that the unanswered questions which it raises and the uncertainties which it creates may be of equal if not greater significance.

In the *du Pont* decision the Supreme Court held, 4 to 2, that the purchase by du Pont in 1917–19 of a 23 per cent stock interest in General Motors violated Section 7 of the Clayton Act, in that through this purchase "du Pont intended to obtain, and did obtain, an illegal preference over its competitors in the sale to General Motors of its products, and a further illegal preference in the development of chemical discoveries made by General Motors." [3] The proceeding began in June 1949 as a civil action in the United States District Court for the Northern District of Illinois, the government charging that du Pont's stock ownership in General Motors violated both Sections 1 and 2 of the Sherman Act and Section 7 of the Clayton Act. . . .

Judge La Buy dismissed the government's complaint, holding that du Pont did not control General Motors, that there had been no limitation or restraint upon General Motors' freedom to deal and that there was no basis for a finding that there was or had been any reasonable probability of an illegal restraint within the meaning of the Clayton Act.[4] The government appealed despite the fact that, reportedly, government attorneys felt that the District Court's decision was "airtight." [5] However, in appealing, the government limited the complaint to du Pont, General Motors,

[2] "Brennan on Bigness," *Fortune,* July 1957, LVI, 91.

[3] *U.S. v. du Pont,* p. 608.

[4] *U.S. v. E. I. du Pont de Nemours and Co. et al.,* 126 F. Supp. 235 (1954).

[5] "The Bite of the G. M. Decision," *Business Week,* June 8, 1957, p. 42.

and the two holding companies. . . . The appeal, like the original complaint, charged violations both of Sections 1 and 2 of the Sherman Act and Section 7 of the Clayton Act, but the latter apparently was included only as an afterthought or make-weight; according to Justice Burton the government referred to it only in the closing pages of its brief and for a few minutes in its oral argument. Nevertheless the majority of the Supreme Court rested its decision solely on the ground that a violation of Section 7 of the Clayton Act was involved.[6] The decision of the District Court was reversed and the case remanded to it for determination, after further hearing, of the equitable relief necessary and appropriate to eliminate the effects of the unlawful stock acquisition involved.

In reaching the foregoing conclusion the majority of the Supreme Court extended the scope of the Clayton Act in three ways. First, it was held that Section 7, even prior to the Celler amendments of 1950, covered vertical as well as horizontal acquisitions of stock; that is, acquisitions of stock of customer or supplier companies as well as stock of competitors. . . .

Second, it was held that, although prior cases under Section 7 were brought at or near the time of the stock acquisition involved, this fact does not mean that the government is foreclosed from bringing an action at any time when a threat of substantial lessening of competition or restraint or monopoly of any line of commerce is evident. The Court pointed out that the purpose of the Clayton Act was to arrest the foregoing tendencies in their incipiency and that: " 'Incipiency' in this context denotes not the time the stock was acquired, but any time when the acquisition threatens to ripen into a prohibited effect. . . . To accomplish the congressional aim, the Government may proceed at any time that an acquisition may be said with reasonable probability to contain a threat that it may lead to a restaint of commerce or tend to create a monopoly

---

[6] The relevant portion of Section 7 in its original form reads as follows: "That no corporation engaged in commerce shall acquire, directly or indirectly, the whole or any part of the stock or other share capital of another corporation engaged also in commerce where the effect of such acquisition may be to substantially lessen competition between the corporation whose stock is so acquired and the corporation making the acquisition or to restrain such commerce in any section or community or tend to create a monopoly of any line of commerce."

of a line of commerce." [7] In the present case the suit was brought 30 years after the stock acquisition involved took place.

Third, the relevant market for purposes of determining whether there had been a substantial lessening of competition as a result of the stock acquisition in question was held to be the market for automobile finishes and fabrics and not the entire industrial market for finishes and fabrics of all sorts. The Court held that "automotive finishes and fabrics have sufficient peculiar characteristics and uses to constitute them products sufficiently distinct from all other finishes and fabrics to make them a 'line of commerce' within the meaning of the Clayton Act." [8] It was noted that General Motors accounted for upwards of two-fifths of the total sales of automotive vehicles in the United States and that in 1946 and 1947 du Pont supplied approximately two-thirds of General Motors' requirements for finishes and 40 to 50 per cent of its requirements for fabrics. Hence the requirements for establishing a violation of Section 7, namely, that the market involved be "substantial" and that the firm involved supply a "substantial" part of that market, were satisfied.

This holding stands in sharp contrast to that in the *Cellophane*[9] case a year earlier, in which du Pont was held not to have violated the Sherman Act despite the fact that it was one of only two producers of cellophane and accounted for 75 per cent of the output of that commodity. It was held that the relevant market was not that for cellophane but for all flexible wrapping materials and that cellophane's 17.9 per cent share of the latter market was too small to sustain a finding that du Pont was guilty of monopolizing within the meaning of Section 2 of the Sherman Act.

In addition to the foregoing specific findings the Court by implication made two further points. First, the percentage of stock ownership necessary to establish control may be substantially less than a majority. Under the circumstances of the present case du Pont's 23 per cent ownership in General Motors was found to be sufficient to establish control. Second, while it must be shown

[7] *U.S. v. du Pont*, p. 597.

[8] *Ibid.*, pp. 593–94.

[9] *U.S. v. E. I. du Pont de Nemours and Co.*, 351 U.S. 377 (1956). See also G. W. Stocking and W. F. Mueller, "The Cellophane Case and the New Competition," *Am. Econ. Rev.*, March 1955, XLV, 29–63.

that a vertical stock acquisition results in excluding competitors from a "substantial" share of the relevant market in order to establish a violation of Section 7 it is not necessary that they be completely excluded. In the present case competitors of du Pont supplied a substantial share of General Motor's requirements for finishes and fabrics and the bulk of its requirements for a number of other products which could have been secured from du Pont. As with the definition of the relevant market, the significance of the foregoing features of the present decision will depend upon future interpretations.

The Court also found it necessary to demonstrate that du Pont's commanding position as supplier of finishes and fabrics to General Motors was not achieved on competitive merit alone but resulted from the elimination of competitive suppliers consequent upon du Pont's stock acquisition. In support of its conclusion the Court reviewed the circumstances antecedent to the acquisition and documents purporting to show du Pont's purpose in making the acquisition. Some years prior to the acquisition of the General Motors stock the du Pont Company, long dominant in the manufacture of military and commercial explosives, had decided to expand its business into other fields. The expansion program was barely started, however, when the first world war intervened and made it necessary for du Pont greatly to enlarge its facilities for producing explosives. The need to find post-war uses for these enlarged facilities stimulated du Pont to continue its expansion program into other fields during the war years, $90 million being set aside for this purpose.

The trial court found evidence that at or near the time of du Pont's purchase of General Motors stock officials of du Pont were well aware that the latter was a large consumer of some of the commodities which their organization was producing in increasing quantities. John J. Raskob, then treasurer of du Pont, apparently was the principal promotor of the idea that his company should make an investment in General Motors in order to insure that it would supply a predominant share of the latter's requirements for finishes, fabrics, and other products. He was supported in this view by Pierre S. du Pont, then president of the du Pont Company, who had acquired personal holdings of General Motors stock in 1914, and by William C. Durant, founder and, for some time, president of General Motors. Two circumstances facilitated the eventual purchase of General Motors stock by du Pont. First, when Durant and the banking interests controlling General Motors deadlocked on the choice of a Board of Directors in 1915 they resolved the deadlock by agreeing to name Pierre S. du Pont chairman of the General Motors Board, and to make Pierre du Pont, Raskob, and two nominees of Pierre du Pont neutral directors. Second, $50 million of du Pont's $90 million expansion fund was still in hand. The first block of General Motors stock was purchased by du Pont in 1917. In recommending this purchase to the du Pont Finance Committee Raskob said that "Our interest in the General Motors Company will undoubtedly secure for us the entire Fabrikoid, Pyralin [celluloid], paint and varnish business of those companies, which is a substantial factor." [10] Du Pont's annual reports to its stockholders in 1917 and 1918 likewise emphasized that the purchase would result in the company obtaining a new and substantial market for its products. In view of the foregoing evidence the majority of the Supreme Court felt that there was no basis for concluding that the acquisition could qualify for Section 7's exemption of purchases made "solely for investment."

Immediately after the stock acquisition J. A. Haskell, du Pont's sales manager and vice president, became General Motors' vice president in charge of the operations committee, and documentary evidence revealed his intention to pave the way for more general adoption of du Pont products. . . .

The Court concluded that whereas prior to the stock acquisition du Pont's sales to General Motors were relatively insignificant, as a result of the foregoing activities "du Pont quickly swept into a commanding lead over its competitors, who were never afterwards in serious contention." [11] By 1921, 4 of General Motors' 8 operating divisions bought from du Pont their entire requirements of paints and varnishes; 5, their entire requirements of Fabrikoid; 4, their entire requirements of rubber cloth; and 7, their entire requirements of Pyralin. The Fisher Body division for many years refused to use du Pont products. The explanation probably is that

[10] Quoted in *U.S. v. du Pont*, p. 602.
[11] *Ibid.*, p. 603.

when General Motors acquired the Fisher Body Company a voting trust was established which gave the Fisher brothers more autonomy in the management of the business than was enjoyed by the other operating divisions and enabled them to withstand efforts of high-ranking du Pont and General Motors executives to induce them to switch to du Pont from their accustomed sources of supply.

The Court conceded that "Competitors did obtain higher percentages of the General Motors business in later years although never high enough at any time substantially to affect the dollar amount of du Pont's sales." [12] It also conceded that "considerations of price, quality and service (of the products concerned) were not overlooked by either du Pont or General Motors" but held that the wisdom of this business judgment could not obscure the fact "plainly revealed by the record, that du Pont purposely employed its stock to entrench itself as a primary supplier of General Motors' requirements for automotive finishes and fabrics." [13] Finally, the fact that the executives of both companies acted fairly and on the basis of honest conviction concerning the best interests of their respective companies, without any attempt to overreach du Pont's competitors or anyone else, was dismissed as irrelevant on the ground that it was not necessary to show intent to restrain competition or to create a monopoly in order to prove a violation of Section 7.

Justice Burton, joined by Justice Frankfurter, in a long minority opinion attacked the reasoning and conclusions of the majority. The minority's reading of the legislative history of the Clayton Act convinced them that vertical acquisitions of stock were to be reached, if at all, only by provisions of the Clayton Act other than Section 7. They pointed out that for 40 years this interpretation of Congressional intent had been followed administratively by the Department of Justice and Federal Trade Commission and contended that this should be regarded as persuasive evidence of the proper scope of Section 7. They objected to the majority's ruling that lawfulness at the time of the suit rather than at the time of the stock acquisition was controlling, on the ground that "The result is to subject a good-faith stock acquisition, lawful when

[12] *Ibid.*, p. 605.
[13] *Ibid.*, p. 606.

made, to the hazard that the continued holding of the stock may make the acquisition illegal through unforeseen developments," and that "such a view is not supported by the statutory language and violates elementary principles of fairness." [14]

The majority were accused of being guilty of a logical fallacy in concluding that "because du Pont over a long period supplied a substantial portion of General Motors' requirements of paints and fabrics, its position must have been obtained by misuse of its stock interest rather than competitive considerations." [15] In support of the contrary interpretation the minority pointed out that each of the General Motors operating divisions bought independently and that the volume of purchases from du Pont varied greatly from one division to another; that although du Pont is General Motors' principal paint supplier the latter in recent years had bought as much as 30 per cent of its paint from competitors; that du Pont has had much less success than its competitors in selling to General Motors products other than finishes and fabrics; and that the fact that du Pont supplies a larger proportion of General Motors' requirements of finishes and fabrics than of other automobile manufacturers can be explained on grounds other than its stock interest in General Motors. For example, Ford follows the policy of making most of its own finishes and fabrics, with du Pont supplying most of these materials which the company itself does not manufacture. Chrysler follows the policy of selecting for each product a single supplier to whom it can be the most important customer, choosing Pittsburgh Plate Glass for paint and Texileather for fabrics.

The minority dismissed the documentary evidence relied upon by the majority to prove du Pont's intent to secure noncompetitive preferences—the letters and reports of Raskob, Haskell, and others—as being in each case "a matter of disputed significance which cannot be evaluated without passing on the motivation and intent of the author." [16] It was said that, read in the context of the situations to which they were addressed, they were consistent with the District Court's conclusion that no restriction was placed

[14] *Ibid.*, p. 622.
[15] *Ibid.*, p. 643.
[16] *Loc. cit.*

on General Motors' freedom to buy as it chose and that General
Motors' buyers did not regard themselves as being in any way
restricted. The minority also contended that the Supreme Court
should have accepted the lower court's interpretation of the facts
in the case, since its findings were supported both by contemporaneous documents and by oral testimony and since the question
of the credibility of the witnesses was of great importance and
the trial judge was in a position to evaluate their credibility at
first hand.[17]

Finally, economists may be interested in the minority's criticism
of the Court's concept of the relevant market. They held that the
record did not support the majority's decision that the relevant
market was that for automotive finishes and fabrics; on the other
hand, the record did show that other finishes and fabrics were
competitive with those in question, and that therefore the relevant
market was that for all industrial finishes and fabrics. The
majority were criticized for including sales of du Pont's "Dulux,"
which is not used on automobiles, in computing du Pont's share
of the market for automotive finishes and for excluding the sales
of its "Duco" automotive finishes which are made for nonautomotive uses.[18] The comment was made, à la Schumpeter,[19] that "If

---

[17] Two principal criticisms of the *du Pont* decision from a legal standpoint
are suggested by the above discussion of the minority opinion. One concerns
the proper scope of judicial review; it is said that the lower court's findings
of fact should have been sustained since they were not clearly erroneous and
were supported both by oral testimony and contemporaneous documents. The
other criticism is that in holding that the original Section 7 applied to vertical
as well as horizontal acquisitions and that lawfulness at the time of bringing
suit rather than at the time of acquisition was controlling, the Court disregarded 40 years of administrative interpretation and all the precedents
except one lower-court decision. Underlying this criticism is the contention
that regard for precedent gives predictability to law and guards against ca-
pricious or illogical changes in rulings, and that if precedents become out-
moded as a result of changing conditions or changing social policies the
proper remedy is legislative action.

[18] If the relevant market were taken to be that for all du Pont finishes for
both automotive and nonautomotive uses General Motors' share in recent
years, according to the minority, would range from 14 to 25 per cent. While
this is considerably smaller than the share as computed by the majority's
method it would still seem to be "substantial."

[19] J. A. Schumpeter, *Capitalism, Socialism and Democracy,* 3rd ed. (New
York, 1950), Ch. 7, 8.

Duco is to be treated as a separate market solely because of its initial superiority, du Pont is being penalized rather than rewarded for contributing to technological advance." [20] On the basis of the minority's definition, du Pont's share of the relevant market in 1947 was less than 3.5 per cent for finishes and about 1.6 per cent for fabrics. From this it was concluded that the Clayton Act was not violated by du Pont's stock acquisition because it did not foreclose competitors from a substantial share of the relevant market or significantly limit the competitive opportunities of others trading in that market.

Economists would disagree with the minority's contention that automotive finishes are indistinguishable from other industrial finishes or that Duco is indistinguishable from other finishes. The mere fact that the latter was a patented product is at least presumptive evidence that it is significantly differentiated from other finishes. Moreover each such differentiated product has a distinct market; whether the "relevant market" for antitrust purposes is to be considered the market for a single product in the narrowest sense or as comprising a group of markets of closely related products is necessarily a policy question depending upon what degree of monopoly power is regarded as permissible.

While the present decision extends the scope of the antitrust laws in ways described above this conclusion is subject to certain qualifications. First, the holding which extends the Clayton Act in its pre-1950 form to vertical stock acquisitions is not likely to be of great importance. It was early discovered that the original Clayton Act covered acquisitions of stock but not of assets;[21] in view of this loophole it is unlikely that there were many vulnerable stock acquisitions in the pre-1950 period. For the period since 1950 the holding is superfluous in view of the Celler amendments which extend the coverage of the Clayton Act to all types of mergers and acquisitions, vertical, horizontal, and conglomerate, whether achieved by the purchase of stock or the purchase of assets. Second, there are definite limitations on the retroactive

[20] *U.S. v. du Pont,* p. 651.

[21] See *F.T.C. v. Western Meat Co., Thatcher Mfg. Co. v. F.T.C., Swift and Co. v. F.T.C.,* 272 U.S. 554 (1926); *Arrow-Hart and Hegemann Electric Co. v. F.T.C.,* 291 U.S. 587 (1934).

aspect of the holding which permits suit to be brought at any time, following a stock acquisition, when a probable violation of the Clayton Act can be established. This is both because of the probable fewness of vulnerable stock acquisitions in the pre-1950 period and because of the need on the part of the antitrust enforcement agencies to conserve their time and resources for dealing with important current cases. Where acquisition of assets is involved there is the additional limitation that suit must be brought before the assets become scrambled to such an extent as to make divestiture impracticable. However, the holding in the present case is important in that it will enable the enforcement agencies to deal retroactively with some recent, post-1950, acquisitions, and by removing the time factor, especially in the case of stock acquisitions, should materially strengthen enforcement in the future.

The significance of the present case, as indicated at the outset, perhaps depends less upon what it decided, important though these points are, than upon the answers which will ultimately be given to the numerous important questions which it poses. For the case raises more questions than it answers. Since the decision rests to a large extent upon facts peculiar to the du Pont-General Motors relationship much uncertainty has been created concerning the extent to which a similar conclusion will be reached in future cases under Section 7 of the Clayton Act which involve different fact situations.[22] One area of uncertainty concerns the definition of the relevant market which will be adopted in future acquisition cases. Will a narrow concept of the relevant market comparable to that adopted in the present decision be retained in future Clayton Act cases? Will a narrow concept of the relevant market be adopted in Clayton Act cases while a broader definition is retained (following the precedent of the *Cellophane* decision) in Sherman Act cases?

A second area of uncertainty concerns the percentage of ownership by one corporation in another which will be vulnerable under Section 7. Under the circumstances of the present case du Pont's 23 per cent ownership of General Motors stock was held to be

---

[22] See also Betty Bock, "Antitrust Polarity: The Two du Pont Decisions," *Conference Board Bus. Record,* July 1957, XIV, 325–31.

sufficient to establish the fact of control. However, it cannot be assumed that this is necessarily a firm figure; the percentage of ownership which will be held to establish the fact of control may be higher or lower in future cases under Section 7 depending upon the degree of interference by the acquiring corporation in the affairs of the corporation a stock interest in which has been acquired, the absolute size and market shares of the acquiring and acquired corporations, and other factors.

A related question concerns the extent to which the rulings in the du Pont case with regard to the relevant market and percentage of ownership necessary to establish the fact of control will serve as precedents in future cases involving joint stockholdings by two or more corporations in a third corporation. Another related question concerns the possible bearing of the present case upon vertical integration involving the acquisition of the entire capital stock or assets of a customer or supplier corporation. In view of the fact that since 1950 the Clayton Act has applied to acquisitions of assets as well as of stock the question arises whether a corporation will be more or less vulnerable if it acquires, or has acquired, a customer or supplier corporation outright than if it acquires merely partial stock ownership. More specifically, will a concept of the relevant market comparable to that adopted in the present case be adopted in cases involving complete vertical integration? In this connection much importance attaches to the outcome of the pending Federal Trade Commission complaint against the acquisition by the Union Carbide and Carbon Corporation of the assets of the Visking Corporation, one of its principal customers. This is the Commission's first action against a so-called "forward-vertical" merger.

A third area of uncertainty concerns the bearing of the absolute size and market shares of the acquiring and acquired firms upon the vulnerability of acquisitions under Section 7. Would the present decision have been different if one or both of the industries represented by du Pont and General Motors were less concentrated, or if the market share of either or both of these firms had been smaller? What is the minimum market share which could qualify as "substantial" within the meaning of the Clayton Act? Would the decision have been different if the absolute size, as distinct from the market share, of du Pont and/or General Motors had been materially smaller?

A final question concerns the remedies which will be invoked to give effect to the Supreme Court's decision in the du Pont case. The Supreme Court in remanding the present case to the District Court noted that the latter had "wide discretion" in adapting remedies to the requirements of the individual case. The question of remedies in the present proceeding is particularly difficult because of the magnitude of the divestiture involved. The sale of du Pont's holdings of some 63 million shares of General Motors, currently worth about $2.4 billion, would represent the largest government-ordered disposal of property ever made. Sale of the stock in the open market over any short period would drastically depress the price of the shares and might have other undesirable repercussions. Even assuming that it were possible to dispose of the stock on the open market without appreciable depression of its price this solution would be undesirable from du Pont's standpoint because of tax considerations. The Company would be subject to a huge capital gains tax—estimated at between $500 and $600 million—while the du Pont stockholders would pay income taxes at the regular rates on such part of the proceeds as might be distributed in dividends.

The government has filed a divestiture plan intended to accomplish the eventual disposal of the General Motors stock while minimizing the foregoing difficulties. The plan calls for depositing all of the General Motors stock with a court-appointed trustee who, in turn, would parcel it out over a ten-year period to du Pont stockholders other than Christiana Securities Company, Delaware Realty and Investment Corporation, and stockholders of the latter. The distribution would be made in proportion to each shareholder's interest in the du Pont Company. . . . The purpose of these arrangements is to prevent an important residue of common control of du Pont and General Motors from remaining in the hands of the du Pont family.

The government's plan prohibits du Pont, Christiana, and Delaware from acquiring or holding, directly or indirectly, any General Motors stock or from exercising any kind of influence or control over General Motors. Du Pont and General Motors are prohibited from having interlocking directorates and common officers; from entering into any agreement, understanding, or arrangement for joint ownership or operation of any commercial or manufacturing enterprise; and from granting exclusive patent rights to each other. In addition, du Pont and General Motors are prohibited from entering into any contract, agreement, or understanding which requires that General Motors purchase any specific percentage of its requirements of any product from du Pont, or which grants to du Pont the first or a preferential right to manufacture or sell any chemical discovery made by General Motors.

The foregoing analysis, in the opinion of the writer, demonstrates that the *du Pont* decision materially increases the ability of the enforcement agencies to maintain if not enhance the strength of competitive forces in the economy, and that potentially its influence in this direction could be much greater. The decision will, therefore, be applauded by those who favor a strong antimonopoly policy, but even those who oppose such a policy and the larger number who are defeatists concerning its possibilities would find it difficult to deny that stockholdings of the type here involved make little or no economic contribution from the social viewpoint and that, potentially at least, they may be socially disadvantageous. The Celler amendments and the *du Pont* decision have materially increased the stature of Section 7 of the Clayton Act, but whether the decision deserves the appellation of "sleeping giant" will depend upon future judicial rulings concerning the numerous important questions which the decision poses.

11 BETHLEHEM-YOUNGSTOWN:

A Test Case

Present merger law centers about Section 7 of the Clayton Act as amended in 1950. The first case under the revised Section 7 involved the proposed merger between the Bethlehem Steel Company and the Youngstown Sheet and Tube Company.[1] All of the elements of a major decision were present in this litigation. Because it was recognized as a test case and both sides presented and concentrated their efforts on economic arguments pertinent to the statute, the case became a landmark in merger litigation. The arguments and decisions revolved about the market and the product definitions, since these are central to the lessening of competition and the creation of monopoly problems. More than any of the earlier cases, the Bethlehem case involved several alternative decisions on each issue. As will be noted, there is no necessary inconsistency in either arguing or upholding the existence of several relevant lines of commerce or market areas, as each overlaps with one or more of the other alternatives.

The existence of alternative market areas or lines of commerce would be accepted by most economists. Nevertheless, the relevance of a particular market would vary with the business practices, time,

[1] United States v. Bethlehem Steel Corporation and The Youngstown Steel and Tube Corporation, 168 F. Supp. 576 (1958).

and other considerations. In this antitrust suit Bethlehem sought to show that the merger would permit expansion into new areas and facilitate greater competition with United States Steel, the country's largest steel producer. The argument was not accepted by the court, which argued: "A merger may have a different impact in different markets—but if the proscribed effect is visited on one or more relevant markets then it matters not what the claimed benefits may be elsewhere." The court, therefore, held that the anticompetitive effects, which were held to exist on both vertical and horizontal bases, precluded the merger. The court also rejected Bethlehem's claim that flexibility of production resources rather than their peculiar characteristics and uses, identified the relevant product lines. Bethlehem contended, in effect, that the merger was a conglomerate one, since only *de minimus* competition existed within common product lines. With its philosophical argument thus structured, the court was able to consider alternative proposals; these considerations are indicated in the following excerpts from the decision.

....

UNITED STATES
v.
BETHLEHEM STEEL CORPORATION AND THE YOUNGSTOWN SHEET AND TUBE COMPANY
168 F. SUPP. 576 (1958)

Weinfeld, District Judge.

The Government seeks to enjoin a proposed merger between the defendants, Bethlehem Steel Corporation and The Youngstown Sheet and Tube Company, on the ground that it would violate section 7 of the Clayton Act, as amended.

Under the proposed merger Bethlehem is to acquire all the assets and properties of Youngstown pursuant to an agreement between them entered into on December 11, 1956. Prior to the execution of the agreement the defendants applied to the Department of Justice for clearance and submitted in support of their request detailed data pertaining to themselves, to other companies in the iron and steel industry, and to the industry in general. The Department of Justice was of the opinion that the contemplated merger came within the ban of section 7 and refused clearance. When the defendants nonetheless executed the merger agreement the Government commenced this suit to block its consummation.

The contending positions of the parties can be understood only against the background and general pattern of the iron and steel industry, the making and distribution of steel and steel products, the nature, size and location of the companies in the industry, the nature of competition in the industry generally, and the relative positions of Bethlehem and of Youngstown. The parties are in irreconcilable dispute on what are the relevant markets both as to products and areas. The difficulty recognized by the Supreme Court "of laying down a rule as to what areas or products are competitive, one with another" is highlighted in this case.

I. THE IRON AND STEEL INDUSTRY

The iron and steel industry is one of the most important, if not the most important of all American industries. Indeed, in contemporary international terms, steel production is viewed as a basic measure of the strength and status of a country. The industry is commonly recognized as set apart and as a separate and distinct segment of American industry. . . .

The Process of Making Steel and Steel Products

The finished steel products sold to consuming industries by companies in the iron and steel industry have their origin in iron ore, coal and limestone. These raw materials, after preliminary processing, are combined in blast furnaces to produce molten pig iron. The iron is then combined with scrap steel in steel making furnaces, principally open hearth, to produce steel in a molten state. The molten steel is poured into moulds where it solidifies into ingots. The ingot is the first solid form in which most steel is made; it is the raw product from which all steel products except castings are made. Most ingots are not sold as such but are further processed by the steel producing company.

The Steel Consumer

The principal consumers of finished steel products include the automotive industry, warehouses and distributors, and the construction, container, oil and gas, rail transportation, electrical machinery and equipment and appliances industries. . . .

Size, Nature and Location of Companies in the Iron and Steel Industry

The iron and steel industry is a highly concentrated one. It is an oligopoly. Twelve integrated companies control 83% of the industry capacity. In all, as of January 1, 1957, the iron and steel industry consisted of 247 companies engaged in one or more processes of making steel products. There were 23 integrated, 61 semi-integrated, and 140 nonintegrated companies. In addition there were 12 producers of ferroalloys and 11 operators of merchant blast furnaces.

Integrated companies begin the manufacture of steel by mining the raw materials. They operate coke ovens, blast furnaces, steel making furnaces and rolling and finishing facilities. Semi-integrated companies do not operate blast furnaces which make pig iron. They purchase pig iron or steel scrap from which they manufacture steel. Nonintegrated companies purchase steel from integrated or semi-integrated companies and begin their manufacturing operations with the rolling of steel.

The 23 integrated companies own approximately 90% of the industry capacity for coke, blast furnace products, ingots and hot rolled products. The semi-integrated companies own over 9%

of the industry capacity for ingots and hot rolled products. The output of these companies is measured in millions of tons. Their gigantic size becomes graphic when it is noted that 39 of these companies are included in the 500 largest American industrial companies and that 16 of the 39 are not fully integrated.

The American Iron and Steel Institute, the acknowledged industry association, divides the country into six production districts for the purpose of reporting statistics of production and capacity. Four of these districts, which coincide with the highly industrialized northeast quadrant of the United States, contain about 89% of the industry's total ingot capacity, produce about 90% of the nation's ingots and consume approximately 83% of the national consumption of steel.

Position of Bethlehem and Youngstown in the Iron and Steel Industry

Bethlehem is the second largest company in the iron and steel industry; Youngstown is the sixth largest. . . .

Bethlehem and Youngstown are fully integrated from the mining of iron ore through the production of pig iron, steel ingots and various finished steel products. Both companies are further integrated vertically into the manufacture and sale of oil field equipment and other fabricated products. Both operate oil field supply stores in the oil producing regions of the country. Bethlehem has carried its integration into a number of fabricating fields not occupied by Youngstown. Youngstown is a source of supply for independent fabricators who compete with Bethlehem in the sale of certain fabricated products.

Bethlehem and Youngstown both produce and sell the principal products of the iron and steel industry including coke oven byproduct chemicals, pig iron, steel ingots, strip mill plates, hot rolled bars, track spikes, sucker rods, concrete reinforcement bars, wire rods, wire, hot rolled sheets, cold rolled sheets, hot rolled strip, cold rolled strip, electrolytic tinplate, hot dipped tinplate, black plate, buttweld pipe and electricweld pipe. In addition Bethlehem produces some

35 classes of finished steel products that Youngstown does not make. Youngstown produces and sells seamless pipe, stampings and pressed steel parts which are not produced by Bethlehem. However, Bethlehem competes with Youngstown in the sale of seamless pipe which Bethlehem does not manufacture but obtains from United States Steel.

About 75% of the combined capacity of Bethlehem and Youngstown for the production of finished steel products is represented by products which both companies produce and sell in common. In 1955 the combined sales of Bethlehem and Youngstown of these common products amounted to approximately $1.5 billion. . . .

Mergers and Acquisitions of Bethlehem and Youngstown

Much of the growth of both Bethlehem and Youngstown is attributable to mergers and acquisitions. . . .

Competition in the Iron and Steel Industry

There is no real price competition in the iron and steel industry. The record in this case establishes that United States Steel initiates the price changes for steel products and that its lead is followed by all other steel producers. With few exceptions, the mill price for each steel product does not vary significantly from company to company.

A principal form of competition in the steel industry is the assurance to buyers of continuing sources of supply. . . . An assured source of supply is extremely important; it is so important to a steel consumer that he regards a stable and continuing relationship with a supplier of greater importance than price. . . .

Another consideration influencing the buyer's choice is the desire to purchase from a steel company which does not manufacture the same products to avoid dependency on a competitor for his raw material. . . .

Competition in the steel industry is sometimes reflected in the absorption of freight. . . .

II. THE RELEVANT MARKET

A horizontal merger can affect competition in at least two ways. It can have an impact not only on the competitors of the merged companies but also on the buyers who must rely upon the merged companies and their competitors as sources of supply. The purpose of section 7 is to guard against either or both effects of a merger—if the likely consequence is substantially to lessen competition or to tend to create a monopoly. The section 7 market must therefore be considered with reference to the two groups—(1) the competitors of the merged companies and (2) the buyers who would be dependent upon the merged companies and their competitors as sources of supply. While both impacts of a merger are interrelated and in an ultimate sense feed on each other, the major impact in some cases will be on the buyers and in other cases on the competitors of the merged companies. . . .

Line of Commerce

The Government contends that a line of commerce is any product or group of products that has peculiar characteristics and uses, which make it distinguishable from all other products. It predicates its position upon the definition of line of commerce by the Supreme Court in the du Pont-General Motors case. . . .

The defendants reject all the lines of commerce advanced by the Government. While they do not deny that a number of these products have peculiar characteristics and uses, they challenge the standard of peculiar characteristics and uses as appropriate for determining the lines of commerce in the steel industry and for assessing the competitive consequences of the merger. Their position is that lines of commerce must be defined with primary emphasis on the process of producing steel products and also with emphasis on the availability of substitute products. They refer to (1) the production flexibility concept and (2) the substitute products concept. The former relates to the capacity of a steel producer to shift from product to product; the latter to competition offered by substitute products.

. . . Since the availability of ingots limits the ultimate output of finished products, the defendants would regard ingots as the basic line of commerce because ingot capacity best reflects the competitive potential of each company; however, they do not urge it because ingots are not ordinarily sold as such. Instead, since the ingot is further processed into finished steel products, the defendants contend that the finished steel products produced by both Bethlehem and Youngstown—"common finished steel products"—constitute a line of commerce. They urge that this is the appropriate line of commerce because it comprises the products that are actually sold by both companies and takes into account the ability of each to allocate ingots among such products.

At this point a recapitulation of the lines of commerce with respect to steel products[1] as advocated by the parties may be helpful to the ensuing discussion.

Government's Line of Commerce	Defendants' Line of Commerce	
Broad Line	Broad Line	
Iron and steel industry	*Common finished steel products*	
Separate Lines	Separate Lines	
1. Hot rolled sheets 2. Cold rolled sheets	(1)	*sheet and strip mill products,* including hot rolled sheets, cold rolled sheets, galvanized sheets and hot and cold rolled strip
3. Hot rolled bars 4. Track spikes	(2)	*bar mill products,* including merchant bars, hot rolled bars, bar size shapes, track spikes, cold finished bars and sucker rods
5. Tin plate	(3)	*tin mill products,* including electrolytic and hot dipped tin plate, hot dipped terne plate and black plate
6. Buttweld pipe 7. Electricweld pipe 8. Seamless pipe	(4)	*pipe,* including buttweld pipe, electricweld pipe, seamless pipe, nonferrous metal and plastic pipe

[1] Oil field equipment and supplies are treated separately.

. . . But however competition is defined and whatever its form or intensity, it always involves interplay among and between both buyers and sellers. Any definition of line of commerce which ignores the buyers and focuses on what the sellers do, or theoretically can do, is not meaningful.

The evidence establishes that the defendants' production flexibility of mill product line theory is indeed pure theory. In practice steel producers have not been quick to shift from product to product in response to demand. Moreover, the evidence establishes that the continuing relationships between buyers and sellers in the steel industry make such shifts unlikely. The inappropriateness of the defendants' production flexibility or mill product line theory is further exposed by the inconsistent positions they have themselves taken.

The products of the iron and steel industry as a group are generally standardized, are not subject to the vagaries of style appeal, and have peculiar characteristics and uses for which there are no effective substitutes. The manufacture of such products requires special know-how and experience, huge capital investment and a trained labor force. The products of the iron and steel industry are generally distinct one from the other and as a group distinct from the products of other industries. They are sold in a recognized market with its own competitive standards. The iron and steel industry is commonly recognized by its members as well as the community at large as a separate industry. It has its own trade association, treating the industry as separate and distinct. In the light of these facts the conclusion is warranted that the sum of all the products of the iron and steel industry constitute a line of commerce. Since Bethlehem and Youngstown both produce and sell the principal products of the iron and steel industry, it is an appropriate line of commerce for analyzing the effect of this merger.

With respect to the iron and steel industry, four sets of statistics serve as guides in considering the impact of the proposed merger on competition—(1) blast furnace capacity and production, (2) ingot capacity and production, (3) shipments of all finished steel products and (4) shipments of "common finished steel products." . . .

Upon all the evidence the Court finds that the following are the appropriate lines of commerce: (1) the iron and steel industry as a whole; (2) hot rolled sheets; (3) cold rolled sheets; (4) hot rolled bars; (5) track spikes; (6) tin plate; (7) buttweld pipe; (8) electricweld pipe; (9) seamless pipe; (10) oil field equipment and (11) oil field equipment and supplies.

It is not necessary to analyze separately and in detail each line of commerce as found by the Court, since a merger violates section 7 if the proscribed effect occurs in any line of commerce "whether or not that line of commerce is a large part of the business of any of the corporations involved" or "where the specified effect may appear on [an] * * * industry-wide scale. The purpose of [section 7] is to protect competition in each line of commerce in each section of the country." . . .

Section of the Country

The Government's basic position is that for the iron and steel industry as a whole and for the various component lines of commerce included therein the appropriate geographic market is the nation as a whole. In addition it proposes several alternative sections, from the single states of Michigan and Ohio to several groupings of states, the largest of which coincides with the northeast quadrant of the United States. These separate areas which the Government proposes as alternatives to the nation as a whole are predicated on the fact that they are areas into which Bethlehem and Youngstown each ships substantial percentages of its total shipments and are the areas which are the most substantial and significant consuming centers for the industry as a whole—appreciable segments of the market.

The defendants reject all the sections of the country advanced by the Government. They divide the country into three parts, Eastern, Mid-Continent and Western which they urge as the relevant sections of the country. The defendants' basic position is that the geographic market is the area in which a company is an "effective competitor" in the sense of being a strong factor in competition. . . . The effect of the defendants' tri-partite division is that the productive capacity of each defendant is separate from the other —that in no section do both companies have steel producing capacity. Thus all the Bethlehem plants are confined to the Eastern and Western Areas and all of Youngstown's to the Mid-Continent Area.

The substance of the defendants' argument is: that within each of the three areas there are natural or regional markets adjacent to the locations of the steel plants; that steel consumers prefer to purchase from steel plants which are located nearby in order to avoid excess freight charges; that steel producers prefer customers located nearby in order to reduce freight absorption when that is necessary; that the greater the distance between the customer and the steel plant, the less effective is the steel plant in the competition for the customer's business; that the competitive force of a steel plant's shipments decreases as sales are made further away from the so-called natural market. . . .

Assuming arguendo that the defendants' standard for determining sections of the country is proper, although this is disputed by the Government, the facts do not support their tri-partite division of the country. . . .

The defendants seek to mitigate the force of their shipments into Michigan and other areas distant from their plants by contending that such shipments are unique because they are made to so-called deficit areas. However, the imbalance between local supply and local demand is a normal condition of this industry. . . .

The imbalance between local supply and local demand makes freight costs only a marginal factor. The steel companies in order to keep their plants at as close to capacity as costs dictate must ship into shortage areas, and freight costs and absorption are simply incidents of doing business. . . .

Many theoretical concepts were advanced to support the defendants' claim that neither is an "effective competitor" of the other and that as to each submarket that may exist in the Mid-Continent Area, Bethlehem is a relatively minor factor; that as to each submarket that may exist in the Eastern and Western Areas, Youngstown is a relatively minor factor. But these theoretical concepts must yield to the facts which have persisted in this industry through the years and reflect an industry pattern. . . .

The persistent and substantial shipments by Bethlehem indicate that it does overcome freight barriers and competes effectively with

Youngstown and the other steel companies whose plants are located in the Mid-Continent Area. . . .

Application of these criteria to the facts of this case lead to the conclusion that the proposed merger may be analyzed against the nationwide market for steel, as well as against the smaller geographic areas where the impact may be felt. . . .

. . . But while the heart of the nation's market for steel is the northeast quadrant there is no reason for separating from it the remaining 27 states which consume but 17% of national consumption and which are affected directly by the competitive situation in the northeast quadrant; particularly since 25 of these 27 states receive but fractional shares, less than 1%, of total industry shipments. The competitive standards in all other consuming centers are so dependent on, and influenced by, what happens in the dominant northeast quadrant that they should be analyzed together.

An economically significant area in an industry cannot be determined with the precision of a surveyor. In considering the anticompetitive consequences of a merger there is nothing sacred about the boundary lines of a state. The impact may manifest itself in an appreciable segment of a market which may coincide with a political subdivision of a state, a state, a combination of states or the nation.

III. IMPACT OF THE PROPOSED MERGER ON COMPETITION

There may be a substantial lessening of competition or tendency to monopoly when a merger substantially increases concentration, eliminates a substantial factor in competition, eliminates a substantial source of supply, or results in the establishment of relationships between buyers and sellers which deprive their rivals of a fair opportunity to compete. The proposed merger between

Bethlehem and Youngstown would have each of these proscribed effects. The substantiality of these effects is beyond question.

Increase in Concentration

A major purpose of section 7 is to ward off the anticompetitive effects of increases "in the level of economic concentration resulting from corporate mergers and acquisitions." . . .

Both United States Steel (with 30%) and Bethlehem (with 15%) are at present substantially larger than their competitors. . . . Increasing the concentration in United States Steel and Bethlehem would make even more remote than at present the possibility of any real competition from the smaller members of the industry who follow the leadership of United States Steel.

The increased concentration which would result from the merger cannot be considered in a vacuum; it cannot be divorced from the history of mergers and acquisitions, which in large measure accounts for the existing high degree of concentration in the industry. The substantiality of the shares of ingot capacity and shares of shipments of steel products held by Bethlehem and Youngstown take on added significance in the light of this history.

. . . The prospect of a new entrant to replace an absorbed Youngstown, either in terms of capital investment or experience, is in the light of the history of this industry, practically nihil. . . .

The new entrants have made no real dent as far as the larger integrated companies are concerned. . . .

These considerations compel the conclusion that the merger offends the statute, and that in end result there is more than a reasonable probability that it would substantially lessen competition and tend to create a monopoly. But apart from the adverse consequence of increased concentration of economic power, other factors even more directly establish that there would, in fact and in immediate terms, be a substantial lessening of competition—

the elimination of actual and direct competition between the two defendants.

Lessening of Competition

. . . Bethlehem's and Youngstown's combined 1955 shipments of these three principal products to common customers in Michigan and Ohio totaled 1,131,000 tons or about 40% of their combined shipments of 2,948,510 tons of "common finished steel products" to all their customers in these states. The 2,948,510 tons represented 14.8% of the 19,930,000 tons of total industry shipments of "common finished steel products" to the two states. Bethlehem's and Youngstown's sales of the three principal products to common customers in Michigan and Ohio represented 5.7% of total industry shipments of all "common finished steel products" to the two states. These *shipments* by the defendants of but three common products to common customers in only two states involved more tonnage than the *ingot capacity* of each of 64 of the nation's 84 companies with such capacity as of January 1, 1957.

The situation with respect to the iron and steel industry as a whole, buttweld pipe, hot rolled sheets, cold rolled sheets, and hot rolled bars demonstrates the substantiality of each defendant's competitive force in the relevant markets and the substantial anticompetitive effects which would follow in the wake of the proposed merger. But other constrictions of competition are also evident.

Vertical Aspects of the Proposed Merger

The proposed merger is primarily horizontal. Both Bethlehem and Youngstown are engaged in the same business—producing and selling the principal products of the iron and steel industry. However, there are also significant vertical aspects of the merger. Bethlehem is integrated into a number of steel fabricating fields not occupied by Youngstown. There are small independent fabricators of steel, competitors of Bethlehem, who would be deprived of the availability of Youngstown as a substantial source of supply of the steel products which are the raw materials for the products they sell in competition with Bethlehem. These small independent competitors of Bethlehem would also be deprived of Youngstown as a market for various of their products which are also made by Bethlehem but not by Youngstown and which Youngstown presently purchases from them.

Oil Field Equipment and Supplies

. . . Thus the proposed merger would have both horizontal and vertical impact with respect to oil field equipment and supplies. As to the sale of all these products and the production of some, the impact would be horizontal. To the extent that Youngstown purchases some of these products from others and to the extent that Bethlehem produces some of these products, like wire rope and slush pumps, not produced by Youngstown, there would be a foreclosure of substantial outlets for the companies which have been supplying Youngstown's requirements.

The proposed merger would (1) eliminate the substantial competition between Bethlehem and Youngstown in the production and sale of oil field equipment and supplies; (2) result in the foreclosure of a substantial portion of the market for oil field equipment and supplies produced by other companies; and (3) result in a substantial increase in concentration in the oil field equipment industry in the hands of the integrated steel companies since Bethlehem, Youngstown, United States Steel and Armco account for about 47% of the total industry shipments of oil field equipment; thereafter three instead of four integrated companies would control this percentage.

IV. CONCLUSION

To sum up the Court's conclusions as to the impact of the merger, it is clear that the acquisition of Youngstown, by Bethlehem, would violate section 7 in that in each of the relevant markets considered the effect may be substantially to lessen competition or to tend to create a monopoly.

The proposed merger would eliminate the present substantial competition between Bethlehem and Youngstown in substantial relevant markets. It would eliminate substantial potential competition between them. It would eliminate a substantial independent alternative source of supply for all steel consumers. It would eliminate Youngstown as a vital source of supply for independent fabricators who are in competition with Bethlehem in the sale of certain fabricated steel products. It would eliminate Youngstown as a substantial buyer of certain fabricated steel products.

Any alleged benefit to the steel consumer in the Chicago district because of reduced freight charges and an increased supply, cannot, under the law, be bought at the expense of other consumers of numerous other steel products where the effects of the merger violate the Act. A merger may have a different impact in different markets—but if the proscribed effect is visited on one or more relevant markets then it matters not what the claimed benefits may be elsewhere. . . .

The Court concludes that there is a reasonable probability that the merger of Bethlehem and Youngstown would, in violation of section 7, substantially lessen competition and tend to create a monopoly in:

1. the iron and steel industry
2. hot rolled sheets
3. cold rolled sheets and
4. hot rolled bars, in
    a. the United States as a whole
    b. the northeast quadrant of the United States
    c. Michigan, Ohio, Pennsylvania and New York
    d. Michigan and Ohio
    e. Michigan, and
    f. Ohio
5. buttweld pipe
6. electricweld pipe
7. seamless pipe
8. oil field equipment
9. oil field equipment and supplies
10. tin plate

11. track spikes, and
12. wire rope, in
    a. the United States as a whole.

．．

[The *Bethlehem* decision has been strongly criticized on "economic" grounds by Professor M. A. Adelman,[2] among others. A principal criticism (directed toward the court's economic reasoning) is that the court should have recognized the merger as a conglomerate one (thus lacking any competitive or structural competitive effects) while holding that conglomerate mergers could violate the antitrust laws. The failure to adopt this stance resulted in the court's particular definition of products and markets, designed to show that merger was not a conglomerate one. In Adelman's opinion, the case is important for holding that, in a concentrated market with a lack of strong competition, a merger serving to increase concentration would be violative of Section 7 of the Clayton Act; this is, of course, a lesser requirement than under the Sherman Act. The court's market definition was concerned with product attributes and area components rather than with the scope of adjustments in supply in response to price changes to which Adelman and most other economists would adhere. With this definition as his restraint, Adelman is then unable to accept the Bethlehem definition. With a professed belief that both du Pont cases stated the same requirements for defining product lines, the court is attacked for its product-line definition. If the producers do shift between the several specific iron and steel products, then the iron and steel industry is the relevant product line; if not, then the industry should not be identified as the relevant product line. The court considered the general industry and the individual products as alternatives, along with a third possibility, the share of ingot capacity controlled by the parties. This seems to be a superfluous confusion. Additionally, dissatisfaction

[2] M. A. Adelman, "Economic Aspects of the Bethlehem Opinion," *Virginia Law Review*, 45 (1959), 684–696.

has also been directed toward the importance of very short-term substitution as a factor in determining a Section 7 market. The use of alternative markets is subject to criticism on the same grounds as the alternative product lines used by the court. Critics argue that a given area cannot simultaneously be a market less than and more than the same market. If it is recognized that the degree of competition will vary throughout a market and probably be strongest at a focal point, then this condition defines a single market and not several separate ones. In this instance the market might be the northeast quadrant of the United States, since this binds the several sources and users of iron and steel products. Adelman has speculated that the alternative product and market lines were provided as a safeguard against reversal upon appeal. Some other issues, such as the statement that the possible benefits of a merger will not be sufficient to overcome any illegal features, serve to spice the criticisms of this decision and of the general trend of merger decisions.

On the other hand, an article by Dr. L. S. Keyes is concerned with the standards employed by the court in reaching a decision. Keyes fears that a concentration level or market-share standard will be adopted for antitrust cases rather than a criterion concerning competition. She suggests that the competitiveness of firms be defined in each instance; this practice would aid in the judge's determination as to whether a noneligible share of commerce was concerned. Although antitrust economists are concerned with competition in the steel industry, some place more emphasis on the court's analysis while others are more concerned with the alternative applicable standards.]

....

The Bethlehem-Youngstown Case and
the Market-share Criterion
Lucile Sheppard Keyes

....

One of the most important unsolved problems in antitrust policy concerns the precise significance of the market share of the defendant in determining whether or not certain violations have occurred. Under Section 2 of the Sherman Act [1], it is apparently no longer true (if it ever was) that one-firm production of some (unspecified) large percentage of any more or less homogeneous product is usually sufficient to prove violation and justify dissolution. But beyond this, the content of the law remains uncertain. The leading recent decision [10] leaves unsettled two key points of interpretation: (1) the definition of "market control" or "monopoly power" as a necessary element in violation; (2) the need for some additional factor—such as exclusionary practices—to complete the crime of monopolizing.

At least until the new Section of the Clayton Act [2] [1] is interpreted by the Supreme Court, the role of the market-share concept in merger regulation must be similarly uncertain. However, the administration of the new Section [7, p. 519] and in particular the interpretation accepted by the District Court in what seems to be

Abridged from Lucile Sheppard Keyes, "The Bethlehem Youngstown Case and the Market-share Criterion," *The American Economic Review,* LI (September 1961), 643–657.

[1] In 1950, Section 7 of the original 1914 Act was strengthened by an amendment making it applicable to acquisitions of assets as well as of securities; eliminating the provision which limited the "substantial lessening of competition" relevant under the Act to that "between the acquiring and the acquired corporation"; and substituting the phrase "in any line of commerce in any section of the country" for the older "in any community" as a description of the sector of commerce within which illegal restraint might occur.

the major relevant case [9] tend to support the belief that this role will be of great practical significance in the treatment of "horizontal" mergers. It may well be that in this area the law will prohibit those mergers, and only those mergers, which would combine suppliers of "large" percentages of the output of some "product," or would increase the share of the "product" accounted for by a firm with an already "large" existing share. The aspects of the Bethlehem-Youngstown decision which appear to support such a prediction are, first, the amount of attention devoted to the definition of markets and to the calculation of the shares in these markets accounted for by the participants in the proposed merger, both individually and in combination; and, second, the treatment of the degree of concentration in the industry as a factor relevant to legality.

Let it be said at once that the same practical outcome—that is, the decision to enjoin the merger—could very likely have been wholly justified without any reference to shares or concentration, and this indeed without adducing any evidence not cited by Judge Weinfeld. It is what appears to be the main line of argument, rather than the resulting action, which can be criticized on economic grounds. This main line of argument is discussed in the first section of the present study. The second section outlines certain objections to the policy implied by this argument. Finally, an alternative approach to the problem of merger control is suggested.

I. THE COURT'S ARGUMENT

There is no doubt that Judge Weinfeld considered the definition of the affected markets to be one of the two most important questions to be considered in applying Section 7. In denying a motion for summary judgment, he declared [8, p. 879]:

> In broad outline, the essential ultimate issues which the Court is called upon to determine and as to which the Government has the burden of proof in order to sustain its charge that the proposed merger comes within the prohibition of Section 7 are: the line or lines of commerce and the section or sections of the country in which the effects of the merger may be felt, or as phrased by the

Supreme Court, the relevant market—"the area of effective competition" [11, p. 593]—and whether the merger may substantially lessen competition or tend to create a monopoly.

The main decision itself is to a large extent devoted to the selection of "lines of commerce" and "sections of the country" with reference to which the prospective impact of the proposed merger is to be measured.

Perhaps the most interesting aspect of this part of the decision is its attempt to distinguish between the market definition relevant under Section 2 of the Sherman Act and that appropriate under Section 7 of the Clayton Act—a distinction which would, in brief, make "reasonable interchangeability" the proper classificatory guide in the former context as against "peculiar characteristics and uses" in the latter. The significance of both definitions lies, of course, in their use to delimit the nature and quantity of outputs to be included in the global total—"the area of effective competition"—with which the defendants' outputs are to be compared. Needless to say, the definitional distinction made in Bethlehem-Youngstown does not indicate the real or purported discovery of some new economic principle which would take the place of substitutability in indicating competitiveness among the products of different firms. The distinction serves rather to epitomize the doctrine that a (somehow) different view of market definition is appropriate under Section 7 than under Section 2 of the Sherman Act, and in particular that the Cellophane case is not a proper precedent in cases involving the former Section. On this point, the decision reads [9, pp. 593–94, note]:

. . . the basic issue in the Cellophane case was that of monopoly power and the Supreme Court expressly limited the market definition there to the monopolization clause of §2 of the Sherman Act. There is a basic distinction between §2 of the Sherman Act and §7 of the Clayton Act. Further, monopoly power was defined by the Supreme Court in the Cellophane case as "the power to control prices or exclude competition." Obviously, when the question is power over price, substitute products may be relevant because they can limit that power. The issue under §7 . . . is not whether a merger may result in a company having power over price or the power to exclude competition . . . [it] is whether there is a reasonable probability of a substantial lessening of competition. There can be a substantial lessening of competition with respect to a product whether or not there are reasonably interchangeable substitutes. The merger of two producers of a product may substantially lessen competition or tend to create a monopoly in the market for that product even though it does not substantially lessen competition or tend to create a monopoly in the broader market embracing all the products which are reasonably interchangeable with that product. . . . This does not, however, mean that interchangeability can be ignored—a high degree of interchangeability may under certain circumstances make it more or less the same product. [Citations omitted.]

A simpler and, in the long run, probably more expedient way around the Cellophane doctrine would appear to have been available: that is, to accept the general relevance of imperfect substitutes in assessing the competitive position of a given firm (as is done by indirection in the last sentence of the passage quoted); but to require a smaller percentage share for a violation of Section 7 of the Clayton Act than would be necessary under the antimonopolization law. For the argument used here tends to undermine the entire orthodox rationale for the consideration of market shares in merger cases: If "the power to control prices or exclude competition" is not at issue under Section 7, then why invoke the elaborate apparatus of market definition and percentage share computation which is alleged to be specifically designed to measure "market control" or "monopoly power"—i.e., the power to control prices or exclude competition? Why not, for example, simply demonstrate that the two steel companies were satisfactory alternative sources of supply of the same or substitute products to some of the same buyers, and that the purchases of these buyers were "substantial" in terms of money value? Let me hasten to say that I do not believe that the orthodox case is valid under either Section: I merely mean to suggest that the attempted distinction does not seem entirely consistent with the rest of the Bethlehem-Youngstown decision.

At any rate, it does not appear that this decision has furnished an acceptable rule for market definition in merger cases which is any

more satisfactory in practice—that is, any more objectively de-
terminate—than that which would be appropriate under Section 2
of the Sherman Act. The suggestion that competition among imperfect substitutes can always be ignored under Section 7 must,
of course, be rejected. A merger involving two producers of imperfect substitutes obviously could have as much anticompetitive impact, in depriving buyers of alternative independent sources
of effective substitutes, as a merger between producers of perfect substitutes. And if it is admitted that the imperfect competition between the participants must be considered in determining
their premerger competitive relations, then it must also be admitted
that imperfect competition between the participants, on the one
hand, and the firms remaining outside, on the other, must be considered in assessing the expected competitive status of the proposed
combination.

An "asymmetrical" market definition—one which would use one
criterion for interparticipant competition and another for competition between the participants and outsiders—cannot be defended
in any way that I can see. In some circumstances, admitting the
relevance of nonhomogeneous competition will tend to weaken
the case against a proposed merger by enlarging the admitted area
of competition remaining after the merger, without any commensurate increase in the estimated amount of interparticipant competition (which the merger would quash). In other circumstances, the
effect may be reversed. The choice of market definition, like the
choice of a maximum legal percentage for market share, remains
subject to the same basic uncertainty here as under the Sherman
Act.

The purpose of the "line-of-product" discussion in the Bethlehem-
Youngstown decision was to define statistical categories of output
in order that the sales of each output by the participant firms might
be compared, in a given area, with the corresponding total sales
figure for all producers. Since it was quite properly concluded
that the steel companies compete for business throughout the United
States, subareas were selected simply by choosing sections accounting for a large proportion of total sales, and of the sales of each
defendant. . . . The list does not purport to exhaust the areas of
competition among the participant firms.

At the beginning of the present study, it was suggested that the Bethlehem-Youngstown case tends to support an interpretation of the law which could prohibit only those mergers which combine suppliers of "large" percentages of the output of some "product" or increase the share of a firm with an already "large" existing share. On the other hand, it must be admitted that the percentages at issue in this case, while certainly large as compared with the negligible share attributable to the member of a pure-competition industry, are small compared to the shares considered significant in Sherman Act cases, as may be seen in the accompanying tables (Tables 1 and 2). This relative smallness becomes more impressive when it is noted that the proposed merger was found to be (prospectively) in violation of the statute in *each* of the markets considered. The essential point is, however, that some minimum share may well be crucial in the law's application; furthermore, what may be large enough for one judge may be much too small for another.

TABLE 1—Percentage Ownership of Industry Capacity to Produce for the Twelve Largest Steel Producers (1957)

Company	Per Cent of Industry Capacity (Ingots)
U. S. Steel Corporation	29.7
Bethlehem Steel Company	15.4
Republic Steel Corporation	8.3
Jones and Laughlin Steel Corporation	4.9
Youngstown Sheet and Tube Company	4.7
National Steel Corporation	4.6
Armco Steel Corporation	4.5
Inland Steel Corporation	4.1
Colorado Fuel and Iron Corporation	2.1
Wheeling Steel Corporation	1.6
Sharon Steel Corporation	1.4
Ford Motor Co.	1.4

Source: [9, p. 585].

Nowhere in the decision is it actually stated that elimination of an independent source of an appreciable supply of a given product is *insufficient* to make a merger illegal if the resulting market share is not large enough. Moreover, it is expressly found, and therefore presumably considered relevant, that an amount of direct competition

TABLE 2—Percentage of Industry Shipments Accounted for by Bethlehem and Youngstown, Calendar Year 1955 (Except as Noted)

	Bethlehem	*Youngstown*	*Bethlehem-Youngstown*
Hot Rolled Sheets	20.1	5.7	25.8
Cold Rolled Sheets	16.9	7.7	24.6
Hot Rolled Bars	16.9	4.4	21.3
Track Spikes	19.1	9.9	29.0
Tin Mill Products[a]	16.3	5.1	21.4
Buttweld Pipe	11.1	13.6	24.7
Seamless Pipe	4.1	8.0	12.1
Electricweld Pipe[b]	1.3	6.9	8.2

[a] Principally tin plate.
[b] 1957 figures. Bethlehem has been producing electricweld pipe in commercial quantities only since May 1957.
Source: [9, p. 606].
Note: On page 614 of the decision, it is noted that "Bethlehem's supply stores accounted for 5.7% and Youngstown's for 6.7% of total industry sales" of oil field equipment and supplies in 1956.

both absolutely and relatively substantial would be eliminated by the merger of the two steel companies.[2] However, Judge Weinfeld's general statement of the meaning of the statute leaves this question in doubt;[3] and, as has been noted, the extended consideration of market shares and the emphasis on the concentration ratio tend to support the view suggested here. If it had been desired merely to show competitiveness between the two participants, this could have been accomplished without any excursion into the theory and practice of market definition. It would have been necessary only to show that some nonnegligible amount of dollar sales by each company was accounted for by orders for which the other company was a significant competitor: that is, for which the buyers would have substituted the other company's product, had it been offered at

[2] "About 75 per cent of the combined capacity of Bethlehem and Youngstown for the production of finished steel products is represented by products which both companies produce and sell in common. In 1955 the combined sales of Bethlehem and Youngstown of these common products amounted to approximately $1.5 billion" [9, p. 586].

[3] "There may be a substantial lessening of competition or tendency to monopoly when a merger substantially increases concentration, eliminates a substantial factor in competition, eliminates a substantial source of supply, or results in the establishment of relationships between buyers and sellers which deprive their rivals of a fair opportunity to compete" [9, p. 603].

the lowest cost-covering price, if the actual seller had withdrawn his supplies. (This suggested definition of "significant competitiveness" will be further discussed in Part III, below.)

Since it would not be necessary in this connection to calculate the degree of monopoly power resulting from the merger, or to predict the extent to which buyers are probably going to be worse or better off, there would be no need to define the relevant market, or to attempt to measure the effectiveness of competition either before or after the combination. Similarly, differences of opinion regarding the precise boundaries of competitive areas would not present crucial difficulties. It would be sufficient to show that there is some area of significant competition (as defined above) which would be eliminated by the proposed merger.

Apart from the significance attributed to the market shares accounted for by the participants themselves, and hence to the proposed merged firm, the decision apparently ascribes an independent importance to concentration of ownership in the steel industry as a whole: that is, to the fact that the concentrating effect of the merger would be added to an already high degree of over-all concentration. The following quotation illustrates this point [9, pp. 604–5]:[4]

A major purpose of Section 7 is to ward off the anticompetitive effects of increases "in the level of economic concentration resulting from corporate mergers and acquisitions" [12, p. 3]. . . . If Bethlehem were to acquire Youngstown the Big Two would have 50 per cent [of the national steel market]. . . . In sum, the merger of Bethlehem and Youngstown would bring together the second

---

[4] The following statement should also be considered in this connection [9, p. 583]: "A fair reading of both the Senate and House Committee Reports [regarding the 1950 amendment of Section 7] leaves no doubt as to its major objectives. As stated in those Reports they were, in some instances *in haec verba*, (1) to limit future increases in the level of economic concentration resulting from corporate mergers and acquisitions; (2) to meet the threat posed by the merger movement to small business fields and thereby aid in preserving small business as an important competitive factor in the American economy; (3) to cope with monopolistic tendencies in their incipiency and before they attain Sherman Act proportions; and (4) to avoid a Sherman Act test in deciding the effects of a merger." An intent to deter concentration does not, of course, justify *limiting* antimerger action to those cases where significant concentration exists or threatens to occur.

and sixth largest integrated steel companies with 23,000,000 and 6,500,000 tons of ingot capacity, respectively, giving Bethlehem almost 21 per cent of industry capacity. This would add substantially to concentration in an already highly concentrated industry and reduce unduly the already limited number of steel companies. The merger would increase concentration in the hands of the Big Four and the next three companies after U.S. Steel by 4.6 percentage points, which would be the greatest increase in concentration in the iron and steel industry [roughly, in any decade] from 1901 to 1958 . . . with the exception of the decade 1920 to 1930 when Bethlehem and other large companies were engaged in a series of important mergers and acquisitions.

Only if at least one of the participants is relatively large can an overall industrial concentration ratio be significantly affected by a merger. It is for this reason that the emphasis on the over-all ratio tends to reinforce the probable legal importance of the market shares of the participants.

Some aspects of the treatment of concentration in the Bethlehem-Youngstown decision may be thought of as differentiating this case from the general run of mergers, and as limiting the applicability of its doctrine to firms which are absolutely large [9, p. 586], show a past history of growth through merger [9, pp. 586–87], and are in industries where entry is extraordinarily difficult [9, pp. 606] or which are already characterized by a high degree of concentration. (On the other hand, the presence of "vertical" anticompetitive aspects [9, pp. 611–15] does not serve to differentiate this case, since prospective violation was found in several markets unaffected by these aspects.) However, it is hardly to be expected that Section 7 is henceforth to be enforced only with respect to giants in concentrated industries, or that an entirely different set of principles will be used with respect to nongiants. A somewhat less drastic differentiation appears more likely. For example, a larger share of the market, on the part of one or both participants, may well turn out to be legal in industries of smaller size, more favorable entry characteristics and less concentration, and with respect to applicants with little or no past history of growth through merger. Such a development as this would still leave the concept of market share in a key position in the application of Section 7.

II. OBJECTIONS TO THE COURT'S ARGUMENT

There are three main objectives to injecting the question of market share into the regulation of mergers. The first is that the definition of the relevant market and the determination of a proper limit for the share of any one firm are essentially wide-open questions, not subject to judicial determination in any one case and not subject to discovery by examination of similar past instances and averaging the results. The second is that the injection of this concept may very well unduly limit the application of the statute so that economically undesirable mergers may be permitted to escape its prohibition; moreover, it is also possible that certain economically desirable mergers may be prevented. The third is that these fundamental faults do not appear to be balanced by any compensating advantage. Certainly at least some of the advantages claimed for the suggested doctrine turn out upon examination to be nonexistent. These three objections will be discussed in turn.

As has been pointed out above, the question of market definition and determination of a proper limit for the share to be accounted for by any one firm is no less difficult here than under the Sherman Act. Moreover, the use of market share as a policy guide appears to have no real economic justification under either statute. In connection with monopolizing or merger, such a justification can hardly be found in any analogy with the virtually negligible share of industrial supply attributable to the pure competitor. Nor does it appear that a justification can be found in terms of the theory of "workable competition." As I have written [6, pp. 298–99] in connection with Section 2 of the Sherman Act, this theory:

> as applied to the antitrust problem issues in little more than a generalized prescription that any group of goods that "we think of as the 'same' product" should be sold by more than one firm (or "a considerable number of firms") none of which accounts for a "large" percentage of sales. In this form, the doctrine is too vague and too unreliable to be of use as a policy guide: too vague, because of the indistinct boundaries of the "product" concept fixing the area to be considered as within the industry (i.e., belonging to the relevant market), because of the lack of any clue as to how

many competitors within this boundary would be sufficient or as to what percentage of sales would be too large for any one firm, and because of the uncertain status (if any) given to the competition of substitutes outside the industry; too unreliable, because the mere counting of firms and figuring of percentages within any defined area of production is not an accurate measure of either the stimulus to the producer or protection to the consumer afforded by the presence and/or possibility of competition.

In view of the failure of these attempts to trace a dependable causal connection between market share and economic performance, with results suitable for use as a legislative or judicial guide, it is not surprising that more recent advocates of a policy of deconcentration have preferred to defend their proposals on essentially political grounds. Thus, Kaysen and Turner, in a work [4] which I have discussed in detail elsewhere [5], assert their belief that the adoption of improved economic performance as the primary goal of antitrust policy would "present definitional and administrative problems of such magnitude that consistent and sensible enforcement would be well-nigh impossible" [4, p. 49]. Their own program of deconcentration is justified as a means of eliminating "unreasonable market power"—an entity whose operational definition turns out to be rather complicated, but which appears to occur whenever a business management exercises some degree of continuing discretion with regard to price policy, and cannot prove that the ability to exercise this discretion arises from one or some of a short, enumerated list of causal factors [4, pp. 265–70]. The following passage sets forth their reasons for regarding the elimination of this "power" as a proper primary target for antitrust policy [4, pp. 48–49]:

Our positive reasons rest ultimately on a value judgment. The most important aspect of the competitive process is that it is self-controlling with regard to private economic power. For all the important qualifications and limitations of the doctrine of the invisible hand which modern economic analysis has produced, that doctrine remains the basic political justification for an enterprise economy in which major economic decisions are compelled and coordinated through the market. It is the fact that the competitive market *compels* the results of its processes which is the ultimate defense against the demand that economic decisions be made or supervised by politically responsible authorities. Without such market compulsion, that demand appears ultimately irresistible in a society committed to representative government.

It does not seem likely that this sort of demand will in fact be made; but be that as it may, the primary objective of the suggested policy is clearly to avoid certain alleged political dangers rather than to improve the functioning of markets in an economic sense.

The second argument against the percentage-share limitation is the practical consequence of the first: that is, that its economic influence may well be undesirable. A merger need not be relatively large-scale in order to be economically objectionable. The absorption of a small maverick by an average-sized competitor may easily have a more harmful effect than the marriage of two apathetic giants, in that in the former instance a promising source of new techniques of production or product variation, or of independent price experimentation, may be removed from the scene, whereas the latter might well leave everything essentially the same. Again, the disappearance of a firm is perhaps seldom just a matter of subtracting one from a list of sources of identical goods; there are in many cases certain needs, certain markets, which are less well served after any merger. There is, moreover, the ever-present possibility that the small firm might grow because of its superior merit. That this possibility cannot be predicted or assessed in advance does not make it any less real or important. Where a firm disappears as a result of losing business to its competitors, there is a presumption that these competitors' relative growth at the expense of the defunct firm is accompanied by some superiority in product or price; as will be pointed out below, there is no such presumption in connection with disappearance by merger.

In support of a policy of permitting all relatively small-scale mergers, certain arguments are frequently advanced which on examination do not appear valid. It is said that such a policy is necessary (1) to permit transactions that bring about cost savings and/or product improvements; (2) to provide that free market for the disposal of business assets which is necessary to promote maximum mobility of resources and justified investment of capital [7, p. 493]; and (3) to bring the treatment of mergers into line with the treatment of other restraints of trade which are subject to equally vague permissive limits.[5] The first point is cogent only with respect to mergers not merely sufficient but actually *necessary* to bring about the improvements involved. Should these instances turn out to be frequent enough or important enough individually to warrant a modification of antimerger policy for their accommodation, there seems to be no reason to suppose that an appropriate modification would take the form of a percentage-share limitation. A similar observation applies to the narrowing of the asset market by prohibiting firms from selling out to their competitors. Indeed, if the price offered by a competitor is markedly above that available from others, does not the excess probably represent the "protective" value to the competitor of removing independent competition, and permitting its payment therefore an undesirable method of promoting liquidity? If, on the other hand, the excess is due to considerations of superior efficiency, this case reduces to that identified by the first point, and could be dealt with (if necessary) by the same policy modification. As to the third point, suffice it to say that the value of these other percentage criteria is at least as doubtful as the value of those applied to mergers.

On the other hand, some relatively large-scale mergers may be economically desirable, in the sense that they are necessary to produce an otherwise unavailable economic benefit. To the extent that such transactions are prevented by a policy of merger control based on a percentage-share criterion, the results of such a policy are disadvantageous. It would seem, on the basis of present evidence, that this sort of effect would not often occur; however, its possibility certainly should not be ignored.

III. PROPOSED BASIS FOR MERGER REGULATION

Although there seems to be no economic case for a policy of merger regulation aimed at limitation of the share of a given market accounted for by one firm, there is an alternative basis which ap-

[5] See, for example, the discussion of "exclusive dealing" in [3].

pears to be more promising. This rationale is based on the general economic case against practices restricting the choices open to sellers or buyers: that is, against activities by which a seller (or buyer) makes it more difficult—or impossible—for buyers (or sellers) to obtain access to the products of (or to sell to) his independent competitors. In brief, acquisition of a competitor may, by depriving some set of buyers of a formerly available source of supply, enable the acquiring firm to charge a higher price and/or to make an alteration in product (broadly defined so as to include all the nonprice aspects of his sales) which would not otherwise have been profitable. *Unless the merger is necessary for the achievement of cost reductions or product improvement,* it can be shown that, if actual (unrestricted) expenditures and revenues are acceptable indicators of the costs and benefits of any resulting change in output, the increase in net profit accruing to the combined firm as a result of such a stratagem is almost certain to be less than the losses incurred by others; indeed, this is almost self-evident, since any such output change would *ex hypothesi* produce no net revenue gain in the absence of restriction. (Increased profits from higher prices on outputs which would have been sold anyway, however, represent merely transfers of income from buyer to seller, without any net benefit or loss.) The argument is essentially the same as the general case supporting free entry and free mobility of resources, and is open to the same objections; if the general case is accepted, so is the case for an antirestrictive merger policy.

There appears to be a considerably greater probability of net economic loss when a competitor is eliminated by merger than when he is displaced through loss of business to other firms. Product change and/or price reduction would almost certainly be necessary to attract customers away from an existing firm and thus to eliminate it by simple displacement. Except in instances of cutthroat tactics, which should be dealt with directly in law, simple growth through displacement of competitors does not imply net economic loss even though the choice of firms available to customers is thereby rendered less extensive. It is otherwise with mergers, which will be undertaken if the total prospective gains—possibly originating wholly or in large part from the protected status to be obtained thereby—appear sufficient to cover whatever incidental costs may arise, and if a suitable distribution of the proceeds can be agreed upon. This does not mean, of course, that no merger could result in economic gains sufficient to justify it regardless of an appreciable protective effect, but only that we cannot presume that any merger will have some desirable results, as we can in the case of simple expansion.

For reasons admirably set forth by Markham [7, pp. 493–95] it seems probable that few mergers can be shown to be indispensable to the production of cost savings or other economic benefits. Thus, to prohibit mergers between firms significantly competitive with one another might well be the best available course.

The chief conceptual problem connected with such a policy is the provision of a suitable definition of "significant competitiveness." It is necessary to draw a definite and defensible line between the competitiveness which will make a merger subject to legal control and the general competitiveness between each pair of firms in the economy; and the rough distinction between "potential" and "actual" competition is not sufficiently precise to serve this purpose. It has been suggested (in Section I) that the legal test of significant competitiveness among merger participants be satisfied by a showing that some nonnegligible amount of dollar revenues of one participant is accounted for by sales for which buyers would have substituted the other participant's product, had it been offered at the lowest cost-covering price, if the actual seller had withdrawn his supplies. In a sense, this test is an indicator of potential rather than actual competition. Not *actual* price relationships nor *immediate* product availability are referred to in assessing competitiveness, but rather the possibility of substitution of the products of firm A for those of firm B under the most favorable conditions for such substitution, given the actual costs and (with an exception to be noted below) the product-lines of firm A. But some such set of conditions must be chosen in any assessment of competitiveness.

Since only one firm can in fact supply each particular shipment actually bought, *any* criterion of competitiveness relates to potential rather than actual substitution; and potential substitution—or substitutability—has different meanings according to the conditions under which the opportunity for substitution is supposed to take place. If we attempt to assess competitiveness, or potential substitution, while allowing for all possible readjustments in the production plan and cost levels of the competitors, we soon see that not only producers of similar products but also every entrepreneur, and indeed every potential entrepreneur, must be accounted a significant competitor. On the other hand, to regard firms as competitive only where they are so evenly matched that the buyers must flip a coin to choose between them is most certainly to underestimate the extent of effective competition—i.e., the area in which the existence of a particular competitive source exerts a limiting effect on the willingness of the supplier to raise prices or reduce quality.

What is needed here is an indicator of effective competition between the firms in question in so far as this competitiveness exceeds the "background level" of potential competition—the competition of entrepreneurs in general—which may be regarded as practically unaffected by the disappearance of any one firm. Thus, while a merger of two firms in dissimilar and noncompetitive industries would not be ordinarily regarded as having any significant anticompetitive impact, an indicator of effective competition *should* take into account potential product-lines which the firm in question is able to enter more quickly or more efficiently than the average potential new entrant into the field. Effects too small to justify the cost of policing and prosecution could presumably be eliminated from consideration by exempting transactions involving companies below a certain minimum size. (This discussion has referred only to the horizontal aspect of mergers; a vertical integration may have an entirely dissimilar anticompetitive effect.)

It should be remembered that any proposed expansion is not blocked by denial of permission to acquire a competitor, but simply confined to a channel where it cannot ordinarily take place unless accompanied by some desirable consequences. Moreover, it is often possible to achieve substantial cost savings by eliminating duplicate facilities and by limited cooperation short of merger. In these instances, proper policy would prevent merger but would not prevent these economies. Many of the advantages brought about by rail consolidation are examples of this sort of saving.

Alternatively, if future experience should suggest a need for selective permission of some mergers between competitors, a screening process could be set up, perhaps to be administered by the

Federal Trade Commission, with the burden of proof on the applicant firms to show that their merger measures up to the rigorous test of indispensability. Permission for an anticompetitive merger might well be followed by special surveillance for a period of years with a view to determining whether or not price control should be instituted.

Finally, in spite of the above-mentioned presumption that the expansion of a firm which occurs through simple growth rather than combination, and without cutthroat tactics, is economically justified, there appear to be good grounds for some sort of limit on the size of the individual enterprise, a limit which may or may not require present embodiment in law. The psychological costs involved in such a limit may perhaps be minimized by avoiding its formulation in absolute terms; I do not mean to suggest that a satisfactory result cannot be achieved by a policy of gradual braking on expansion rather than building a blank wall. From the economic point of view, it is evidently very desirable that what has been termed the background level of potential competition be kept high: that is, that each existing firm be always kept aware of the possibility of new competition originating outside the circle of his existing significant competitors, if any, ready to materialize in the event of unsatisfactory performance by the incumbent. A limitation on the size of individual enterprises would serve this end by helping to insure the maintenance of many independent sources of productive factors, including initiative and financing, in sufficient abundance to make their influence felt in every market.

From a broader point of view, such a limitation would help to insure the existence of "many" independent sources of employment and income in order to prevent, or to reduce to a minimum, coercion of the individual in matters rightfully reserved to his own judgment. I trust there is no need to labor this point in principle. What is desired is that each man threatened with dismissal or refused employment can in the majority of cases (preferably in all cases) find alternative employment. The important thing is not, of course, merely the *number* of available alternative employers, but also their collective capacity for hiring. (That is, if 99 per cent of the total jobs in the country were controlled by one employer, it would be of little importance that the remaining 1 per cent were controlled by a thousand employers. The probability that a man dismissed by the giant could find a job with another employer would still be small, since the total number of "independent" jobs would be relatively small.) Therefore, what would be called for would be a limit—formally elastic or otherwise—on the percentage of the jobs within the political unit (i.e., unit of free migration) which is controlled by any single employer or other entity—e.g., a single trade union.

REFERENCES

1. 15 U.S.C.A. §§ 1–7.
2. 15 U.S.C.A. § 18.
3. ATTORNEY-GENERAL'S NATIONAL COMMITTEE TO STUDY THE ANTITRUST LAWS, *Report*. Washington 1955.
4. C. KAYSEN AND D. F. TURNER, *Antitrust Policy: An Economic and Legal Analysis*. Cambridge 1959.
5. L. S. KEYES, Review of Kaysen and Turner [4], *George Washington Law Rev.*, Oct. 1960, *29* 184–88.
6. ———, "The Shoe Machinery Case and the Problem of the Good Trust," *Quart. Jour. Econ.*, May 1954, *68*, 287–304.
7. J. W. MARKHAM, "Merger Policy Under the New Section 7: A Six-Year Appraisal," *Univ. Virginia Law Rev.*, May 1957, *43*, 489–524.
8. *United States v. Bethlehem Steel Corporation and The Youngstown Sheet and Tube Company*, 157 F. Supp. 877 (1958).
9. *United States v. Bethlehem Steel Corporation and The Youngstown Sheet and Tube Company*, 168 F. Supp. 576 (1958).
10. *United States v. E. I. duPont de Nemours and Co.*, 351 U.S. 377 (1956).
11. *United States v. E. I. duPont de Nemours and Co.*, 353 U.S. 586 (1957).
12. U.S. Senate Report No. 1775, 81st Cong., 2d Sess., 1950. *Amending Act to Supplement Existing Laws Against Unlawful Restraints and Monopolies.*

12 BROWN SHOE:

Guide to Future Merger Cases

Appraisal of mergers will probably offer the toughest problems in the future as more emphasis is placed on mergers involving vertical and conglomerate considerations. The Brown Shoe[1] case, involving vertical considerations, offers an interesting contrast to the Alcoa case and the "squeeze" problems that allegedly existed in the aluminum industry. Although this situation is not to be found in every industry, the contrast is direct. Where in the development of an industry does one preclude additional integration, via merger at least, in an effort to maintain competitive conditions and the independent businessman?

The Brown Shoe case involved many issues that will undoubtedly be among the more important and troublesome in future merger litigation. Brown, a major shoe producer, and Kinney, a major distributor of shoes, each specialized in its own separate industry, while operating to a much smaller extent in the other industry. The Court's opinion reveals many of the problems in the case, concerning the analysis of integration, the evaluation of structural factors in a meaningful manner, and the consideration of efficiency and industry trends. The Court's determinations of relevant market and product line are particularly pertinent, and it is noteworthy that the dissent agrees with the decision while advocating a more limited product line and relevant market. The analysis of the Brown Shoe case may be compared with that employed by Judge Hand in the

[1] Brown Shoe Co., Inc. v. United States, 370 U.S. 294 (1962).

Alcoa decision. In part the contrasts in the apparent treatment of oligopoly in the two cases probably stem from the differences in the purposes of the cases: One was designed to cure a monopolistic industry, the other to prevent a lapse from competitive conditions. The cases highlight the generally more restrictive views toward restraint of competition in merger as contrasted with monopoly situations. These differences in attitudes are also seen in the narrower lines of commerce and of market areas accepted in merger cases.

The definition of the relevant line of commerce is crucial. The defendants obviously benefit whenever the definition is so broad that no large market share is affected by the merger, or so narrow that no common activity relates to the defendants. As already indicated, no automatic formula facilitates these product definitions. The lower court cited the "peculiar characteristics and uses" standard to select men's, children's, and women's shoes as separate products regardless of price. The court also held that cities of 10,000 or over and their immediate areas identified the geographical markets, since all Kinney stores were located in such areas. A trend in the industry toward forward vertically integrated manufacturer-retailer chains was also noted by the trial judge, who cited evidence from independent nonintegrated retailers and manufacturers indicating that they were adversely affected by this trend. Thus the divestiture was ordered and the decision appealed. The case is especially notable for the Court's guidelines in defining products and markets. Concerning products, the cross-elasticity concept was employed in setting forth the limits as those products that compete with each other; however, subproduct lines are permitted where they are identified by common acceptance or use or specialized production facilities. The Court also carried this concept into the identification of submarkets within one overall market, such as the entire United States. Additionally, the Court's pronouncements on the competitive impact of the merger were directed toward both vertical and horizontal effects. Concerning vertical effects, the Court recognized that the contract's terms and purpose, structural trends, and general congressional intent were all important considerations. In regard to horizontal mergers, the

Court considered size relative to traditional structure in assessing the likely competitive impact of this merger.

Not all of these facets are, of course, original to this case. In Brown Shoe the Court was willing to accept flexibility of production as a factor in identifying the product line. In this instance the actuality of such flexibility was indicated, while in Bethlehem the argument was not supported by actual practice and the Court rejected its relevancy. At least this source of potential competition is thus seemingly accorded little attention unless it has shown some actual realization. The Court may have laid down some guides for conglomerate mergers in its decision: the possible use of partial divestiture as well as the examination of the new relationship relative to prior conditions and the nature of the industry may be factors in determining the legality of conglomerate mergers.

....

BROWN SHOE CO., INC.
v.
UNITED STATES
370 U.S. 294 (1962)

Mr. Chief Justice Warren delivered the opinion of the Court.

I.

This suit was initiated in November 1955 when the Government filed a civil action in the United States District Court for the Eastern District of Missouri alleging that a contemplated merger between the G. R. Kinney Company, Inc. (Kinney), and the Brown Shoe Company, Inc. (Brown), through an exchange of Kinney for Brown stock, would violate § 7 of the Clayton Act. . . . The complaint sought injunctive relief under § 15 of the Clayton Act, . . . to restrain consummation of the merger.

A motion by the Government for a preliminary injunction *pendente lite* was denied, and the companies were permitted to merge provided, however, that their businesses be operated separately and that their assets be kept separately identifiable. The merger was then effected on May 1, 1956.

In the District Court, the Government contended that the effect of the merger of Brown—the third largest seller of shoes by dollar volume in the United States, a leading manufacturer of men's, women's, and children's shoes, and a retailer with over 1,230 owned, operated or controlled retail outlets—and Kinney—the eighth largest company, by dollar volume, among those primarily engaged in selling shoes, itself a large manufacturer of shoes, and a retailer with over 350 retail outlets—"may be substantially to lessen competition or to tend to create a monopoly" by eliminating actual or potential competition in the production of shoes for the national wholesale shoe market and in the sale of shoes at retail in the Nation, by foreclosing competition from "a market represented by Kinney's retail outlets whose annual sales exceed $42,000,000," and by enhancing Brown's competitive advantage over other producers, distributors and sellers of shoes. . . .

The Industry

The District Court found that although domestic shoe production was scattered among a large number of manufacturers, a small number of large companies occupied a commanding position. Thus, while the 24 largest manufacturers produced about 35% of the Nation's shoes, the top 4—International, Endicott-Johnson, Brown (including Kinney) and General Shoe—alone produced approximately 23% of the Nation's shoes or 65% of the production of the top 24.

The public buys these shoes through about 70,000 retail outlets, only 22,000 of which, however, derive 50% or more of their gross receipts from the sale of shoes and are classified as "shoe stores" by the Census Bureau. These 22,000 shoe stores were found generally to sell (1) men's shoes only, (2) women's shoes only, (3) women's and children's shoes, or (4) men's, women's, and children's shoes.

The District Court found a "definite trend" among shoe manufacturers to acquire retail outlets. . . .

And once the manufacturers acquired retail outlets, the District Court found there was a "definite trend" for the parent-manufacturers to supply an ever increasing percentage of the retail outlets' needs, thereby foreclosing other manufacturers from effectively competing for the retail accounts. Manufacturer-dominated stores were found to be "drying up" the available outlets for independent producers.

Another "definite trend" found to exist in the shoe industry was a decrease in the number of plants manufacturing shoes. . . .

Brown Shoe

Brown Shoe was found not only to have been a participant, but also a moving factor, in these industry trends. Although Brown had experimented several times with operating its own retail outlets, by 1945 it had disposed of them all. However, in 1951, Brown again began to seek retail outlets by acquiring the Nation's largest operator of leased shoe departments, Wohl Shoe Company. . . .

The acquisition of these corporations was found to lead to increased sales by Brown to the acquired companies. . . .

During the same period of time, Brown also acquired the stock or assets of seven companies engaged solely in shoe manufacturing. As a result, in 1955, Brown was the fourth largest shoe manufacturer in the country, producing about 25.6 million pairs of shoes or about 4% of the Nation's total footwear production.

Kinney

Kinney is principally engaged in operating the largest family-style shoe store chain in the United States. At the time of trial, Kinney was found to be operating over 400 such stores in more than 270 cities. These stores were found to make about 1.2% of all national retail shoe sales by dollar volume. . . .

In addition to this extensive retail activity, Kinney owned and operated four plants which manufactured men's, women's, and children's shoes and whose combined output was 0.5% of the national shoe production in 1955, making Kinney the twelfth largest shoe manufacturer in the United States.

Kinney stores were found to obtain about 20% of their shoes from Kinney's own manufacturing plants. At the time of the merger, Kinney bought no shoes from Brown; however, in line with Brown's conceded reasons for acquiring Kinney, Brown had, by 1957, become the largest outside supplier of Kinney's shoes, supplying 7.9% of all Kinney's needs. . . .

III. LEGISLATIVE HISTORY

This case is one of the first to come before us in which the Government's complaint is based upon allegations that the appellant has violated § 7 of the Clayton Act, as that section was amended in 1950. . . .

The dominant theme pervading congressional consideration of the 1950 amendments was a fear of what was considered to be a rising tide of economic concentration in the American economy. . . .

What were some of the factors, relevant to a judgment as to the validity of a given merger, specifically discussed by Congress in redrafting § 7?

First, there is no doubt that Congress did wish to "plug the loophole" and to include within the coverage of the Act the acquisition of assets no less than the acquisition of stock.

Second, by the deletion of the "acquiring-acquired" language in the original text, it hoped to make plain that § 7 applied not only to mergers between actual competitors, but also to vertical and conglomerate mergers whose effect may tend to lessen competition in any line of commerce in any section of the country.

Third, it is apparent that a keystone in the erection of a barrier to what Congress saw was the rising tide of economic concentration, was its provision of authority for arresting mergers at a time when the trend to a lessening of competition in a line of commerce was still in its incipiency. Congress saw the process of concentration in American business as a dynamic force; it sought to assure the Federal Trade Commission and the courts the power to brake this force at its outset and before it gathered momentum.

Fourth, and closely related to the third, Congress rejected, as inappropriate to the problem it sought to remedy, the application to § 7 cases of the standards for judging the legality of business combinations adopted by the courts in dealing with cases arising under the Sherman Act, and which may have been applied to some early cases arising under original § 7.

Fifth, at the same time that it sought to create an effective tool for preventing all mergers having demonstrable anticompetitive effects, Congress recognized the stimulation to competition that might flow from particular mergers. . . . Taken as a whole, the legislative history illuminates congressional concern with the protection of *competition,* not *competitors,* and its desire to restrain mergers only to the extent that such combinations may tend to lessen competition.

Sixth, Congress neither adopted nor rejected specifically any particular tests for measuring the relevant markets, either as defined in terms of product or in terms of geographic locus of competition, within which the anticompetitive effects of a merger were to be judged. Nor did it adopt a definition of the word "substantially," whether in quantitative terms of sales or assets or market shares or in designated qualitative terms, by which a merger's effects on competition were to be measured.

Seventh, while providing no definite quantitative or qualitative tests by which enforcement agencies could gauge the effects of a given merger to determine whether it may "substantially" lessen competition or tend toward monopoly, Congress indicated plainly that a merger had to be functionally viewed, in the context of its particular industry. . . .

Eighth, Congress used the words *"may be* substantially to lessen competition"* (emphasis supplied), to indicate that its concern was with probabilities, not certainties. . . .

IV. THE VERTICAL ASPECTS OF THE MERGER

The Product Market

The outer boundaries of a product market are determined by the reasonable interchangeability of use or the cross-elasticity of demand between the product itself and substitutes for it. However, within this broad market, well-defined submarkets may exist which, in themselves, constitute product markets for antitrust purposes. *United States* v. *E. I. du Pont de Nemours & Co.,* 353 U.S. 586, 593–595. The boundaries of such a submarket may be determined by examining such practical indicia as industry or public recognition of the submarket as a separate economic entity, the product's peculiar characteristics and uses, unique production facilities, distinct customers, distinct prices, sensitivity to price changes, and specialized vendors. . . .

Applying these considerations to the present case, we conclude that the record supports the District Court's finding that the relevant lines of commerce are men's, women's, and children's shoes. These product lines are recognized by the public; each line is manufactured in separate plants; each has characteristics peculiar to itself rendering it generally noncompetitive with the others; and each is, of course, directed toward a distinct class of customers.

This is not to say, however, that "price/quality" differences, where they exist, are unimportant in analyzing a merger; they may be of importance in determining the likely effect of a merger. But the boundaries of the relevant market must be drawn with sufficient breadth to include the competing products of each of the merging companies and to recognize competition where, in fact, competition exists. Thus we agree with the District Court that in this case a further division of product lines based on "price/quality" differences would be "unrealistic." . . .

The Geographic Market

We agree with the parties and the District Court that insofar as the vertical aspect of this merger is concerned, the relevant geographic market is the entire Nation. The relationships of product value, bulk, weight and consumer demand enable manufacturers to distribute their shoes on a nationwide basis, as Brown and Kinney, in fact, do. The anticompetitive effects of the merger are to be measured within this range of distribution.

The Probable Effect of the Merger

Since the diminution of the vigor of competition which may stem from a vertical arrangement results primarily from a foreclosure of a share of the market otherwise open to competitors, an important consideration in determining whether the effect of a vertical arrangement "may be substantially to lessen competition, or to tend to create a monopoly" is the size of the share of the market foreclosed. However, this factor will seldom be determinative. . . .

A most important such factor to examine is the very nature and purpose of the arrangement. Congress not only indicated that "the tests of illegality [under § 7] are intended to be similar to those which the courts have applied in interpreting the same language as used in other sections of the Clayton Act," but also chose for § 7 language virtually identical to that of § 3 of the Clayton Act, 15 U. S. C. § 14, which had been interpreted by this Court to require an examination of the interdependence of the market share foreclosed by, and the economic purpose of, the vertical arrangement. Thus, for example, if a particular vertical arrangement, considered under § 3, appears to be a limited term exclusive-dealing contract, the market foreclosure must generally be significantly greater than if the arrangement is a tying contract before the arrangement will be held to have violated the Act. . . .

. . . Moreover, it is apparent both from past behavior of Brown and from the testimony of Brown's President, that Brown would use its ownership of Kinney to force Brown shoes into Kinney stores. Thus, in operation this vertical arrangement would be quite analogous to one involving a tying clause.

Another important factor to consider is the trend toward concentration in the industry. It is true, of course, that the statute prohibits a given merger only if the effect of *that* merger may be substantially to lessen competition. But the very wording of § 7 requires a prognosis of the probable *future* effect of the merger.

Moreover, as we have remarked above, not only must we consider the probable effects of the merger upon the economics of the particular markets affected but also we must consider its probable effects upon the economic way of life sought to be preserved by Congress. . . .

The District Court's findings, and the record facts, many of them set forth in Part I of this opinion, convince us that the shoe industry is being subjected to just such a cumulative series of vertical mergers which, if left unchecked, will be likely "substantially to lessen competition." . . .

V. THE HORIZONTAL ASPECTS OF THE MERGER

An economic arrangement between companies performing similar functions in the production or sale of comparable goods or services is characterized as "horizontal." The effect on competition of such an arrangement depends, of course, upon its character and scope. . . .

The Product Market

Shoes are sold in the United States in retail shoe stores and in shoe departments of general stores. These outlets sell: (1) men's shoes, (2) women's shoes, (3) women's or children's shoes, or (4) men's, women's or children's shoes. Prior to the merger, both Brown and Kinney sold their shoes in competition with one another through the enumerated kinds of outlets characteristic of the industry.

In Part IV of this opinion we hold that the District Court correctly defined men's, women's, and children's shoes as the relevant lines of commerce in which to analyze the vertical aspects of the merger. For the reasons there stated we also hold that the same lines of commerce are appropriate for considering the horizontal aspects of the merger.

The Geographic Market

The criteria to be used in determining the appropriate geographic market are essentially similar to those used to determine the relevant product market. . . . Congress prescribed a pragmatic, factual approach to the definition of the relevant market and not a formal, legalistic one. The geographic market selected must, therefore, both "correspond to the commercial realities" of the industry and be economically significant. Thus, although the geographic market in some instances may encompass the entire Nation, under other circumstances it may be as small as a single metropolitan area. . . .

The parties do not dispute the findings of the District Court that the Nation as a whole is the relevant geographic market for measuring the anticompetitive effects of the merger viewed vertically or of the horizontal merger of Brown's and Kinney's manufacturing facilities. As to the retail level, however, they disagree.

The District Court found that the effects of this aspect of the merger must be analyzed in every city with a population exceeding 10,000 and its immediate contiguous surrounding territory in which both Brown and Kinney sold shoes at retail through stores they either owned or controlled. By this definition of the geographic market, less than one-half of all the cities in which either Brown or Kinney sold shoes through such outlets are represented. . . .

We believe, however, that the record fully supports the District Court's findings that shoe stores in the outskirts of cities compete effectively with stores in central downtown areas, and that while there is undoubtedly some commercial intercourse between smaller communities within a single "standard metropolitan area," the most intense and important competition in retail sales will be confined to stores within the particular communities in such an area and their immediate environs.

We therefore agree that the District Court properly defined the relevant geographic markets in which to analyze this merger as those cities with a population exceeding 10,000 and their environs in which both Brown and Kinney retailed shoes through their own outlets. Such markets are large enough to include the downtown shops and suburban shopping centers in areas contiguous to the city, which are the important competitive factors, and yet are small enough to exclude stores beyond the immediate environs of the city, which are of little competitive significance.

The Probable Effect of the Merger

Having delineated the product and geographic markets within which the effects of this merger are to be measured, we turn to an examination of the District Court's finding that as a result of the merger competition in the retailing of men's, women's and children's shoes may be lessened substantially in those cities in which both Brown and Kinney stores are located. . . .

In the case before us, not only was a fair sample used to demonstrate the soundness of the District Court's conclusions, but evidence of record fully substantiates those findings as to each relevant market. . . .

The market share which companies may control by merging is one of the most important factors to be considered when determining the probable effects of the combination on effective competition in the relevant market. In an industry as fragmented as shoe retailing, the control of substantial shares of the trade in a city may have important effects on competition. If a merger achieving 5% control were now approved, we might be required to approve future merger efforts by Brown's competitors seeking similar market shares. The oligopoly Congress sought to avoid would then be furthered and it would be difficult to dissolve the combinations previously approved. Furthermore, in this fragmented industry, even if the combination controls but a small share of a particular market, the fact that this share is held by a large national chain can adversely affect competition. . . . The retail outlets of integrated companies, by eliminating wholesalers and by increasing the volume of purchases from the manufacturing division of the enterprise, can market their own brands at prices below those of competing independent retailers. Of course, some of the results of large integrated or chain operations are beneficial to consumers. Their expansion is not rendered unlawful by the mere fact that small independent stores may be adversely affected. It is competition, not competitors, which the Act protects. But we cannot fail to recognize Congress' desire to promote competition through the protection of viable, small, locally owned businesses. Congress appreciated that occasional higher costs and prices might result from the maintenance of fragmented industries and markets. It resolved these competing considerations in favor of decentralization. We must give effect to that decision.

Other factors to be considered in evaluating the probable effects of a merger in the relevant market lend additional support to the District Court's conclusion that this merger may substantially lessen competition. One such factor is the history of tendency toward concentration in the industry. As we have previously pointed out, the shoe industry has, in recent years, been a prime example of such a trend. Most combinations have been between manufacturers and retailers, as each of the larger producers has sought to capture an increasing number of assured outlets for its wares. Although these mergers have been primarily vertical in their aim and effect, to the extent that they have brought ever greater numbers of retail outlets within fewer and fewer hands, they have had an additional important impact on the horizontal plane. . . .

The Judgment is   *Affirmed.*

Mr. Justice Clark, concurring.

 . . . It would appear that the relevant line of commerce would be shoes of all types. This is emphasized by the nature of Brown's manufacturing activity and its plan to integrate the Kinney stores into its operations. The competition affected thereby would be in the line handled by these stores which is the full line of shoes manufactured by Brown. This conclusion is more in keeping with the record as I read it and at the same time avoids the charge of splintering the product line. Likewise, the location of the Kinney stores points more to a national market in shoes than a number of regional markets staked by artificial municipal boundaries. Brown's business is on a national scale and its policy of integration of manufacturing and retailing is on that basis. I would conclude, therefore, that it would be more reasonable to define the line of commerce as shoes—those sold in the ordinary retail store—and the market as the entire country.

On this record but one conclusion can follow, *i. e.,* that the acquisition by Brown of the 400 Kinney stores for the purposes of integrating their operation into its manufacturing activity created a "reasonable probability" that competition in the manufacture and sale of shoes on a national basis might be substantially lessened. I would therefore affirm.

Mr. Justice Harlan, dissenting in part and concurring in part.

I would dismiss this appeal for lack of jurisdiction, believing that the case in its present posture is prematurely here because the judgment sought to be reviewed is not yet final. Since the Court, however, holds that the case is properly before us, I consider it appropriate, after noting my dissent to this holding, to express my views on the merits because the issues are of great importance. On that aspect, I concur in the judgment of the Court but do not join its opinion, which I consider to go far beyond what is necessary to decide the case.

THE MERITS

. . . The question presented by this case can be stated in narrow and concise terms: Are the District Court's conclusions that the effect of the Brown-Kinney merger may be, in the language of § 7 of the Clayton Act, "substantially to lessen competition, or to tend to create a monopoly" in "any line of commerce in any section of the country" sustainable? In other words, does the indefinite and general language in § 7 manifest a congressional purpose to proscribe a combination of this sort? Brown contends that in finding the merger illegal the District Court lumped together what are in fact discrete "lines of commerce," that it failed to define an appropriate "section of the country," and that when the case is properly viewed any lessening of competition that may be caused by the merger is not "substantial." For reasons stated below, I think that each of these contentions is untenable.

The dispositive considerations are, I think, found in the "vertical" effects of the merger, that is, the effects reasonably to be foreseen from combining Brown's manufacturing facilities with Kinney's retail outlets. In my opinion the District Court's conclusions as to such effects are supported by the record, and suffice to condemn the merger under § 7, without regard to what might be deemed to be the "horizontal" effects of the transaction.

1. "Line of Commerce." In considering both the horizontal and vertical aspects of this merger, the District Court analyzed the probable impact on competition in terms of three relevant "lines of commerce"—men's shoes, women's shoes, and children's shoes. It rejected Brown's claim that shoes of different construction or of different price range constituted distinct lines of commerce. Whatever merit there might be to Brown's contention that the product market should be more narrowly defined when it is viewed from the vantage point of the ultimate consumer (whose pocketbook, for example, may limit his purchase to a definite price range), the same is surely not true of the shoe manufacturer. Although the record contains evidence tending to prove that a shoe manufacturing plant may be managed more economically if its production is limited to only one type and grade of shoe, the history of Brown's own factories reveals that a single plant may be used in successive years, or even at the same time, for the manufacture of varying grades of shoes and may, without undue difficulty, be shifted from the production of children's shoes to men's or women's shoes, or vice versa.

Because of this flexibility of manufacture, the product market with respect to the merger between Brown's manufacturing facilities and Kinney's retail outlets might more accurately be defined as the complete wearing-apparel shoe market, combining in one the three components which the District Court treated as separate lines of commerce. Such an analysis, taking into account the interchangeability of production, would seem a more realistic gauge of the possible anticompetitive effects in the shoe manufacturing industry of a merger between a shoe manufacturer and a retailer than the District Court's compartmentalization in terms of the buying public. . . .

. . . In light of the production flexibility demonstrated by the undisputed facts in this case, I think the line of commerce by which the vertical aspects of the Brown-Kinney merger should be judged is the wearing-apparel shoe industry generally.

2. "Section of the Country." This merger involves nation-wide concerns which sell and purchase shoes in various localities throughout the country, so that it appears that the most suitable geographical market for appraising the alleged anticompetitive effects of the vertical combination is the Nation as a whole. This finding of the District Court (limited to the vertical aspect of the merger) is not contested by Brown and is properly accepted here. One *caveat* is in order, however. In judging the anticom-petitive effect of the merger on the national market, it must be recognized that any decline in competition that might result need not have a uniform effect throughout the entire country. It is sufficient if the record proves that as a result of the merger competition will generally be lessened, though its most serious impact may be felt in certain localities.

3. "Substantially to Lessen Competition." The remaining question is whether the merger of Brown's manufacturing facilities with Kinney's retail outlets "may . . . substantially lessen com-petition" or "tend to create a monopoly" in the nationwide market in which shoe manufacturers sell to shoe retailers. The findings of the District Court, supported by the evidence, when taken together with undisputed facts appearing in the record, justify the conclusion that a substantial lessening of competition in the relevant market is a "reasonable probability." S. Rep. No. 1775, 81st Cong., 2d Sess. 6 (1950).

Prior to 1955 Kinney had bought none of its outside-source shoes from Brown, and its records for 1955 reveal that the year's purchases were made from a diverse number of independent shoe manufacturers. . . .

That the merger between Brown's shoe production plants and

Kinney's retail outlets will tend to foreclose some of the large market which smaller shoe manufacturers found in sales to Kinney hardly seems open to doubt. This conclusion is supported by the following facts which emerge indisputably from the record: (1) In the shoe industry, as in many others, the purchase of a retail chain by a manufacturer results in an increased flow of the purchasing manufacturer's shoes to the retail store. Hence independent shoe manufacturers find it more difficult to sell their shoes to an acquired retail chain than to an independent one. (2) The result of Brown's earlier acquisition of two retail chains was, in each instance, a substantial increase in the quantity of Brown shoe purchases by the previously independent chains.[1] (3) The history of many of Brown's plants proves that they may be readily adapted to the production of the grade and style of shoes customarily sold in Kinney stores.[2] (4) Although Brown supplied none of Kinney's requirements before the merger, it was supplying almost 8% of these requirements just two years thereafter.

If the controlling test were, as it may be under the similar language of § 3 of the Clayton Act, one of "quantitative substantiality," . . . the probable foreclosure of independent manufacturers from this substantial share of the available retail shoe market would be enough to render the vertical aspect of this merger unlawful under § 7.

[1] In 1951 Brown purchased the Wohl Shoe Company, which operated leased shoe departments in department stores throughout the country. Before its acquisition of Wohl, Brown had supplied 12.8% of Wohl's shoe requirements; by 1957, it was supplying 33.6% of Wohl's needs.

In 1953, Brown purchased a partial interest in a small chain of retail stores in Los Angeles known as Wetherby-Kayser. Before this purchase, Brown had supplied 10.4% of Wetherby's shoes; within one year this percentage increased to almost 50%.

[2] In addition, it appears from the record that shortly after the merger was effected, Kinney abandoned its earlier policy of selling only Kinney-brand shoes (80% of which were "made up" for it by its manufacturers) and began selling a considerable number of Brown's branded and advertised shoes. Along with the indications in the record that Kinney was beginning also to sell higher-priced shoes in its suburban outlets, this suggests that Brown could supply much of Kinney's needs with only a minimal additional capital investment.

Not only may this merger, judged from a vertical standpoint, affect manufacturers who compete with Brown; it may also adversely affect competition on the retailing level. With a large manufacturer such as Brown behind it, the Kinney chain would have a great competitive advantage over the retail stores with which it vies for consumer patronage. As a manufacturer-owned outlet, the Kinney store would doubtless be able to sell its shoes at a lower profit margin and outlast an independent competitor. The merger would also effectively prevent the retail competitor from dealing in Brown shoes, since these might be offered at lower prices in Kinney stores than elsewhere.[3]

Brown contends that even if these anticompetitive effects are probable, they touch upon an insignificant share of the market and are not, therefore, "substantial" within the meaning of § 7. Our decision in *Tampa Electric Co.* v. *Nashville Coal Co.,* 365 U.S. 320, is cited as authority for the proposition that a foreclosure of about 1% of the relevant market is necessarily insubstantial. . . . When, as here, the foreclosure of what may be considered a small percentage of retailers' purchases may be caused by the combination of the country's third largest seller of shoes with the country's largest family-style shoe store chain, and when the volume of the latter's purchases from independent manufacturers in various parts of the country is large enough to render it probable that these suppliers, if displaced, will have to fall by the wayside, it cannot, in my opinion, be said that the effect on the shoe industry is "remote" or "insubstantial."

I reach this result without considering the findings of the District Court respecting the trend in the shoe industry towards "oligopoly" and vertical integration. The statistics in the record fall short of convincing me that any such trend exists.[4] I consider the District Court's judgment warranted apart from these findings.

---

[3] The change in Kinney policy whereby it now carries shoes bearing the Brown brand (see note 2, *supra*) tends to make retailer competition still more difficult.

[4] There is no suggestion in the record as to whether earlier purchases of retail chains by shoe manufacturers reduced the number of independent manufacturers or otherwise harmed competition. Consequently, while the record does establish that manufacturers have been increasing the number of their retail outlets, it is entirely silent on the effects of this vertical expansion.

Accordingly, bowing to the Court's decision that the case is properly before us, I join the judgment of affirmance.

■■

[The major responsibility of economists in merger cases is clearly evident from Section 7; that is, to identify market and industry boundaries in an effort to discern whether a monopoly is created or competition is restricted by the merger in question. To be meaningful, these market boundaries must include relevant competitors, or suppliers of substitute products. However, these boundaries cannot be so excessively broad as to include specious competitors, that is, producers whose products cannot reasonably be considered substitutes. Unfortunately, these seemingly sophisticated social science objectives cannot be met by equally sophisticated and objective procedures. As a practical matter, the process of market delineation turns upon the individual analyst's judgment. To be sure, this judgment is based both on training in economic analysis and on familiarity with the particular industry in question. Still, the process does center about the individual's judgment in applying his analytical tools to the industry's identified attributes.

Professionally, this issue was first clearly articulated in Chamberlin's *The Theory of Monopolistic Competition,*[2] which first appeared in 1933. Although the conceptual approach to market definition and delineation has been refined considerably since then, the analytical procedures remain difficult to implement in particular cases. Both the "line of commerce" and the "section of the country" delineations are largely matters of judgment. Properly undertaken, these delineations would rest on (1) sufficient empirical evidence and (2) a thorough analytical background of market operations (both in general and in particular). Seemingly, the courts are aware of the legal and economic problems and the difficulties in selecting reasonable boundaries. A most incisive

---

[2] Edward H. Chamberlin, *The Theory of Monopolistic Competition,* 7th ed. (Cambridge: Harvard University Press, 1956).

statement of these economic problems is contained in the Supreme Court's statement of the issues it faced in the Brown Shoe case:

> The outer boundaries of a product market are determined by the reasonable interchangeability of use or the cross-elasticity of demand between the product itself and substitutes for it. However, within this broad market, well-defined submarkets may exist which, in themselves, constitute product markets for antitrust purposes. . . . The boundaries of such a submarket may be determined by examining such practical indicia as industry or public recognition of the submarket as a separate economic entity, the product's peculiar characteristics and uses, unique production facilities, distinct customers, distinct prices, sensitivity to price changes, and specialized vendors. . . .[3]

A review of the Court's analysis of product markets in various antitrust cases indicates an exercise of judgment and adoption of highly diverging market boundaries in different cases. In Brown Shoe, for example, the Court adopted an intermediate view of the relevant products from among those advanced—men's, women's, and youth's shoes—but it demonstrated that nationally, and in some selected local markets, the market shares based on such product-market delineation paralleled those based on both broader and more narrow definitions. By contrast, in the du Pont (GM) case the Court rejected an argument by du Pont and GM that the relevant product market was one of all finishes (paints or lacquers) and fabrics and ruled that it was one of automotive finishes and fabrics. (Indeed, at points the Court adopted the argument that the relevant markets were GM's purchases of finishes and fabrics.)

> . . . The record shows that automotive finishes and fabrics have sufficient peculiar characteristics and uses to constitute them products sufficiently distinct from all other finishes and fabrics to make them a "line of commerce" within the meaning of the Clayton Act. . . . Thus, the bounds of the relevant market for the purposes of this case are not coextensive with the total market for finishes and

[3] *Op. cit.,* 325.

fabrics, but are coextensive with the automotive industry, the relevant market for automotive finishes and fabrics.[4]

In Brown Shoe (as in the District Court's treatment of Bethlehem) the Supreme Court somewhat arbitrarily cut the cord on the definitions of product—"line of commerce"—and geographical market—"section of the country." However, the distinctions between Brown Shoe and many other earlier, and later, cases are not arbitrary ones. In all cases the courts, and indeed anyone charged with delineating a market, have pragmatically asserted that some particular product or group of products constituted the relevant "line of commerce" and that some market or many markets of particular geographical dimensions constituted the relevant "section of the country," to use the language of Section 7 of the Clayton Act as amended by the 1950 Celler-Kefauver Act. To us, the crucial distinction between Brown Shoe and the analysis in later cases considered by the Supreme Court is the stage at which the Court exercised its judgment as to the pertinent products and markets in the case. In Brown Shoe the Court rather carefully considered an extensive body of evidence concerning trade practices, interchangeability in production and in consumption, and so on, before making its pronouncement as to *the* relevant markets and products.

In all cases the courts must pragmatically assert some definitions of product and market as the relevant ones. This is not unique to any case or to the courts. What is of concern is the sophistication and subtlety buttressing the courts' exercise of their judgment— or choice among alternatives as to the market and product definitions. However, it may not be possible to directly appraise the act or processes of the courts' exercise of judgment; by their nature the decision, or individual judge's thought, processes may be unconscious, inarticulate, or even firmly misunderstood by a human being capable of great rationalizations. To appraise the exercise of discretion by the Court in Brown Shoe, we must therefore, turn to the Court's preliminary analysis, review of the facts, and so forth, which are background to its exercise of

[4] *Op. cit.*, 593–595.

judgment. The care, thoroughness, and sophistication in stripping
the lint of controversy in self-serving statements of adversaries
from the fabric of market phenomenon is therefore revealing of
the sophistication and aptness of the Court's final judgment. It is
this judgment that Professor David Dale Martin subjects to scrutiny
in the following article.]

···

The Brown Shoe Case and the New Antimerger Policy

David Dale Martin

···

In June, 1962, the United States Supreme Court unanimously declared illegal the Brown Shoe Company's 1956 acquisition of the
G. R. Kinney Company. After eleven and a half years, the Supreme
Court for the first time decided a case requiring a detailed analysis
of the 1950 amendments of Section 7 of the Clayton Act. Brown
Shoe is undoubtedly one of the few truly landmark antitrust cases
on close-knit combinations. The Court confirmed the fact that the
Celler-Kefauver Act of 1950 constitutes a major substantive change
in public policy toward the allowable degree of centralization of
corporate control and not just a mere plugging of a loophole in the
1914 legislation. In an opinion that liberally dispensed interpretations of the statute, the Court enunciated a policy that would have
prevented the development of oligopoly structure in American
industry had it been adopted in 1895, when the problem of regulating corporate mergers was temporarily relegated to the states in
the E. C. Knight case.

Abridged from David Dale Martin, "The Brown Shoe Case and the
New Antimerger Policy," *The American Economic Review*, LIII, No. 3
(June 1963), 340–358.

A number of cases must reach the Supreme Court before enough specific criteria will have emerged for easy judgment of the legality of mergers. In this case, however, the Court greatly narrowed the area of uncertainty. The merger had vertical and horizontal characteristics, both of which the Court considered even though it might have disposed of the case on either of the two grounds alone. It also examined both the "line of commerce" and the "section of the country" questions, as well as the all-important issue of measuring a merger's probable competitive impact. Thus, the high Court has finally spoken on many of the key merger questions that have risen and will continue to arise in the lower courts and the Federal Trade Commission.

I. THE DISTRICT COURT OPINION

Shoe manufacturing and distribution have not traditionally been characterized by oligopoly structure. In the district court, Brown's attorneys contended that the industry enjoyed healthy competition that would not be diminished by the merger because Kinney manufactured less than one-half of one per cent and retailed less than 2 per cent of the nation's shoes. Although Brown was the fourth largest U.S. shoe manufacturer in 1955, it produced only a little less than 4 per cent of the total shoe output of the industry.

Of the total 1957 national production, the largest 24 companies together accounted for only about 35 per cent, the four largest companies accounting for about 23 per cent. International, the largest producer, was followed by Endicott-Johnson. Joined with Kinney, Brown displaced General Shoe as the third largest producer in 1957, whether size is measured by value of assets, physical volume of production, or net dollar volume of sales. Nearly a thousand other smaller firms were engaged in the manufacture of shoes.

Shoe retailing is even more decentralized than shoe manufacturing. In 1954 shoes were sold through over 70,000 retail outlets in the United States, of which some 22,000 were classified as "shoe stores" by the Bureau of the Census. These did about half of the shoe business, and about half the sales of shoe stores—that is,

about one-fourth of total shoe sales—was made by the chain operators. In 1956 the six firms with the largest number of retail "shoe
store" outlets owned 18 per cent of such stores, and the top 13
firms owned 21 per cent. Thus, in both shoe production and shoe
retailing a few firms are large relative to the great number of
small firms, but the degree of concentration is low compared with
such industries as tobacco, petroleum, aluminum, shoe machinery,
and steel, in which important Sherman Act cases have dealt with the
basic question of market structure.

The question before the court, however, was not whether Brown
had monopolized the shoe industry, but whether the acquisition violated the Clayton Act. Judge Weber, who tried the case after the
death of Judge Hulen, singled out three basic issues for decision:
the lines of commerce, the sections of the country, and the probable impact of the merger. Brown's attorneys contended that the
merger would be shown not to lessen competition substantially or
tend to create a monopoly if the lines of commerce and sections of
the country were properly determined.

The defense, of course, gains in a merger case if it can show that
the only relevant markets are defined in such a way that the
merger has no impact on competition. This showing may be made
by defining the markets in which the two firms operate either (1) so
narrowly that the merging firms have no markets in common, or
(2) so broadly that the merging firms are but two small firms among
so many others that any impact is negligible. Brown's attorneys
chose the first of these alternatives. Following the 1930 International Shoe Company case, Brown argued for a product breakdown not only on the basis of age and sex of the ultimate consumer of the shoes, but also for a further breakdown on the basis of
different grades of materials, quality of workmanship, price, and
type of use of shoes.[1] The government argued that the relevant line

[1] International Shoe Company v. Federal Trade Commission, 280 U.S. 291
(1930).

The International Shoe case was the only case before 1950 in which the
Supreme Court interpreted the standard of legality of the original Section
7 of the Clayton Act. The Court ruled that the International Shoe Company's
acquisition of the stock of the McElwain Company did not violate the law
primarily on the grounds that "in respect of 95 per cent of the business [of
each of the two companies] there was no competition in fact and no contest,

of commerce was "footwear" or, alternately, "men's, women's, and children's shoes," separately considered.

Judge Weber concluded from his analysis of the cases "that a 'line of commerce' cannot be determined by any process of logic and should be determined by the processes of observation." He asked what the testimony revealed about "the practices in the industry, the characteristics and uses of the products, their interchangeability, price, quality and style." He concluded:

> There is this noticeable fact, however, that there is one group of classifications which is understood and recognized by the entire industry and the public—the classification into "men's", "women's" and "children's" shoes separately and independently. Brown and Kinney each manufacture and sell men's, women's and children's shoes. While there is a close question as to whether "shoes—as such" could be treated as "a line of commerce" and, while there is argument for a breakdown into quality, style, price and intended use, there can be no question or argument either legal, logical or evidentiary, but that it can be said that all "men's shoes," regardless of quality, style, price and intended use, have sufficient peculiar characteristics and uses to make them distinguishable and a "line of commerce." The same can be said separately as to all "women's shoes" and all "children's shoes." On this the government has sustained its burden.

On the related question of the proper geographical delimitation of the markets, the defendants agreed with the government that the nation as a whole is the relevant "section of the country" for shoe manufacturing. But for shoe retailing the defendants' attorneys argued that the relevant sections of the country should be defined by the flow of local commerce, varying from the central business district of large cities to the "standard metropolitan area" as de-

---

or observed tendency to contest, in the market for the same purchasers; and it is manifest that, when this is eliminated, what remains is of such slight consequence as to deprive the finding that there was substantial competition between the two corporations, of any real support in the evidence. . . ." A most important change made in the statute by the 1950 amendment, however, was the removal of the test of lessening of competition *between* the acquiring and acquired firms and its replacement by the test in terms of lessening of competition in the market.

fined by the Bureau of the Census for smaller communities. The acceptance of this position by the court would have placed suburban shoe stores in separate markets from downtown stores. The government argued first that the whole United States was the relevant market, and alternately, in case the judge would not accept this definition, that it should be defined as a city, or a city and the immediate surrounding area. As in the case of the product dimension of the market, the defense was arguing for a narrow definition to show that an insubstantial part of the business of the two firms was done in competition with each other.[2]

Judge Weber was satisfied that in cities like St. Louis, where the trial was held and for which information was available, the downtown shoe stores were competing for business with the neighborhood shopping centers in outlying areas. He found that seven million pairs of Kinney shoes were sold in one year in the same cities in which twelve million pairs of Brown shoes were sold, and noted at least 141 cities with more than 10,000 population in which both firms had outlets. Brown's and Kinney's shares of the retail market in these cities were held to be substantial. Judge Weber concluded that the relevant sections of the country were cities of 10,000 or more inhabitants and the immediate surrounding areas in which both firms had outlets. He explained the limitation of the definition to cities of 10,000 or more population by the fact that all Kinney stores were located in cities of such size and the evidence presented in the case dealt with such cities.

Judge Weber's reasoning with respect to the probable impact of the merger on the degree of competition and monopoly in the markets as defined was based on a definite recognition of a difference between the Sherman Act and Clayton Act standards. He said:

> Certainly it is evident that Congress intended to encompass minute acquisitions which tend toward monopoly and to do so in their incipiency. . . . What difference can it make that Brown has only 5% of the shoe production and Kinney 0.5%, when Brown is the fourth largest firm in the United States and Kinney with only 1.2%

[2] In many of the post-1950 cases under Section 7 of the Clayton Act, the defense attorneys have argued for a broader market definition than the government in order to show a lower degree of concentration of control.

of all retail shoe sales is the largest family shoe chain retailer. Their combination moves Brown to third place in the industry. Does it then make sense to say that this is imperceptible because the percentages are small? Or rather, doesn't it make sense to say, that regardless of percentages or size, the test is, what do the facts show as to the trends in the industry and the true economic impact of this particular merger, which takes place among an industry having a few large firms that control a sizeable segment of the total with the balance divided among hundreds of others having only minute segments.

Thus on the impact question Judge Weber was much more concerned with rather vaguely defined general circumstances in the industry than with the structure of the specific markets he had defined as the relevant ones.

As to the trend in the industry, Judge Weber found substantial evidence of a change in its organization, of which this merger was a part. In 1945 two of the large shoe manufacturers—International and Brown—had no retail outlets. By 1956 International had acquired 130 and Brown 845. By 1958 Brown had over 1,800 outlets in operation, counting the 416 Kinney stores. Between 1945 and 1956 General Shoe increased its retail outlets from 80 to 526; Shoe Corporation of America increased its number from 301 to 842; Melville Shoe Company from 536 to 947; and Endicott-Johnson stepped up slightly from 488 to 540. Judge Weber noted that between 1950 and 1956 nine independent shoe firms became subsidiaries of large firms, the acquired companies having operated 1,114 of the nation's 22,000 shoe stores.

The trend in the industry was toward vertical forward integration brought about primarily by acquisition. Judge Weber viewed this development as an incipient lessening of competition because of its effect on the opportunity of the remaining non-integrated shoe producers to find buyers of their products. The limitation on the markets of independent manufacturers was accompanied by a definite downward trend in the number of shoe manufacturing plants—from 1,207 in 1950 to 1,048 in 1956. In 1956, 20 per cent of all plants were operated by only 10 firms, which acquired seven companies with 25 plants between 1950 and 1956.

Besides the effect of vertical integration on the remaining non-integrated manufacturers, Judge Weber found injury to the remaining nonintegrated retailers. Independent retailers testified that they were having a harder time competing with company-controlled retail outlets benefiting from increased brand-name acceptability resulting from national advertising, availability of credit, inventory control, and price control. As a result, independent retailers were forced to concentrate their business in the higher quality and higher priced lines for which the market is smaller. Judge Weber concluded that the independent retailer was placed in this disadvantageous position "not by choice, but by necessity."

The district court ordered Brown to divest itself completely of all the stock, assets, or other interests held in Kinney and to file with the court within 90 days a plan for effecting the divestiture.

II. SUPREME COURT INTERPRETATION
OF THE STATUTE

The Brown Shoe Company appealed the lower court's decision directly to the Supreme Court on the basis of the Expediting Act of 1903. The Court's opinion discussed in detail the legislative history of the 1950 amendments to the statute in order to lay the foundations for its interpretation of the law. Congress, the Court decided, not only intended to make asset acquisitions subject to the Clayton Act's provisions, but also intended to change the standard of illegality contained in Section 7 of the Clayton Act. The Court cited seven factors specifically considered in the legislative history to be relevant to a judgment on the legality of a particular merger:

1. Congress intended to apply the statute to vertical and conglomerate as well as horizontal acquisitions. This intention was evidenced by the removal from the statute of that part of the standard of illegality having to do with the effect of an acquisition on competition *between* the acquiring and the acquired firm and its replacement with language stating the criteria in terms of the effect of the acquisition "in any line of commerce in any section of the country."

2. Congress intended to erect a barrier to the "rising tide of economic concentration." A keystone in the erection of this barrier was the provision enabling the Federal Trade Commission and the courts to stop mergers when the trend to lessening of competition in a market was still incipient.

3. Congress rejected the application of Sherman Act. standards in Section 7 cases.

4. Recognizing that stimulation to competition might result from a particular merger, Congress did not intend to prohibit all acquisitions or mergers. The Court found two examples in legislative history of mergers thought to be acceptable by supporters of the bill: mergers of small companies that make possible more effective competition with dominant firms, and acquisition of failing companies that can no longer compete effectively in the market.

5. Congress did not adopt or reject particular tests for defining either product or geographical limits of the relevant markets within which the probable impact is to be judged. Nor did Congress define the word "substantially" by which the probable lessening of competition is to be measured.

6. Although Congress provided no specific qualitative or quantitative tests with which to gauge whether a given merger's effect may be substantially to lessen competition or tend to create a monopoly, it did indicate that a merger must be viewed functionally in the context of its particular industry, taking into account market structure, changes in market structure, and the condition of entry. Adoption of the amendment in 1950 had been urged as a means of preventing the Congressionally perceived trend toward concentration from reaching those industries as yet unaffected.

7. Congress intended the word "may" to indicate a concern with probabilities rather than certainties.

Thus the net result was a change in the law to prohibit some mergers that would have been permitted under Sherman Act standards; yet per se rules were not provided by Congress. A rule of reason still must be used by the Supreme Court in judging each merger case. Gradually, a new body of law will emerge from a series of cases decided by the highest court. The Brown Shoe case was the first of the series, and it provides new law on a number of questions.

A. The Relevant Market Question

The Court's problem of defining the relevant market is complicated by the fact that the defendants gain by either an extremely broad or an extremely narrow market definition. Per se rules are clearly inappropriate for such a question. In each merger case the trial court or Federal Trade Commission hearing examiner, constrained both by the particular facts at hand and the purposes of the statute, must find reasonable market definitions. In Brown Shoe the Supreme Court laid down some guidelines on both the product and geographical aspects of the problem.

1. *Line of Commerce.* Until this case, the most important Supreme Court precedents on the line of commerce question were the du Font-Cellophane and the du Pont-General Motors cases. Both of these were cases in which the defense chose to argue for a sufficiently *broad* definition to reduce its market share enough to show no undesirable anticompetitive effects. The broad definition was accepted and the defense won in the Cellophane case against a charge of monopolization in violation of the Sherman Act. A narrow definition was accepted in the G.M. case and the defense lost against a charge of violating the pre-1950 Clayton Act. Neither case was a binding precedent in Brown Shoe, and neither dealt with the question of how *narrowly* a market can be defined.

Since the Court recognized a Congressional intent to strengthen the prohibitions against mergers, it was necessary to find guidelines for market definition that would serve to lessen the government's burden of proof. The Court found such guidelines while accepting both the Cellophane and G.M. precedents.

The cross-elasticity or reasonable interchangeability criterion was accepted as the proper determinant of the outer boundaries of a product market. The Court insisted that "the boundaries of the relevant market must be drawn with sufficient breadth to include the competing products of each of the merging companies and to recognize competition where, in fact, competition exists." Presumably, the Court was also accepting reasonable interchangeability as the criterion for deciding the question of "outer boundaries" in cases in which the defense argues for extremely broad definitions. But this acceptance does not mean that the Court has adopted the Sherman Act guidelines. The government's burden has been significantly eased by the Supreme Court's acceptance of the argument that subcategories included within a broader line may also be considered relevant. The boundaries of such relevant lines within lines may be ascertained by ". . . examining such practical indicia as industry or public recognition of the submarket as a separate economic entity, the product's peculiar characteristics and uses, unique production facilities, distinct customers, distinct prices, sensitivity to price changes, and specialized vendors."

The Court went on to say that a merger is proscribed if the probable impact is found in *any* one of such economically significant submarkets. In other words, a merger is unlawful if the government can find a subproduct line, supportable as relevant on any of a number of grounds, for which the unlawful probable impact can be proven. The defense cannot rely on a proof of no unlawful impact in other product lines; it must fight on whatever battlegrounds the government chooses. Congress has said *"any* line of commerce" and the Court has accepted "any" at face value so long as some reasonable ground exists for the definition used. Applying these principles to the Brown Shoe case, the Court was able to uphold Judge Weber's decision that the relevant lines for both the vertical and horizontal parts of the case were men's, women's and children's shoes. The Court found these three product lines (1) to be recognized by the public, (2) to be manufactured in separate plants, (3) to have peculiar characteristics making each one "generally noncompetitive" with the others, and (4) to be directed toward distinct classes of customers.

2. Section of the Country. Using criteria essentially the same as those laid down in arriving at product limits, the Court, while accepting the lower court's findings, offered several important conclusions of law relating to the geographical delimitation of a market. The line-within-a-line concept was extended to include a section within a section of the country. Thus the Court recognized the existence of relevant markets within relevant markets. A relevant geographic market may be as extensive as the whole nation or a small as a single metropolitan area. The whole nation was used for the vertical part of the Brown Shoe case, and cities of over 10,000 and their environs in which both Brown and Kinney had stores were used for the horizontal part.

In a footnote, the Court stated that the fact that the unlawful impact is found in only a small portion of the markets in which the merging firms operate "would, of course, be properly considered in determining the equitable relief to be decreed." This statement may open the door to partial divestiture orders, thereby giving the government incentive to prove the unlawful effect in as many markets as possible, in spite of the fact that proof for any one market is sufficient to establish the violation. This question of partial divestment can be expected to arise in future cases.

A strong case can be made for ordering divestment of only those specific assets for which the probable effect is a substantial lessening of competition. If antitrust policy were implemented by the institution of cases to remedy all unlawful situations, such remedies would not be questionable. Antitrust policy, however, has always been based on deterrence. Society relies on the business community to avoid committing the unlawful acts. Such a deterrence policy requires that cases be brought both to clarify the law and to insure a reasonable probability that those who knowingly violate the law will be prosecuted. In the case of Section 7 of the Clayton Act no criminal penalties apply. A policy of deterrence requires, therefore, that the remedies used by courts or commissions in merger cases be sufficiently stringent to provide incentives to business firms to make only those acquisitions that are clearly lawful. If the Court interprets the law to require complete divestment of any going concern illegally acquired, then more selective acquisition policies by business would be necessary. If partial divestment becomes the rule, then business will have little to lose by making acquisitions and waiting for government action to be brought. The government, on the other hand, would have little incentive to restrict the case to the one or two best relevant markets but would feel impelled to demonstrate anticompetitive effects in enough markets to assure maximum divestiture. With a limited enforcement budget, bigger cases would result in fewer cases. In short, this interpretation of the statute could result in little deterrence. The purpose of the 1950 amendments would not be achieved, and the Clayton Act would serve merely to harass business without preserving and promoting competition.

Fortunately, the Court only refers to the propriety of *consideration* of the degree of overlap in arriving at a remedy. In the case at bar, less than half the cities in which one or the other of the two firms operated outlets were represented. The Court concluded, and the defendants had not even questioned the fact, that the number of included cities was large enough to invalidate the entire merger, if the unlawful impact were found.

B. The Competitive Impact Question

The statute prohibits an acquisition only "where in any line of commerce in any section of the country, the effect of such acquisition may be substantially to lessen competition, or to tend to create a monopoly." As noted above, the Court explicitly recognized that the amended statute applies to vertical and conglomerate as well as to horizontal mergers. The criteria for evaluating the probable effect on competition in each relevant market cannot be identical, of course, for these three types of factual situations. In disposing of the Brown Shoe case, the Supreme Court only hinted at criteria for judging conglomerate mergers, but Chief Justice Warren and the other four justices joining in his opinion were willing to offer criteria on both the vertical and horizontal questions.

1. *Competitive Impact Vertically.* The Court's opinion defines "vertical arrangements" generally as "economic arrangements between companies standing in a supplier-customer relationship." The effect of a vertical arrangement that ties a customer to a supplier, whether by merger or otherwise, may be to foreclose the competitors of either the supplier or customer from a segment of the market otherwise open to them. Neither Section 3 nor Section 7 of the Clayton Act, both of which deal with such vertical arrangements, forbids all of them. The probable anticompetitive impact on a relevant market must be demonstrated.

The Court reasoned that since the primary evil in a vertical acquisition stems from foreclosure of a share of the market, the magnitude of the market share foreclosed is an important consideration. But rather than adopting some specific market share and thus establishing a precedent in quantitative terms, the Court decided to depart from the market share criterion and to look at other factors for the answer. It specified three: (1) the nature and purpose of the contract, (2) the trend toward concentration in the industry, and (3) the merger's probable effects upon the economic way of life sought to be preserved by Congress.

Since the Clayton Act is not a criminal statute, the relevance of evidence on the purpose of the acquisition stems not from a need to prove intent to violate the law, but from the aid that such evidence may give the courts "in predicting the probable future conduct of the parties and thus the probable effects of the merger." The nature and purpose of a merger must be evaluated in the same way as the nature and purpose of a contractual vertical arrangement in a Section 3 case. The Court reviewed the interpretation of Section 3, pointing out the necessity under that part of the Clayton Act of examining the interdependence between the magnitude of the market share foreclosed and the economic purpose of a contractual vertical arrangement. A tying contract is by nature inherently anticompetitive, since it forces a customer to buy something he doesn't want to buy from the seller in order to get something he does want to buy. It is therefore ordinarily unlawful even if the amount of commerce affected is very small. In the case of a limited term exclusive-dealing contract, the market share foreclosed could be much greater without the law being violated. Such a contract, under which a buyer agrees to buy all he requires of a particular type of product from the seller, is not inherently anticompetitive since the buyer may have freely chosen the product and its seller. It might escape censure if its purpose is to insure the purchaser of a sufficient supply of a vital product. Also, the Court said a requirements contract might be lawful if the share foreclosed is small and there is no trend toward concentration.

Similar considerations of purpose and nature are necessary in vertical acquisition cases. The Court found the Brown-Kinney merger to be neither an acquisition of a failing company nor the combination of two small firms attempting to compete better with large dominant companies. Kinney was the largest independent chain, so the potential foreclosure was as large as possible with a merger of an independent retailer and a manufacturer. As to the question whether the potential foreclosure would likely become actual, it was apparent that foreclosure was the purpose of the acquisition. The Court therefore considered the nature of this vertical acquisition to be inherently anticompetitive like a tying clause. Shoes that otherwise would not have been bought by an independent Kinney were forced into the Kinney stores. The opinion also noted the more permanent nature of a tie by acquisition.

It is not clear that the Court's findings on the nature and purpose of vertical integration in the Brown Shoe case would by themselves have provided sufficient grounds for upholding the lower court decision without the companion finding of a trend toward vertical integration in the industry. Justice Harlan was willing to rely on the nature and purpose alone. But the majority accepted Judge Weber's finding of a trend toward concentration and considered this trend to be an important factor, saying that "remaining vigor [of competition] cannot immunize a merger if the trend in that industry is toward oligopoly."

The Court was convinced by the record that the shoe industry was in danger of a change in organization that would probably foreclose competition from "a substantial share" of the relevant markets without resulting in sufficient countervailing advantages— competitive, economic, or social. It did recognize the elimination of wholesalers and increased volume of purchases from the firm's manufacturing division as possible sources of lower costs and lower prices that benefit consumers. But such offsetting advantages of vertical integration were given little weight. The Court's reasoning on this question is not entirely clear, but it appears to have been influenced by three considerations. (1) Independent retailers may be hurt. The Court, however, was not willing to accept injury to competitors in and of itself as a substantial lessening of competition in the market. The statute, it said, protects competition rather than competitors. (2) The weighing of the disadvantages of vertical foreclosure against the advantages of efficiency had been done by Congress when it enacted the legislation. The Court said:

But we cannot fail to recognize Congress' desire to promote competition through the protection of viable, small, locally owned business. Congress appreciated that occasional higher costs and prices might result from the maintenance of fragmented industries and markets. It resolved these competing considerations in favor of decentralization. We must give effect to that decision.

(3) The Court also seems to have recognized that the efficiency advantages, if great enough, can always be achieved by internal expansion rather than by merger.

In summary, the seven Supreme Court justices who participated in the decision agreed that it is the foreclosing nature of a vertical acquisition rather than the magnitude of the share of the market foreclosed that is of primary importance in judging such arrangements under Section 7 as well as under Section 3 of the Clayton Act. The government's case was strengthened, no doubt, by evidence of a trend toward concentration through acquisition. Offsetting economic or competitive advantages were considered relevant, but insufficient, by the five-man majority. Thus, vertical acquisitions are not per se unlawful, but the new law of mergers puts much less burden on the government than before. The criteria used in judging vertical arrangements brought about by a transfer of property rights in a going concern are now essentially the same as the criteria used when the connection between seller and buyer is achieved through a loose-knit contractual agreement.

2. Competitive Impact Horizontally. In formulating criteria for evaluating the probable impact in the relevant market of the horizontal aspects of an acquisition, the Court did not move quite so far toward bringing together the law on loose-knit contractual agreements and close-knit combination through property transfers. In the case of a contractual agreement to centralize pricing decisions among firms on the same side of a market, the law has long considered the nature of the arrangement so obviously anticompetitive as to make it unlawful per se without regard to the reasonableness of the prices fixed. Although centralization horizontally by means of transfer of property confers the same, if not more, power to centralize decision-making, the antitrust laws have until now been interpreted by the Supreme Court to require a showing by the government of power to exclude entry and enhance the price of a product sufficiently to injure the public. The nature and purpose of a transfer of ownership of property was presumed to be inherently consistent with public policy, so such an arrangement had to confer a very large share of the relevant market to a single owner in order to be unlawful under the Sherman Act.

In this first case under the new law the Court has provided a more stringent prohibition of horizontal acquisitions by accepting much smaller market shares than have been considered sufficient to confer illegal monopoly power in past cases. With three products and over one hundred separate geographical markets, the number of relevant markets in which to consider market shares was very large. In spite of the failure of the government to produce testimony and precisely defined statistical information on each of the markets, the Supreme Court accepted the findings of the district court as adequately supported by evidence. Judge Weber had accepted evidence on market shares based on census information for cities, but he defined the market as "cities and their environs."

The largest combined share of Brown and Kinney outlets was 55.7 per cent of the sales of women's shoes in Dodge City, Kansas, in 1955. The Court noted that the combined share exceeded 5 per cent in at least one of the three product lines in 118 of the cities in which both firms had outlets. On the significance of a 5 per cent market share the Court had this to say:

> In an industry as fragmented as shoe retailing, the control of substantial shares of the trade in a city may have important effects on competition. If a merger achieving 5% control were now approved, we might be required to approve future merger efforts by Brown's competitors seeking similar market shares. The oligopoly Congress sought to avoid would then be furthered and it would be difficult to dissolve the combinations previously approved.

Thus the Court considered the magnitude of the market share of the merging firms in the light of the degree of fragmentation that exists in the industry. A merger resulting in a 5 per cent market share might be lawful under different circumstances. Particularly, the Court would appear reluctant to prohibit the use of a merger to achieve a market share less than that already permitted for a firm's competitors. Thus, if a line is to be drawn someplace, it can best be drawn so as to prevent relatively large firms from getting larger market shares through merger, irrespective of the magnitude of the share. It would seem that the Court has adopted a policy on market shares in horizontal mergers similar to that used with vertical tying arrangements. The shares of the relevant market united by the merger is relevant, but the standard of legality is to be multidimensional. No particular percentage is to be used either to condemn or condone a merger. The market shares united by the acquisition must be evaluated in the light of several other factors.

In this particular case of a horizontal merger of retail chains, the Court considered several characteristics of the firm controlling a specific share of a particular market to be important. A specific share in the hands of a firm also operating in many other markets need not be as large to be unlawful as the same share in the hands of a firm operating only in the particular market. If a firm can price in such a way as to achieve higher profits from some of its markets than from others, it is certainly justified in doing so from a profit-maximizing point of view. The effect may be a lessening of competition, however, since a firm with some profitable markets can last longer in a price war in the more competitive low-profit markets. The existence of such unbalanced market power may serve to inhibit competition and promote price leadership even though the largest firm's market share is relatively small compared with that which would be necessary for price leadership to develop if all firms operated only in one market. . . .

Finally, as in the case of the vertical-integration question, the Court also considered the trend toward concentration in the industry. The Court found this merger to be the "appropriate place at which to call a halt." This incipiency doctrine requires prohibition of mergers that in and of themselves do not appear to have the effect of public injury. The prohibition of the Brown-

Kinney merger is a means of forestalling a large number of other potential mergers in the shoe industry. Thus the general pattern of control in many markets will be affected by the decision.

In short, the Court has greatly narrowed the range of uncertainty about the new law on horizontal mergers. The Sherman Act requirement of proof of the achievement of power to enhance price and exclude entry is clearly inapplicable, having been replaced by the incipiency doctrine. Rather than simply looking to the past, the Court will look primarily to the future, forecasting in broad terms the probable effect on the structure and performance of an industry if such mergers as the one at hand are condoned.

The relevant markets must be defined, but market definition is not likely to be the crux of many horizontal merger cases for three reasons. (1) Markets within markets were clearly recognized by the Court so that the quest for the one and only right market definition is no longer useful to either party to a case. (2) The Court definitely rejected the idea that the existence of only a small amount of overlap of the business of the merging firms, and thus little competition between them, justifies a merger. Defendants can no longer hope to gain by arguing for the market definition that minimizes the percentage of each firm's business done in competition with the other. (3) Market share statistics have themselves been relegated to a subsidiary role, and the definition of the base on which shares are computed is less crucial to the outcome of a case.

III. CONCLUSIONS

The Supreme Court had to be concerned with the effect of the Brown-Kinney merger on competition in the relevant markets. Far more important, however, is the effect of the Court's interpretation of the law on competition generally in the markets of our economy. With this decision and the opinions accompanying it, the changes in the law on corporate acquisitions made by Congress in 1950 finally have been given specific content. In essence the new policy is simple: both vertical and horizontal mergers are likely to be held illegal unless the companies can demonstrate clearly that the mergers are likely to increase competition and thus promote the public interest. Unless a company is able to so demonstrate, any vertical or horizontal acquisition in any significant market is particularly subject to challenge if a trend toward concentration exists.

PART IV _Tying Contracts and Exclusive Dealing Contracts_

13 EXCLUSIVE DEALINGS AND TIE-IN SALES:

Strangers No More

In this section we turn to certain more complex areas of business behavior, for example, exclusive dealings and full-line forcing, with a view toward their effect upon competition. Regrettably, the importance of these forms of business behavior is easily underestimated. A substantial portion of industrial sales is subject to conditions—such as requiring the purchase of one or more commodities as a part of the transaction—in addition to simply price and quantity factors. Thus the emphasis in this section is in counterdistinction to that upon the structural aspects of monopoly of the preceding sections on monopoly and merger. The heart of the problem lies in determining the effects of particular types of behavior and reconciling such behavior with competitive results, or our norm for industrial performance and antitrust policy. These considerations are complicated by the implicit problem of deciding whether, as technology and other facets of modern industry become more complex with the passage of time, laws should provide for continuance of competition or competitive structure. Although the problem may appear to be semantic, a conflict is posed when competition eliminates entrepreneurs who are assumed to be in "competition." One reason for the problem is the "can't see the forest for the trees" environment of antitrust, as many past cases have been concerned with particular behavior patterns or even incidents rather than with the resultant market performance. An economic analysis of business environment and behavior facilitates identification of competitive effects, or market performance, stemming from various behavior patterns. For social or other reasons, it may seem desirable to take action regardless of the economic effect of that action. Then the action should be explicitly based on those noneconomic objectives, and thus avoid garbing such action in the robe of economics.

In this section several aspects of business behavior are examined and their legally assumed economic effects are compared with their expected, or predicted, effects in an economic sense. Throughout the following material various situations are compared to determine the degree of divergency between the use of contractual agreements governing purchases and sales between two parties and the ownership of all stages of business in a single vertically integrated company. These positions must be reconciled before our antitrust policy can be considered logically structured.

One common business practice, *exclusive dealing,* involves a contractual agreement that the purchaser utilize only the seller's output of a particular product and no other. Exclusive-dealing contracts were involved in the Standard Fashion and Standard Stations[2] cases considered later in this section. The essence of an exclusive-dealing contract is embodied in Magrane-Houston's contract with Standard Fashion whereby it could "not sell or permit to be sold on its premises during the term of the contract any other make of patterns." Similarly, Standard's contracts with service-station operators were "of several types, but a feature common to each is the dealer's undertaking to purchase from Standard all his requirements of one or more products . . . [including] written agreements . . . [that] bind the dealer to purchase of Standard all his requirements of petroleum products only."

Tying arrangements involve the concomitant purchase-sale of two or more commodities. As indicated above, exclusive-dealing arrangements might involve the purchase of a single commodity.

---

[1] Standard Fashion Co. v. Magrane-Houston Co., 258 U.S. 346 (1922).

[2] Standard Oil Company of California and Standard Stations, Inc. v. United States, 337 U.S. 293 (1949).

Typically, a tying contract involves the requirement that a purchaser acquire a second product from the seller as a condition for acquiring the first. This essential feature of tie-in sales was effectively achieved when American Can leased its "closing machines only to customers who purchase[d] their cans from it . . ." [3]

It is not always possible to distinguish unambiguously between exclusive dealings and tying-arrangement contracts. At times the two blend to provide a situation identified as "full-line forcing." One economist, M. L. Burstein, defines *full-line forcing* "as the practice of requiring that the purchaser of product A purchase stated quantities or 'requirements' of products B, C, . . . from the seller of A . . ." [4] It can be readily appreciated that full-line forcing, as Burstein defines it, would include the examples of tying arrangements and exclusive dealing discussed above. Ordinarily the term, if not the conceptual formulation, is applied to cases where an extended line of products is forced upon a buyer. Such was the case when Standard's contracts bound "the dealer to purchase of Standard all his requirements of gasoline and other petroleum products as well as tires, tubes, and batteries . . . [and in] some instances dealers . . . also orally agreed to purchase of Standard their requirements of other automobile accessories."

Although exclusive-dealing and tying contracts have been attacked under Section 1 of the Sherman Act and Section 5 of the Federal Trade Commission Act, these practices have most frequently been fought under Section 3 of the Clayton Act, which states:

> . . . it shall be unlawful for any person engaged in commerce . . . to lease or make a sale or contract for sale of goods, . . . whether patented or unpatented, . . . on the condition . . . that the lessee or purchaser thereof shall not use or deal in the goods . . . of a competitor . . . where the effect of such lease, sale, or contract for sale or such condition . . . may be to substantially lessen competition or tend to create a monopoly in any line of commerce.

[3] United States v. American Can Co., 87 F. Supp. 18 (1949).
[4] Meyer L. Burstein, "A Theory of Full-Line Forcing," *Northwestern University Law Review,* 55 (1960), 62.

This provision is applicable in those instances in which the courts find a decline in competition resulting from the contractual commitment. However, the interpretation of Section 3 has varied over time, and a concern with the likelihood of noncompetitive results ("may be to substantially lessen . . .") has dominated the courts' views on the matter.

As indicated, exclusive-dealing and tying contracts involve two or more distinct products. In each instance control of one product apparently enables its seller to exert some "extra" control over the sale of a second product. However, the tying situation seemingly requires—or provides room for—considerably greater finesse and variety than does the exclusive-dealing situation. Many of its applications are related to alternative means of conducting modern business operations. Not infrequently tying contracts are alleged to improve business efficiency. Consequently there is perhaps greater legal and economic interest in the tying cases than in the exclusive-dealing situations.

Tying cases antedate exclusive-dealing cases by several years in antitrust; further, tying situations have received greater attention from antitrust enforcers. To fully grasp the evolution of antitrust law in this area of business practice, one must consider a wide number of cases, including at least six important ones: United Shoe[5] (1918); United Shoe[6] (1922); IBM [7] (1936); International Salt[8] (1947); Times-Picayune[9] (1953); and Northern Pacific[10] (1957). However, the evolution of the antitrust law of exclusive dealing can be summarized in three cases: Standard Fashion (1922); Standard Stations (1949); and Tampa Electric[11] (1960). Other decisions have provided legal refinements, but these cases

[5] United States v. United Shoe Machinery Corporation, 247 U.S. 32 (1918).

[6] United States v. United Shoe Machinery Corporation, 258 U.S. 451 (1922).

[7] International Business Machines Corporation v. United States, 298 U.S. 131 (1936).

[8] International Salt Co. v. United States, 332 U.S. 392 (1947).

[9] Times-Picayune v. United States, 345 U.S. 594 (1953).

[10] Northern Pacific Railway Co. v. United States, 356 U.S. 1 (1958).

[11] Tampa Electric Co. v. Nashville Coal Co., 365 U.S. 320 (1961).

contain the essence of the Court's position on exclusive dealings.

Reflecting the earlier and more extensive concern with the legal and economic issues inherent in the tying situations, we will first focus on the six tying-contract cases cited above. Then we will consider exclusive dealing. These nine cases indicate the judicial evaluation of readily identifiable business practices over time. These decisions also indicate how the application of a legal statement has varied as our (business and legal) institutions have evolved. However, the cases also indicate the consequences of an increasing sophistication—or continuing change—in the nature of economic reasoning. This is most clearly reflected in the concepts of competition applied in the first United Shoe case as contrasted to our contemporary concepts of competition. The question posed by the exclusive-dealing and tying cases is whether the application of this evolving economic thought has been sufficiently rapid or whether applied economics, in this area, has lagged significantly behind the zealousness of statutory enforcement.

Tying contracts have been the subject of Supreme Court decisions since the 1912 A. B. Dick[12] case. In this decision the Court held that the patentee could tie the use of nonpatented items to the purchase and use of the patented item. This tie-in of several goods was justified by virtue of the control exercised by the patent holder over his product. The position taken in these early cases was modified following the passage of the Clayton Act, with its Section 3. In the 1917 Motion Picture Patents[13] case the Supreme Court held that the patent of an item permitted only the restricted sale of that item, but not the restriction of any other product not covered by the patent.

However, the real shifts of contemporary antitrust law on tying practices lie in a pair of lawsuits brought by the federal government against the United Shoe Machinery Corporation.[14] United Shoe Company was the result of a five-firm merger in 1899 that then accounted for a 70 to 80 per cent share of the shoe-machinery

[12] Henry v. A. B. Dick Co., 224 U.S. 1 (1912).

[13] Motion Picture Patents Co. v. Universal Film Co., 243 U.S. 502 (1917).

[14] See Carl Kaysen, *United States v. United Shoe Machinery Corporation* (Cambridge: Harvard University Press, 1956) for a more detailed analysis of this case.

market. Subsequently it was involved in fifty-nine mergers, from 1899 through 1911, and from an initial stock offering of $15 million, it grew to an asset size of $40.8 million by 1910. About 25 per cent of United's total growth in this period resulted from acquisitions. Unfortunately, no serious estimate of market share exists for this latter period, although the Justice Department generally claimed 95 per cent. The market-share figures are only for some relatively small number of the most important machine types, and no method for weighing these machine types was presented. Sections 1 and 2 Sherman Act antitrust charges were filed in 1911. The government alleged that the 1899 merger creating United had violated Section 1 because it restrained trade. In addition the government charged a violation of Section 2 by the original mergers and the leasing system itself. In finding for United Shoe, the Court held:

1. Intent was not to monopolize but to maintain efficiency.
2. Companies had not competed with each other; machines produced were complementary and not competitive.
3. The leasing system (and its tying aspects) were within the valid patent rights of United.[15]

After passage of the Clayton Act in 1914 and after the first case was decided for United, the government filed a new suit, charging United with violating Section 3 of the Clayton Act. The government complained that a number of United's lease clauses violated Section 3. The District Court upheld the government on a number of these clauses, thus effectively overturning the decision of several years earlier.[16] Among the clauses found objectionable were:

1. Clauses prohibiting use of machines to shoes upon which many specified basic operations were undertaken only on United machines.

[15] United States v. United Shoe Machinery Company, 222 Fed. Rep. 350 (1915); affirmed, 247 U.S. 32 (1918).
[16] United States v. United Shoe Machinery Corporation, 264 Fed. Rep. 138 (1920).

2. Clauses restricting use of machines only to certain work.
3. Requiring supplies for some machines to be purchased from United.
4. Requiring additional machinery to be obtained from United.
5. United's right to cancel all leases for breach of one lease.
6. Granting United royalties on all operations, even those not performed on its machines, in lessee's factory.
7. United's restriction of some operations (on its patented insole) to be worked only on United's machines.
8. Increasing United's royalties on some machines when some operations were performed on other's machines.

Although the Court held these clauses violative of Section 3, it permitted three other clauses to stand:

1. United's machines to be used to full capacity if suitable work available
2. Parts and attachments to be purchased from United; repair and service only by United
3. United's right to order return of machines in excess of those needed for lessee's volume

Two clauses (1 and 3) were held necessary to protect royalty revenues, while the other clause (2) was deemed a reasonable protection of the "functional efficiency" of the machines. However, neither the seventeen-year-lease term nor the leasing system itself were found to violate the law. These lower court findings were upheld by the Supreme Court.[17]

In the first United Shoe case the definition of competition was much narrower than it is today. The Court overlooked the fact that the machines may have differed in the process used, but the shoes were competitive and thus (indirectly) the machines had to be competitive. Also, the research and development programs instituted by these companies to develop new machines indicated the extent of potential competition existing prior to the merger.

The second United Shoe case thus struck down some aspects

[17] United States v. United Shoe Machinery Corporation, 258 U.S. 451 (1922).

of tying contracts, but left intact the principle that "clean" tying contracts (those without the noncompetitive clauses) would be considered valid under law. Two justifications of the tying contracts remained: (1) The need to protect royalty revenues; and (2) the need to protect the machines through assuring proper use and care.

The 1936 International Business Machines decision was important because it passed on the legitimacy of one important defense—product protection—for using tying clauses. IBM had tied the sales of tabulating cards to the leasing of its tabulating machines. The Supreme Court held that IBM dominated the market for tabulating machines, and so the tying arrangement permitted the expansion of this dominance to the new punch-card market. In its decision the Court denied the possibility that product protection would justify the anticompetitive effects of the tying contract. The protection was available, according to the decision, in a variety of ways, including instructional warnings to purchasers or lessees of the equipment. However, even after this decision, some doubt remained as to the scope of prohibition of the tying clauses, since the Court specifically cited IBM's dominance in the tying product's market. Thus, after the IBM case, the importance of market domination and the possible enclave of justified tying still remained to be defined.

The 1947 International Salt decision provided some light on the nature of foreclosure necessary to violate the antitrust law. The case was brought under Section 1 Sherman Act and Section 3 Clayton Act. International Salt was the largest producer of salt for industrial purposes and owned the patents on two salt-selling machines. These machines were distributed primarily through leases that required the lessees to use International's salt in the machines. The Court held that, just as price fixing was unreasonable per se, so was it unreasonable per se to foreclose competitors from any substantial market. In this instance the salt for use in the patent machines sold under the contested agreements totaled 119,000 tons annually and cost about $500,000. This volume was declared "not insignificant and, though the tendency to monopoly was growing slowly, the law did not preclude an antitrust action prior to the monopoly's creation." The decision was important precisely because it defined market substantiality in terms of the volume of business affected by the contracts. The gist of the decision seemed to make patent tie-ins illegal per se. The substantiality test itself was analogous to that applied two years later in the Standard Stations exclusive-dealings case. The Supreme Court recognized the manufacturer's necessity to protect the machines, but the Court declared a need to provide reasonable standards of machine use (for protection and so forth) rather than promulgate rules that were disguised restraints on free competition. The case presented a confrontation of two arguments: one, that the tying clause was necessary to assure proper use of machines (i.e., that salt of proper characteristics would be used); and, two, that the tying restrictions (ostensibly for machine protection) were merely a thinly disguised form of noncompetitive exclusion of other suppliers from a market—in this instance, other salt manufacturers. The problem as to whether the tie-in arrangement serves a real economic function arises in each of the exclusion cases. The value of striking the tying clause varies from suit to suit, depending on whether other, permissible devices exist to provide the same purpose as the tie-in.

In International Salt a charge was filed and sustained under both the Clayton and Sherman Acts, and the decision indicated no differentiation between the standards to be applied under the two laws. However, the 1953 Times-Picayune decision seemed to differentiate between the Sherman and Clayton Acts tying charges and the proof required under each law. As indicated below, the suit was filed under Sections 1 and 2 of the Sherman Act, and for some unknown reason, there was no alternative allegation of a Section 3 violation:

At issue is the legality under the Sherman Act of the Times-Picayune Publishing Company's contracts for the sale of newspaper classified and general display advertising space. The Company in New Orleans owns and publishes the morning Times-Picayune and the evening States. Buyers of space for general display and classified advertising in its publications may purchase only combined insertions appearing in both the morning and evening papers, and not in either separately. The United States filed a civil suit under the Sherman Act, challenging these "unit" or "forced combination" contracts as unreasonable restraints of interstate trade, banned by §1, and as tools in an attempt to monopolize a segment of interstate commerce, in violation of §2. After intensive trial of the facts, the District Court found violations of both sections of the law and entered a decree enjoining the Publishing Company's use of these unit contracts and related arrangements for the marketing of advertising space.[18] . . .

As indicated, the case was filed only under the Sherman Act. Commentators were troubled by this decision, which seemed to differentiate in the standards to be applied under Sherman and Clayton Act violation. In the Court's words:

. . . When the seller enjoys a monopolistic position in the market for the "tying" product, *or* if a substantial volume of commerce in the "tied" product is restrained, a tying arrangement violates the narrower standards expressed in §3 of the Clayton Act because from either factor the requisite potential lessening of competition is inferred. And because for even a lawful monopolist it is "unreasonable, *per se,* to foreclose competitors from any substantial market," a tying arrangement is banned by §1 of the Sherman Act whenever *both* conditions are met. In either case, the arrangement transgresses §5 of the Federal Trade Commission Act, since minimally that section registers violations of the Clayton and Sherman Acts.[19]

The Court's examination of the facts in this situation are, at least, interesting to the antitrust practitioner. Unfortunately, space precludes this presentation; for current purposes the suit's importance lay in its apparent distinguishing among the tests applied by the Sherman and Clayton Acts. From 1953 until 1957 this apparent distinction existed, but the 1958 Northern Pacific case has apparently erased this distinction with a decision that may have made tying contracts illegal per se.

In this instance Northern Pacific sold or leased much of its great land holdings under a requirement that any originating rail shipments were to go via Northern Pacific routing—provided that

[18] *Op. cit.,* 596–598.
[19] *Ibid.,* 608–609.

Northern Pacific's rates (and sometimes service) were competitive. No patent was involved and no dominance over the total supply of land existed, although the Court ruled that the size of the land holdings was substantial. The majority opinion cited many of the other cases considered in this chapter. However, the portions especially relevant for our purposes were:

The defendant attempts to evade the force of *International Salt* on the ground that the tying product there was patented while here it is not. But we do not believe this distinction has, or should have, any significance. In arriving at its decision in *International Salt* the Court placed no reliance on the fact that a patent was involved nor did it give the slightest intimation that the outcome would have been any different if that had not been the case. If anything, the Court held the challenged tying arrangements unlawful *despite* the fact that the tying item was patented, not because of it. . . .

The defendant argues that the holding in *International Salt* was limited by the decision in *Times-Picayune Publishing Co.* v. *United States.* . . . There the Court held that a unit system of advertising in two local newspapers did not violate §1 of the Sherman Act. . . . But the Court was extremely careful to confine its decision to the narrow record before it. . . .

While there is some language in the *Times-Picayune* opinion which speaks of "monopoly power" or "dominance" over the tying product as a necessary precondition for application of the rule of *per se* unreasonableness to tying arrangements, we do not construe this general language as requiring anything more than sufficient economic power to impose an appreciable restraint on free competition in the tied product (assuming all the time, of course, that a "not insubstantial" amount of interstate commerce is affected). . . . *Times-Picayune* . . . makes clear . . . that the vice of tying arrangements lies in the use of economic power in one market to restrict competition on the merits in another, regardless of the source from which the power is derived and whether the power takes the form of a monopoly or not.

. . . [I]f these restrictive provisions are merely harmless sieves with no tendency to restrain competition, as the defendant's argument seems to imply, it is hard to understand why it has expended so much effort in obtaining them in vast numbers and upholding their validity, or how they are of any benefit to anyone, even the defendant. But however that may be, the essential fact remains that these arguments are binding obligations held over the heads of vendees which deny defendant's competitors access to the fenced-off market on the same terms as the defendant. . . . All of this is only aggravated, of course, here in the regulated transportation industry where there is frequently no real rate competition at all and such effective competition as actually thrives takes other forms.[20]

Thus, despite Justice Clark's absence from consideration of this case and the dissenting opinion of Justices Harlan, Frankfurter, and Whittaker, the 1958 Northern Pacific case provided the culmination of over forty years of antitrust efforts against tying contracts. In almost every situation the practice is viewed as illegal per se. The preceding examination of cases has indicated a steady trend from a "rule of reason" evaluation to a per se violation status. A similar evolution can be observed in the treatment of exclusive-dealing contracts, which are considered next.

A standard exclusive-dealing contract was the subject of the Standard Fashion decision of 1922. Magrane-Houston Company, a retail store, had contracted to sell Standard's fashion patterns exclusively for a two-year period. The contract provided for subsequent renewal on a term-to-term basis, and it included provisions of minimum stocks, "transfer of the agency," and other considerations. As indicated below, the Court rejected the agency defense, and the decision included the following finding of facts and application of law:

> The contract contains an agreement that . . . [Magrane-Houston] shall not sell or permit to be sold on its premises during the term of the contract any other make of patterns. It is shown that on or about July 1, 1917, . . . [Magrane-Houston] discontinued the sale of . . . [Standard Fashion's] patterns, and placed on sale in its store patterns of a rival company known as the McCall Company.
>
> It is insisted by . . . [Standard Fashion] that the contract is not one of sale, but is one of agency or joint venture, but an analysis of the contract shows that a sale was in fact intended and made. . . .
>
> Section 3 condemns sales or agreements where the effect of such sale or contract of sale "may" be to substantially lessen compe-

[20] *Op. cit.*, 9–12.

tition or tend to create monopoly. It thus deals with consequences to follow the making of the restrictive covenant limiting the right of the purchaser to deal in the goods of the seller only. But we do not think that the purpose in using the word "may" was to prohibit the mere possibility of the consequences described. It was intended to prevent such agreements as would, under the circumstances disclosed probably lessen competition, or create an actual tendency to monopoly. That it was not intended to reach every remote lessening of competition is shown in the requirement that such lessening must be substantial.

Both courts below found that the contract interpreted in the light of the circumstances surrounding the making of it was within the provisions of the Clayton Act as one which substantially lessened competition and tended to create monopoly. These courts put special stress upon the fact found that, of 52,000 so-called pattern agencies in the entire country, . . . [Standard Fashion], or a holding company controlling it and two other pattern companies, approximately controlled two fifths of such agencies. As the Circuit Court of Appeals summarizing the matter pertinently observed:

"The restriction of each merchant to one pattern manufacturer must in hundreds, perhaps in thousands, of small communities amount to giving such single pattern manufacturer a monopoly of the business in such community. Even in the larger cities, to limit to a single pattern maker the pattern business of dealers most resorted to by customers whose purchases tend to give fashions their vogue, may tend to facilitate further combinations; so that the plaintiff, or some other aggressive concern, instead of controlling two-fifths, will shortly have almost, if not quite, all the pattern business." [21]

The Standard Fashion case thus indicated that a showing of probable noncompetitive effects would be sufficient to find a violation of Section 3. This implicitly suggests the permissibility of such practices when they provide economic benefits. The Standard Fashion decision held that competition was restricted by a producer's contracts precluding the retailer from selling a rival manufacturer's product. Standard Fashion banned the use of exclusive dealings as the tool of a dominant seller; this practice was viewed as a means of extending and maintaining the dominant seller's

[21] *Op. cit.*, 554–557.

primacy. It should be stated that these agreements subsequently have been permitted in the absence of dominant market power or danger that competitors would be excluded from significant sectors of the market. However, in 1949 the Standard Stations opinion held that economic justifications would not condone an otherwise illegal exclusive-dealing control.

In the Standard Stations case the government attacked (under Sherman Act, Section 1, and Clayton Act, Section 3) Standard's use of "exclusive supply contracts with . . . independent dealer(s) in petroleum products and automobile accessories." These exclusive-dealing or full-line-forcing contracts

> . . . [were of] several types, but a common feature to each is the dealer's undertaking to purchase from Standard all his requirements of one or more products. Two types . . . bind the dealer to purchase of Standard all his requirements of gasoline and other petroleum products as well as tires, tubes and batteries. The remaining written agreements . . . bind the dealer to purchase of Standard all his requirements of petroleum products only. It was found that independent dealers had entered 742 oral contracts by which they agreed to sell only Standard's gasoline. In some instances, dealers who contracted to purchase from Standard all their requirements of tires, tubes, and batteries, had also orally agreed to purchase of Standard their requirements of other automobile accessories.[22] . . .

The Standard Stations opinion held that Section 3 of the Clayton Act was violated by a given requirements contract that covered "a substantial number of outlets and a substantial amount of products, whether considered on a comparative basis or not." Showing these conditions sufficed as proof that the contracts caused an actual or potential decline in competition or that the contracts tended to establish a monopoly. The Court rejected, as mitigating factors, the possible benefits of the agreements if they were found to otherwise violate Section 3. The excerpts below provide a summary of the facts and of the majority's reasoning; parts of the dissenting views are included to facilitate a comparison

[22] *Op. cit.,* 296.

of the arguments, pro and con, concerning the necessity to show that a contract actually lessened competition or tended to create a monopoly.

The Standard Stations case seemed to resolve the "may . . . substantially lessen competition" issue through the simple expediency of considering the substantiality of the product sales as indicative of substantial lessening of competition. The decision was thus consistent with the principles indicated in International Salt. Further, the cases considered to this point provide comparable treatment of tying and exclusive-dealing situations; in both instances we are provided with a virtual quantitative substantiality test leading to an almost complete per se illegality. Apart from its economic merits (which should be considered in evaluating the material in this and the following two chapters), this approach quite successfully meets the certainty test to which all good law must conform. However, two relatively recent decisions indicate that the Court is willing to allow exceptions to this principle. The two decisions (both involving exclusive-dealing contracts) were the 1951 J. I. Case Company[23] decision and the 1961 Tampa Electric decision.

The J. I. Case decision was apparently based on the government's failure to establish that the defendants had (1) market power or (2) attempted to coerce their customers. In this situation Case was a major agricultural-implement manufacturer with about 3,738 dealers in 1948. The Court's finding of facts and comments included:

> During the last World War . . . many dealers in farm machinery handling competing lines were induced by Case to take on its line. . . . And when the war ended . . . Case recognized that it would have to make a survey of all of its dealers, and where inadequate representation was had, new dealers would have to be obtained. And where a dealer was handling another full line with Case and could not do justice to both lines, he was given in many instances a choice as to which line he preferred to handle, and if the competing line was chosen, Case looked for another dealer. . . . Generally, the result . . . would be that there became a Case dealer

[23] United States v. J. I. Case Co., 101 F. Supp. 856 (1951).

and the competitive dealer in the community. Therefore, not only did competition continue, but the free flow of farm machinery rather than being impeded was usually increased. There is no showing that any farm machinery manufacturer had difficulty in obtaining dealers as outlets for its particular line under such circumstances. . . .

. . . The advent of power-drawn machinery on the farms . . . has entirely changed the farm machinery business. . . . A full supply of parts for the machinery handled is required to be kept by the dealer. Service men who can promptly respond to the farmer's call when machines break down in the field are indispensable to a successful dealer, and a progressive dealer in farm machinery generally recognizes that, if he is identified in a community as the representative of one of the major lines of farm machinery, he assumes a certain standing and reputation in the community as a dealer with adequate parts and personnel for servicing the particular line which he handles. Just as an automobile owner prefers to go to the agency for service which handles his car for sale and specializes in that car for service, the tractor owner naturally prefers to go to the farm machinery dealer who sells and specializes in that particular line.

It cannot be gainsaid that, in pursuit of a bona fide business policy, Case has the right to select its own customers in absence of any scheme or purpose to effect a monopoly. . . .[24]

Section 3 of the Clayton Act is directed to the preserving of a free flow of goods to the ultimate market—here, the users of farm machinery. If there are agreements . . . made with dealers that they shall not handle competitive lines, . . . competition may be lessened or there may be a tendency to create a monopoly. . . .

Realistically considered, it is difficult to understand from the evidence how Case's acts and conduct would have any tendency to lessen competition substantially, or that the outlet for farm machinery has been, or would be, narrowed or endangered thereby. There are some 20,000 farm equipment dealers in the United States and of these dealers the Government relies upon evidence which pertains to 108—less than ½ of one percent of the entire number of farm equipment dealers. Moreover, generally when a Case contract was not renewed as to any one of its dealers, the merchandise

[24] *Ibid.*, 862–863.

of both Case and the competitor continued to flow in commerce as before—the competitor's through the former Case dealer, and Case's through another dealer established by it. . . . Not only is there failure in the evidence to establish any substantial restrictions on outlets for the retail distribution of farm machinery, but the evidence reflects that there is healthy competition among all farm machinery manufacturers.[25]

The decision forces one to rethink whether Standard Stations really laid down a quantitative substantiality standard. Here the criteria was based on the reasonableness of the market restriction in light of other case situations. However, the decision does not indicate either a return to the rule of reason or an altering of the Court's general standards, because the otherwise illegal practices will not be excused by the beneficial aspects of that practice. However, the Case decision indicates that the beneficial aspects of an exclusive-dealing contract will be considered in evaluating the contract's role in the given situation.

The J. I. Case decision recognized the legitimacy of some exclusive dealings; that decision effectively permitted exclusive dealings in support of a distribution-and-service organization in those situations in which (1) customers would not be faced with a monopolistic situation and (2) similar practices could be adopted by other producers. In the Tampa Electric case, the Supreme Court was faced with a contract obligating Tampa Electric Company to purchase its coal from a single supplier for a twenty-year period. These coal needs were estimated at an eventual 2,250,000 tons per year. However, about 700 coal suppliers were located in that area and the amount of coal represented only one per cent of the total area production of that type. The Court summed up its general statement of facts and law as follows:

To determine substantiality in a given case, it is necessary to weigh the probable effect of the contract on the relevant area of effective competition, taking into account the relative strength of the parties, the proportionate volume of commerce involved in relation to the total volume of commerce in the relevant market area, and the

[25] *Ibid.*, 865–866.

probable immediate and future effects which pre-emption of that share of the market might have on effective competition therein. It follows that a mere showing that the contract itself involves a substantial number of dollars is ordinarily of little consequence.[26]

With this rather surprising statement behind it, the Court then proceeded to apply the law to this given situation. The statement is surprising because it denies that quantitatively substantial amounts of commerce are sufficient to violate Section 3. The following quote indicates the Court's decision and its succinct differentiation of the case from the previous bench-mark situations.

It may well be that in the context of antitrust legislation protracted requirements contracts are suspect, but they have not been declared illegal *per se*. Even though a single contract between single traders may fall within the initial broad proscription of the section, it must also suffer the qualifying disability, tendency to work a substantial—not remote—lessening of competition in the relevant competitive market. It is urged that the present contract pre-empts competition to the extent of purchases worth perhaps $128,000,000, and that this "is, of course, not insignificant or insubstantial." While $128,000,000 is a considerable sum of money, even in these days, the dollar volume, by itself, is not the test, as we have already pointed out.

The remaining determination, therefore, is whether the pre-emption of competition to the extent of the tonnage involved tends to substantially foreclose competition in the relevant coal market. We think not. That market sees an annual trade in excess of 250,000,000 tons of coal and over a billion dollars—multiplied by 20 years it runs into astronomical figures. There is here neither a seller with a dominant position in the market as in *Standard Fashions, supra*; nor myriad outlets with substantial sales volume, coupled with an industry-wide practice of relying upon exclusive contracts, as in *Standard Oil, supra*; nor a plainly restrictive tying arrangement as in *International Salt, supra*. On the contrary, we seem to have only that type of contract which "may well be of economic advantage to buyers as well as to sellers." *Standard Oil Co.* v. *United States, supra*, . . . In the case of the buyer it "may assure supply," while on the part of the seller it "may make possible the

[26] *Op. cit.,* 329.

substantial reduction of selling expenses, give protection against price fluctuations, and . . . offer the possibility of a predictable market." *Id.,* . . . The 20-year period of the contract is singled out as the principal vice, but at least in the case of public utilities the assurance of a steady and ample supply of fuel is necessary in the public interest. Otherwise consumers are left unprotected against service failures owing to shutdowns; and increasingly unjustified costs might result in more burdensome rate structures eventually to be reflected in the consumer's bill. The compelling validity of such considerations has been recognized fully in the natural gas public utility field. This is not to say that utilities are immunized from Clayton Act proscriptions, but merely that, in judging the term of a requirements contract in relation to the substantiality of the foreclosure of competition, particularized considerations of the parties' operations are not irrelevant. In weighing the various factors, we have decided that in the competitive bituminous coal marketing area involved here the contract sued upon does not tend to foreclose a substantial volume of competition.[27]

Thus Tampa Electric mitigated the strict quantitative-substantiality doctrine to the extent of recognizing the desirability, or need, of requirements contracts in modern business—at least to the extent that (1) relative substantiality was not a concomitant of quantitative substantiality and (2) alternative outlets existed for similar products.

This review of the evolution of the antitrust laws concerning exclusive-dealing and tying contracts has revealed some of the conflicts frequently existing between economic and legal considerations in antitrust. The conflicts emerge in the transition from general competitive principles to the detailed investigation needed to distinguish necessary business practices from those malpractices designed to frustrate competition. In any given situation one must consider (1) how the situation compares to the philosophy and requirements of the Sherman and Clayton Acts, (2) the significance of patents and of industry conditions and practices, (3) the relative market (area and product) affected, (4) the possibilities of utilizing other practices to achieve the alleged purposes of the tying practices and exclusive dealings, (5) the validity of "quantita-

[27] *Ibid.,* 333–335.

tive substantiality," (6) the harmoniousness of the decision, (7) the importance and extent of a rule of reason application, and (8) the extent to which the practice has beneficial aspects. Particularly in light of a workable competition goal, what is a desirable yardstick in these matters? Can a general rule or guide be provided to secure this workable competitive result? The following chapter considers the changes stemming from the application of Section 3 to a particular tying situation. However, the question is reconsidered in the chapter following that.

....

STANDARD OIL COMPANY OF CALIFORNIA AND STANDARD STATIONS, INC.
v.
UNITED STATES
337 US 293–324 (1949)

Mr. Justice Frankfurter delivered the opinion of the Court.

The Standard Oil Company of California, a Delaware corporation, owns petroleum-producing resources and refining plants in California and sells petroleum products in what has been termed in these proceedings the "Western area"—Arizona, California, Idaho, Nevada, Oregon, Utah and Washington. It sells through its own service stations, to the operators of independent service stations, and to industrial users. It is the largest seller of gasoline in the area. In 1946 its combined sales amounted to 23% of the total taxable gallonage sold there in that year: sales by company-owned service stations constituted 6.8% of the total, sales under exclusive dealing contracts with independent service stations, 6.7% of the total; the remainder were sales to industrial users. Retail service-station sales by Standard's six leading competitors absorbed 42.5% of the total taxable gallonage; the remaining retail sales were divided between more than seventy small companies. It is undisputed that Standard's major competitors employ similar exclusive dealing arrangements. In 1948 only 1.6% of retail outlets were what is known as "split-pump" stations, that is, sold the gasoline of more than one supplier.

Exclusive supply contracts with Standard had been entered into, as of March 12, 1947, by the operators of 5,937 independent stations, or 16% of the retail gasoline outlets in the Western area, which purchased from Standard in 1947, $57,646,233 worth of gasoline and $8,200,089.21 worth of other products. Some outlets are covered by more than one contract so that in all about 8,000 exclusive supply contracts are here in issue. These are of several types, but a feature common to each is the dealer's undertaking to purchase from Standard all his requirements of one or more products. . . . Before 1934 Standard's sales of petroleum products through independent service stations were made pursuant to agency agreements, but in that year Standard adopted the first of its several requirements-purchase contract forms, and by 1938 requirements contracts had wholly superseded the agency method of distribution.

Between 1936 and 1946 Standard's sales of gasoline through independent dealers remained at a practically constant proportion of the area's total sales; its sales of lubricating oil declined slightly during that period from 6.2% to 5% of the total. Its proportionate sales of tires and batteries for 1946 were slightly higher than they were in 1936, though somewhat lower than for some intervening years; they have never, as to either of these products, exceeded 2% of the total sales in the Western area.

Since § 3 of the Clayton Act was directed to prohibiting specific practices even though not covered by the broad terms of the Sherman Act, it is appropriate to consider first whether the enjoined contracts fall within the prohibition of the narrower Act. . . .

Obviously the contracts here at issue would be proscribed if § 3 stopped short of the qualifying clause beginning, "where the effect of such lease, sale, or contract for sale. . . ." If effect is to be given that clause, however, it is by no means obvious, in view of Standard's minority share of the "line of commerce" involved, of the fact that that share has not recently increased, and of the claims of these contracts to economic utility, that the effect of the contracts may be to lessen competition or tend to create a monopoly. It is the qualifying clause, therefore, which must be construed.

The District Court held that the requirement of showing an actual or potential lessening of competition or a tendency to establish monopoly was adequately met by proof that the contracts covered "a substantial number of outlets and a substantial amount of products, whether considered comparatively or not." . . .

The issue before us, therefore, is whether the requirement of showing that the effect of the agreements "may be to substantially lessen competition" may be met simply by proof that a substantial portion of commerce is affected or whether it must also be demonstrated that competitive activity has actually diminished or probably will diminish.

It is thus apparent that none of these cases controls the disposition of the present appeal, for Standard's share of the retail market for gasoline, even including sales through company-owned stations, is hardly large enough to conclude as a matter of law that it occupies a dominant position, nor did the trial court so find. The cases do indicate, however, that some sort of showing as to the actual or probable economic consequences of the agreements, if only the inferences to be drawn from the fact of dominant power, is important, and to that extent they tend to support appellant's position.

Two of the three cases decided by this Court which have held § 3 inapplicable also lend support to the view that such a showing is necessary. . . . The third went off the ground that the contract involved was one of agency and so is of no present relevance. . . .

But then came International Salt Co. v. United States, . . . That decision, at least as to contracts tying the sale of a nonpatented to a patented product, rejected the necessity of demonstrating economic consequences once it has been established that "the volume of business affected" is not "insignificant or insubstantial" and that the effect of the contracts is to "foreclose competitors from [a] sub-

stantial market.". . . Upon that basis we affirmed a summary judgment granting an injunction against the leasing of machines for the
utilization of salt products on the condition that the lessee use in
them only salt supplied by defendant. . . . It was not established
that equivalent machines were unobtainable, it was not indicated
what proportion of the business of supplying such machines was
controlled by defendant, and it was deemed irrelevant that there was
no evidence as to the actual effect of the tying clauses upon competition. It is clear, therefore, that unless a distinction is to be drawn
for purposes of the applicability of § 3 between requirements contracts and contracts tying the sale of a nonpatented to a patented
product, the showing that Standard's requirements contracts affected a gross business of $58,000,000 comprising 6.7% of the total
in the area goes far toward supporting the inference that competition has been or probably will be substantially lessened.[1]

In favor of confining the standard laid down by the International
Salt Case to tying agreements, important economic differences may
be noted. Tying agreements serve hardly any purpose beyond the
suppression of competition. The justification most often advanced
in their defense—the protection of the good will of the manufacturer
of the tying device—fails in the usual situation because specification
of the type and quality of the product to be used in connection with
the tying device is protection enough. If the manufacturer's brand
of the tied product is in fact superior to that of competitors, the
buyer will presumably choose it anyway. The only situation, indeed,
in which the protection of good will may necessitate the use of tying
clauses is where specifications for a substitute would be so detailed
that they could not practicably be supplied. In the usual case only
the prospect of reducing competition would persuade a seller to
adopt such a contract and only his control of the supply of the
tying device, whether conferred by patent monopoly or otherwise
obtained, could induce a buyer to enter one. . . . The existence
of market control of the tying device, therefore, affords a strong

---

[1] It may be noted in passing that the exclusive supply provisions for tires,
tubes, batteries, and other accessories which are a part of some of Standard's
contracts with dealers who have also agreed to purchase their requirements
of petroleum products should perhaps be considered, as a matter of classification, tying rather than requirements agreements.

foundation for the presumption that it has been or probably will be used to limit competition in the tied product also.

Requirements contracts, on the other hand, may well be of economic advantage to buyers as well as to sellers, and thus indirectly of advantage to the consuming public. In the case of the buyer, they may assure supply, afford protection against rises in price, enable long-term planning on the basis of known costs,[2] and obviate the expense and risk of storage in the quantity necessary for a commodity having a fluctuating demand. From the seller's point of view, requirements contracts may make possible the substantial reduction of selling expenses, give protection against price fluctuations, and—of particular advantage to a newcomer to the field to whom it is important to know what capital expenditures are justified—offer the possibility of a predictable market. . . . They may be useful, moreover, to a seller trying to establish a foothold against the counter-attacks of entrenched competitors. . . . Since these advantages of requirements contracts may often be sufficient to account for their use, the coverage by such contracts of a substantial amount of business affords a weaker basis for the inference that competition may be lessened than would similar coverage by tying clauses, especially where use of the latter is combined with market control of the tying device. A patent, moreover, although in fact there may be many competing substitutes for the patented article, is at least *prima facie* evidence of such control. And so we could not dispose of this case merely by citing International Salt Co. v. United States, . . .

Thus, even though the qualifying clause of § 3 is appended without distinction of terms equally to the prohibition of tying clauses and of requirements contracts, pertinent considerations support, certainly as a matter of economic reasoning, varying standards as to each for the proof necessary to fulfill the conditions of that clause. If this distinction were accepted, various tests of the economic usefulness or restrictive effect of requirements contracts would become relevant. Among them would be evidence that competition has flourished despite use of the contracts, and under this test much of

---

[2] This advantage is not conferred by Standard's contracts, each of which provides that the price to be paid by the dealer is to be the "Company's posted price to its dealers generally at time and place of delivery."

the evidence tendered by appellant in this case would be important. . . . Likewise bearing on whether or not the contracts were being used to suppress competition, would be the conformity of the length of their term to the reasonable requirements of the field of commerce in which they were used. . . . Still another test would be the status of the defendant as a struggling newcomer or an established competitor. Perhaps most important, however, would be the defendant's degree of market control, for the greater the dominance of his position, the stronger the inference that an important factor in attaining and maintaining that position has been the use of requirements contracts to stifle competition rather than to serve legitimate economic needs. . . .

Yet serious difficulties would attend the attempt to apply these tests. We may assume, as did the court below, that no improvement of Standard's competitive position has coincided with the period during which the requirements-contract system of distribution has been in effect. We may assume further that the duration of the contracts is not excessive and that Standard does not by itself dominate the market. But Standard was a major competitor when the present system was adopted, and it is possible that its position would have deteriorated but for the adoption of that system. When it is remembered that all the other major suppliers have also been using requirements contracts, and when it is noted that the relative share of the business which fell to each has remained about the same during the period of their use, it would not be farfetched to infer that their effect has been to enable the established suppliers individually to maintain their own standing and at the same time collectively, even though not collusively, to prevent a late arrival from wresting away more than an insignificant portion of the market. If, indeed, this were a result of the system, it would seem unimportant that a short-run by-product of stability may have been greater efficiency and lower costs, for it is the theory of the antitrust laws that the long-run advantage of the community depends upon the removal of restraints upon competition. . . .

Moreover, to demand that bare inference be supported by evidence as to what would have happened but for the adoption of the practice that was in fact adopted or to require firm prediction of an increase of competition as a probable result of ordering the abandonment of the practice, would be a standard of proof, if not virtually impossible to meet, at least most ill-suited for ascertainment by courts. . . . So long as these diverse ways of restricting competition remain open, therefore, there can be no conclusive proof that the use of requirements contracts has actually reduced competition below the level which it would otherwise have reached or maintained.

We are dealing here with a particular form of agreement specified by § 3 and not with different arrangements, by way of integration or otherwise, that may tend to lessen competition. To interpret that section as requiring proof that competition has actually diminished would make its very explicitness a means of conferring immunity upon the practices which it singles out. Congress has authoritatively determined that those practices are detrimental where their effect may be to lessen competition. . . . We are faced, not with a broadly phrased expression of general policy, but merely a broadly phrased qualification of an otherwise narrowly directed statutory provision.

. . . Yet the economic investigation which appellant would have us require is of the same broad scope as was adumbrated with reference to unreasonable restraints of trade in Board of Trade v. United States. . . . To insist upon such an investigation would be to stultify the force of Congress' declaration that requirements contracts are to be prohibited wherever their effect "may be" to substantially lessen competition. If in fact it is economically desirable for service stations to confine themselves to the sale of the petroleum products of a single supplier, they will continue to do so though not bound by contract, and if in fact it is important to retail dealers to assure the supply of their requirements by obtaining the commitment of a single supplier to fulfill them, competition for their patronage should enable them to insist upon such an arrangement without binding them to refrain from looking elsewhere.

We conclude, therefore, that the qualifying clause of § 3 is satisfied by proof that competition has been foreclosed in a substantial share of the line of commerce affected. It cannot be gainsaid that observance by a dealer of his requirements contract with Standard does effectively foreclose whatever opportunity there might be for competing suppliers to attract his patronage, and it is clear that the affected proportion of retail sales of petroleum products is substantial. In view of the widespread adoption of such contracts by Standard's competitors and the availability of alternative ways of obtaining an assured market, evidence that competitive activity has not actually declined is inconclusive. Standard's use of the contracts creates just such a potential clog on competition as it was the purpose of Section 3 to remove wherever, were it to become actual, it would impede a substantial amount of competitive activity.

Since the decree below is sustained by our interpretation of Section 3 of the Clayton Act, we need not go on to consider whether it might also be sustained by Section 1 of the Sherman Act. . . .

[The majority opinion recognized that some pre-International Salt precedents were inapplicable because (1) Standard did not occupy a dominant power in the retail market or (2) Standard did not involve an agency relationship. However, the court placed considerable emphasis on the International Salt decision, the importance of a patent-based restriction, the benefits of the agreement, and other considerations. Although the substantial amount of commerce foreclosed by the agreement was crucial to five justices, four found stronger bases of dissent; three felt that quantitative substantiality itself was not sufficient to violate Section 3. Justice Douglas's dissent centered about the likely conditions under a violation decision versus current conditions.]

Mr. Justice Douglas.

The economic theories which the Court has read into the Anti-Trust Laws have favored rather than discouraged monopoly. As a result of the big business philosophy underlying United States v. United Shoe Machinery Co. . . . United States v. United States Steel Corp. . . . United States v. International Harvester Co., . . . big business has become bigger and bigger. Monopoly has flourished. Cartels have increased their hold on the nation. The trusts wax strong. There is less and less place for the independent.

The full force of the Anti-Trust Laws has not been felt on our economy. It has been deflected. Niggardly interpretations have robbed those laws of much of their efficacy. There are exceptions. Price fixing is illegal *per se*. The use of patents to obtain monopolies on unpatented articles is condemned. Monopoly that has been built as a result of unlawful tactics, e. g., through practices that are restraints of trade, is broken up. But when it comes to monopolies built in gentlemanly ways—by mergers, purchases of assets or control and the like—the teeth have largely been drawn from the Act.

We announced that the existence of monopoly power, coupled with the purpose or intent to monopolize, was unlawful. But to date that principle has not shown bright promise in application. Under the guise of increased efficiency big business has received approval for easy growth. United States v. Columbia Steel Co. . . . represents the current attitude of the court on this problem. In that case United States Steel—the giant of the industry—was allowed to fasten its tentacles tighter on the economy by acquiring the assets of a steel company in the Far West where competition was beginning to develop.

The increased concentration of industrial power in the hands of a few has changed habits of thought. A new age has been introduced. It is more and more an age of "monopoly competition." Monopoly competition is a regime of friendly alliances, of quick and easy accommodation of prices even without the benefit of trade associations, of what Brandeis said was euphemistically called "co-operation." While this is not true in all fields, it has become alarmingly apparent in many.

The lessons Brandeis taught on the curse of bigness have largely been forgotten in high places. Size is allowed to become a menace to existing and putative competitors. Price control is allowed to escape the influences of the competitive market and to gravitate into the hands of the few. But beyond all that there is the effect on the community when independents are swallowed up by the trusts and entrepreneurs become employees of absentee owners. Then there is a serious loss in citizenship. . . .

It is common knowledge that a host of filling stations in the country are locally owned and operated. Others are owned and operated by the big oil companies. This case involves directly only the former. It pertains to requirements contracts that the oil companies make with these independents. It is plain that a filling station owner who is tied to an oil company for his supply of products is not an available customer for the products of other suppliers. The same is true of a filling station owner who purchases his inventory a year in advance. His demand is withdrawn from the market for the duration of the contract in the one case and for a year in the other. The result in each case is to lessen competition if the standard is day-to-day purchases. Whether it is a substantial lessening of competition within the meaning of the Anti-Trust Laws is a question of degree and may vary from industry to industry.

The elimination of these requirements contracts sets the stage for Standard and the other oil companies to build service-station empires of their own. The opinion of the Court does more than set the stage for that development. It is an advisory opinion as well, stating to the oil companies how they can with impunity build their empires. The formula suggested by the Court is either the use of the "agency" device, which in practical effect means control of filling stations by the oil companies . . . , or the outright acquisition of them by subsidiary corporations or otherwise. . . . Under the approved judicial doctrine either of those devices means increasing the monopoly of the oil companies over the retail field.

When the choice is thus given, I dissent from the outlawry of the requirements contract on the present facts. The effect which it has on competition in this field is minor as compared to the damage which will flow from the judicially approved formula for the growth of bigness tendered by the Court as an alternative. Our choice must be made on the basis not of abstractions but of the realities of modern industrial life.

Today there is vigorous competition between the oil companies for the market. That competition has left some room for the survival of the independents. But when this inducement for their survival is taken away, we can expect that the oil companies will move in to supplant them with their own stations. There will still be competition between the oil companies. But there will be a tragic loss to the nation. The small, independent business man will be supplanted by clerks. Competition between suppliers of accessories (which is involved in this case) will diminish or cease altogether. The oil companies will command an increasingly larger share of both the wholesale and the retail markets.

That is the likely result of today's decision. The requirements contract which is displaced is relatively innocuous as compared with the virulent growth of monopoly power which the Court encourages. The Court does not act unwittingly. It consciously pushes the oil industry in that direction. The Court approves what the Anti-Trust Laws were designed to prevent. It helps remake America in the image of the cartels.

Mr. Justice Jackson, with whom The Chief Justice and Mr. Justice Burton join, dissenting.

I am unable to join the judgment or opinion of the Court for reasons I will state, but shortly.

Section 3 of the Clayton Act does not make any lease, sale, or contract unlawful unless "the effect of such lease, sale, or contract for sale or such condition, agreement or understanding may be to substantially lessen competition or tend to create a monopoly in any line of commerce." . . . It is indispensable to the Government's case to establish that either the actual or the probable effect of the accused arrangement is to substantially lessen competition or tend to create a monopoly.

I am unable to agree that this requirement was met. To be sure, the contracts cover "a substantial number of outlets and a substantial amount of products, whether considered comparatively or not." . . . But that fact does not automatically bring the accused arrangement within the prohibitions of the statute. The number of dealers and the volume of sales covered by the arrangement of course was sufficient to be substantial. That is to say, this arrangement operated on enough commerce to violate the Act, provided its effects were substantially to lessen competition or tend to create a monopoly. But proof of their quantity does not prove that they had this forbidden quality; and the assumption that they did, without proof, seems to me unwarranted.

Moreover, the trial court not only made the assumption but he did not allow the defendant affirmatively to show that such effects do not flow from this arrangement. Such evidence on the subject as was admitted was not considered in reaching the decision that these contracts are illegal.

But if they must decide, the only possible way for the courts to arrive at a fair determination is to hear all relevant evidence from both parties and weigh not only its inherent probabilities of verity but also compare the experience, disinterestedness and credibility of opposing witnesses. This is a tedious process and not too enlightening, but without it a judicial decree is but a guess in the dark. That is all we have here and I do not think it is an adequate basis on which to upset long-standing and widely practiced business arrangements.

However, if the Court refuses to do that, I cannot agree that the requirements contract is *per se* an illegal one under the anti-trust law, and that is the substance of what the Court seems to hold. I am not convinced that the requirements contract as here used is a device for suppressing competition instead of a device for waging competition. If we look only at its effect in relation to particular retailers who become parties to it, it does restrain their freedom to purchase their requirements elsewhere and prevents other companies from selling to them. Many contracts have the effect of taking a purchaser out of the market for goods he already has bought or contracted to take. But the retailer in this industry is only a conduit from the oil fields to the driver's tank, a means by which the oil companies compete to get the business of the ultimate consumer—the man in whose automobile the gas is used. It means to me, if I must decide without evidence, that these contracts are an almost necessary means to maintain this all-important competition for consumer business, in which it is admitted competition is keen. The retail stations, whether independent or company-owned, are the instrumentalities through which competition for this ultimate market is waged.

14 AMERICAN CAN:

A Tied-up Package

Among the important antitrust cases decided in the immediate post-World War II period was the 1949 District Court decision in United States v. American Can Co.

The government alleged several distinct violations of Sections 1 and 2 of the Sherman Act and Section 3 of the Clayton Act. The District Court judgment centered on the Can Company's use of "requirements contracts and closing machine leases [tie-in contracts] . . ." The requirements contracts were common agreements that American supply all the cans required by a user who in turn purchased cans only from American. Judge Harris noted that the tying arrangement involved American's leasing of "closing machines only to customers who purchase their cans from it, and closing machine leases run for terms concurrent with the can contracts . . ." These dual arrangements were found to be in violation of the antitrust laws; especially, Section 3 of the Clayton Act. The case extracts, presented below, provide a meaningfully detailed description of the American's use of these contracts prior to the suit and some cursory explanation of how they buttressed American's dominant position in tin-can production.

The significance of the material presented here, especially that dealing with the tying arrangements and the prices, emerges fully only after the material is reexamined in light of later analysis, especially the articles by McKie[1] and Bowman.[2] It is worthwhile

[1] McKie, "The Decline of Monopoly in the Metal Container Industry,"

to analyze the role of tying arrangements as counting devices as does Bowman in an attempt to evaluate American's tying of cans to the closing equipment whose lease rates did not "cover the complete cost of furnishing and servicing the machines . . ." Similar issues are discussed by McKie in his article immediately following the case material. The case excerpts also provide an abstract of the legal reasoning, which will indicate the critical factors in the court's analysis and decision. Despite its concern with other manufacturers, the court recognizes the real need for some mutual commitment between buyer and seller. This concern is fully reflected by the final decision and remedy in which the court sought to create competitive conditions in this duopolistic industry.

....

UNITED STATES
v.
AMERICAN CAN CO.
87 F. SUPP. 18 (1949)

Harris, District Judge.

This action was instituted by the government under the Sherman Act, Sections 1 and 2, . . . and the Clayton Act, Section 3, seeking to enjoin the American Can Company from unlawful practices, allegedly in violation of both acts. The primary question for determination is whether defendant's requirements contracts and closing machine leases are illegal in the particulars specified.

The facts are not in serious dispute save with respect to a conspiracy charged against American Can Company and Continental Can Company, hereinafter referred to as American and Conti-

---

The American Economic Review, XLV, No. 2, Proceedings (May 1955), 499–508.

[2] Ward S. Bowman, Jr., "Tying Arrangements and the Leverage Problem," *The Yale Law Journal,* 67 (1957), 19–36.

nental, respectively, for purposes of brevity. The alleged conspiracy will be dealt with at a later stage in this opinion.

Historically the proceeding is not novel. In 1916 Judge John C. Rose, in U.S. v. American Can Company, D. C., 230 F. 859, after an extended hearing under the Sherman Act, Sections 1 and 2, and after finding a monopoly to exist concluded: although American Can Company was designed as a monopoly, dissolution should not be ordered as it is too drastic a remedy.

In 1924 the matter was heard before the Federal Trade Commission. The result of this extensive hearing was that American Can Company consented to remove a tying provision from its closing machine leases.

Today for a third time, the Government has instituted proceedings against defendant under the anti-trust laws. A brief statement of the instant case should suffice at this juncture:

Plaintiff attacks defendant's contracts under which it sells its metal and fiber containers; plaintiff also challenges the legality of defendant's closing machine leases under which it lets its can closing machines which complete the metal and fiber containers. Plaintiff contends that the can contracts and closing machine leases constitute unreasonable restraints of trade and commerce and, in addition, that such contracts and leases, together with certain specified devices, means, methods which will be discussed below, constitute a violation of Section 3 of the Clayton Act. Plaintiff further contends that defendant's contracts and closing machine leases constitute a mode of operation which gives rise to an attempt to monopolize trade and commerce and has effectuated such a monopoly in certain parts of the trade and commerce in canning, in violation of Sections 1 and 2 of the Sherman Act.

The ultimate remedy sought by the Government is sweeping: it asks for elimination of requirements contracts and complete divestiture of the closing machine phase of the business. In connection with the requirements contracts, American contends that, if the relief sought is granted, the user-customers will be relegated to an uncertain mode of supply and demand not based upon contracts giving rise to enforceable obligations.

Viewed from the standpoint of competitive sales . . . American's percentage is . . . impressive. Some canning concerns manufacture their own cans and are thus not in the buying market. Among the can manufacturers who sell on a competitive basis, the total received for cans in 1946 was $433,621,729. American's percentage of the total was 46.4 per cent.

What does the evidence disclose as to the business conducted by American's competitors? It shows that of not more than 125 manufacturers of cans, up to 25 make tin containers for their own use; of the competitive can companies only five manufacture what are known as packers' and general line cans.

American and Continental in 1946 together manufactured approximately 70 per cent of the cans produced in the industry and approximately 80 per cent of all cans made for sale. These figures may be raised to 81 per cent and 93.6 per cent respectively, if the output of four additional companies—Crown, National, Heekin, and Pacific—is added. Their combined sales of both kinds of cans that year totaled approximately 461 million dollars. Their combined sales of general line cans in the amount of $151,736,000 was equivalent to approximately 66.9 per cent of all cans made and 81 per cent of all made for sale. In this group of six companies in 1946, American accounted for 47.9 per cent of the sanitary cans and 52.2 per cent of the general line cans. American and Continental together sold 86.1 per cent of all the cans made.

Thus we see that the canmaking industry is concentrated in a handful of companies and that American achieves dominant stature among this handful with an output of 49 per cent of all cans made by the group in 1946.

By graphical representation and statistical supporting data, the trial record is convincing, clear, and complete, that the defendant's domination of the industry has grown over the intervening years; that Continental and American manufacture about 80 per cent of all cans made for sale; that there are six companies in the United States, making both packers' and general line cans, and they manufacture 93.6 per cent of all cans made for sale.

Viewed from the standpoint of growth, American's position continues to be impressive; because of its size at the outset of the war period defendant's percentage of growth during the war and subsequent thereto has not been as rapid as that of its smaller and aggressive rivals. However, in terms of business realized, American has continued to be the mammoth manufacturer of cans. . . .

From the above recital of facts, it is clear that from a national standpoint, defendant is the leader in the manufacture of cans, although it has competition in its business and is not in a position of complete monopoly. From a regional standpoint, the story of control is different. Thus, in such an area as Utah, defendant has the only plant which serves the needs of the packers in that state. A similar monopoly exists in Hawaii, while in Alaska defendant has 80 per cent of the can business. As might be expected American is the dominant influence in specific sections of the United States.

Viewed from another standpoint—type of container manufactured—defendant far outdistances its competitors in several lines. For example, in the sale of beer cans, coffee cans, shortening cans, and meat cans, American is the major manufacturer.

The foregoing should suffice to indicate the dominant position of American in the industry.

With respect to closing machines:

Since the canning industry progressed from the hole and cap cans, which were used at the turn of the century, to the sanitary or packers' cans which are closed by machines, American has moved into leadership in the manufacture and leasing of closing machines. Today it makes and leases to its customers substantially all of their closing machines. The leasing practice by American is followed by its competitors, with Continental also making its own closing machines for this purpose. The number of independent concerns engaged in the manufacture of closing machines is limited to two—Max Ams Machine Company and The Angelus.

In terms of closing machines leased to canners, American controls 54 per cent of all such machines. In excess of 17,000 closing machines were on lease by the canning industry at the time of commencement of this litigation in 1946. Of this number, American had 9,258 machines. Continental far outdistances other canning concerns with approximately 36 per cent of the total machines on lease. The independent can-closing machine makers are thus limited in their sales to a market of 12 per cent of the closing machine business.

It is the fixed and uniform policy of American to lease rather than sell its closing machines. The only exceptions to this policy arise in the few instances in which American sells machines abroad or sells a few single spindle semi-automatic machines in the Ozarks. Other canmaking concerns follow American's policy. Therefore, the two independent can-closing machine makers, Angelus and Max Ams, have a market limited to the small canmakers, for the ordinary canner will not purchase a can-closing machine as long as he can lease it from his can supplier. An important factor which induces canners to lease their machines has been the low rentals charged for such machines. The defendant admits that low rentals provide an effective "sales tool."

American, over the years, has imposed rentals ranging from the purely nominal to a rate sufficient to pay for the cost of the equipment furnished. Recently defendant standardized its charges so that today they represent an amount equivalent to 8.2 per cent of the original cost or 12 per cent of the depreciated value of the machines. Such a charge approaches a fair standard, but even present rentals are insufficient to cover the complete cost of furnishing and servicing the machines. Other canmakers, on a competitive basis, have followed American's policy of imposing low or nominal rentals on their closing machines. Rental figures appear to have been purely arbitrary, depending upon the exigencies and the desirability of the customers' business.

The present case is not directed toward American in its capacity as manufacturer of closing machines. However, it should be noted that the practice of defendant in leasing at below cost figures has tended to restrict the market for closing machine manufacturers and has limited the number of concerns engaged in this business. The record disclosed that others would engage in the manufacture of closing machines if there were a free market in which sellers might compete on an equal basis with the canmakers who now lease their machines. Of American's canmaking competitors, at least one, namely Pacific Can Company, is willing to lease or sell its closing machines to its customers.

With respect to the requirements contracts:

The Government contends that defendant's contracts are the

major tool by which it is able to exclude or limit competition in the canning business and, hence, is able to maintain its dominant position. American now has a standard form of contract which the plaintiff chooses to call "total requirements contract." In a practical sense, defendant does enter into such a total requirements contract with most of its customers. Canners, according to the record, prefer to deal with a single can manufacturer in obtaining their products for a single plant. American's 1946 contract permits a customer to purchase a single line of cans or any number of kinds of cans on a requirements basis. In 1945 American did 92 per cent of its business in sanitary cans on this basis. Over the years defendant has handled only minute portions of its sales on an open order basis.

. . . In a single plant it is most exceptional for a canner to obtain his cans from two or more sources. The record discloses two instances in which customers used other than American cans in their plants.

Throughout its business life American has entered into requirements contracts of varied duration. These have ranged from three to twenty years. Recently, defendant prepared a standardized contract of uniform length of five years. . . .

American offers an attractive discount on quantity purchases. The scale serves as an inducement for canners to purchase all of their needs from a single manufacturer. The discount rate has varied over the years. . . . In the 1946 contract, which is applicable to both sanitary and general line cans, requirements contract customers enjoy a price differential in discounts which are not granted to open order customers. Prior to 1946 there was a flat differential of 5 per cent in general line cans which were purchased by requirements contract purchasers as against open order customers.

The defendant's degree of market control:
The statistical data in this case is voluminous. . . .

Such is the history, as the record discloses it, of the genesis of the defendant, such the story of its organization and of its conduct during the first years of its existence. It is clear an attempt was made both to restrain and monopolize the interstate trade in tin cans.

The closing machine Leases executed by customers with the defendant are violative of Section 3 of the Clayton Act:

In the light of Standard Oil Company v. United States, . . . this phase of the case is reduced to comparative simplicity. In reaching the conclusion that the leasing practices must be proscribed, we must trace briefly the practices of American since the "tying provision" was admittedly removed from the lease contracts covering closing machines.

In May 1917, in the course of an investigation of American by the Federal Trade Commission, the defendant agreed to eliminate from its forms of contract and lease any clauses which the Commission considered objectionable. Defendant now asserts that it struck the offending "tying clause" from its leases in the latter part of 1917, and, that since the elimination of the clause, the provisions in the contract for the lease of closing machines has remained substantially identical, embodying the usual covenants customarily found in lease contracts.

The Government contends that the provision, although eliminated from the lease forms, has been kept alive and in effect as a result of the practices engaged in by American of a "subtle and refined" character. The practices, in substance, are as follows:

Defendant leases closing machines only to customers who purchase their cans from it, and closing machine leases run for terms concurrent with the can contracts. Sales policies, as contained in memoranda and directives from the executive officers, bear out the Government's contentions that the "tying provision" for all practical purposes has remained in the contract negotiations. The evidence introduced by the Government in this connection abundantly supports this contention and no useful purpose could be served herein by lengthy excerpts from the record.

Defendant asserts that "unless the lessee, as a condition of his closing machinery lease, is obligated to buy from the defendant all the containers he closes on that machine, the Clayton Act has no application." That is precisely what American achieves as a matter of over-all policy!

. . . the Court is inclined to view the written record as disclosing a pattern as to policy, pointing unerringly to the conclusion that, in the main, American would not lease closing machines without a corresponding sale of cans.

That the closing machines represent a most valuable sales tool becomes increasingly manifest when it is considered that defendant has in excess of 9,000 machines on lease of an approximate value of 12 million dollars, many of which have been rented at nominal or low rental values in order to foreclose competition. The evidence herein discloses that American owns and controls more closing machines than the rest of the industry together, and demonstrates that defendant effectively ties the leasing of such machines to the sales of its cans. Defendant owns approximately 54 per cent of all closing machines available for lease to the industry.

It may be noted that the closing machines manufactured by American, with slight adjustment, may be used to close the cans of the other can manufacturers; that there are no basic patent rights involved as was the case in the International Salt controversy, . . .

Finally, American contends that "in the absence of proof of the alleged condition, agreement or understanding not to use the goods of a competitor, and a proof that any such understanding may substantially lessen competition or tend to create a monopoly the Clayton Act has not been violated."

. . . Section 3 of the Clayton Act is satisfied by proof that competition has been foreclosed in a substantial share of the line of commerce affected.

It is manifest to this Court from the record herein that abundant proof has been supplied by the Government, and the Court accordingly finds that the leasing practices of can closing machines violate the said Act for they affect injuriously a sizable part of interstate commerce, i. e., an appreciable segment of interstate commerce.

The devices, means and methods used by defendant in accomplishing the monopoly:

Suffice it to say, that no useful purpose could be served by recounting herein the details of all the transactions spread over a period of years from 1930. They represent a saga of American business—so-called "big business." Taken alone, or disassociated from the general configuration or picture, many of the transactions would appear to be without probative value. However, as a composite they set a pattern of operations evidencing the extremes defendant saw fit to go in perpetuating the contractual relationship between defendant and the customer-user. The devices took many forms: defendant provided discounts in ancillary contracts; defendant paid large sums of money to obtain business of its customers; defendant furnished equipment, in addition to closing machines, at nominal rentals; defendant paid large claims when it appeared propitious and good policy; defendant purchased can-making equipment from its customers for inflated values in order to obtain can business. The foregoing represent only part of the claims set up by the Government under the "inducements" phase of the case. . . .

Defendant, in responding to the Government's contention that these transactions and incidents must be taken as part of the general configuration in interpreting the effect of the requirements contracts and the closing machine leases, says in part: "Certainly there is no evidence in this record that these 'inducements' were conditioned on the signing of a requirements contract."

To the contrary there is evidence in the record, and inferences to be drawn therefrom, that the inducements referred to, in many instances, formed an important and vital part in the renewal or re-negotiation of requirements contracts.

The incidents, when examined realistically and not as mere abstractions, are deeper than the typical run-of-the-mill, day-to-day business transactions. They represent a studied, methodical and effective method of retaining and acquiring by refined, gentlemanly and suave means, plus an occasional "commercial massage," the dominant position which American has had and maintained for at least a generation on and over the canning industry. A detailed analysis of this phase of the Government's case convinces that there is little room left in a competitive sense, for the independent small business man. As a competitive influence, he has slowly and sadly been relegated into the limbo of American enterprise.

The evidence establishes violations of Sections 1 and 2 of the Sherman Act:

The proof in this case compels the conclusion that the five year requirements contracts and closing machine leases unreasonably restrain trade in violation of the Sherman Act. The evidence discloses that competitors have been foreclosed from a substantial market by the contracts and leases.

The practices surrounding the leasing of closing machines, in view of Section 3 of the Clayton Act, have received appropriate treatment and discussion, supra; although the "tying provision" has ostensibly been deleted from the leases, nevertheless, as a matter of practice and policy, the machines are still "tied" to the sale of cans.

As demonstrative of the control and domination exercised by American in and over the industry, we have referred to statistical information which stands uncontradicted.

With the premise established that American is in a dominant role and a position of preeminent power in the industry, we may then examine the record to determine whether: (a) competition has been foreclosed; (b) from any substantial market. . . .

In the instant case the Government's proof shows the use by defendant of approximately 4,000 requirements contracts involving 250 million dollars in business annually, and a domination in the canmaking industry for a period of almost 50 years. The evidence reveals the ownership and control of more closing machines than the rest of the industry as a whole, and it further demonstrates that defendant effectively ties in the leasing of the closing machines with the sale of cans under requirements contracts. Thus, Government argues that domination and control having been demonstrated, this Court must hold as a matter of law, in the light of the contracts entered into and the business controlled under the contracts, implemented with the devices, means and methods already alluded to, that competition is foreclosed over a period of many years with respect to a sizeable segment of the canmaking business, to wit, approximately 40 per cent.

In short, it is contended that from the foregoing an *automatic* result follows and that where competition under such circumstances is excluded, that the restraint and monopolistic practices are unreasonable.

Defendant contends that traditionally, in view of practices surrounding requirements contracts, this Court must undertake a comparative analysis in determining the merit or de-merit of such contracts; whether they are apt in their use in this particular industry; whether they are favored by the user-consumer, etc.

The Supreme Court has held such evidence immaterial and has stated that "serious difficulties would attend the attempt to apply these tests," in concluding a violation with respect to requirements contracts under Section 3 of the Clayton Act, . . .

Apart from the inevitable conclusion reached that the requirements contracts and closing machine leases, backgrounded by the configuration of the devices and practices, offend against the Sherman Act, Sections 1 and 2 thereof, there is the problem of the user-consumer which must be approached not as a legal abstraction, but realistically. He should not be left without a source of supply. The canners are subject in many instances to the whims of nature over which they have no control. They are, therefore, required to have available a supply of tin containers, fluid in amount, and appropriate from the technological and marketing viewpoints. The general reason assigned for requirements contracts was that canners wished to be assured of receiving containers when, as, and if needed, regardless of any contingency which might affect the raw material supply or the market.

During the course of the trial the question was posed in several instances whether the term of the contracts under consideration was reasonable or unreasonable in the light of the five year period. . . . the question of reasonableness must to some degree be determined by the force and effect of the contract upon trade and commerce, and, when we take the requirements contract in and of itself and examine it in the light of its possible effect upon trade and commerce, it must be concluded that the *five year* term creates an unreasonable restraint in the light of all the facts, factors, circumstances and background.

In finding the five year requirements contract illegal, we are not thereby compelled to declare void any and all requirements contracts. We *cannot* ignore the testimony of countless witnesses who indicated the vital necessity of some sort of supply contract. Several of them, of course, vigorously denounced the long-term period. Others believed emphatically in a term not to exceed one year for, as it was pointed out, at the expiration date of such a period of time they could cast about in the open market.

Mindful that requirements contracts are not per se unlawful, and that one of the elements which should be considered is the length thereof, it is only fair to conclude after a careful review of the evidence, that a contract for a period of one year would permit competitive influences to operate at the expiration of said period of time, and the vice which is now present in the five year requirements contracts, would be removed. . . .

To strike down the requirements contracts and to declare them totally void as violative of the Sherman Act, without at the same time affording to the user-consumer a supply over a limited period of time, would be destructive, illogical, unsound and not in consonance with the acute and particular problems confronting the canning industry.

In this *particular case* we have concluded that the Court is not foreclosed from an examination into the needs and requirements of the industry with respect to a finding as to whether an unreasonable restraint and monopoly exist under Sections 1 and 2 of the Sherman Act. The requirements of the industry in our opinion have a bearing upon the problem herein although admittedly not finally determinative of the ultimate question to be resolved.

We find, therefore, that, in the light of the evidence, the requirements contracts herein are unreasonable for the period or duration of five years and that a reasonable period of time for said duration is one year.

The Government contends that the requirements contracts also offend against Section 3 of the Clayton Act. From a review of the record, the Court perceived that these contracts properly fall within the proscription of Sections 1 and 2 of the Sherman Act and that their provisions must be dealt with accordingly. Defendant's requirements contracts do not come within either the language or the intent of Section 3 of the Clayton Act.

The agreement to fix prices between American and Continental:
Prior to trial, plaintiff moved to consolidate this cause with that of a similar anti-trust suit now pending between U. S. of America and Continental Can Company. After lengthy argument by counsel, the Court denied the motion. It was contended then, as it is now, that the practices, devices, and general pattern of operation of Continental are identical in practically all respects with those of American.

It becomes unnecessary, under the issues as framed in this case, to make any finding with respect to a so-called conspiracy or to otherwise allude thereto. The conspiracy, or its absence, cannot serve as a premise in any logical reasoning leading to a conclusion with respect to the practices that are at issue. However, we do find that American and Continental, through their officers, agents, and servants, did directly agree to fix prices. This is manifest from the evidence, as well as the pattern of the price lists which appeared in the exhibits.

Defendant claims that the relief sought is drastic and unjustified. The Government claims with equal vigor that the closing machine phase of the business should be divested and that the closing machine leases and requirements contracts should be stricken and declared void. We are satisfied that it will take an additional hearing or several hearings to clarify this case on the sweeping remedies asked by the Government.

The Court's conclusion being that there has been a violation of the Sherman Act as well as the Clayton Act, the final question is one of determining the equitable relief to be had.

■■■

AMERICAN CAN AFTERMATH:
ON OPENING A CLOSED MARKET

[In some respects the 1949 American Can case posed few issues that were new. When formed in 1901, the American Can Company was the industry's dominant firm, and in the late 1940s it remained much the largest can manufacturer. Despite an initial rapidly declining market share, in 1916 it accounted for about one-half of the industry's output. In 1916 a District Court—in a Sherman Act proceeding against the company—found an unlawful monopoly but refused to order dissolution, partly hoping that American Can's market position would be further eroded by newly emerging competition.[3] This hope was futile since American Can's market share thereafter ceased to decline. In a later antitrust proceeding, the Can Company's use of tying contracts was attacked and the company then consented to terminate the practice. Although it formally ceased using tying contracts in 1924, American—according to the conclusions reached by the District Court in 1949—was able to obtain the same result through the use of requirements contracts that ran concurrent with its leasing agreements.

Thus the eventual impact of the 1949 American Can case is of considerable interest: Would the remedy, as in the earlier cases, be an empty one? or Would the remedy this time have a meaningful influence on American Can's conduct and, in turn, on competition and market performance? In large part these are the issues probed by Professor James W. McKie in his important consideration of the decision and the impact of the resultant remedy.

McKie's review and analysis of the results of this case provide a fuller understanding of the use of Section 3 in this instance. His article neatly describes the manner in which Clayton Act, Section 3 enforcement helped reverse a duopolistic industry orientation and initiated an increase in competition. This was done through

---

[3] United States v. American Can Co., 230 Fed. Rep. 859 (1916), decree rendered 234 Fed. Rep. 1019 (1916).

elimination of such devices and marketing practices as long-term requirements contracts buttressing the positions held by American and Continental. The result of this Section 3 action differs from the avowed purpose of the Clayton Act of preventing monopoly from arising by permitting the government to act during the incipient stages of lessened competition.

The American Can decision and its analysis do not portray any necessary conflict between legal and economic approaches to a particular problem. Instead, the two selections together reveal how more freely, if not perfectly, competitive market situations can be provided through antitrust action in basically noncompetitive situations. As McKie's review of developments in the industry clearly indicates, the elimination of the tying arrangements removed substantial barriers to the emergence of new competition in this industry. The demonstration of desirable results stemming from the remedy in this case, however, does not resolve one pressing question: Were equally or more desirable procedures and remedies available to the courts in this instance (and in parallel cases)?]

··

The Decline of Monopoly in the Metal Container Industry

James W. McKie

··

I

The American Can case of 1950 illustrates in almost unexpected circumstances the force that the indirect and peripheral approach

Abridged from James W. McKie, "The Decline of Monopoly in the Metal Container Industry," *The American Economic Review*, XLV, No. 2, Proceedings (May 1955), 499–508.

of the Clayton Act may have to make competition more effective. This was a case in which a specific market practice was the key to market power. The practice had nothing to do with the creation of market power, since it supervened upon a monopolistic structure that was already there; but it played a decisive part in the maintenance of market control after the foundations of monopoly had been undermined.

A cursory examination of the structure of the metal container industry just before the antitrust suit began in 1948 might well have made anyone skeptical of the success of a policy which did not involve fundamental structural reorganization. The industry was highly concentrated, and still is: the two leading firms, American Can Company and Continental Can Company, together accounted for nearly 80 per cent of total sales, and American alone had over 45 per cent. There were in addition a number of small sellers—no one of them more than one-eighth as large as American—which occupied sheltered and specialized positions or else appeared to subsist on a margin of tolerance. The major companies manufacture a product-mix of containers for different purposes, but differentiation within each product line was and is insignificant. Cross-elasticities of demand between metal cans and substitute containers are very small. The prices of the two leaders, as well as their other market policies, have long been substantially identical. Prices for given products in given sales regions were set by one of the large firms, the other following; a policy of universal freight equalization eliminated the uncertainties of geographical differentiation; and prices exhibited the characteristic rigidity that we have come to associate with tacit oligopolistic collusion.

Tacit collusion in circumstances like these might be expected to result in the maximization of joint profits. However, the maximization of joint profits is always subject to limitations in any oligopoly structure, and in some instances the limitations are so severe that the principle loses its explanatory value. Economists have long preferred an eclectic approach to this problem. No universal solvent has yet been found that will exempt us from a detailed examination of the structure of particular oligopolistic markets and their history, as a prerequisite to explaining their behavior. The limitations upon monopoly power are often hidden from immediate view. A detailed analysis of the metal container industry reveals a number of them.

II

There is time for only a brief summary here. The first thing to be noted is that the limited-duopoly structure in the can industry is a relatively recent development. . . . American Can was organized originally as a trust controlling virtually the entire capacity of the industry. It suffered the fate of many of the trusts organized at the turn of the century: the umbrella it held over the industry encouraged the growth of competition, and within a dozen years its share of the market had fallen to 50 per cent. It was about this time, in 1916, that American was first charged with monopoly under the Sherman Act. . . .

The court refrained from dissolving it principally because of the rapid decline in its market share, and the judge expressed the hope that the growth of rivals would soon restore competition in the industry.

Competition was not quickly restored. American possessed nothing approaching pure monopoly after 1916, but it remained the dominant firm. Its market share ceased to fall, and its capacity remained for a time enormously greater than its rivals'. American's prices determined the prices for the whole industry. It maintained its lead by rapid development and expansion from within. Nevertheless, its power to control the industry was considerably weaker in 1948 than it was in 1916.

This slow metamorphosis was due partly to developments within the industry, partly to the impact of the antitrust laws. . . . In 1916, Continental was a small cloud on American's horizon, . . . Continental grew rapidly with a bold program of acquisition and merger as well as by rapid expansion from within. By 1939, it was half as large as American; by 1950 it was three-fourths as large. Its growth eventually put it in a position that rivalled American's. Prior to the middle thirties, American was the only metal container manufacturer with an important research program and was practically solely responsible for the progress and development that had occurred up to that time. Moreover, it was the only manufacturer up to then that was fully able to realize certain other advantages of scale. These are not production economies, but are achieved through the interlocking of separate plants so that the extreme uncertainties of demand for food containers in any one area are diffused along a chain of production sites. The ability of American to offer certainty of supply, together with its facilities for research and customer service, made it the only acceptable source of supply to many buyers of cans, including most of the large and stable ones, until a second large seller appeared.

By the end of the thirties, American was at last confronted with a powerful, efficient, and progressive rival in practically every geographical region and every product, including many in which American had earlier enjoyed a monopoly. . . .

Conditions were more stringent for the smaller firms. No other was able to achieve anything like the growth of Continental; in fact, several of those which had begun to grow to substantial size were acquired by Continental. A few producers of food cans managed to build up integrated regional organizations, securing at least part of the advantage of size, and compensated for their inferior research and service facilities by charging somewhat lower prices. Two firms even succeeded in entering the industry and establishing themselves in the food can market. All of these smaller producers were potential bases for expanded competition; that this potential was not fully realized was due to certain market practices of the larger firms which held the smaller ones in check.

A significant change was forced by the tightening of the law against price discrimination after 1936. The Robinson-Patman Act affected two markets: tin plate and tin cans. Tin plate accounts for 60 per cent of metal container costs. In the days of the Steel Trust and the Can Trust the tin plate market was almost a classic bilateral monopoly. The monopolies on both sides lost their near-exclusive control, but the "leading bargain" between U.S. Steel and American Can continued to determine the price of tin plate. In this market it appeared that monopoly power was offset by monopoly power. The benefits of this countervailing power, however, were mixed. Improvement and development in the tin plate industry, for instance, have been rapid and considerable, and there is no doubt that the large buyers, especially American, have pressed the steel producers closer to the maximum attainable rate of progress— both in product improvement and cost reduction—than would have been the case if buyers had been small and impotent. On the other hand, the price benefits of countervailing power filtered down to consumers very slowly. . . . After a second buyer of sub-stantial size had entered the market a new dimension of strategy emerged, and price reductions negotiated between individual buyers and sellers became more difficult to confine to the largest buyers. Nevertheless, systematic discrimination continued in various forms up to the passage of the Robinson-Patman Act, at which time American actually capitalized its claims to discriminatory treatment and liquidated them by accepting substantial lump-sum settlements from United States Steel and other suppliers. After 1937, counter-vailing power was exercised in behalf of all buyers of tin plate. This benefited the ultimate buyers of cans only insofar as there were limits to the exercise of monopoly power in the can market.

The buyers of cans were themselves not entirely helpless. . . . Backward integration is not extremely difficult for a large user, and it would have taken only a slight widening of the profit margin on cans to make it economical. Potential entry from the buying side limited monopoly power on the selling side. At first the result was systematic, secret discrimination in favor of the buyers who could offer this threat. After a second seller grew to large size, the bar-gaining position of the large buyers was strengthened, since they could play one off against the other. The Robinson-Patman Act obliged the major can companies to abandon secret discrimina-tion. It was replaced, not by uniform prices to all buyers, but by an open schedule of volume discounts, which eventually came to be based on total purchases of all kinds of containers from the supplier. The discounts were greater for large-volume purchas-ers than any concession that the smaller can companies could easily offer, and there is no doubt that these discounts worked to their disadvantage. On the other hand, the continuous altera-tion and reshaping of the discount structure did afford a means of limited price competition between the two leaders; and the large buyers had at least the potential power to enforce this com-petition between them.

III

Though the monopoly power once possessed by the dominant firm had been markedly eroded by 1950, the effect of the underlying structural changes on competition remained more potential than actual. The reason was that the leading firm followed several policies which concentrated its remaining market power in the most effective way, and its large rival did likewise. There were three important instruments of commercial dominance. The first was the volume discounts just mentioned. The second was the practice of selling under long-term requirements contracts. It is fair to say that neither of these could have had a powerful enough effect to justify action under the antitrust laws, though they did tend to reinforce each other. The contracts were written for specific containers for use at specific plants. Smaller can companies occasionally succeeded in becoming secondary suppliers of large buyers, but it was the usual practice for a buyer to concentrate all his purchases on a single source of supply. There were some buyers whose purchases considerably exceeded the volume necessary to get the highest discount that was offered, but most of these also had long-term requirements contracts with a single supplier or, less frequently, split their purchases between American and Continental. The amount of business that the smaller can companies were eligible to compete for at any given time was thus restricted. Volume discounts were partly responsible, but the superiority of the two large sellers in research and customer service may have been equally important in determining the result.

The third instrument of control was the practice of tying the lease of can closing machinery to the sale of cans. (This was not done through an explicit tying clause, but by arranging the expiration dates of separate contracts so that no canner would be able to retain American's machinery to close competitors' cans. There were minor exceptions.) This requires a word of explanation. If the manufacture of closing machinery had been perfectly competitive, the larger can companies would have gained no net advantage by this practice. But American's can machinery has long been recognized as the best and most complete in the industry, and its progressiveness in this field is beyond dispute. Continental began late, but was over-taking American rapidly in the late thirties. Both large firms followed the same policy. Rentals on closing machinery, which also covered servicing by the manufacturer, were set below actual cost, to induce buyers to lease machines. Most can buyers were allowed to retain the machinery only as long as they purchased the cans to be closed on it from the same firm. The moderate advantage which the major sellers possessed in closing machinery was thus extended forward and magnified in the can market. The relation between supplier and customer became harder to break. (Closing machinery is generally unimportant for nonfood cans, and both major companies faced much more vigorous competition from independents in this field.) In markets for food cans, the smaller manufacturers were forced to imitate the leasing practices of the majors; but since they had to buy somewhat inferior closing machines on the open market and lease them at below-cost rentals, they reaped no comparable advantage. (One or two of the smaller companies also entered the manufacture of closing machinery, without much success until recently.) A side effect of the practice was that no canner would buy machinery in preference to renting it, and independent machinery manufacturers faced an uneconomically thin market.

IV

The government might have attempted a major Sherman Act case, with wholesale dissolution and structural reorganization of the industry as the objective. But this would have been risky, since the specific charge of monopolization had been tried in an earlier case and the judge had refused the suggested remedy of dissolution. Instead, the government attacked the practice of tie-in sales directly under Section 3 of the Clayton Act, retaining a Sherman Act charge to scoop in the requirements contracts if possible and to provide for equitable relief. There is some evidence that the Antitrust Division was not entirely satisfied with the form that its case eventually took in consequence, but it won the case nevertheless.

The court decided that American had violated both the Clayton Act and the Sherman Act.[1] In addition to a number of minor matters, which need not concern us here, the 1950 decree altered market practice in the metal container industry in three ways. (Continental accepted the same judgment in a consent decree.)

1. The major firms were prohibited from offering any annual cumulative volume discounts.

2. Requirements contracts were limited to one year. American Can had presented convincing evidence that requirements contracts are necessary to protect food canners, in view of the great uncertainty of crop yields and timing, and that canners preferred them to fixed-quantity contracts; hence the court did not prohibit them altogether. The court also ordered that separate contracts be written for individual plants when the customer had more than one cannery. The buyer could still place all his contracts with a single seller if he chose, but smaller can manufacturers would find it easier to bid at least for the business of a single plant of a multiplant buyer.

3. The tie between machine leasing and the sale of cans was broken. The major companies were permanently enjoined from conditioning the lease of machines on the sale of cans, by any subterfuge. In addition, they were ordered to sell their existing closing machines at bargain prices to anyone who wanted to buy them, giving priority to existing lessees. This order applied to all machines to be built in the future as well, for a period of ten years. The can companies were required to make all technological information and know-how available to buyers, to set up schools to train service men employed by the canneries, and to license closing machinery patents without royalty. The court recognized that there were certain advantages to integration between machinery manufacture and can manufacture, since can manufacture and can closing involve much the same technology, and so it did not order divestiture. The can companies were required to lease to everyone any machine that they were then leasing to anyone. Moreover, rentals had to be fully compensatory, including a fair profit,

---

[1] 87 F. Supp. 18 (1949). A simultaneous case against Continental was not brought to trial, Continental having agreed in advance to accept any judgment entered against American, short of divestiture.

after the end of 1953. . . . No more could below-cost rentals be used as an inducement to lease.

V

This decree knocked out practically all the remaining props of market control. The decree has been in effect now for over three years. Some of its consequences have been striking. One instance is the sale of closing machines, which has greatly exceeded everyone's expectations. The can manufacturers had claimed that customers would be reluctant to buy them—that customers would prefer to lease instead and pay the supplier the appropriate fee for bearing the risk of obsolescence and the task of servicing and maintenance. If this reluctance ever existed it was quickly overcome. The bargain prices the court set on the machines existing in 1950 made it uneconomical not to buy them, and in addition American and Continental, in wholehearted compliance with the letter and the spirit of the decree, have made vigorous efforts to sell both old and newly manufactured machines. By the middle of 1954 both American and Continental had sold over 75 per cent of the closing machines they were leasing in 1950. While the lease market may revive in the future, can buyers are no longer heavily dependent on their can suppliers for closing machinery, and there is no way now for the machinery supplier to apply commercial leverage to the can market. After the transition period is over, the independent manufacturers of machinery will be able to market closing machines directly to the canning industry, and they have already responded to this broadening of their opportunities.

A second result has been an extensive breakdown of exclusive supplier-customer relations. While fruit and vegetable canneries have largely continued their requirements contracts, the large packers operating several canneries have begun to allocate them to different suppliers. Other canners have begun to split requirements within the plant, closing cans from several suppliers indiscriminately on the machines of several manufacturers. . . . The vertical partitions in the market which formerly made the ties between particular buyers and sellers very strong have been demolished, and competitive forces, wherever they originate, can sweep across it largely unimpeded. The market position of smaller manufacturers has been greatly strengthened.

It is interesting to note that these changes in the can market have been accompanied by some instability in the tin plate market. At least part of this instability has been transmitted backward from the can market. Prices have become more flexible; open-order purchasing has grown in volume; the leadership of the leading bargain between U.S. Steel and American Can has weakened further. The tin plate suppliers still feel the weight of the large buyers' bargaining power, but this is more likely now to work to the benefit of ultimate consumers of cans.

It is possible of course to expect too much of the decree. The gross structure of the industry has not changed very much and probably will not change much in the immediate future. Doubtless the effects of a decree of dissolution, if American had been convicted of illegal acquisition and maintenance of monopoly, would have been more spectacular. Several firms could have been fashioned out of either of the leaders without an appreciable loss of efficiency, and the market would in time have enforced a high degree of competition among the fragments. However, such a monopoly charge could not have been sustained. We must decide whether we have any better ground now than the court did in 1916 for expecting workable competition in the future.

American and Continental together would still be able to dominate the industry in the short run if they maintained effective collusion in every dimension of the market. But instead the two large firms are in a state of intense rivalry. The challenger is staging a vigorous drive on the markets of the leader. A number of large accounts previously held by American have now been split. Technological rivalry is unrestrained. While open price warfare has been avoided, except in a few local instances, there is protracted maneuvering in an atmosphere of great uncertainty when the time for quoting new prices and renewing contracts comes round every year. American's price leadership is now merely barometric, and it cannot count on being followed by Continental or by any other seller.

The smaller firms, aided by a strong growth trend in the industry, have been establishing themselves on a more secure footing and have also been edging into the markets of both the leaders. In several instances recently the price structure of the majors has had to be adapted to the independent competitive tactics of a smaller firm aggressively reaching for a larger share. Although the oligopoly structure remains, enough has been said to show that the competitive pattern is in a state of flux.

No outsiders have entered can manufacture in the last three years, but the threat of entry from the buying side has been intensified. Large buyers can no longer be pacified with volume discounts. During the past year the very largest consumer of packers cans began to manufacture part of its own requirements, and another large buyer, located in one of American's few remaining monopoly territories, has announced plans to manufacture all its own containers. The effect of these events is incalculable. Both of the large sellers are constrained as never before by the threat of backward integration, and the restraints exercised on profit margins in cans work to the benefit of all buyers.

American itself has no monopoly weapons left in its hands. Any firm which relies on size and the momentum of past achievements alone to protect it against competition is likely to find its position deteriorating with alarming speed. What American can do is to take advantage of the moderate superiorities it evidently has in efficiency and research. It can maintain its leading position by reducing costs and continuing its rapid rate of product development, passing along the benefits to consumers. Its large rival will push it, or perhaps lead it, in this respect. Its smaller rivals will offer a stronger competitive challenge as time goes on. And its large customers will never be more than a few years behind in potential efficiency if they should decide to produce their own supplies. A forecast of workable competition appears to be justified. Thus it seems that the Antitrust Division, in choosing to make a limited attack on market practices—however much it may later have doubted its own wisdom—made a good decision after all.

15 TYING CONTRACTS:

Protection of Competition or Competitors?

In the following article Professor Ward S. Bowman, Jr., considers the economic logic underlying tying arrangements. In large part Professor Bowman's analysis is intended as background for an appraisal of the per se illegality of contracts in which the sale of a good is tied to the sale of a patented good. Bowman first considers the view that tie-in sales involving a patented tying product are held illegal because they represent an extension of monopoly from the tying product to a new area, the tied product. His primary thesis contradicts this view that tie-in sales using patented products necessarily involve the exercise of monopolistic leverage to create a second monopoly. He contends instead that some contracts are simply a "revenue maximizing device" that does not create new monopolies and that hence should not be subject to a per se illegality. Bowman identifies several situations in which a product might be tied to a patented item:

1. Evasion of price regulation
2. Single-product discrimination—a counting device
3. Product complementarity; in variable proportions
4. Technological interdependence
5. Economies of joint production or distribution

Of these, he feels, only product complementarity with variable proportions should be considered illegal as creating a new monopoly. He contends that a new monopoly power is created, when profits of a given good are maximized, if less of the tied product is available than in the absence of a tie-in contract. This contention, of course, rests upon a view of monopoly as power over supply in a very broad, impersonal sense. However, in this context Donald F. Turner[1] has noted that the antitrust laws are concerned, not with this overall view of competitive or noncompetitive results for the industry, but with a more personal or individual objective of providing each competitor with unrestricted access to markets. Under this view attention is focused more on the other sellers of the tied good. In some respects the issue here comes very close to the traditional philosophical problem as to whether antitrust laws are intended to preserve competition of competitors. It seems clear that, at least in regard to tying contracts, the courts have preferred to protect the competitors, apart from any competitive need to do so.

[1] Donald F. Turner, "The Validity of Tying Arrangements under the Antitrust Laws," *Harvard Law Review,* 72 (1958).

Tying Arrangements and the Leverage Problem

Ward S. Bowman, Jr.

In antitrust law, the conclusion that tying the sale of a second product to a patented product is automatically illegal has been accepted by courts for forty years. Under this theory, tying is harmful because it creates a new monopoly wholly outside the patent. Conditioning the sale or lease of one commodity on the sale or lease of another, a practice known as a tying agreement or a tie-in, is generally considered a trade-restraining device. The recent *Report of the Attorney General's Committee to Study the Antitrust Laws* declares that the purpose of a tying contract is monopolistic exploitation. This exploitation is achieved by "artificially extending the market for the 'tied' product beyond the consumer acceptance it would rate if competing independently on its merits and on equal terms." The view that tying contracts allow the wielding of monopolistic leverage is widely accepted.

"Wielding monopolistic leverage" is an ambiguous phrase. A distinction can usefully be made between leverage as a revenue-maximizing device and leverage as a monopoly-creating device. The first involves the use of existing power. The second requires

Abridged from Ward S. Bowman, Jr., "Tying Arrangements and the Leverage Problem," *The Yale Law Journal*, 67, No. 1, (November 1957), 19–36.

This Article attempts to explore the relationship between product complementarity and tying sales as contrasted with other explanations which have been offered. A "complementarity" view of tying sharply contrasts with other positions in terms of what is called the "leverage" problem. In particular, two explanations have been formulated by Professor Aaron Director—tying as an evasion of price regulation and tying as a counting device for price discrimination. . . .

the addition of new power.[1] In both cases monopoly is involved and the buyers of the first product have a second product forced upon them. But if the tying sale is only a means of utilizing effectively a power already possessed, different conclusions may well be reached about the propriety of the practice than if the tie-in created a second monopoly beyond the scope of the first. The term "leverage," in this article, specifically describes the establishment of a new or second monopoly. The existence of such leverage depends upon the effect of the tying arrangement on the output of the tied product. If the tying seller is maximizing his return on the tying product and the same output of the tied product can still be produced under circumstances consistent with competitive production of the tied product, no additional or new monopoly effect should be assumed.[2] Conversely, if the amount of production of the tied product is less than any output which could exist when the return on the first product can be maximized, a monopoly in the tied product has been created. The description of this effect as leverage derives from the economic concept of monopoly as the equivalent of control over supply. A finding that supply is not restricted is a finding that no monopoly as been created.

Analysis of the situations in which sellers find tie-ins useful casts doubt upon the validity of the statement that the only purpose of tie-ins is monopolistic exploitation. Present legal methods of treating tying contracts are based upon a false notion of leverage. When the suggested definition of leverage is employed, analysis reveals the need for critical revaluation of the law in this area.

---

[1] A similar distinction can be made in the field of price discrimination. Thus price discrimination may be used to increase revenue or to drive out competitors. The Robinson-Patman Act, for example, embodies the assumption that cutting the price of a product in a discriminatory manner is a means of driving out competitors and creating monopoly, whereas the economic analysis stresses its usefulness in maximizing monopoly revenue.

[2] Monopoly is commonly described as the power to set a price. Where the sale of only one product is involved, the definition is satisfactory because price and output are inversely related. To change the price is to change the output. With a tie-in, however, under certain circumstances a supplier may raise the price of the tied product and lower the price of the tying product without affecting the output of the former. Consequently supply restriction on the tied product must be emphasized here.

AN ANALYSIS OF TYING: FIVE EXAMPLES

The Tie-in, a Monopoly Problem

To sell or lease one commodity, the tying product, advantageously on condition that it be used with another commodity, the tied product, requires the existence of monopoly power—in economic theory, the ability to control supply. A competitive supplier, selling at the prevailing price and attempting to impose a tie-in upon a buyer, would merely be displaced by a seller who did not.[3] "It is plain," Professor Watkins has pointed out, "that the sale or lease of one article upon condition that a stipulated quantity or number of another article or articles be bought or leased from the same concern imposes a handicap, other things being equal, upon the distribution of the first article. . . . Under freely competitive conditions, therefore, the adoption of the policy of the tying contract would tend to hinder distribution of one product as much as it fostered distribution of the other or 'tied' product. There could be no advantage in the employment of such a policy. . . ."[4]

The idea of a compensating disadvantage advanced by Professor Watkins is not unique to free competition. It might equally well be applied to a monopoly situation. A monopolist cannot necessarily improve his position—increase his monopoly revenue—by imposing restrictions on his customers. A monopolist who is charging a price which maximizes his return under given demand and cost conditions is still confronted by the problem of imposing an additional restriction on his customers—the equivalent of a higher price—without giving up as much as he gains. To put the problem in this form is to emphasize the central prerequisite for a successful tie-in: what is sacrificed in the way of return from the sale or lease of the tying product must be more than compensated by increased return from the tied product.[5] Four different situations

---

[3] If the tying seller gave a compensating advantage to the buyer, he might not be displaced. But in that event the tie-in would no longer be useful.

[4] Watkins, Public Regulation of Competitive Practices in Business Enterprise 220–21 (3d ed. 1940).

[5] The right to buy a product from whom one chooses and the availability

may be suggested in which tying might give rise to an increased return. These include evasion of price regulation; single product discrimination, a counting device; product complementarity in a variable proportion context; and technological interdependence, a questionable case. A fifth example is also discussed, which appears to involve a tie-in but is to be explained by economies of joint production or sale.

Evasion of Price Regulation

Whenever two products are used together in fixed proportions, such as one bolt and one nut, a cup and a saucer, or a left shoe and a right shoe, from the buyer's point of view the two together might as well be a single product. The price of the combination is the only matter of interest. Certainly the buyer of a fifteen dollar pair of shoes does not care when he is told that the left shoe costs ten dollars and the right one only five. Furthermore, a monopolist who sold one part of such a combination while the other part was sold competitively could exact as much monopoly revenue from the sale of one part as from the sale of both. Here is a monopoly case —more precisely a nondiscriminating monopoly case—comparable to that described by Professor Watkins in the area of free competition—an illustration of compensating disadvantage. For example, if the price of bolts were set by a monopolist and the price of nuts were set by competition, tying the sale of nuts to the sale of bolts would not increase the monopoly profit. Every increase in the price of nuts, even if the monopolist could produce them as cheaply as competitors, would require reduction in the price of bolts by a compensating amount. If the monopolist acted otherwise, he would be creating a situation which reduced his total monopoly return.

If the assumption that the bolt monopolist is free to set the bolt price at the level maximizing his return is abandoned—if, for example, the government were to place a ceiling on the price of bolts and leave the price of nuts uncontrolled—a tying arrange-

---

of alternative sources of supply is a consideration in the purchase when no tie-in is present. Therefore the demand for the tying product at any price will be less than the demand before the imposition of the tie-in. The effect of the tie-in must more than compensate this loss.

ment would become beneficial. By this means, the seller could increase the nut price to maintain the profit-maximizing price for the bolt-nut combination. Only when freedom to set the price of the monopolized product is denied can a tie-in of two products used in fixed proportions become useful.[6] This principle, however, does not limit the evasionary use of a tie-in to the fixed proportion case alone. Wartime whiskey purchasers, for example, bought unregulated rum and wine in order to secure price-controlled whiskey. The sellers were thus able to employ tie-ins advantageously even though whiskey and rum need not be used in fixed proportions.

Where fixed proportions are involved, no revenue can be derived from setting a higher price for the tied product which could not have been made by setting the optimum price for the tying product. The imposition of a tie-in under these circumstances determines the identity of the seller, but the amount of the tied product actually sold will not differ at all from that which could be sold if the optimum price for the tying product were set.[7] Another monopoly is not created. The seller has only established a new method of exercising his already existing monopoly in the regulated product. Leverage, therefore, does not exist when the proportions of the two products are fixed.

Single Product Discrimination— A Counting Device

A similar conclusion follows when different buyers use different quantities of the second commodity with one unit of the first. If the first commodity is worth more to the intensive users than to the less intensive users—in economic terms, if the formers' demand is less elastic—tying the second commodity to the first can in effect achieve the goal of discriminatory pricing for the first. In

[6] An example may be found in the facts of FTC v. Gratz, 253 U.S. 421 (1920). See Stevens, *Tying Arrangements,* in CONFERENCE ON THE ANTITRUST LAWS AND THE ATTORNEY GENERAL'S COMMITTEE REPORT 145–47 (1955). . . .

[7] Critics of the Robinson-Patman Act make the same point when they suggest that harm to competitors, caused by discrimination, is not to be confused with harm to competition.

this situation, the tied product serves as a counting device to measure how intensively the first product is being used.

An illustration may perhaps be drawn from an early tying case.[8] A machine was invented for stapling buttons to high-button shoes, an operation formerly done by hand at higher cost. The patentee had a number of prospective customers for his machine, some of whom made a great many shoes, others only a few. The invention saved each user a fixed amount on each button attached. Thus the machine was worth more to the more intensive users. If the patentee attempted to sell it at different prices to the different users, however, he would have encountered two problems. To determine in advance how intensively each buyer would use the machine would have been difficult; to prevent those who paid a low price from reselling to those who paid a high price might have proved impossible. A tie-in would resolve these difficulties. The machine might be sold at cost, on condition that the unpatented staples used in the machine be bought from the patentee. Through staple sales, the patentee could obtain a device for measuring the intensity with which his customers used the machines. Hence by charging a higher than competitive price for the staples, the patentee could receive the equivalent of a royalty from his patented machines.[9]

Although a tying sale may thus be used as a "counting device" for setting discriminatory prices on the tying product, the patentee creates no new and additional monopoly over the tied product. He could have achieved exactly the same return by attaching a meter to the button-stapling machine to measure the intensity of use, leasing the machine and charging a meter rate.[10] As in the first

[8] Heaton-Peninsular Button-Fastener Co. v. Eureka Specialty Co., 65 Fed. 619 (C.C.W.D. Mich. 1895).

[9] The same "discrimination" result could conceivably have been achieved by giving the machine away and charging a still higher price for staples, except for the fact that the machine might be provided to infrequent users. Under these circumstances the patentee might not even secure a return which would cover the cost of supplying the machine.

[10] Although each user of a patented button-fastening machine pays the same rate per pair of shoes manufactured, use of the tying device or of a meter has the effect of a different sales price for the machine according to intensity of use. This is discrimination, since the large user pays the higher price. When the desired result is to charge the less intensive user the higher

example, tying is used simply as a means of insuring the full monopoly return on the tying product, where a monopoly already existed. No leverage can be found because the output of tied product, staples, is exactly the same when machine payment is charged directly and staples are sold competitively as when the staples are tied to the machine. The two outputs under the two equivalent methods of discrimination are identical.

Although the use of a tie-in sale as a counting device is consistent with the facts of a large number of tying cases—for example, the tying of ink to mimeographs, punch cards to computers or rivets to riveting guns—it does not provide the only rational explanation of tying practice when variable proportions are involved. The example suggests a means by which a monopolist can separate markets to achieve the maximum return from each of the various markets in which the single product can be sold. In this instance, the higher price charged for the tied product is in lieu of the proper pricing of the tying product without the tie-ins. But the fact that profit maximization on only a single product is involved must be emphasized. The example takes no account of the possible effect that the price or the quantity sold of the tying product may have on the sales of the tied product, or of the effect that the price or the quantity sold of the tied product may have on the sales of the tying product when the demands for the two are related.

Product Complementarity in a Variable Proportion Context

If two products complement each other, so that an increase in the price of one will not only result in fewer sales of that product

---

price, the tie-in is ineffective. Whether or not the machine manufacturer's royalty comes from the sale or lease of the machine or from the sale of the staples or the buttons, the maximum that can be charged is fixed by the amount the machine saves the machine users. If the users to whom the machine is "worth" more can be charged more for the machine, either in the form of a machine charge or indirectly by compulsory purchase of a tied product, the patentee is being rewarded for his machine patent. Interestingly enough, Mr. Justice Lurton used almost precisely this reasoning in deciding both Heaton-Peninsular Button-Fastener Co. v. Eureka Specialty Co., 77 Fed. 288 (6th Cir. 1896), and Henry v. A. B. Dick Co., 224 U.S. 1 (1912).

but also in fewer sales of the other, the price which maximizes return from the sale of one will depend upon the price at which the other sells. If product *A,* for which no close substitutes exist, is sold by only one seller, and product *B,* its complement, is offered by many competing sellers, the maximum monopoly profit from the sale of *A,* arising from the "best" price of *A* when *B* is competitively priced, may possibly be increased by tying the sale of *B* to the sale of *A.* Increase of the total profit will depend upon the existence of a situation—unlike the first example—in which the profit lost on sales of product *A* by imposition of the tie-in is more than compensated by the profit obtained from the higher price charged for product *B.* This condition alone is the generalization which explains the rational use of any tie-in. When cross-elasticity of demand is involved, a price increase in one product affects the demand for the other. Thus in the first example, the price of left shoes will influence the demand for right shoes and the price of right shoes will affect the demand for left shoes in the same manner. On the other hand, when two complements are used in variable proportions, even after the market has been separated into segments in which different prices can be charged—the counting device—the cross-elasticity of the complements creates the condition calling for two distinct prices in order to maximize profit, just as if a single firm had the monopoly of each product. When product complementarity is involved, the higher price charged for product *B* is not a substituted means of charging for product *A.* On the contrary, output of product *B* for use with product *A* is less than any output of product *B* for such use which would exist by manipulation of the price or output of product *A* when product *B* is competitive. In other words, the result of the tie-in is to create the equivalent of another monopoly, a monopoly over product *B* for use with product *A.* The tie-in thus yields the equivalent of monopoly by a single seller over both *A* and *B.* Leverage is present; and the tie-in provides the leverage, since the price and output of one product will necessarily affect the price and output of the other. Of the three examples given, only under these circumstances does a tying sale create leverage. Thus, as the term is used in this article, leverage did not exist in the counting case because the same result could have been obtained by metering the first product with no control over the second. In the complementarity case, however, control over the second product, product *B*, is required even though latent power over product *B* may be said to reside in product *A* for those uses of *B* with *A*. Here, in the complementarity case, control over *B* is essential to securing revenue which could not be realized from *A* alone; and the tie-in creates the equivalent of a new monopoly of *B* in addition to the monopoly of the complementary product *A*.

Even though product complementarity exists, a tie-in may not be feasible despite the possibility of increased profits. A pen seller, for example, would have difficulty conceiving of an arrangement assuring that only ink cartridges of his own make were being used with his pen. After a pen sale, the cost of policing the tie-in would be prohibitive. And leasing a ballpoint pen is hardly to be recommended in the name of sound merchandising. But if, rather than pens and cartridges, an example of two complementary machines is assumed, and if for two maximizing sale prices equivalent lease rental charges are substituted, a tying arrangement will result in increased profits.[11] The United Shoe Machinery Company, for example, made extensive use of the practice of leasing a monopolized or patented machine only on the condition that another machine—either unpatented, unmonopolized or precariously monopolized—would also be rented.[12]

Technological Interdependence

The usefulness of a particular product or device may depend not only upon its own adaptability but equally upon the adaptability of some essential complement. If the essential complement did not conform to exact specifications, it might impair the operation or usefulness of the principal product. For example, if a very slight imperfection in an unpatented card were to make a patented

[11] A machine and a product would provide an equally good example. The button-fastening machine and the staples, used as an illustration of a counting device, might conceivably involve interrelated demands as well. The two discrete prices could add some monopoly in addition to the advantage achieved by counting.

[12] See United States v. United Shoe Mach. Co., 247 U.S. 32 (1918).

tabulating machine operate inefficiently, or in a more extreme case actually cause costly damage, a patentee lessor or seller of such a machine would have an understandable interest in protecting the good will which arises from satisfactory performance. When the exact source of poor performance is difficult to trace, the supplier will be especially concerned that no foreign elements are being used with his machines. This defense for tying clauses has often been raised in the litigated cases. Thus in *Henry v. A. B. Dick Co.,* defendant claimed that ink supplied by others would or might impair the proper functioning of a mimeograph machine which he manufactured.[13] Nor is the example of cards and tabulators fanciful; such a defense was invoked in a tying case by I.B.M.[14] Again, in the early shoe machinery cases, the United Company stressed the very close technological interdependence of a wide variety of machines each of which, although doing a separate task, was only efficient if properly co-ordinated with the others.[15]

In many cases involving technological interdependence, a careful description of the specifications necessary for successful performance might overcome the objections of the manufacturer. However, in one respect interdependence differs from the other examples described: the interests of the prospective "tyer" and the "tyee" are not in conflict. Each has a rational interest in technological efficiency. One would rarely expect objections from a buyer or lessee that a complementary product is being forced upon him, if the technological reasons advanced by the seller are valid. In the *Pick* case, General Motors insisted that its dealers sell and install only those parts authorized by the company.[16] The substance of the court's holding was that substandard parts installed in a General Motors car by a General Motors dealer would have a deleterious effect on the company's good will because users would not ordinarily associate the improper functioning of their automobiles with the use of non-General Motors parts. Why the dealers'

[13] 224 U.S. 1 (1912).

[14] International Business Machines Corp. v. United States, 298 U.S. 131 (1936).

[15] United States v. United Shoe Mach. Co., 247 U.S. 32 (1918).

[16] Pick Mfg. Co. v. General Motors Corp., 80 F.2d 641 (7th Cir. 1935).

interest in this problem should not parallel that of General Motors was not discussed in the case. An absence of conflict of interest at least would support a strong presumption that the difficulties arising from problems of technological interdependence between products can be resolved by means other than tying contracts.

Economies of Joint Production or Sale

Occasionally tie-ins are alleged to exist under circumstances in which no tying is intended and in fact no tie-in, in any economic meaning of the word, can be found. Probably no one has bought shoes without buying shoelaces at the same time, and the sale of that combination of mechanical parts generally called an automobile is not usually thought of as a tie-in. Of course, shoelaces may be purchased separately, as may automobile parts, but this condition does not preclude the possibility that a tie-in is involved. Still, when the cost of producing and selling the combination is less than the cost of producing and selling the parts separately, no tie-in can be said to exist. Cost justification excludes the rational use of a tie-in. No coercion is required when a cost advantage exists, for these lower costs will be reflected in lower prices.

That the separate offering of a complementary product does not preclude the existence of a tie-in is apparent from an extreme example in which the condition imposed on a buyer for not taking both products from the same seller requires the alternative of paying a higher price for one product than for both. In contrast is another extreme example. Suppose the publisher of both a morning and an evening newspaper found that the cost of running a want ad in both papers was no higher than running it in one paper only. For this reason, the publisher quoted the same price for running the ad in both papers as for running it in one, to the disadvantage of a competitor, the publisher of an afternoon newspaper alone. The cost justification assumed in this example should preclude a finding that a tie-in exists.[17] The larger publisher's find-

---

[17] No necessary relationship to the facts of Times-Picayune Publishing Co. v. United States, 345 U.S. 594 (1953), should be assumed. If a cost justification had been present in that case, defendants would almost certainly have brought it to the Court's attention.

ing that resetting the want ads in type for the afternoon paper was more expensive than merely reprinting the morning's ads seems a reasonable basis for his course of action—a case of economy of scale. If such an arrangement were to be struck down, efficient operations would have to be sacrificed.

Use of tying sales is not necessarily conclusive proof that the seller is wielding leverage. The analysis of the motives and purposes which may underlie utilization of the tying device suggests that the legal conclusion of automatic illegality is too facile. The device may be employed to achieve a number of goals, some of which are clearly legitimate. Of the five examples discussed, only one, that of product complementarity in the variable proportion context described, involves leverage.

LEVERAGE AND THE LAW

The Clayton Act, passed in 1914, contains the only specific statutory language forbidding tie-ins. In section three of this act, prohibition of tie-ins extends to both patented and unpatented products, covers both selling and leasing, but is limited to commodities. The tie-in, to be found illegal, must be likely "to substantially lessen competition or tend to create a monopoly." The section contains no direct reference to leverage, but in a very real sense the conception of the whole Clayton Act depends upon the leverage notion. The declared purpose of the sponsors of this legislation was to strengthen the anti-trust laws by outlawing particular practices. These practices, beyond the reach of the Sherman Act, were believed to lead to or "ripen into" monopoly. Among such practices, tying arrangements were emphasized. The very language "substantially lessen competition or tend to create a monopoly" reflects the leverage presumption.

The relationship of tying to the creation of monopoly—the leverage problem—had been faced by courts in the area of patent law before the passage of the Clayton Act. In the *Button-Fastener* case, the Court of Appeals for the Sixth Circuit considered a patentee's right to sell a patented machine for stapling buttons to shoes with the attached condition that staples be purchased from the patentee. The court decided the issue in favor of the patentee. However the tie-in question was not presented to the Supreme Court until 1912, sixteen years later. In a four to three decision Mr. Justice Lurton, who had decided the earlier *Button-Fastener* case, came to the same result when considering the tying sales of a mimeograph machine on condition that ink, stencils, paper and other supplies be bought from the patentee. A vigorous dissent was entered by Mr. Justice White. Stripped to its essential logic, the dissent advanced the proposition that a tie-in to a patented commodity was the equivalent of allowing a monopoly over the tied product. This additional monopoly, White reasoned, went beyond that granted to the patentee and should not be protected by the patent law.

This "patent extension" argument of the minority became the majority opinion five years later in the *Motion Picture Patents* case.[18] Mr. Justice Clarke's opinion makes an unmistakable reference to leverage:

> "Such a restriction is invalid because such a film is obviously not any part of the invention of the patent in suit; because it is an attempt, without statutory warrant, to continue the patent monopoly in this particular character of film after it has expired, and because to enforce it would be to create a monopoly in the manufacture and use of moving picture films, wholly outside of the patent in suit and of the patent law as we have interpreted it." [19]

This legal conclusion relating to patent tie-ins has remained substantially unchanged for forty years. When the sale or lease of a commodity is tied to a patented product, the tie-in is considered per se illegal.[20] No exceptions to the rule have emerged since its estab-

[18] Motion Picture Patents Co. v. Universal Film Mfg. Co., 243 U.S. 502 (1917).

[19] *Id.* at 518.

[20] The rule of per se illegality operates only if the volume of the tied supplies is "significant." See International Salt Co. v. United States, 332 U.S. 392, 396 (1947). Sale of the patented machine was involved in Motion Picture Patents Co. v. Universal Film Mfg. Co., 243 U.S. 502 (1917). Subsequently, in United States v. United Shoe Mach. Co., 247 U.S. 32 (1918), a machine lease was distinguished and the tie-in allowed under patent law. In a later case brought under § 3 of the Clayton Act and involving the

lishment; and indeed its acceptance may be gauged by the fact that no defendant has even questioned the doctrine in recent years.[21]

The attitude of the law toward tying to unpatented products, covered by section three of the Clayton Act, is not so clear. Although the per se rule has no application here, a recent summary of the law by the Supreme Court in the *Times-Picayune* case does profess to narrow the area for relevant inquiry.[22] According to this opinion, a court may find illegal activity, in the absence of a patent on the tying product, whenever the supplier enjoys a monopolistic position in the tying product or if a substantial volume of commerce in the tied product is restrained.[23] For purposes of economic analysis this "clarification" is not helpful. A tie-in is a useless device unless the supplier possesses substantial monopoly over the tying product. How much economic monopoly must exist before the law's monopoly, which will result in illegality, may be found? In determining whether a substantial volume of the tied product is restrained, should a lower court emphasize "substantial" or "restrained"? If the former, the equivalent of the "quantitative substantiality test" of the *Standard Oil Company* case suggests itself.[24] If the latter, application of the kind of criteria embodied in an economic description of leverage seems proper. These questions must be answered if the advice about tie-in law in the absence of patents given in *Times-Picayune* is to be of use. To attempt to provide answers to these broader problems, however, is beyond the scope of an article concerned with leverage.

Leverage necessarily involves the creation of new monopoly. Only when the original monopoly can be assumed to serve some

---

same facts, the result was reversed. See United Shoe Mach. Corp. v. United States, 258 U.S. 451 (1922).

The term "patented product" includes a machine, a process or a combination as well as a commodity.

[21] As a measure of the doctrine's present accepted status, see *Report of the Attorney General's National Committee to Study the Antitrust Laws* (Washington, D.C.: Government Printing Office, 1955), p. 145.

[22] Times-Picayune Publishing Co. v. United States, 345 U.S. 594 (1953).

[23] *Id.* at 608.

[24] Standard Oil Co. v. United States, 337 U.S. 293 (1949). See *Attorney General's Report,* p. 141.

useful public purpose, as in a patent situation, need the relevance of the leverage question arise. If the first monopoly is without conceivable justification, the creation of a second is irrelevant to the public interest. Either the justifications for the first monopoly should be attacked directly, or, if the first is an acceptable monopoly, the effect of tying should be scrutinized to determine whether it leads to the establishment of an unacceptable second. The following evaluation is confined to the leverage problem as it relates to an acceptable first monopoly, here exemplified by the existence of the patent.

EVALUATION OF PATENT TIE-IN LAW
IN TERMS OF LEVERAGE

Writing a fifth and concluding part of a long article on patent practice and the antitrust laws in 1942, Mr. Giles Rich summarized what a patentee may legitimately do in exercising his right to exclude others from making, vending or using his invention.[25] The patentee has the right to maximize the monopoly profit from the invention. He can sell or not sell, lease or not lease. He can restrict production or fix the price of his own sales or the sales of his licensees.[26] What a patentee may do involves "restraining trade and maintaining a monopoly, but permission to do so with respect to inventions is the basis of the patent system. This is the reward offered to induce invention, disclosure and enterprise." [27] Mr. Rich then provides several examples of licensing which are clearly permissible because they make possible only a more profitable exploitation of the proper patent monopoly. Examples of permissible practice include the retention or reservation by a patentee of a particular field of use for himself or for others; a reservation of this kind is allowed even though the other fields of use have been licensed to someone else. Such division of fields is permissible because it has not "created a monopoly in anything more than the

[25] Rich, *The Relation Between Patent Practices and the Anti-Monopoly Laws,* 24 J. PAT. OFF. SOC'Y 422 (1942).

[26] *Id.* at 424.

[27] *Ibid.*

patented invention." [28] A reservation or a division of geographical areas leads Mr. Rich to exactly the same result. "Nothing has been added to the patent monopoly." [29] A similar conclusion is also reached about restrictions upon a licensee's output. "He has not enlarged his monopoly nor has he extended it to anything *other than the invention protected by the patent.*" [30] Summarizing his conclusions, Mr. Rich cites with approval the *Motion Picture Patents* case to the effect that a patentee's monopoly cannot be expanded beyond the boundaries claimed:

> "The test is always the same: will the enforcement of the restriction be a mere enforcement of the right to exclude others from making, using, or selling the patented invention *or will it enlarge the rights of the patentee as against the public?* If to enforce it gives a partial monopoly in an unpatented commodity, there has been an extension." [31]

This test which Mr. Rich applies is the equivalent of the question posed in this Article: is leverage involved? Mr. Rich then goes on to conclude, without proof, that tie-ins inevitably involve monopoly over a second product. One need not disagree with any of Mr. Rich's conclusions to hold the position that if a patent tie-in can be found which does not involve leverage, it cannot be ruled illegal by the logic of the leading cases. The finding that leverage exists has been the central determinant to a reasoned conclusion that patent tie-ins should not be allowed.

Although a rule holding illegal the sale or lease of a patented product or machine to which another product is tied is sometimes supported on the ground that the wisdom of a public policy sponsoring any patent monopoly is doubtful,[32] such an argument is in effect a direct attack upon the first monopoly and seems to be a

[28] *Id.* at 425.

[29] *Ibid.*

[30] *Id.* at 426. (Emphasis added.)

[31] *Id.* at 427. (Emphasis added.) See Motion Picture Patents Co. v. Universal Film Mfg. Co., 243 U.S. 502, 518 (1917).

[32] See Plant, *Economic Theory Concerning Patents for Invention,* 1 ECONOMICA (n.s.) 30 (1934).

better subject for separate inquiry. The validity of the original monopoly is not questioned here.

Other arguments may be advanced to support the desirability of a per se rule against patent tie-ins, whether or not leverage is present. One would justifiably assert that non-leverage tie-ins foster either the evasion of price regulation, as in the first example, or price discrimination, as in the second, the counting case. A per se rule to stamp out all evasion of price regulation is unacceptable. Given fixed proportions, tie-ins can be used to evade privately regulated as well as publicly regulated prices. But gray markets may result in better allocation of resources than would exist if the fixed prices were observed,[33] and, unlike black markets, they are not publicly condemned. Moreover, in the combination patent cases, products in fixed proportions cannot be sold without the use of tie-ins; and the interest so protected seems valid.[34] To make a tie-in illegal in the price discrimination situation is arbitrary, for it resolves a very complicated problem in a manner totally different from the law directly concerned with price discrimination. If a tie-in is declared automatically illegal because of discrimination, the result is effective elimination of the necessary showing, required even by the Robinson-Patman Act, that "the effect of such discrimination may be substantially to lessen competition or tend to create a monopoly." [35] Secondly, the contention that a tie-in prolongs the effective life of a patent rests on a belief that entry will be less prompt after the expiration of a patent, when a tie-in is used, because two entries, one into the field of the tying product and another into the field of the tied, are then required.[36] The requisite "know-how" is enlarged, the argument runs, and a longer life for the monopoly is thus created. The argument has no validity when the tied product has other uses than with the tying product, for the essential know-how is already in the market. Moreover, to

---

[33] See STIGLER, THE THEORY OF PRICE 83–87 (rev. ed. 1952).

[34] See text following note 36 *infra.*

[35] 49 STAT. 1526 (1936), 15 U.S.C. § 13(a) (1952). See ATT'Y GEN. REP. 160–67.

[36] For a fuller discussion of the double entry problem, see Bork, *Vertical Integration and the Sherman Act,* 22 U. CHI. L. REV. 157, 195 (1954).

support the entry argument, the patentee himself must be able to produce everything the market demands. If the patentee buys the tied product from others, using the tie-in to become an exclusive seller of the tied product, the other manufacturers will acquire the know-how. A per se rule takes no account of this common pattern. Finally, know-how concerns the tying product as well as the tied. Once the patent on the tying product has expired, any relevant know-how must also be acquired by new producers of this tying product. The tie-in will only delay entry, therefore, when the time required to obtain tying product know-how is shorter than that for the tied product. Under any other circumstances, no time extension can be attributed to the existence of a tie-in. But if the know-how for manufacture of the tied product is actually longer, no reason may exist for the patentee to establish a tie-in in the first place. The relationship of tie-ins to new entry seems far too doubtful to justify per se treatment.

The legal rule which has developed has been based upon an imprecise evaluation of the economic effects of tying practice in extending monopoly. Analytically, the per se rule depends upon a prior finding of leverage. This dependence suggests the relevance of a proposal which would not condemn patent tie-ins when leverage clearly is not involved. No conclusive method can be prescribed which will make possible a neat division of cases into two mutually exclusive categories of "leverage" and "no leverage." A clearer understanding of what is involved in distinguishing the "counting" case and the "complimentarity" case might lead to the eventual establishment of a more satisfactory and certainly a more logical legal rule.

Reason neither in law nor economics will justify concern over leverage unless separate prices of both the tying and the tied products are set. Advantageous use of leverage necessarily depends upon effective pricing of the first and the second product.[37] The "one price" cases involving economies of joint production or sale, therefore, might be segregated for exclusion not only from the per se rule, but also from the "illegal" category. Courts now hold illegal

---

[37] See pp. 385–387 *supra.*

certain patent tie-in arrangements in which all the revenue is derived from the sale of a single tied product. Most notable of this category are the familiar combination patent cases, where no part of the combination is patentable and no revenue can be derived without the sale of one of the component products. In the absence of the tie-in, the seller can obtain no royalty from the otherwise perfectly proper licensing of the combination. A number of illustrative cases might be cited, cases in which a tie-in could not have a leverage effect. Among them stand such well-known patent tie-in decisions as *Carbice*,[38] *Mercoid*[39] and *B. B. Chemical*.[40] These combination patent cases are special examples of the "fixed proportion" type described in the first example. The absence of freedom to set the price of the monopolized product—in these cases, a process—makes this kind of tie-in useful.[41] A patentee of a combination patent cannot enjoin manufacture of the unpatented parts; he lacks any practical means to control their assembly and sale at the retail level; hence, absent tying, he is unable to exercise any freedom in setting the price of that which is monopolized.

A conclusion that leverage cannot exist if only one price is set is not a conclusion that leverage is involved when more than one price is set. Even when a tie-in is used solely as a counting device, and no revenue from an additional monopoly is involved—the second example—the price of the tying as well as the tied product must be so fixed that the equivalent of a minimum charge to protect against nonuse is created. One of the prices serves the sole purpose of eliminating the undesirable customer in the extreme case. Thus, the existence of a charge for the tying product in addition to the charge for the tied product does not necessarily signal the equivalence of another monopoly. For example, the fact that in both *A. B. Dick* and *Button-Fastener*[42] the machines were sold

[38] Carbice Corp. v. American Patents Development Corp., 283 U.S. 27 (1931).

[39] Mercoid Corp. v. Mid-Continent Inv. Co., 320 U.S. 661 (1944).

[40] B. B. Chemical Co. v. Ellis, 314 U.S. 495 (1942).

[41] See text at note 6 *supra*.

[42] Heaton-Peninsular Button-Fastener Co. v. Eureka Specialty Co., 77 Fed. 288 (6th Cir. 1896).

at cost and the staple price and the ink price were raised does not necessarily indicate that two maximizing prices were set, with a resulting creation of leverage.

Factors given no attention in the opinions and illuminated only by ambiguous evidence must be considered before determining whether such cases as *Button-Fastener, A. B. Dick, Motion Picture Patents* or *Shoe Machinery*[43] are "counting" cases or "complementarity" cases. *Button-Fastener,* for instance, may be viewed more easily than *A. B. Dick* as a "counting" case involving no leverage because only one counter, staples, was involved in the former, while in the latter, the machine was tied to several other products: ink, stencils, paper and other supplies. Any one of them presumably would have provided a perfectly adequate and satisfactory counting device; the counting example cannot explain why all the products are tied.[44]

A counting explanation of the tie-in of films to projectors in the *Motion Picture Patents* case is even less convincing. Any movie house which is not "dark" is using film, and the amount of film used is an unsatisfactory means of finding the exhibitor who should be paying the highest effective rate for the use of a projection machine. Paid admissions would appear a better measure. Although the record does not show that separate prices were set on the projection machine and the films to produce a return larger than could be received from either, the case is consistent with this rationale, and the alternatives offered are unsatisfactory. Similarly, the complicated *Shoe Machinery* case, while not susceptible of an easy explanation, in certain aspects fits the analysis of complementarity.

CONCLUSION

A finding like that of the complementarity example has not been a legal prerequisite to a conclusion of illegality in tie-in cases. In both *Motion Picture Patents* and *Shoe Machinery,* complementarity

---

[43] United States v. United Shoe Mach. Co., 247 U.S. 32 (1918).

[44] This conclusion would seem to follow unless the multiple tie-in can be assumed to represent the kind of carefulness involved in wearing both belt and suspenders.

was not considered. The analysis in this article suggests that the right result may have been reached for the wrong reasons. Doubts must exist about such cases until the relevant information is obtained by something more than pure accident. In the "one price" cases, however, no reasonable basis yet appears for conclusively identifying leverage with tying and automatically declaring tie-ins illegal. At the least, analysis of the patent combination cases suggests their exemption from the per se rule of illegality. More generally, inquiry into the necessary effects of a patentee's adoption of the tying device should be stressed in all patent cases. Outside the patent field, inquiry might be first directed to the monopoly which enables effective use of the tie-in mechanism. Should that monopoly prove consistent with the public interest, examination could then be extended to considerations properly governing patent tie-in cases.

....

[Bowman's incisive analysis raises the rather controversial issue of applying a per se illegality to cover all tie-in contracts, even those involving unpatented tying products. Bowman's arguments against the per se illegality assumption with patented products would, of course, be even more applicable in the absence of patented tying products. The basis of the per se argument is that a monopoly in the tying product is no longer necessary as grounds for illegality. It is to be stressed that much of this argument depends on the evolution of the Supreme Court's view of monopoly power in tying cases. Formerly, a monopoly position and substantial foreclosure were required for illegality under the Sherman Act Section 1, or either of these conditions under the Clayton Act Section 3. However, the "dominance" requirement now appears satisfied by a degree of distinctiveness (such as patent, copyright, or other differentiating facets) that leads consumers to prefer one item to comparable competitive items, and the substantial foreclosure can be met on a quantitative basis, that is, that a large amount of commerce is involved. This interpretation is indicated by the early patent cases, which involved only the patent laws; the 1947 International Salt case, which implicitly applied a distinctiveness interpretation; and the subsequent Paramount[2] case, in which the patent-case principles were used to support a decision on copyrighted films. In the 1953 Times-Picayune case the Court stated that whereas a Sherman Act Section 1 violation required a monopolistic position in the tying good as a foreclosure from a substantial market in the tied good, either of these conditions would support a Clayton Act Section 3 violation.

Although the meaning of "monopolistic position" is not entirely clear, and some doubts exist as to the level of additional proof required for Sherman rather than Clayton Act cases, it seems from the Northern Pacific case that the Court is applying a "dominance" standard requiring some element of distinctiveness. Since the Clayton Act Section 3 relates only to "goods, wares . . . or other commodities," the identity of tests is a delicate issue. In the absence of identical tests, the severity with which tie-ins are treated could reflect only the nature of the product involved and not the economic effect of the agreement; this result does not appear to have been the underlying congressional intent. This issue would, of course, be resolved under a per se illegality ruling. Donald F. Turner has attempted to provide a defense of a per se approach, quite apart from any convenience or certainty involved:

> But despite the obvious advantages of a per se rule, more justification is required. It must be shown to protect a legitimate antitrust interest. In addition, we must ask (1) whether there are other legitimate interests that are served by the practice in question; (2) if so, whether those interests can or cannot be served by less restrictive alternatives; and (3) if they cannot, whether the contribution made by the restrictive practice is likely to be outweighed by the harm, over the range of situations in which it may be used. A per se rule is clearly justified if it protects a legitimate interest and if the restrictive practice serves no other legitimate interest; if the other interests can be equally well or nearly as well served by less restrictive devices; or if the contributions to legitimate interests, though sacrificed by a per se rule, are comparatively small.
>
> There is one further consideration. For the advantages of a per se

[2] United States v. Paramount Pictures, Inc., 334 U.S. 131 (1948).

rule to be realized, we must be able to define the practice in terms that are readily applicable to a substantial number of cases. If this is not possible, if the treatment of cases typically requires a look at a number of varying factors, the area is simply not suitable to a per se approach. But it is by no means necessary that the practice subjected to a per se rule be readily identifiable in all cases. Border-line situations are inevitable. It may often be difficult to identify "price-fixing," as the trade-association cases make manifest. Yet this does not destroy the obvious utility and propriety of the rule that price-fixing is illegal per se. There are obvious kinds of price-fixing; there is no reason for the courts to waste their time over them just because less obvious forms require a more searching examination.[3]

Turner feels that the courts' primary concern in tying cases should be for competing sellers of the tied product whose interest is a free access to markets. He does not consider control over the tying product as the key interest since this could be met by a better stand-ard of defining "control" or "substantial power." However, com-petitive sellers of the tied good will not receive the free access to competitive markets if the tying product enjoys any market power. In this respect four characteristics of tie-ins can be considered:

1. Whether the buyer is unconditionally obligated to buy the tied good
2. Whether the purchases are repetitive and the goods are used over time
3. Whether the tying good differs from the tied good and the two are used in varying amounts over time
4. Whether the tying contract covers users and not distributors.

Turner would apply the per se illegality standard to tying con-tracts with these characteristics. However, even under this stand-ard, tying contracts might serve legitimate purposes: Efficiency or reputation might require the maintenance of high standards when two goods are used together, and the tying arrangements may lead to possible savings where there are high joint costs.

However, the first condition does not require a tie-in to en-

[3] *Op. cit.,* 59–60.

courage proper use and standards, while the second can be provided short of a compulsory tie-in. It should be noted that Turner's proposals do not fully condemn all of the possible tying arrangements. Some of those instances not covered by the per se rule include:

1. If the tying product's rate of return is less than normal and the tied product is priced competitively
2. Tie-in contracts in which both goods are sold at the same time
3. Tie-in sales in which the goods are used in a given proportion
4. Sales to distributors rather than to final users

In each of the above instances, the tie-in contract may be justified by the given context. In regard to distributors, the tie-in would be precluded only upon showing that a substantial amount of commerce was forclosed and if the above-mentioned per se conditions were present. Thus a brief consideration of this material indicates that the matter of per se illegality hinges on whether competition or competitors are the object of our attention. If the former, then the Bowman analysis would be particularly pertinent, while the latter objective seems especially receptive to a per se illegality standard.]

16 RECENT DEVELOPMENTS

An examination of the antitrust opinions issued by the Supreme Court since its 1962 Brown Shoe decision reveals: 1. obvious indications of a strict "hard-line" treatment of mergers and 2. a less obvious decline in sophisticated analyses supporting these decisions.

The Court's hard-line approach is particularly evident in merger cases. Indeed, in all post-du Pont (GM) merger cases decided on their merits, the Supreme Court has found the contested merger in violation of the antitrust laws.

In many recent cases the proscribed mergers involved firms that —given their market shares, product lines, and so forth,—were seemingly outside the guidelines of unlawfulness which, until 1962, the Court appeared to be developing. Although most specialists in this field probably have a bias toward a strong, vigorous antitrust policy, these victories have caused not a few misgivings.

If we do not believe that mergers per se should be proscribed, we must develop criteria that permit discrimination between acceptable and unacceptable mergers. The development of such criteria and their implementation should be based on (1) an understanding of the effects of varying types of mergers and (2) evidence permitting one to infer and appraise the effects of these mergers. Unfortunately, in these cases the Court seems to have been so determined to take a hard line that a careful analysis of the economic issues was considered unnecessary. Only when one rigorously examines these complex factors can analytical standards be high; the use of ambiguous proxy measures is indicative of low analytical standards, which can easily result in inapt conclusions. The substantive issues, their measures and proxies, are examined in each of the following sections: (1) market definition, (2) market structure, and (3) potential competition. These three sets of considerations and their component subsets must be considered in any serious economic evaluation of competitive conditions and the subsequent impact of structural change on competition.

1. MARKET DEFINITION

The clear identification of the relevant economic activity is the truly essential consideration when evaluating competitive conditions. Basically, the fundamental issue in appraising competition is one of delineating market and industry boundaries. If the market's scope is rigorously defined, then subsequent stages of the analysis can be undertaken in alternative ways with satisfactory results. However, if the market is defined in a rough or meaningless fashion, then the best quantitative measures will not provide a meaningful analysis. Meaningful market boundaries must be broad enough to include substitute products and, in turn, relevant competitors. On the other hand these boundaries must not be so broad as to include products that are not reasonably interchangeable and, in turn, specious competitors. Although the objectives may be scientific, the practice of market delineation is one of judgment—to be sure, judgment that is based both on training and on familiarity with the industry at hand, but judgment nevertheless.

For economists, this issue was most articulately posed by the publication of Chamberlin's *The Theory of Monopolistic Competition.*[1] Three decades later, economists can identify the necessary data and analysis needed to answer this question, but, nevertheless, the question still remains one requiring individual case resolution. The delineation of market and industry boundaries—both in terms

[1] Chamberlin, Edward H., *The Theory of Monopolistic Competition* (Cambridge: Harvard University Press, 1933); also, see Joe S. Bain, "The Theory of Monopolistic Competition After Thirty Years: The Impact on Industrial Organization," and related papers, *The American Economic Review,* LIV, No. 2, Proceedings (May 1964), 28–57; and Robert E. Kuenne, ed., *Monopolistic Competition Theory: Studies in Impact* (New York: Wiley, Inc., 1967).

of products or "line of commerce" as well as relevant market area or "section of the country"—is also a judgmental matter in very large part. Ideally, this would be a judgment based on adequate evidence and a firm analytical background as well as substantial general knowledge of the operations of markets in general and in the particular. The courts seemingly have been aware of these problems, both in terms of the legal issues posed and the special efforts by economists in grappling with them. The Supreme Court's most incisive statement of these economic problems was in the *Brown Shoe* decision.

A review of the Court's antitrust analyses indicates its adoption of highly divergent concepts in selecting market boundaries. In Brown Shoe the Court adopted an intermediate view—men's, women's, and youth's shoes—of the relevant products from among those advanced, but it demonstrated that nationally and in some selected local markets, the market shares based on such product-market delineation paralleled that based on both broader and more narrow definitions. By contrast, in the earlier du Pont (GM) case the Court rejected an argument by du Pont and GM that the relevant product market was one of all finishes (paints or lacquers) and fabrics; in that instance the Court defined the market to be automotive finishes and fabrics. Indeed, at points the Court adopted the argument that the relevant markets were GM's purchases of finishes and fabrics.

The du Pont (GM) and Brown Shoe decisions indicate that market definition includes both product characteristic and geographic constraints. Both aspects have been considered in recent Supreme Court decisions. Regrettably, the Court has maintained its ambivalence on product characteristics, while its geographic standards have approached the simplistic. In its Alcoa (Rome)[2] and Continental Can (Hazel-Atlas)[3] decisions, the Court adopted seemingly conflicting definitions of the relevant "line of commerce." In the Pabst case[4] the Court largely stripped the connotation of "relevant geographic *market*" from the term "section of the country." Despite the Court's protestations, these cases, which are

[2] United States v. Aluminum Company of America, 377 U.S. 271 (1964).
[3] United States v. Continental Can Co., 378 U.S. 441 (1964).
[4] United States v. Pabst Brewing Co., 384 U.S. 546 (1966).

considered below, would seem to represent a repudiation, rather than an application, of Brown Shoe.

The acquisition of a relatively small company by a relatively large one was at issue in the Alcoa-Rome Cable case decided by the Supreme Court on June 1, 1964. The Aluminum Company of America was a fully integrated aluminum company while Rome was a copper fabricator that also produced some types of aluminum wire. In considering the relevant product lines and geographical areas, the District Court examined several alternative markets and submarkets.[5] The government alleged ten lines of commerce, of which six were disputed. The disputed lines of most significance, both analytically and for eventual resolution of the case by the Supreme Court, were aluminum conductor wire and cable—a composite of bare aluminum wire and cable including ACSR (aluminum-covered steel reinforced)—and insulated or covered aluminum wire and cable. The litigants agreed that the bare aluminum conductor was a separate, and relevant, line of commerce. At issue was whether insulated aluminum conductor constituted a relevant line of commerce and in turn whether the composite of bare and insulated aluminum conductor was a relevant line of commerce. The District Court found that:

> . . . insulated or covered aluminum wire and cable, is not a line of commerce because it is not recognized in the industry as a separate economic entity. While differing in some characteristics and preferred uses from its copper counterpart, they both perform the same functions . . . [In 1959] insulated copper conductor comprised 22.8% of the gross additions to insulated overhead distribution lines. Both aluminum and copper wire may be produced interchangeably, using the same facilities. Covered aluminum wire has no distinct customers as distinguished from covered copper wire purchasers. Neither has it specialized vendors. Insulated aluminum and copper wire are generally functionally interchangeable. Their purchase and use are likewise principally dictated by economic factors. While aluminum wire and cable is sold at prices generally distinct from copper and does not have the same price sensitivity, these

[5] United States v. Aluminum Company of America, 214 F. Supp. 501 (1963).

factors do not destroy the conclusion that covered aluminum wire and cable is in actual competition with its copper counterpart . . .[6]

The District Court then concluded that insulated aluminum conductor did not constitute a relevant line of commerce. The court held in turn that the broader

> . . . combination cannot result in a line of commerce . . . [since it] extends the outer boundaries of the market beyond its legal limits because covered copper wire and cable is interchangeable in use and there is cross-elasticity of the demand, therefore, between insulated or covered aluminum and copper. To constitute a proper line of commerce, same must include the substitutes, therefore, which are reasonably interchangeable in use and for which there is a cross-elasticity of demand.[7]

The District Court's enumeration of the issues and its summary of the evidence leading to this conclusion are certainly palatable. The validity of the conclusion from the standpoint of economic analysis turns on the extent to which the available facts were objectively appraised by the court (or whether one with special competence would be led to an analogous "summary"), and on the exercise of judgment.

The Supreme Court's review of the contentions and evidence concerning the relevant product market in Alcoa (Rome) led it to "conclude (1) that aluminum conductor and copper conductor are separable for the purpose of analyzing the competitive effect of the merger and (2) that aluminum conductor (bare and insulated) is therefore a submarket and for purposes of § 7 a 'line of commerce.' " [8] The Supreme Court thus rejected the product-market definitions adopted by the District Court. The latter had ruled that bare aluminum conductor constituted a separate line of commerce but found that both aluminum- and copper-insulated conductor together constituted a line of commerce and that insulated aluminum

---

[6] *Ibid.*, 509.
[7] *Ibid.*, 510.
[8] *Op. cit.*, 277.

conductor was not separable from insulated copper conductor. In turn, the lower court rejected the broader aluminum-conductor grouping as a line of commerce, arguing that a line of commerce cannot be composed of two parts, one of which constitutes a line of commerce by itself and another which does not.

The Supreme Court's opinion indicates that the appraisal of price differences between aluminum and copper cable was the deciding consideration leading to the rejection of the line-of-commerce definition adopted by the District Court. Referring to one highly important use of insulated conductor, the Supreme Court neatly outlined its logic and possibly revealed its analytical naivete:

> Insulated aluminum conductor is so intrinsically inferior to insulated copper conductor that in most applications it has little consumer acceptance. But in the field of overhead distribution it enjoys decisive advantages—its share of total annual installations increasing from 6.5% in 1950 to 77.2% in 1959. In the field of overhead distribution the competition of copper is rapidly decreasing. As the record shows, utilizing a high-cost metal, fabricators of insulated copper conductor are powerless to eliminate the price disadvantage under which they labor and thus can do little to make their product competitive, unless they enter the aluminum field. The price of most insulated aluminum conductors is indeed only 50% to 65% of the price of their copper counterparts; and the comparative installed costs are also generally less. As the District Court found, aluminum and copper conductor prices do not respond to one another.[9]

Of course, insofar as the cost of the entire package—installed costs—overlapped due to the particular prices of insulated aluminum conductor relative to copper and to the differences in construction costs using one conductor rather than the other, there would be price competition attributable to varying prices of the conductor. This point was recognized by the lower court. Furthermore, the competitive effect of price variations need not be shown by a response of the price of one commodity to that of another. Indeed, insofar as consumers are concerned, the expected response would be in terms of quantity variations as one commodity is substituted for another with a relative decline in price. The significance that the Court imputed to the unresponsiveness of prices is thus based on a non sequitur.

The differences in the interpretation of the importance of relative prices stemmed in turn from diverging views as to the importance of various nonprice economic factors. The District Court found that "copper and aluminum products are completely interchangeable from a performance standpoint, (and) utility companies choose between copper and aluminum insulated overhead products solely on the basis of economics. The decision requires evaluation of numerous economic factors in addition to the cost of the wire or cable itself." [10] But the Supreme Court insisted that "where insulated aluminum conductor pricewise stands so distinctly apart, to ignore price in determining the relevant line of commerce is to ignore the single, most important, practical factor in the business." [11] As the dissent noted, the majority of the Supreme Court did not present any discussion of the bases for its arrival at the conclusion that price was preeminent among the various economic factors. These are economic and technological matters, which, in large part, cannot be evaluated without technological as well as economic data. The impact on apparent market shares is another, and to us, more intriguing issue.

Based on its distinct market definitions, the Supreme Court found that:

> . . . Alcoa was the leading producer of aluminum conductor, with 27.8% of the market; in bare aluminum conductor, it also led the industry, with 32.5%. Alcoa plus Kaiser controlled 50% of the aluminum conductor market and, with its three leading competitors, more than 76%. Only nine concerns (including Rome with 1.3%) accounted for 95.7% of the output of aluminum conductor. In the narrower market of insulated conductor, Alcoa was third with 11.6% and Rome was eighth with 4.7%. Five companies controlled 65.4% and four smaller ones, including Rome, added another 22.8%.

In other words, the line of commerce showed highly concentrated

---

[10] Finding of Fact, quoted by Justice Stewart, *ibid.*, 285.

[11] *Ibid.*, 276.

markets, dominated by a few companies but served also by a small, though diminishing, group of independents. . . .

The acquisition of Rome added, it is said, only 1.3% to Alcoa's control of the aluminum conductor market. But in this setting it seems to us reasonably likely to produce a substantial lessening of competition within the meaning of § 7. . . .[12]

The consequences of the Supreme Court's manipulation of product-market boundaries to include insulated aluminum conductor along with bare aluminum conductor rather than insulated copper conductor was put into apt relief by Justice Stewart's dissent:

. . . In order to prove that this was a horizontal merger in violation of § 7, the Government was . . . faced with the necessity of showing substantial percentages of market shares in competitive products. Alcoa manufactured no copper cable, and in the conductor field was chiefly a producer of bare aluminum cable. Over 90% of Rome's production was in insulated copper products, and its production of bare aluminum cable was *de minimis* (.3% of the market share). The District Court found that conductor wire and cable (both bare and insulated, aluminum and copper), and insulated conductor (both aluminum and copper), were lines of commerce, but that Alcoa and Rome's market shares in these broad product markets were insufficient to support a finding of requisite anticompetitive effect, . . . a conclusion which the Government does not question here. More substantial market share percentages would be forthcoming, however, if aluminum conductors could be set apart from the rest of the conductor manufacturing industry. Accordingly, the Government asked the District Court to find aluminum conductors in general, and insulated aluminum conductors in particular, to be separate lines of commerce.[13]

The crucial facet of the treatment of alternative product market definitions in Alcoa (Rome) was thus that of segregating aluminum and copper conductor, especially insulated or covered. This per-

[12] *Ibid.*, 278–280.
[13] *Ibid.*, 282–283.

mitted the subsequent merging of bare and insulated aluminum conductor. The interindustry product line of insulated conductor adopted by the District Court reflects greater similarities in both production and consumption. Adoption of this interindustry product line, however, would have also indicated smaller market shares for the merging firms. Alcoa would have held .3 per cent of that market, and Rome 1.3 per cent, or together only 1.6 per cent (see table). Similarly, the adoption of the more heterogeneous grouping

Shares of Alternative Product Lines Attributable to Alcoa and Rome, 1958

	ALUMINUM ONLY		COPPER AND ALUMINUM	
	Alcoa	*Rome*	*Alcoa*	*Rome*
Conductor Wire and Cable	27.8	1.3	1.8	1.4
Conductor Wire and Cable, Bare	32.5*	.3*	10.3	2.0
Wire and Cable, Insulated or Covered	11.6	4.7	.3	1.3

* ACSR and Aluminum Cable, Bare.
Source: 214 Fed. Sup. 501 (1963), p. 514.

consisting of copper and aluminum conductor wire and cable—a less creditable market definition that was accepted by the District Court—gives somewhat larger market shares which, nevertheless, remain very small. Indeed, by only two definitions was Alcoa's market share in the neighborhood of the critical threshold of 30 per cent suggested by the Court in the Philadelphia National Bank case.[14] The Supreme Court adopted the broader of these—aluminum conductor wire and cable, both bare and insulated—even though the apparent market positions of each firm was based largely upon sharply differentiated products. As Justice Stewart noted in his dissent, the retention of bare aluminum conductor as a separate line of commerce would also seemingly have placed the merger beyond Section 7 of the Clayton Act: at least in 1964 the Supreme Court probably would have considered a .3 per cent increase in market share trivial, even for one of the industry's leading firms. It is therefore disconcerting, if not surprising, that the Supreme

[14] United States v. Philadelphia National Bank, 374 U.S. 321 (1963).

Court's written opinion (1) does not indicate the basis for combining bare and insulated aluminum conductor in a single market and (2) consists largely of unsupported assertions where the District Court's market definition of insulated conductor is considered and rejected.

By contrast to Alcoa (Rome), the crucial feature of market manipulation in the Continental Can case hinged on combining product markets which are ordinarily considered distinct. For the most part, Continental Can produced metal containers whereas Hazel-Atlas produced glass containers and the two companies did not manufacture and sell any identical products. Metal containers and glass containers are ordinarily considered separate and distinct in an economic as well as a physical sense. If these constituted distinct lines of commerce, the merger would not have effected the structure of any market, and in turn the merger would have been beyond the Clayton Act as it was then interpreted.[15] The Justice Department argued that the metal containers were competitive with glass containers for many uses and urged the courts to adopt definitions of various lines of commerce which would have included both glass and metal containers. The ten urged by the Justice Department were: (1) the canning industry; (2) the beer industry; (3) the soft drink industry; (4) the toiletries and cosmetics industry; (5) the medicine and health industry; (6) the household and chemical industry; (7) the can industry; (8) the glass container industry; (9) metal closures; and, (10) the packaging industry.

Two of the four alleged lines of commerce defined in terms of production cut across industry lines and at least four of the six defined in terms of end uses also cut across industry lines.[16] The de-

---

[15] The Continental Can case, in the eyes of the Supreme Court, also posed an issue of potential competition. The Court's decisions in other cases considered below, pp. 430–436, suggest that the elimination of potential competition by itself would have been sufficient for the Court to have found a Section 7 violation.

[16] Of the first six listed, only the "beer industry," and possibly the "soft drink industry," represented a generally recognized industry. At best, the remainder were meaningless polyglots. The District Court's opinion contains a thorough, but disquieting, discussion of the problems of delineating the "soft drink industry" and, more generally, of compiling data relevant to an appraisal of a product market. United States v. Continental Can Company, 217 F. Supp. 761 (1963), 796–799 et passim.

fendants conceded two of the alleged lines of commerce—the can industry and the glass container industry. After detailed consideration, the District Court also concluded that "containers for the beer industry" constituted a relevant line of commerce.

Both substance and assertion thus led to consideration of this merger under the rubric of "interindustry merger." According to the District Court:

> This case does not fit into any of the classic anti-trust patterns. It deals with three separate and distinct industries manufacturing separate and distinct types of products [metal, glass, and plastic containers].
>
> . . . each type of container is made from different raw materials and each has different physical characteristics and properties. Different plant and machinery are required for each and the processes of manufacture are different. The different types of containers manufactured by these different industries are of wide varieties of sizes and shapes and are put to hundreds, if not thousands, of different end uses.
>
> Concededly there was substantial and vigorous inter-industry competition between these three industries and between various of the products which they manufactured. Metal can, glass container and plastic container manufacturers were each seeking to enlarge their sales to the thousands of packers of hundreds of varieties of food, chemical, toiletry and industrial products, ranging from ripe olives to fruit juices to tuna fish to smoked tongue; from maple syrup to pet food to coffee; from embalming fluid to floor wax to nail polish to aspirin to veterinary supplies, to take examples at random.
>
> Each industry and each of the manufacturers within it was seeking to improve their products so that they would appeal to new customers or hold old ones. Hazel-Atlas and Continental were part of this overall industrial pattern, each in a recognized separate industry producing distinct products but engaged in interindustry competition for the favor of various end users of their products.[17]

The District Court nonetheless ruled that the government did not show "that there was any reasonable interchangeability of use or cross-elasticity of demand between containers made of these differ-

[17] *Ibid.*, 780–781.

ent materials." The two most prominent reasons for rejection of the alleged lines of commerce were that the different containers and products involved were highly dissimilar and that the users generally did not find it feasible to shift from one type of container to another (different packing and closing equipment, for example, was required).

To illustrate, consider:

> Manufacturers grouped in what is called the household and chemical industry manufacture . . . products running into the hundreds, if not the thousands. To mention only a few, there are such disparate products as car wax; embalming fluid; insecticides; silver polish; inks; hydrochloric, nitric, sulphuric and other acids; chlorination liquids; rust removers; pet cleaners; weed killers; glue; blueing; and photographic chemicals. The containers used range from small cans to large glass carboys to fibre drums and include a wide range of materials.[18]

The court's logic in rejecting lines of commerce based on a composite of products paralleled the above:

> . . . the Government conceived of "the packaging industry" as involving a sales volume of more than ten billion dollars. The products which it sought to include fell into 43 general categories, each of which was subdividable into countless individual items. The products ranged from cooperage to grocery boxes, from transparent film to steel drums, from pill boxes to plastic and glass carboys, from fruit and vegetable baskets to plastic tubes and from Christmas wrappings to cigar boxes. Here we are veritably wandering in a sort of Clayton Act Wonderland where there is talk "of shoes—and ships—and sealing wax—of cabbages—and kings. . . ." [19]

The District Court's conclusion concerning substitution of one type of container for another within the fourth, fifth, and sixth "lines of commerce" listed above was characteristic:

> It is true that manufacturers from time to time may shift a product from one type of container to another. But there does not appear

[18] *Ibid.*, 803.
[19] *Ibid.*, 788.

to have been any general shifting back and forth as between the containers used for a given product. Packaging changes are made only after careful research and investigation and are normally permanent in character. For example, switches for a particular end use from glass to plastic and back from plastic to glass do not appear to occur.[20]

Since Continental did not produce glass containers, Hazel-Atlas did not produce metal containers, and neither firm was a major producer of beer containers, the District Court concluded that the merger would not violate Section 7 of the Clayton Act. Instead, the merger was viewed as a conglomerate merger resulting from a legitimate desire by Continental to diversify its operations which would promote rather than deter competition in the relevant product lines. The Supreme Court felt otherwise.

After briefly considering the relevance of the rulings enunciated in du Pont (Cellophane), Brown Shoe, and other cases, the Court conceded that "these guidelines offer no precise formula for judgment and *they necessitate, rather than avoid, careful consideration based on the entire record*" [21] (Emphasis supplied). Nevertheless, the Court's analysis was limited to a few isolated products whose importance—illustratively and quantitatively—was considered to be evident enough not to require documentation, e.g.

Baby food was at one time packed entirely in metal cans. Hazel-Atlas played a significant role in inducing the shift to glass as the dominant container by designing "what has become the typical baby food jar." According to Continental's estimate, 80% of the Nation's baby food now moves in glass containers. Continental has not been satisfied with this contemporary dominance by glass, however, and has made intensive efforts to increase its share of the business at the expense of glass. . . .

In the soft drink business, a field which has been, and is, predominantly glass territory, the court recognized that the metal can industry had "[a]fter considerable initial difficulty . . . developed a can strong enough to resist the pressures generated by carbonated beverages" and "made strenuous efforts to promote the use of metal

[20] *Ibid.,* 805.
[21] *Op. cit.,* 449.

cans for carbonated beverages as against glass bottles. . . ." Continental has been a major factor in this rivalry. . . . its advertising has centered around the advantages of cans over glass as soft drink containers, emphasizing such features as convenience in stacking and storing, freedom from breakage and lower distribution costs resulting from the lighter weight of cans.[22]

In the Continental Can opinion, the Court again repudiated the criteria for delineating markets and measuring their structure which it had earlier set forth. No evidence was presented, and apparently none was considered necessary, as to whether the qualitative (or impressionistic) data concerning interindustry competition was representative or quantitatively substantial vis-a-vis the industries involved.

Moreover, the apparent criteria for combining or separating products and industries in Continental Can contrast sharply with those employed in Alcoa (Rome).[23] Three weeks earlier the Court had expressly considered, and rejected, the argument that copper wire and cable should be included in the same market with like aluminum products. Nevertheless, the reasons for combining products of "different" industries in Alcoa (Rome) appear far more pervasive and compelling than in Continental Can.[24]

The Pabst case concerned *inter alia* the courts' treatment of "section of the country." The government alleged that the effect of the

---

[22] *Ibid.,* 451–452.

[23] And, as well, with PNB in which the Court received, and fumbled, the same issues. *Op cit.* Also, see Bernard Shull, "Commercial Banking as a 'Line of Commerce'," *The National Banking Review,* I (December 1963); and Wm. Paul Smith, "Measures of Banking Structure and Competition," *Federal Reserve Bulletin,* 51 (September 1965).

[24] In a review of the 1964 Supreme Court merger cases marked by an almost studied detachment, Betty Bock concluded: "What emerges from study of the *Continental Can* (Hazel-Atlas) and *Alcoa* (Rome) decisions is the principle that the Supreme Court will not follow any predesigned set of criteria to which it will always give equal weight in drawing the boundaries of relevant product markets and submarkets; nor will it consistently read the evidence to extend or contract product market boundaries. It has, instead, given notice that it will focus on that part of a product market, or set of markets, where third companies may be substantially affected and will use different tests at different times, discarding old tests or fabricating new ones as it deems appropriate in different competitive situations." *Mergers and Markets: An Economic Analysis of the 1964 Su-*

Pabst Brewing Company's 1958 acquisition of the Blatz Brewing Company "may be substantially to lessen competition, or to tend to create a monopoly" in the production and sale of beer in the state of Wisconsin, the three-state area of Wisconsin, Illinois, and Michigan, and in the United States. Pretrial conferences had secured agreement "that the line of commerce involved . . . the production, sale and distribution of beer and that the continental United States is a relevant geographic market;" but the adversaries indicated that they would rather fight than switch "as to whether the State of Wisconsin and the three-state area of Wisconsin, Illinois, and Michigan are also appropriate sections of the country . . . [and] . . . on the probable effect of the acquisition." [25] The Pabst case thus centered on delineating the relevant "section of the country."

Pabst operated four breweries, including its largest in Milwaukee, Wisconsin, while Blatz's only plant was also located in Milwaukee. Pabst was the eleventh largest national seller of beer in 1958 while Blatz was thirteenth largest, with 2.67 and 2.04 percent of national sales, respectively. Blatz was the largest seller in Wisconsin, with 12.99 percent of the state's sales in 1958; Pabst was fourth, with 10.73 percent. The number of both brewers and breweries producing and selling beer had been declining in recent years.

In support of its contention that Wisconsin was a relevant market, the Justice Department argued that (1) the two companies competed most intensively in that state, (2) Wisconsin was a major factor in the domestic beer market, (3) each state is a separate market because each state has separate regulations, (4) Blatz's prices are higher in Wisconsin than in any other state, and (5) Wisconsin's higher consumption and market structure make it a unique market.

The lower court carefully considered the legal precedents cited in support of these market delineating concepts, namely, Brown Shoe, PNB, Bethlehem-Youngstown, Crown-Zellerbach,[26] El

---

preme Court Merger Decisions, 4th ed. (New York: National Industrial Conference Board, Inc., 1965), 51.

[25] United States v. Pabst Brewing Company, 233 F. Supp. 475 (1964), 478.

[26] Crown Zellerbach Corporation v. Federal Trade Commission, 296 F. 2d 800 (1961).

Paso,[27] and Lexington.[28] Each of these precedents was related by the District Court to a key aspect of the industry. In each instance the Pabst case facts were held to differ substantially from the precedents cited, although some of the distinctions drawn by the District Court were questionable.

The PNB and Lexington cases involved a service industry in which competition was localized by an inconvenience factor ("Individuals and corporations . . . find it impractical to conduct their banking business at a distance"). The beer industry is not a service industry and neither production nor competition in Pabst was localized by an analogous inconvenience characteristic. In Brown Shoe, metropolitan areas were considered the relevant geographic markets for evaluating the merger at the retail level (for manufacturing and the vertical integration facets of that case, it was the entire nation). Blatz and Pabst both appeared to distribute beer through distributors and wholesalers, but the "breweries' relationship with these distributors has not been revealed, nor has the relationship of retail outlets to either the breweries or the distributors or wholesalers." To the court, those data were necessary to establish a precedent.

The District Court also concluded that neither the total beer sales in Wisconsin nor the importance of beer sales in the state to the merging firms was sufficient to permit reliance on Crown-Zellerbach and Bethlehem-Youngstown. The three-state west coast market accounted for "the great bulk of the domestic sales" of the merging firm in Crown-Zellerbach; over 70 percent of the acquired firm's sales were in that area. Further, the three west coast states "were unique, possessing qualities setting them apart as a separate [market] area." The states treated as submarkets in Bethlehem-Youngstown each constituted "an appreciable segment of the market" both for the industry and for the merging firms; "the four-state area of Michigan, Ohio, New York, and Pennsylvania received 48.4% of the total industry shipments of common finished steel products, Michigan and Ohio received 31.3% of those shipments, Michigan received 18.2% of those shipments and Ohio received 13.1% of those shipments." While the Wisconsin citizenry was not adverse

[27] United States v. El Paso Natural Gas Co., 376 U.S. 651 (1964).

[28] United States v. First National Bank & Trust Company of Lexington, 376 U.S. 665 (1964).

to the Pabst and Blatz brews, the companies' sales in the state
were small compared to Crown-Zellerbach. Similarly, Wisconsin's
beer consumption of 3.66 to 3.75 percent of the national consumption did "not set it aside as an area in which the beer market
is concentrated" a la Bethlehem-Youngstown. Although Wisconsin
was a major producer of beer, there was no evidence that such
production was strongly tied to sales. The court also concluded
that individual state regulations did not define separate markets
since they affected all companies impartially and did not affect the
extent of competition between these companies.

By thus considering the several precedents for subnational geographic markets, the court differentiated the Pabst case and ruled
that Wisconsin did not constitute a relevant market. The government also alleged that the three-state areas of Wisconsin, Illinois,
and Michigan also constituted a relevant subnational market. Presumably, the court would have evaluated this three-state area
using the criteria applied in its evaluation of Wisconsin as a separate and distinct relevant market. However, the government's evidence consisted only of data concerning the area's share of beer
sales that were provided by Pabst and Blatz and also of data showing the importance of the area to Pabst's and Blatz's total sales.
Consequently, the court ruled that:

> . . . nor did the plaintiff amplify its position on oral argument. It
> appears therefore that the plaintiff itself relies solely on the reve-
> lations . . . as to percentages of Pabst and Blatz sales in the three
> state area and Pabst and Blatz shares of the market as satisfying its
> burden of proof and considers no other facts relevant on this issue.
>
> Unquestionably, both Pabst and Blatz were successful in the three
> state area. However, we find no precedent for permitting the plain-
> tiff to select an area in which the two companies, which competed
> nationally, realized success and, solely because of that success, desig-
> nate the area a relevant geographic market.[29]

The scope of the relevant market was the principal concern of
the lower court. Thus, upon dismissing these possibilities, the only
remaining issues were the effect on national competition (which

---

[29] *Op. cit.*, 488.

discussion focused on market shares and the "trend toward concentration"). When the plaintiff's case failed to support charges related to these remaining issues, the court dismissed the complaint.

However, like so many other of the interesting contemporary cases, the lower court's decision was reversed by the Supreme Court. Five separate decisions were issued in this reversal, due largely to the Court's difficulty in defining and applying a workable concept of the relevant market. The majority opinion ruled that:

> We first take up the court's dismissal based on its conclusion that the Government failed to prove either Wisconsin or the three-state area constituted "a relevant section of the country within the meaning of Section 7." Apparently the District Court thought that in order to show a violation of §7 it was essential for the Government to show a "relevant geographic market" in the same way the corpus delicti must be proved to establish a crime. But when the Government brings an action under §7 it must, according to the language of the statute, prove no more than that there has been a merger between two corporations engaged in commerce and that the effect of the merger may be substantially to lessen competition or tend to create a monopoly in any line of commerce *"in any section of the country."* (Emphasis supplied). The language of this section requires merely that the Government prove the merger may have a substantial anticompetitive effect somewhere in the United States—"in *any* section" of the United States. This phrase does not call for the delineation of a "section of the country" by metes and bounds as a surveyor would lay off a plot of ground. The Government may introduce evidence which shows that as a result of a merger competition may be substantially lessened throughout the country, or on the other hand it may prove that competition may be substantially lessened only in one or more sections of the country. In either event a violation of §7 would be proved. Certainly the failure of the Government to prove by an army of expert witnesses what constitutes a relevant "economic" or "geographic" market is not an adequate ground on which to dismiss a §7 case. . . . Congress did not seem to be troubled about the exact spot competition might be lessened; it simply intended to outlaw mergers which threatened competition in any or all parts of the country. Proof of the

section of the country where the anticompetitive effect exists is entirely subsidiary to the crucial question in this and every §7 case which is whether a merger may substantially lessen competition anywhere in the United States.[30]

Three justices concurred in the reversal but stated their belief that the government must prove its alleged relevant "markets" or "section of the country." Their support of the reversal reflected their belief that the government had created a prima facie case for its alleged market areas. This need for defining and reconciling alternative submarkets was effectively eliminated by the court's principal opinion. It appears that, until the Pabst opinion is repudiated expressly or by implication, the Court will be without criteria for determining where and a fortiori how a contested merger may affect competition.

2. MARKET STRUCTURE

Economists generally recognize several different elements of market structure. These elements include, among others, the number of firms, the size distribution of firms (relative size or "concentration"), barriers of entry, and, less commonly, product differentiation. Of these, the number and the size distribution of firms are most closely interrelated and most frequently stressed as crucial to the analysis of a given market structure. Implicitly at least, the courts have long recognized that these two measures of market structure are not independent. For example, at the moment of consummation, horizontal mergers must simultaneously reduce the number of competitors and increase the market share of the acquiring firm. Nevertheless, until recently the courts gave greatest—often exclusive—emphasis to (1) the market shares of the merging, and largest, firms in the market and (2) changes in these market shares; that is, the legality of particular mergers was determined after only incidental consideration was given to (1) the number of firms and (2) changes in their number.

[30] *Op. cit.,* 548–550.

Market Concentration

The nature of the Court's reliance on, and treatment of, market concentration in recent merger cases appears to have deteriorated *pari passu* with the erosion of the market definitions and the delineation of the relevant product and geographic markets. In Brown Shoe, the first case under the amended Section 7 of the Clayton Act, the Supreme Court carefully reviewed the contentions as to alternative relevant market definitions and the evidence bearing on the delineation of both product and geographic markets.[31] The impact of the contested merger on market shares and concentration was then considered in terms of this background. It was in this context that the Supreme Court asserted:

> The outer boundaries of a product market are determined by the reasonable interchangeability of use or the cross-elasticity of demand between the product itself and substitutes for it. However, within this broad market, well-defined submarkets may exist which, in themselves, constitute product markets for antitrust purposes. . . . The boundaries of such a submarket may be determined by examining such practical indicia as industry or public recognition of the submarket as a separate economic entity, the product's peculiar characteristics and uses, unique production facilities, distinct customers, distinct prices, sensitivity to price changes, and specialized vendors.
>
> The criteria to be used in determining the appropriate geographic market are essentially similar to those used to determine the relevant product market. . . . Moreover, just as a product submarket may have §7 significance as the proper "line of commerce," so may a geographic submarket be considered the appropriate "section of the country." . . . Congress prescribed a pragmatic, factual approach to the definition of the relevant market and not a formal, legalistic one. The geographic market selected must, therefore, both "correspond to the commercial realities" of the industry and be economically significant. Thus, although the geographic market in some instances may encompass the entire Nation, under other circumstances it may be as small as a single metropolitan area. . . .

[31] For a detailed analysis of the Brown Shoe case, see Chapter 12, *supra.*

The fact that two merging firms have competed directly on the horizontal level in but a fraction of the geographic markets in which either has operated, does not, in itself, place their merger outside the scope of §7. That section speaks of "any . . . section of the country," and if anticompetitive effects of a merger are probable in "any" significant market, the merger—at least to that extent—is proscribed.[32]

This position was in part a logical outgrowth of the Court's thorough treatment of a wide range of economic issues raised by the case, especially in its investigation of the rationale of various product- and geographic-market definitions. These statements have also been taken by many as an indication of the issues and evidence that the Supreme Court would consider in deciding on future merger cases.

In its dicta on market concentration in merger decisions following Brown Shoe, however, the Court first appeared to be developing guidelines whereby a merger would be held unlawful if it led to an increase of concentration—or market share of merging firms—of some specified percentage or if it involved a leading firm in an industry with some particular threshold level of concentration. The suggestion of such rules was clearly drawn in the Philadelphia National Bank case, the Supreme Court's second decision involving the amended Section 7 of the Clayton Act:

> . . . we think that a merger which produces a firm controlling an undue percentage share of the relevant market, and results in a significant increase in the concentration of firms in that market, is so inherently likely to lessen competition substantially that it must be enjoined in the absence of evidence clearly showing that the merger is not likely to have such anticompetitive effects. . . .
>
> Such a test lightens the burden of proving illegality only with respect to mergers whose size makes them inherently suspect in light of Congress' design in §7 to prevent undue concentration. . . .
>
> The merger of appellees will result in a single bank's controlling at least 30% of the commercial banking business in the four-county Philadelphia metropolitan area. Without attempting to specify the smallest market share which would still be considered to threaten

[32] *Op. cit.,* 325, 336–337.

undue concentration, we are clear that 30% presents that threat. Further, whereas presently the two largest banks in the area (First Pennsylvania and PNB) control between them approximately 44% of the area's commercial banking business, the two largest after the merger (PNB-Girard and First Pennsylvania) will control 59%. Plainly, we think, this increase of more than 33% in concentration must be regarded as significant.

Our conclusion that these percentages raise an inference that the effect of the contemplated merger of appelleees may be substantially to lessen competition is not an arbitrary one . . . [33]

However, to some, the inference was not merely arbitrary, but simply wrong.[34] Aside from the validity and merits of the Court's logic and inferences, most authorities would argue that the Court was not altogether successful in honoring its contention that PNB presented "only a straightforward problem of application to particular facts" of the tests for lawfulness of a merger under Section 7 enumerated in Brown Shoe.

The arguments favoring the adoption of per se rules include definiteness and consistency as well as simplicity in their application to new cases. A "mixed per se and rule-of-reason approach to merger case problems" poses both internal inconsistencies in logic and inherent indefiniteness in application, as it would remain uncertain which pole of the spectrum the Court would find guiding in a particular case.[35] The decisions in the post-PNB merger cases seemingly reflect this quandary. To be sure, once the Court had adopted the peculiar product- and geographic-market definitions in PNB, it was similarly led to conclude that the First National— Security Trust merger was unlawful.[36] The resulting bank's market share in the Lexington case was considerably in excess of that held

---

[33] Op. cit., 363–365.

[34] See, for example, the discussion appearing in The National Banking Review and reprinted in Studies in Banking Competition and the Banking Structure (Washington: The Administrator of National Banks, 1966).

[35] Betty Bock, "The Relativity of Economic Evidence in Merger Cases— Emerging Decisions Force the Issue," Michigan Law Review, 63, No. 8 (June 1965), 1359.

[36] Op. cit. The Lexington case, however, was brought under the Sherman Act rather than the Clayton Act. Ostensibly, it thereby posed distinct questions concerning both jurisdiction and standards of lawfulness.

crucial in PNB—52 percent compared to 35 percent, which was adjusted to 30 percent. Again, the PNB market share was almost equaled by the market share of the resulting firm in Alcoa (Rome) —29 percent of aluminum conductor. A somewhat lower level of concentration—25 percent—in the combined metal- and glass-container industries resulted from Continental Can's acquisition of Hazel-Atlas, but the Court argued that: "The resulting percentage of the combined firms approaches that held presumptively bad in *United States v. Philadelphia National Bank* . . . and is almost the same as that involved in *United States v. Aluminum Co. of America.*" [37] As discussed above, an unsympathetic critic could readily infer from the Alcoa (Rome) and Continental Can cases that the manipulation of product or geographic markets can serve to generate the undesired levels of concentration.

In terms of the attention given to levels of concentration or market shares and to possibly enumerating some threshold level of market shares that would be unacceptable, the Von's Grocery[38] and Pabst decisions are in sharp contrast to the above cases. As in Continental Can, neither of these cases involved the industry's largest firm; Von's Grocery involved the acquisition of the sixth-ranked grocery retailer in the Los Angeles SMSA by the third largest, while the acquiring firm in Pabst ranked tenth and the acquired firm was the eighteenth-largest brewer in the Nation.

The importance assigned to shares of the market held by either the merging firms or the several largest in the market in the Von's Grocery opinion is reasonably clear—*none*. The District Court,[39] on reviewing the evidence concerning the combined market shares of the largest grocery retailers in Los Angeles concluded: "There has been no increase in concentration in the retail grocery business in the Los Angeles Metropolitan Area either in the last decade or since the merger. On the contrary, economic concentration has decreased . . ." [40] After noting that the District Court had also found a steady decline in the number of individual grocery store owners, the Supreme Court dismissed the above conclusion as

---

[37] *Op. cit.,* 461.
[38] United States v. Von's Grocery Company, 384 U.S. 270 (1966).
[39] United States v. Von's Grocery Company, 233 F. Supp. 976 (1964).
[40] Finding of Fact, quoted by the Supreme Court, *op. cit.,* 273.

follows: "It is apparent that the District Court . . . used the term 'concentration' in some sense other than a total decrease in the number of separate competitors which is the crucial point here." The Supreme Court thus repudiated any attempt that might have been ascribed to it to establish a per se rule whereby some threshold level of concentration—as measured by the merging or the largest firms' combined share of sales or some other economic magnitude—would be applicable and determining in individual merger cases.

The Supreme Court's written opinion in Pabst, in contrast, emphasized concentration in terms of market shares, although the tenor of the language and the treatment of market delineation lead one to wonder whether concentration was really a factor in the actual decision. As noted earlier, however, the Court held the government's "evidence as to the probable effect of the merger on competition in Wisconsin, in the three-state area, and in the entire country was amply sufficient to show a violation of § 7 in each and all of these three areas." In Wisconsin, Pabst was the largest seller of beer while Blatz ranked fourth, and their resultant share of sales—23.95 percent at the time of merger and 27.41 percent three years later—was similar to that found in Continental Can. But by comparison, the 4.49 percent share of sales nationally in Pabst was less than one-fifth, and the 7.5 percent of sales in Los Angeles in Von's Grocery was less than one-third of that found in Continental Can. The importance that the Court assigned to the percentages for the entire country in Pabst is not clear, but it would appear to be small. Instead, attention directed to the two smaller areas was considerable and may have been overriding.

Number of Firms

One of the few apparently consistent and substantive patterns emerging from the Supreme Court's consideration of recent merger cases is the increasingly heavier emphasis given to the number of competitors—either actual or potential—along with the trends in those numbers. In the first cases under the amended Section 7 of the Clayton Act, the Court's attention was addressed primarily to a trend of mergers and increasing concentration in the affected industry or markets. Most recently, however, the Court's rulings suggest that the declining number of firms per se is presumptive evidence that the contested merger may violate Section 7, and is to be rebutted by the merging firms. This position seems to hold irrespective of the reasons for the decline in the number of firms.

In the PNB decision the Supreme Court noted the declining number of commercial banks in the Philadelphia four-county area as well as the difficulties facing prospective entrants. In this case the declining number of competitors was not only associated with increasing market shares, but stemmed from merger activity by the banks involved:

> The present size of both PNB and Girard is in part the result of mergers. Indeed, the trend toward concentration is noticeable in the Philadelphia area generally, in which the number of commercial banks has declined from 108 in 1947 to the present 42. Since 1950, PNB has acquired nine formerly independent banks and Girard six; and these acquisitions have accounted for 59% and 85% of the respective banks' asset growth during the period, 63% and 91% of their deposit growth, and 12% and 37% of their loan growth. During this period, the seven largest banks in the area increased their combined share of the area's total commercial bank resources from about 61% to about 90%.[41]

However, the discussion of the PNB-Girard merger's lawfulness under Section 7 of the Clayton Act turned almost exclusively on percentage shares of the market. Indeed, as noted earlier, it appeared as if the Court might be developing the initial outline of per se rules of a merger's legality based on prevailing market shares and the resultant changes in them.

In reading the merger cases following PNB one gets the impression that successively more emphasis and increasingly heavier weight was directed to merger activity. Nevertheless, it was not unambiguously clear whether substantial merger activity leading to, or associated with, a marked decline in the number of firms

[41] *Op. cit.,* 331.

would be considered sufficient to bar mergers involving the larger firms in a market. For example, Alcoa (Rome) and Continental Can involved a declining number of firms, but the acquiring and resulting firms also accounted for comparatively large shares of the market. This is illustrated in part by the Court's observations in Alcoa (Rome): (1) that "the line of commerce showed highly concentrated markets, dominated by a few companies but served also by a small, though diminishing, group of independents" and (2) an accompanying footnote outlining recent merger activity which had left "only four nonintegrated fabricators of aluminum conductor whose individual shares of total industry production . . . amounted to more than 1%." [42] Within this context, the Court's analysis and conclusions turned more on the high, increasing levels of concentration than on merger activity and trends in the number of competitors as such. To our way of thinking, these decisions do not imply the Court's reasoning in either Von's Grocery or Pabst.

Faced with different structural conditions in Von's Grocery, the Supreme Court apparently was forced to reexamine and redefine its position with respect to acceptable levels of concentration (or condone the contested merger), or to rely primarily on other criteria for evaluating the lawfulness of the merger. The Von's Grocery decision appears to most clearly reflect a view toward merger trends that is evident in all of the Court's decisions in merger cases tried under the amended Section 7 of the Clayton Act:

> . . . the basic purpose of the 1950 Celler-Kefauver Act was to prevent economic concentration in the American economy by keeping a large number of small competitors in business. . . . "The dominant theme pervading congressional consideration of the 1950 amendments was a fear of what was considered to be a rising tide of economic concentration in the American economy." To arrest this "rising tide" toward concentration into too few hands and to halt the gradual demise of the small businessmen, Congress decided to clamp down with vigor on mergers. It both revitalized § 7 of the Clayton Act by "plugging its loophole" [whereby asset acquisitions were immune from attack] and broadened its scope so as not only to prohibit mergers between competitors, the effect of which "may

[42] *Op. cit.,* 278–279.

be substantially to lessen competition, or to tend to create a monopoly" but to prohibit all mergers having that effect.[43]

The Supreme Court's strictures on the "trend toward concentration" in the Pabst case are direct and pragmatic, yet represent the clearest reasoning contained in the Court's principal opinion. Evidence of a historically increasing concentration—for example, a decrease in the number of brewers from 750 in 1935 to 229 in 1961, and an increase in market share of the top brewers in 1948 from 32.68 percent to 52.60 percent in 1961 for the ten largest and from 49.2 percent in 1948 to 76.96 percent in 1961 for the twenty-five largest—was rejected as irrelevant by the District Court on the grounds that this was not shown to be the result of previous mergers.

On review the Supreme Court maintained that:

These facts show a very marked thirty-year decline in the number of brewers and a sharp rise in recent years in the percentage share of the market controlled by the leading brewers. If not stopped, this decline in the number of separate competitors and this rise in the share of the market controlled by the larger beer manufacturers are bound to lead to greater and greater concentration of the beer industry into fewer and fewer hands. The merger of Pabst and Blatz brought together two very large brewers competing against each other in 40 States. . . . In accord with our prior cases, we hold that the evidence as to the probable effect of the merger on competition in Wisconsin, in the three-state area, and in the entire country was amply sufficient to show a violation of § 7 in each and all of these three areas.

We have not overlooked Pabst's contention that we should not consider the steady trend toward concentration in the beer industry because the Government has not shown that the trend is due to mergers. There is no duty on the Government to make such proof. It would seem fantastic to assume that part of the concentration in the beer industry has not been due to mergers but even if the Government made no such proof, it would not aid Pabst. Congress, in passing § 7 and in amending it was concerned with arresting concentration in the American economy, whatever its cause, in its

[43] *Op. cit.*, 275–277.

incipiency. It passed and amended on the premise that mergers do tend to accelerate concentration in an industry. We hold that a trend toward concentration in an industry, whatever its causes, is a highly relevant factor in deciding how substantial the anticompetitive effect of a merger may be.[44]

From one standpoint, the Supreme Court's position on a "trend toward concentration" represents a clear and consistent logic. Whether this logic is faithful to congressional intent is for the Court to decide, and for others to debate, until Congress further clarifies its intent. Whether its implication for competition and market performance are desirable is a different matter. The Court seems to assume that there is a direct relationship between (1) any particular decline in the number of firms or (2) any particular increase in the disparity of relative sizes of firms in an industry and (3) the intensity of competition in the industry. By implication then, the elimination of firms, through exit or merger, would have the same impact on competition as when the underlying forces and motivation were responses to technological advance.

3. POTENTIAL COMPETITION

In dealing with potential competition, the Supreme Court's recent opinions have seemingly reflected the Court's development—or, better, adoption—of more sophisticated economic analysis. Potential competition was a decisive issue in the El Paso and Penn-Olin[45] cases decided in 1964. In addition to being the first cases in which the Court squarely faced the issue of potential competition, each represented other distinctive developments in antitrust law and economics. The El Paso case involved a merger of two natural gas distributors that had been approved by the Federal Power Commission. This litigation also involved the Court's first handling of a clear market-extension situation, while Penn-Olin represented the Court's first explicit consideration of joint ventures under the amended Section 7 of the Clayton Act.

[44] *Op. cit.*, 551–553.
[45] United States v. Penn-Olin Chemical Company, 378 U.S. 158 (1964).

The El Paso case, decided on April 6, 1964, involved the 1959 acquisition of Pacific Northwest Pipeline Corporation by El Paso Natural Gas Company. Prior to the merger, the two companies operated in separate but adjacent geographical market areas; El Paso was the only out-of-state company that transported natural gas to utilities within California while Pacific Northwest—the only other important interstate pipeline west of the Rocky Mountains—distributed natural gas in Colorado, Idaho, Oregon, Utah, and Washington. Thus there was not direct competition between the two at the time of the merger. In dismissing the case the District Court found: (1) that the companies did not compete with each other; (2) that it was unlikely that they would in the future compete; and (3) that Pacific Northwest was not a potential competitor of El Paso.

On review, the Supreme Court held that while there was no existing competition between the companies, Pacific Northwest did represent an important source of competition for El Paso. The Court's inference of potential competition rested on evidence of, and the effect from, Pacific Northwest's unsuccessful negotiations to supply natural gas to the Southern California Edison Co., the largest industrial user of natural gas in southern California.

(Edison) . . . used El Paso gas, purchased through a distributor. It had, however, a low priority from that distributor, being on an "interruptible" basis, *i.e.,* subject to interruption during periods of peak demand for domestic uses. Edison wanted a firm contract and, upon being advised that it was El Paso's policy to sell only to distributors, started negotiations with Pacific Northwest in May 1956. The idea was for Pacific Northwest to deliver to Edison at a point on the California-Oregon border 300 million cubic feet of Canadian gas a day. In July 1956 they reached a tentative agreement. Edison thereupon tried to develop within California an integrated system for distributing Canadian gas supplied by Pacific Northwest to itself and others. El Paso decided to fight the plan to the last ditch, and succeeded in getting (through a distributor) a contract for Edison's needs. Edison's tentative agreement with Pacific Northwest was terminated. Before Edison terminated that agreement with Pacific Northwest, Edison had reached an agreement with El Paso for firm deliveries of gas; and while the original El Paso offer was 40¢ per Mcf, the price dropped to 38¢ per Mcf, then to 34¢ and finally to 30¢. Thereafter, and while the merger negotiations were pending, Pacific Northwest renewed its efforts to get its gas into California.[46]

To the Court this incident clearly indicated that:

Pacific Northwest, though it had no pipeline into California, is shown . . . to have been a substantial factor in the California market at the time it was acquired by El Paso.

. . . We would have to wear blinders not to see that the mere efforts of Pacific Northwest to get into the California market, though unsuccessful, had a powerful influence on El Paso's business attitudes within the State.[47]

The Court was, therefore, led to the basically valid, if somewhat overstated, position that: "Unsuccessful bidders are no less competitors than the successful one." [48] The Court then concluded: "If El Paso can absorb Pacific Northwest without violating § 7 of the Clayton Act, that section has no meaning in the natural gas field." [49]

The El Paso decision was soon followed by the Penn-Olin case, which also turned on potential competition. The Penn-Olin decision was also the Supreme Court's first statement on the applicability of Section 7 to joint ventures, a facet of the case that is of more intrinsic interest to most antitrust practitioners than the issue of potential competition considered here.

The Penn-Olin Chemical Company was jointly formed by the Pennsalt Chemicals Corporation and the Olin Mathieson Chemical Corporation to produce and sell sodium chlorate in the Southeastern United States. Neither company operated in that area although Pennsalt produced and Olin consumed these same chemicals in other parts of the country. Two plants were already in operation —and a third had been announced—for the Southeast. The national market seemed characterized by balanced supply and demand con-

[46] *Op. cit.,* 654–655.
[47] *Ibid.,* 658–659.
[48] *Ibid.,* 660.
[49] *Ibid.,* 662.

ditions. The joint venture had been undertaken for the alleged need to combine capital resources for such a large project. The lower court found that the Pennsalt and Olin Mathieson companies had not competed with each other prior to the merger; the lower court also felt that some balance against two comparable producers was an important competitive consideration in this issue.[50]

The lower court recognized the capability of both Pennsalt and Mathieson to enter the field; but ruled that entry capability was important only to the extent of indicating the probability that both would enter the industry as independent producers. However, inferences, mere capability, or the probable entry of one alone would not provide the substance of potential competition in the lower court's opinion. On appeal, the Supreme Court overruled, holding that potential competition exists even if only one company would probably have entered the market, because the other company's existence on the market's edge would comprise potential market competition. Thus the Court again revealed its unwillingness (or inability) to distinguish between ranges of statistical closeness or probability.

Potential competition also promises to be a particularly important antitrust concept because it may constitute the only effective basis on which courts can hold conglomerate mergers in violation of the antitrust statutes. Conglomerate mergers do not eliminate competition between the merging companies because they involve neither companies in the same market (horizontal merger) nor in markets bearing a buyer-seller relationship (vertical merger). However, the Court's recent opinions suggest the susceptibility of many conglomerate mergers for allegedly "stifling potential competition." The potentiality of this argument is suggested by the Supreme Court's April 11, 1967 Clorox decision upholding an earlier ruling of the Federal Trade Commission.[51] A Court of Appeals decision had (1) reversed the commission's decision that the Procter & Gamble Company's acquisition of the Clorox Chemical Company constituted a Section 7 violation and (2) directed that

[50] United States v. Penn-Olin Chemical Company, 217 F. Supp. 110 (1963).
[51] Federal Trade Commission v. Procter & Gamble Co., 386 U.S. 568 (1967).

the commission's complaint be dismissed. The Supreme Court's decision, reversing that of the Court of Appeals and ordering the enforcement of the commission's judgment, was based largely on the merger's elimination of potential competition.

Clorox, the nation's leading producer of household bleaches, accounted for 48.8 percent of the national production of household liquid bleaches, the undisputed relevant line of commerce. Procter & Gamble, a highly diversified producer of household and other products including detergents and other wash products, produced no liquid bleach. The undisputed geographic markets included the country as a whole as well as a series of regional markets. Clorox, which operated thirteen plants, was the only national producer: most bleach manufacturers distributed in only one region. Two firms provided 65 percent, and six firms almost 80 percent, of all household liquid-bleach sales, and over 200 other firms accounted for the remaining output. Advertising is important in the product markets because all liquid bleaches are identical. Clorox had sales of about $40 million in 1957 and spent about $5.4 million for advertising and other promotional efforts. Procter's 1957 sales were $1.1 billion, of which 54.4 percent included soaps, detergents, and cleansers. Procter and its two nearest competitors accounted for 80 percent of this market. Procter—the nation's largest advertiser in 1957—spent $127 million in advertising and other promotional allowances in 1957; these promotions frequently were conducted on a multiproduct basis.

Prior to its purchase of Clorox, Procter had been "engaged in a vigorous program of diversifying into product lines closely related to its basic products." Procter had, in fact, considered entering the liquid-bleach field independently because of the product's obviously complementary relation to Proctor's line of household cleansing products. Procter's market-research analyses, which led the company to decide against independent entry, were cited in the Court's opinion:

> . . . Since a large investment would be needed to obtain a satisfactory market share, acquisition of the industry's leading firm was attractive. "Taking over the Clorox business . . . could be a way of achieving a dominant position in the liquid bleach market quickly,

which would pay out reasonably well." 63 F.T.C., at—. The initial report predicted that Procter's "sales, distribution and manufacturing setup" could increase Clorox's share of the markets in areas where it was low. The final report confirmed the conclusions of the initial report and emphasized that Procter could make more effective use of Clorox's advertising budget and that the merger would facilitate advertising economies. . . .[52]

However, the Federal Trade Commission believed that Procter's purchase of Clorox would (1) discourage active competition by other liquid-bleach producers, (2) seriously diminish potential competition by precluding Procter's independent entry into the liquid-bleach market, (3) seriously diminish the market's competitive vigor because other producers would realize the extent of Procter's great resources, and (4) raise the barriers to new entry because other potential entrants could reasonably expect higher advertising costs.

The issue of potential competition (its nature and role) thus assumes critical importance, and the Supreme Court's decision included one statement that reveals the philosophical or analytical differences between it (and the commission) and the lower court:

> The Commission also found that the acquisition of Clorox by Procter eliminated Procter as a potential competitor. The Court of Appeals declared that this finding was not supported by evidence because there was no evidence that Procter's management had ever intended to enter the industry independently and that Procter had never attempted to enter. The evidence, however, clearly shows that Procter was the most likely entrant.[53]

The key difference between the lower court and the Supreme Court lies in the lower court's concern with the probability that Procter would have entered the market independently, using its own resources. On the other hand the Supreme Court emphasizes Procter's position as the most likely company to enter this product line. This latter view was based on Procter's product line, the

[52] *Ibid.*, 574.
[53] *Ibid.*, 580.

history of Procter's mergers, and its aggressive success in these mergers. These three factors were cited by the commission in its ruling. In turn, the Supreme Court adopted this view, citing Procter's substantial advertising and sales advantages, diversification experience, management experience in similar fields, and Procter's prior consideration of independently entering the liquid-bleach market. The Court also felt that Procter's mere presence on the market fringe constituted an important competitive pressure, since each firm's behavior is influenced by its expectations of competitor's possible conduct. The Court professed that barriers to entry were not significant for a firm of Procter's size and that since the number of potential competitors in the national market was so limited, Procter's elimination would constitute a major change in competitive conditions.

The Clorox decision does not, of course, automatically preclude all conglomerate mergers. Company size, market conditions, and the extent of complementarity will be among the critical considerations in each case. However, in potential competition, the courts are provided with a new tool whose relevance to antitrust situations is less constrained than any other antitrust enforcement principle.

APPENDIX

Extracts from Antitrust Statutes

Sherman Act, 1890

Be it enacted by the Senate and House of Representatives of the United States of America in Congress assembled,

SECTION 1.

Every contract, combination in the form of trust or otherwise, or conspiracy, in restraint of trade or commerce among the several States, or with foreign nations, is hereby declared to be illegal. Every person who shall make any such contract or engage in any such combination or conspiracy, shall be deemed guilty of a misdemeanor, and, on conviction thereof, shall be punished by fine not exceeding five thousand dollars,* or by imprisonment not exceeding one year, or by both said punishments, in the discretion of the court.

SECTION 2.

Every person who shall monopolize, or attempt to monopolize, or combine or conspire with any other person or persons, to monopolize any part of the trade or commerce among the several States, or with foreign nations, shall be deemed guilty of a misdemeanor, and, on conviction thereof, shall be punished by fine not exceeding five thousand dollars,* or by imprisonment not exceeding one year, or by both said punishments, in the discretion of the court.

SECTION 3.

Every contract, combination in form of trust or otherwise, or conspiracy, in restraint of trade or commerce in any Territory of the

* Amended to "fine not exceeding fifty thousand dollars" in July 7, 1955.

United States or of the District of Columbia, or in restraint of trade or commerce between any such Territory and another, or between any such Territory or Territories and any State or States or the District of Columbia, or with foreign nations, is hereby declared illegal. Every person who shall make any such contract or engage in any such combination or conspiracy, shall be deemed guilty of a misdemeanor, and, on conviction thereof, shall be punished by fine not exceeding five thousand dollars,* or by imprisonment not exceeding one year, or by both said punishments, in the discretion of the court.

SECTION 4.

The several circuit courts of the United States are hereby invested with jurisdiction to prevent and restrain violations of this act; and it shall be the duty of the several district attorneys of the United States, in their respective districts, under the direction of the Attorney General, to institute proceedings in equity to prevent and restrain such violations. Such proceedings may be by way of petition setting forth the case and praying that such violation shall be enjoined or otherwise prohibited. When the parties complained of shall have been duly notified of such petition the court shall proceed, as soon as may be, to the hearing and determination of the case; and pending such petition and before final decree, the court may at any time make such temporary restraining order or prohibition as shall be deemed just in the premises.

SECTION 5.

Whenever it shall appear to the court before which any proceeding under section four of this act may be pending, that the ends of justice require that other parties should be brought before the court, the court may cause them to be summoned, whether they reside in the district in which the court is held or not; and subpœnas to that end may be served in any district by the marshal thereof.

SECTION 6.

Any property owned under any contract or by any combination, or pursuant to any conspiracy (and being the subject thereof) mentioned in section one of this act, and being in the course of transportation from one State to another, or to a foreign country, shall be forfeited to the United States, and may be seized and condemned by like proceedings as those provided by law for the forfeiture, seizure, and condemnation of property imported into the United States contrary to law.

SECTION 7.

Any person who shall be injured in his business or property by any other person or corporation by reason of anything forbidden or declared to be unlawful by this act, may sue therefor in any circuit court of the United States in the district in which the defendant resides or is found, without respect to the amount in controversy, and shall recover threefold the damages by him sustained, and the costs of suit, including a reasonable attorney's fee.

SECTION 8.

That the word "person," or "persons," wherever used in this act shall be deemed to include corporations and associations existing under or authorized by the laws of either the United States, the laws of any of the Territories, the laws of any State, or the laws of any foreign country.

Approved, July 2, 1890.

Clayton Act, 1914

SECTION 2.

That it shall be unlawful for any person engaged in commerce, in the course of such commerce, either directly or indirectly, to discriminate in price between different purchasers of commodities, which commodities are sold for use, consumption, or resale within the United States or any Territory thereof or the District of Columbia or any insular possession or other place under the jurisdiction of the United States, where the effect of such discrimination may be to substantially lessen competition or tend to create a monopoly in any line of commerce: *Provided,* That nothing herein contained shall prevent discrimination in price between purchasers of commodities on account of differences in the grade, quality, or quantity of the commodity sold, or that makes only due allowance for differences in the cost of selling or transportation, or discrimination in price in the same or different communities made in good faith to meet competition: *And provided further,* That nothing herein contained shall prevent persons engaged in selling goods, wares, or merchandise in commerce from selecting their own customers in bona fide transactions and not in restraint of trade.

SECTION 3.

That it shall be unlawful for any person engaged in commerce, in the course of such commerce, to lease or make a sale or contract for sale of goods, wares, merchandise, machinery, supplies, or other commodities, whether patented or unpatented, for use, consumption, or resale within the United States or any Territory thereof or the District of Columbia or any insular possession or other place under the jurisdiction of the United States, or fix a price charged therefor, or discount from, or rebate upon, such price, on the condition, agreement, or understanding that the lessee or purchaser thereof shall not use or deal in the goods, wares, merchandise, machinery, supplies, or other commodity of a competitor or competitors of the lessor or seller, where the effect of such lease, sale, or contract for sale or such condition, agreement, or understanding may be to substantially lessen competition or tend to create a monopoly in any line of commerce.

SECTION 4.

That any person who shall be injured in his business or property by reason of anything forbidden in the antitrust laws may sue therefor in any district court of the United States in the district in which the defendant resides or is found or has an agent, without respect to the amount in controversy, and shall recover threefold the damages by him sustained, and the cost of suit, including a reasonable attorney's fee.

SECTION 5.

That a final judgment or decree hereafter rendered in any criminal prosecution or in any suit or proceeding in equity brought by or on behalf of the United States under the antitrust laws to the effect that a defendant has violated said laws shall be prima facie evidence against such defendant in any suit or proceeding brought by any other party against such defendant under said laws as to all matters respecting which said judgment or decree would be an estoppel as between the parties thereto: *Provided,* This section shall not apply to consent judgments or decrees entered before any testimony has been taken: *Provided further,* This section shall not apply to consent judgments or decrees rendered in criminal proceedings or suits in equity, now pending, in which the taking of testimony has been commenced but has not been concluded, provided such judgments or decrees are rendered before any further testimony is taken.

Whenever any suit or proceeding in equity or criminal prosecution is instituted by the United States to prevent, restrain, or punish violations of any of the antitrust laws, the running of the statute of limitations in respect of each and every private right of action arising under said laws and based in whole or in part on any matter complained of in said suit or proceeding shall be suspended during the pendency thereof.

SECTION 7. *merger*

That no corporation engaged in commerce shall acquire, directly or indirectly, the whole or any part of the stock or other share *Stock* capital of another corporation engaged also in commerce where the effect of such acquisition may be to substantially lessen competition between the corporation whose stock is so acquired and the corporation making the acquisition or to restrain such commerce in any section or community or tend to create a monopoly of any line of commerce.

No corporation shall acquire, directly or indirectly, the whole or any part of the stock or other share capital of two or more corporations engaged in commerce where the effect of such acquisition or the use of such stock by the voting or granting of proxies or otherwise may be to substantially lessen competition between such corporations, or any of them, whose stock or other share capital is so acquired, or to restrain such commerce in any section or community or tend to create a monopoly of any line of commerce.

This section shall not apply to corporations purchasing such stock solely for investment and not using the same by voting or otherwise to bring about, or in attempting to bring about, the substantial lessening of competition. Nor shall anything contained in this section prevent a corporation engaged in commerce from causing the formation of subsidiary corporations for the actual carrying on of their immediate lawful business or the natural and legitimate branches or extension thereof or from owning and holding all or a part of the stock of such subsidiary corporations when the effect of such formation is not to substantially lessen competition.

Nor shall anything herein contained be construed to prohibit any common carrier subject to the laws to regulate commerce from aiding in the construction of branches or short lines so located as to become feeders to the main line of the company so aiding in such construction or from acquiring or owning all or any part of the stock of such branch lines, nor to prevent any such common carrier from acquiring and owning all or any part of the stock of a branch or short line constructed by an independent company where there is no substantial competition between the company owning the branch line so constructed and the company owning the main line acquiring the property or an interest therein, nor to prevent such common carrier from extending any of its lines through the medium of the acquisition of stock or otherwise of any other such common carrier where there is no substantial competition between the company extending its lines and the company whose stock, property, or an interest therein is so acquired.

Nothing contained in this section shall be held to affect or impair any right heretofore legally acquired: *Provided,* That nothing in this section shall be held or construed to authorize or make lawful anything heretofore prohibited or made illegal by the antitrust laws, nor to exempt any person from the penal provisions thereof or the civil remedies therein provided.

Celler-Kefauver Act, 1950
Amending Section 7 of the Clayton Act

SECTION 7.

"That no corporation engaged in commerce shall acquire, directly or indirectly, the whole or any part of the stock or other share capital and no corporation subject to the jurisdiction of the Federal

Trade Commission shall acquire the whole or any part of the assets of another corporation engaged also in commerce, where in any line of commerce in any section of the country, the effect of such acquisition may be substantially to lessen competition, or to tend to create a monopoly.

"No corporation shall acquire, directly or indirectly, the whole or any part of the stock or other share capital and no corporation subject to the jurisdiction of the Federal Trade Commission shall acquire the whole or any part of the assets of one or more corporations engaged in commerce, where in any line of commerce in any section of the country, the effect of such acquisition, of such stocks or assets, or of the use of such stock by the voting or granting of proxies or otherwise, may be substantially to lessen competition, or to tend to create a monopoly.

"This section shall not apply to corporations purchasing such stock solely for investment and not using the same by voting or otherwise to bring about, or in attempting to bring about, the substantial lessening of competition. Nor shall anything contained in this section prevent a corporation engaged in commerce from causing the formation of subsidiary corporations for the actual carrying on of their immediate lawful business, or the natural and legitimate branches or extensions thereof, or from owning and holding all or a part of the stock of such subsidiary corporations, when the effect of such formation is not to substantially lessen competition.

"Nor shall anything herein contained be construed to prohibit any common carrier subject to the laws to regulate commerce from aiding in the construction of branches or short lines so located as to become feeders to the main line of the company so aiding in such construction or from acquiring or owning all or any part of the stock of such branch lines, nor to prevent any such common carrier from acquiring and owning all or any part of the stock of a branch or short line constructed by an independent company where there is no substantial competition between the company owning the branch line so constructed and the company owning the main line acquiring the property or an interest therein, nor to prevent such common carrier from extending any of its lines through the medium of the acquisition of stock or otherwise of any other common carrier where there is no substantial competition between the company extending its lines and the company whose stock, property, or an interest therein is so acquired.

"Nothing contained in this section shall be held to affect or impair any right heretofore legally acquired: *Provided,* That nothing in this section shall be held or construed to authorize or make lawful anything heretofore prohibited or made illegal by the antitrust laws, nor to exempt any person from the penal provisions thereof or the civil remedies therein provided.

"Nothing contained in this section shall apply to transactions duly consummated pursuant to authority given by the Civil Aeronautics Board, Federal Communications Commission, Federal Power Commission, Interstate Commerce Commission, the Securities and Exchange Commission in the exercise of its jurisdiction under section 10 of the Public Utility Holding Company Act of 1935, the United States Maritime Commission, or the Secretary of Agriculture under any statutory provision vesting such power in such Commission, Secretary, or Board."

Robinson-Patman Act, 1936, Amending Section 2 of the Clayton Act

SECTION 2.

"(a) That it shall be unlawful for any person engaged in commerce, in the course of such commerce, either directly or indirectly, to discriminate in price between different purchasers of commodities of like grade and quality, where either or any of the purchases involved in such discrimination are in commerce, where such commodities are sold for use, consumption, or resale within the United States or any Territory thereof or the District of Columbia or any insular possession or other place under the jurisdiction of the United States, and where the effect of such discrimination may be substantially to lessen competition or tend to create a monopoly in any line of commerce, or to injure, destroy, or prevent competition with any person who either grants or knowingly receives the benefit of such discrimination, or with customers of either of them: *Provided,* That nothing herein contained shall prevent differentials which make only due allowance for differences in the cost of manufacture, sale, or delivery resulting from the differing methods or quantities in which such commodities are to such purchasers sold or delivered: *Provided, however,* That the Federal Trade Commission may, after due investigation and hearing to all interested parties, fix and establish quantity limits, and revise the same as it finds necessary, as to particular commodities or classes of commodities, where it finds that available purchasers in greater quantities are so few as to render differentials on account thereof unjustly discriminatory or promotive of monopoly in any line of commerce; and the foregoing shall then not be construed to permit differentials based on differences in quantities greater than those so fixed and established: *And provided further,* That nothing herein contained shall prevent persons engaged in selling goods, wares, or merchandise in commerce from selecting their own customers in bona fide transactions and not in restraint of trade: *And provided further,* That nothing herein contained shall prevent price changes from time to time where in response to changing conditions affecting the market for or the marketability of the goods concerned, such as but not limited to actual or imminent deterioration of perishable goods, obsolescence of seasonal goods, distress sales under court process, or sales in good faith in discontinuance of business in the goods concerned.

"(b) Upon proof being made, at any hearing on a complaint under this section, that there has been discrimination in price or services or facilities furnished, the burden of rebutting the prima-facie case thus made by showing justification shall be upon the person charged with a violation of this section, and unless justification shall be affirmatively shown, the Commission is authorized to issue an order terminating the discrimination: *Provided, however,* That nothing herein contained shall prevent a seller rebutting the prima-facie case thus made by showing that his lower price or the furnishing of services or facilities to any purchaser or purchasers was made in good faith to meet an equally low price of a competitor, or the services or facilities furnished by a competitor.

"(c) That it shall be unlawful for any person engaged in commerce, in the course of such commerce, to pay or grant, or to receive or accept, anything of value as a commission, brokerage, or other compensation, or any allowance or discount in lieu thereof, except for services rendered in connection with the sale or purchase of goods, wares, or merchandise, either to the other party to such transaction or to an agent, representative, or other intermediary therein where such intermediary is acting in fact for or in behalf, or is subject to the direct or indirect control, of any party to such transaction other than the person by whom such compensation is so granted or paid.

"(d) That it shall be unlawful for any person engaged in commerce to pay or contract for the payment of anything of value to or for the benefit of a customer of such person in the course of such commerce as compensation or in consideration for any services or facilities furnished by or through such customer in connection with the processing, handling, sale, or offering for sale of any products or commodities manufactured, sold, or offered for sale by such person, unless such payment or consideration is available on proportionally equal terms to all other customers competing in the distribution of such products or commodities.

"(e) That it shall be unlawful for any person to discriminate in favor of one purchaser against another purchaser or purchasers of a commodity bought for resale, with or without processing, by contracting to furnish or furnishing, or by contributing to the furnishing of, any services or facilities connected with the processing, handling, sale, or offering for sale of such commodity so purchased upon terms not accorded to all purchasers on proportionally equal terms.

"(f) That it shall be unlawful for any person engaged in commerce, in the course of such commerce, knowingly to induce or receive a discrimination in price which is prohibited by this section."

That nothing herein contained shall affect rights of action arising, or litigation pending, or orders of the Federal Trade Commission issued and in effect or pending on review, based on section 2 of said Act of October 15, 1914, prior to the effective date of this amendatory Act: *Provided,* That where, prior to the effective date of this amendatory Act, the Federal Trade Commission has issued an order requiring any person to cease and desist from a violation of section 2 of said Act of October 15, 1914, and such order is pending on review or is in effect, either as issued or as affirmed or modified by a court of competent jurisdiction, and the

Commission shall have reason to believe that such person has committed, used or carried on, since the effective date of this amendatory Act, or is committing, using or carrying on, any act, practice or method in violation of any of the provisions of said section 2 as amended by this Act, it may reopen such original proceeding and may issue and serve upon such person its complaint, supplementary to the original complaint, stating its charges in that respect. Thereupon the same proceedings shall be had upon such supplementary complaint as provided in section 11 of said Act of October 15, 1914. If upon such hearing the Commission shall be of the opinion that any act, practice, or method charged in said supplementary complaint has been committed, used, or carried on since the effective date of this amendatory Act, or is being committed, used or carried on, in violation of said section 2 as amended by this Act, it shall make a report in writing in which it shall state its findings as to the facts and shall issue and serve upon such person its order modifying or amending its original order to include any additional violations of law so found. Thereafter the provisions of section 11 of said Act of October 15, 1914, as to review and enforcement of orders of the Commission shall in all things apply to such modified or amended order. If upon review as provided in said section 11 the court shall set aside such modified or amended order, the original order shall not be affected thereby, but it shall be and remain in force and effect as fully and to the same extent as if such supplementary proceedings had not been taken.

SECTION 3.

It shall be unlawful for any person engaged in commerce, in the course of such commerce, to be a party to, or assist in, any transaction of sale, or contract to sell, which discriminates to his knowledge against competitors of the purchaser, in that, any discount, rebate, allowance, or advertising service charge is granted to the purchaser over and above any discount, rebate, allowance, or advertising service charge available at the time of such transaction to said competitors in respect of a sale of goods of like grade, quality, and quantity; to sell, or contract to sell, goods in any part of the United States at prices lower than those exacted by said person elsewhere in the United States for the purpose of destroying competition, or eliminating a competitor in such part of the United States; or, to sell, or contract to sell, goods at unreasonably low prices for the purpose of destroying competition or eliminating a competitor.

Any person violating any of the provisions of this section shall, upon conviction thereof, be fined not more than $5,000 or imprisoned not more than one year, or both.

Federal Trade Commission Act, 1914

SECTION 5.

That unfair methods of competition in commerce are hereby declared unlawful.

The commission is hereby empowered and directed to prevent persons, partnerships, or corporations, except banks, and common carriers subject to the Acts to regulate commerce, from using unfair methods of competition in commerce.

Whenever the commission shall have reason to believe that any such person, partnership, or corporation has been or is using any unfair methods of competition in commerce, and if it shall appear to the commission that a proceeding by it in respect thereof would be to the interest of the public, it shall issue and serve upon such person, partnership, or corporation a complaint stating its charges in that respect, and containing a notice of a hearing upon a day and at a place therein fixed at least thirty days after the service of said complaint. The person, partnership, or corporation so complained of shall have the right to appear at the place and time so fixed and show cause why an order should not be entered by the commission requiring such person, partnership, or corporation to cease and desist from the violation of the law so charged in said complaint. Any person, partnership, or corporation may make application, and upon good cause shown may be allowed by the commission to intervene and appear in said proceeding by counsel or in person. The testimony in any such proceeding shall be reduced to writing and filed in the office of the commission. If upon such hearing the commission shall be of the opinion that the method of competition in question is prohibited by this Act, it shall make a report in writing in which it shall state its findings as to the facts, and shall issue and cause to be served on such person, partnership, or corporation an order requiring such person, partnership, or corporation to cease and desist from using such method of competition. Until a transcript of the record in such hearing shall have been filed in a circuit court of appeals of the United States, as hereinafter provided, the commission may at any time, upon such notice and in such manner as it shall deem proper, modify or set aside, in whole or in part, any report or any order made or issued by it under this section.

If such person, partnership, or corporation fails or neglects to obey such order of the commission while the same is in effect, the commission may apply to the circuit court of appeals of the United States, within any circuit where the method of competition in question was used or where such person, partnership, or corporation resides or carries on business, for the enforcement of its order, and shall certify and file with its application a transcript of the entire record in the proceeding, including all the testimony taken and the report and order of the commission. Upon such filing of the application and transcript the court shall cause notice thereof to be served upon such person, partnership, or corporation and thereupon shall have jurisdiction of the proceeding and of the question determined therein, and shall have power to make and enter upon the pleadings, testimony, and proceedings set forth in such transcript a decree affirming, modifying, or setting aside the order of the commission. The findings of the commission as to the facts, if supported by testimony, shall be conclusive. If either party shall apply to the court for leave to adduce additional evidence, and shall show to the satisfaction of the court that such additional evidence is material and that there were reasonable grounds for the failure to adduce such evidence in the proceeding before the commission, the court may order such additional evidence to be taken before the commission and to be adduced upon the hearing in such manner and upon such terms and conditions as to the court may seem proper. The commission may modify its findings as to the facts, or make new findings, by reason of the additional evidence so taken, and it shall file such modified or new findings, which, if supported by testimony, shall be conclusive, and its recommendation, if any, for the modification or setting aside of its original order, with the return of such additional evidence. The judgment and decree of the court shall be final, except that the same shall be subject to review by the Supreme Court upon certiorari as provided in section two hundred and forty of the Judicial Code.

Any party required by such order of the commission to cease and desist from using such method of competition may obtain a review of such order in said circuit court of appeals by filing in the court a written petition praying that the order of the commission be set aside. A copy of such petition shall be forthwith served upon the commission, and thereupon the commission forthwith shall certify and file in the court a transcript of the record as hereinbefore provided. Upon the filing of the transcript the court shall have the same jurisdiction to affirm, set aside, or modify the order of the commission as in the case of an application by the commission for the enforcement of its order, and the findings of the commission as to the facts, if supported by testimony, shall in like manner be conclusive.

The jurisdiction of the circuit court of appeals of the United States to enforce, set aside, or modify orders of the commission shall be exclusive.

Such proceedings in the circuit court of appeals shall be given precedence over other cases pending therein, and shall be in every way expedited. No order of the commission or judgment of the court to enforce the same shall in any wise relieve or absolve any person, partnership, or corporation from any liability under the antitrust acts.

Complaints, orders, and other processes of the commission under this section may be served by anyone duly authorized by the commission, either (a) by delivering a copy thereof to the person to be served, or to a member of the partnership to be served, or to the president, secretary, or other executive officers or a director of the corporation to be served; or (b) by leaving a copy thereof at the principal office or place of business of such person, partnership, or corporation; or (c) by registering and mailing a copy thereof addressed to such person, partnership, or corporation at his or its principal office or place of business. The verified return by the person so serving said complaint, order, or other process setting forth the manner of said service shall be proof of the same, and the return post-office receipt for said complaint, order, or other process registered and mailed as aforesaid shall be proof of the service of the same.

SECTION 6.

That the commission shall also have power—

(a) To gather and compile information concerning, and to investigate from time to time the organization, business, conduct, practices, and management of any corporation engaged in commerce, excepting banks and common carriers subject to the Act to regulate commerce, and its relation to other corporations and to individuals, associations, and partnerships.

(b) To require, by general or special orders, corporations engaged in commerce, excepting banks, and common carriers subject to the Act to regulate commerce, or any class of them, or any of them, respectively, to file with the commission in such form as the commission may prescribe annual or special, or both annual and special, reports or answers in writing to specific questions, furnishing to the commission such information as it may require as to the organization, business, conduct, practices, management, and relation to other corporations, partnerships, and individuals of the respective corporations filing such reports or answers in writing. Such reports and answers shall be made under oath, or otherwise, as the commission may prescribe, and shall be filed with the commission within such reasonable period as the commission may prescribe, unless additional time be granted in any case by the commission.

(c) Whenever a final decree has been entered against any defendant corporation in any suit brought by the United States to prevent and restrain any violation of the antitrust Acts, to make investigations, upon its own initiative, of the manner in which the decree has been or is being carried out, and upon the application of the Attorney General it shall be its duty to make such investigation. It shall transmit to the Attorney General a report embodying its findings and recommendations as a result of any such investigation, and the report shall be made public in the discretion of the commission.

(d) Upon the direction of the President or either House of Congress to investigate and report the facts relating to any alleged violations of the antitrust Acts by any corporation.

(e) Upon the application of the Attorney General, to investigate and make recommendations for the readjustment of the business of any corporation alleged to be violating the antitrust Acts, in order that the corporation may thereafter maintain its organization, management, and conduct of business in accordance with law.

(f) To make public from time to time such portions of the information obtained by it hereunder, except trade secrets and names of customers, as it shall deem expedient in the public interest; and to make annual and special reports to the Congress and to submit therewith recommendations for additional legislation; and to provide for the publication of its reports and decisions in such form and manner as may be best adapted for public information and use.

(g) From time to time to classify corporations and to make rules and regulations for the purpose of carrying out the provisions of this Act.

(h) To investigate, from time to time, trade conditions in and with foreign countries where associations, combinations, or practices of manufacturers, merchants, or traders, or other conditions, may affect the foreign trade of the United States, and to report to Congress thereon, with such recommendations as it deems advisable.

INDEX

D

E

M

McGee, John S., 51, *52–60,* 61
McKie, James W., 351–352, *366–376*
Market
 definition, 9, 67–73 *passim,* 103–109, 213–235 *passim,*
  241–268 *passim,* 278–316 *passim,* 404–423 *passim*
 cross elasticity of demand, 9–25 *passim,* 104, 106,
  119–121, 406–409
Market performance, 10–11, 27–35 *passim,* 61–68
  passim
Market structure
 relative size, 11–12, 68–73 *passim,* 182–193 *passim,*
  278–314 *passim,* 323–341 *passim,* 354–368 *passim,*
  406–429 *passim*
 market shares and merging firms, 204–205, 234–239
  passim, 244–271 *passim*
 (*see also* Entry into the market; Merger trends)
Markham, Jesse W., 159, *160–175,* 201
Martin, David Dale, 202, 298–316
Mergers, 199–316
 conglomerate, 257–258, 279
Monopoly, 135–197
 in common law, 31–33
 (*see also* Competition and monopoly, concepts of;
  Market, definition; market structure)
Motion Pictures Patent Co. v. Universal Film Co., 323,
  391, 394, 398
Mueller, Willard F., 107, *108–134*

N

National Lead Co., 183
Nelson, Ralph L., 201
Nicholls, William H., 140, *146–158,* 159, 188
Northern Pacific, 322, 328–330, 400
Northern Securities Co., 35

P

R

S

W

Y

A Note on the Type

The text of this book was set on the Linotype in a face called TIMES ROMAN, designed by Stanley Morison for *The Times* (London), and first introduced by that newspaper in 1932.

Among typographers and designers of the twentieth century, Stanley Morison has been a strong forming influence, as typographical advisor to the English Monotype Corporation, as a director of two distinguished English publishing houses, and as a writer of sensibility, erudition, and keen practical sense.

Printed by The Colonial Press, Clinton, Mass.

Designed by Richard-Gabriel Rummonds